W9-BIC-850

Instant
IE4
Dynamic HTML
IE4 Edition

Alex Homer
Chris Ullman

Wrox Press Ltd.®

Instant IE4 Dynamic HTML *IE4 Edition*

© 1997 Wrox Press

All rights reserved. No part of this book may be reproduced, stored in a retrieval system or transmitted in any form or by any means—electronic, electro static, mechanical, photocopying, recording or otherwise, without the prior written permission of the publisher, except in the case of brief quotations embodied in critical articles or reviews.

The author and publisher have made every effort in the preparation of this book and disk to ensure the accuracy of the information. However, the information contained in this book or disk is sold without warranty, either express or implied. Neither the author, Wrox Press nor its dealers or distributors will be held liable for any damages caused or alleged to be caused either directly or indirectly by this book or disk.

All images supplied are for viewing purposes only within the programs supplied on the disk. Programs, files and images are not for redistribution without express permission from Wrox Press.

Published by Wrox Press Ltd. 30 Lincoln Road, Olton, Birmingham, B27 6PA.

Printed in USA

ISBN 1-861000-68-5

Trademark Acknowledgements

Wrox has endeavored to provide trademark information about all the companies and products mentioned in this book by the appropriate use of capitals. However, Wrox cannot guarantee the accuracy of this information.

Credits

Authors
Alex Homer
Chris Ullman

Additional Material
Brian Francis
Larry Roof
Dan Kohn

Editors
Anthea Elston
Jeremy Beacock

Technical Reviewers
Bob Beauchemin
Jon Bonnell

Technical Reviewers
Muffy Barkocy
Andy Enfield
Brian Francis
Darren Gill
John Harris
Richard Harrison
Stephen Jakab
Sing Li

Design/Layout/Cover
Andrew Guillaume
Graham Butler

Index
Simon Gilks

Cover image by David Maclean. Digital processing by Andrew Guillaume.

About the Authors

Alex Homer

Alex Homer is a software consultant and developer, who lives and works in the idyllic rural surroundings of Derbyshire UK. His company, Stonebroom Software, specializes in office integration and Internet-related development, and produces a range of vertical application software. He has worked with Wrox Press on several projects.

Chris Ullman

Chris Ullman is a computer science graduate who's not let this handicap prevent him becoming a programmer fluent in Visual Basic, Java and SQL. Currently interested in all things web-based, he's trying to figure out how to design a web-bot which drags off every mention of his favourite soccer team, Birmingham City, from the web and displays it within an IE4 desktop component without him lifting a finger.

Table of Contents

Chapter 3: The Dynamic HTML Browser Object Model 57

Chapter 7: Dialogs, Forms and Data Binding 181

Section B: List of Dynamic HTML Tags 297

Section C: Style Sheet Properties 393

Section D: Common HTML Tags by Category 413

Section E: The Browser Object Model 419

xix

Introduction

Dynamic HTML is the latest and most exciting proposal for a language that can provide information in a web browser. It releases the web site creator from the strait-jacket that has previously limited so many of the things that could be done, and the effects that could be achieved. In fact, it provides a whole new way to make pages more interesting, more attractive, more like traditional documents, and—of course—more dynamic.

What is this Book About?

Since mid 1996, the World Wide Web Consortium (W3C) has been working on proposals for the next version of HTML, version 4.0, code named *Project Cougar*. One of the main innovations in HTML 4.0 is the ability to let the user update and manipulate text and graphics on a screen dynamically, without the need for a page refresh. This innovation is the reason why the new update to the language is known as Dynamic HTML.

Dynamic HTML differs from HTML in that it no longer relies on tags alone to achieve these effects, but makes use of JavaScript and VBScript as well. This book aims to bring you up to date with the proposed standard outlines for Dynamic HTML, and to explain what it offers you and how closely the new proposals are followed in Microsoft's new browser, Internet Explorer 4.

Dynamic HTML allows the web author to work with the contents of the page in a fundamentally different way. This book isn't a dry list of specifications and discussion documents. You'll find that it's been split into two distinct sections. The first is a lightning tour and demonstration of all the new features that Dynamic HTML offers. We make references to the HTML standard, detailing what is and what isn't supported, throughout the book. The second section is a comprehensive reference guide to everything an HTML programmer could possibly need. This includes a cross reference of all the new and old properties, events and methods, a listing of all the Dynamic HTML tags that Internet Explorer 4 supports, a browser object model reference and much, much more.

Why Internet Explorer 4 Edition?

Early in 1997, Microsoft released to the public the first preview of their new browser, Internet Explorer version 4, and it supports much of what is currently under discussion by W3C. Netscape have also released a new browser, named Communicator 4—and it too supports a version of Dynamic HTML. Unfortunately, at least at present, this implementation is somewhat removed from the W3C proposals. However, like all W3C "work in progress" documents, the final version of Dynamic HTML/Cougar (or HTML 4.0, as it seems likely to become) is still some way down the road, and likely to change as the ratification process continues.

Browser Compatibility

However, this places HTML authors in a difficult position. We are used to minor differences in the tags and attributes that different browsers support, and the different ways that they sometimes interpret them, but the current situation means that there is very little common ground between the new features in the two main browsers. Producing pages and scripts that will work correctly on both browsers is a very difficult task during this transition period.

In Chapter 8 of this book, you'll see a more detailed discussion of browser, document and script compatibility, plus our opinions on what the future may hold.

What Do I Need to Use This Book?

All you'll need to create Dynamic HTML documents yourself is a text editor capable of saving files in ASCII format, and a browser which supports Dynamic HTML. This book uses Internet Explorer version 4. This can be downloaded from:

```
http://www.microsoft.com/ie4
```

Apart from that, everything you need is here in this book. The examples and screenshots in this book were all taken from a PC running Windows 95, and using Windows Notepad as the text editor. However, HTML is a platform-independent language, so you can just as easily use a Macintosh or other operating system with the same results—again, as long as you have a suitable browser.

Who Should Read This Book?

You should read this book if you want to be able to create exciting and attractive web pages, using the latest techniques. Dynamic HTML is a combination (perhaps even a culmination) of two originally very different web page coding techniques. The appearance of the page is created using **HTML**, but much of the control of the way it looks and works is down to embedded **scripting code**. On top of that, extensions to the way in which **style sheets** work add extra ways of controlling and specifying the final product's layout.

Therefore you should have at least a basic knowledge of a scripting language, preferably JavaScript as this is the one that has been specified by ECMA (a European standards organization) in their document ECMA-262 as the standard scripting language. You should also be reasonably familiar with HTML and style sheets as we won't be providing a full tutorial on these subjects. However, we have included some tips on how they work in our examples, and a full reference section at the back of the book.

As long as you've created a few pages before, and have done a little scripting before, you'll have no problems keeping up with what's going on.

Where you'll find the Samples, Tools and Updates

If you want to try out the examples in this book, you can run them straight from our web site or you can download them as compressed files from the same site. The index page can be found at:
`http://www.rapid.wrox.com/books/0685/`

If you're located in Europe or the United Kingdom, or you find that the site in the United States is down for maintenance, then you may want to try our mirror site which can be found at:
`http://rapid.wrox.co.uk/books/0685/`

Any additional features included in the final release version of IE4 will be covered on our web site at:
`http://rapid.wrox.co.uk/books/0685/`

What is the World Wide Web?

The concept of the World Wide Web, or simply the Web, was born in 1983 at the CERN laboratory in Geneva, when Tim Berners-Lee was looking for a way of disseminating information in a friendly, but platform-independent, manner. The scheme he devised was placed in the public domain in 1992, and the World Wide Web was born.

Most of the activity in developing the many standards and technologies that go into making the World Wide Web function have now been transferred from CERN to the World Wide Web Consortium (W3C). Their web site at `http://www.w3.org` is always a good starting place for discovering more about the Web. Here is the home page of the World Wide Web Consortium:

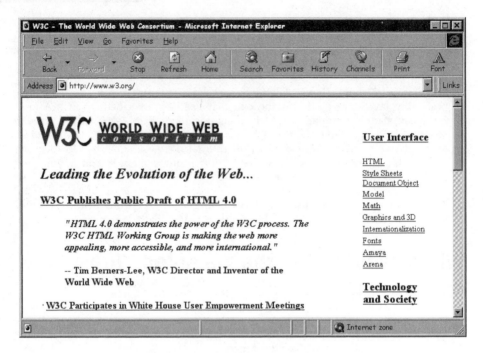

In this book, we aren't going to be examining how the World Wide Web works, but it is important to understand the basics that make it possible. There are three parts to this technology:

 The server that holds the information

 The client that is viewing the information

 The protocol that connects the two

Documents, including text, images, sounds, and other types of information are held on a server computer, viewed on a client computer, and transferred between the two using the HTTP (Hyper Text Transfer Protocol).

When a client (the computer or workstation being used by the person who wishes to view the document) makes a request to the server, it uses the HTTP protocol across a network to request the information—in the form of a URL—from the server. The server processes the request and, again, uses HTTP to transfer the information back to the client. As well as transferring the actual document, the server must tell the client the type of document being returned. This is usually defined as a MIME type. The client must then process the information before it presents it to the human viewer.

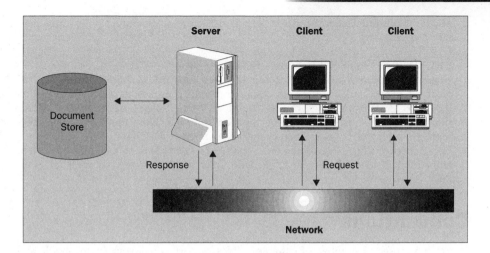

In this simplified diagram, we have shown the documents as fixed; however, in some cases, they can be dynamic documents, created 'on the fly' by the server as the client requests them. Perhaps the simplest example of a dynamic document is the ubiquitous 'hit counter' that appears on many pages.

Some Terminology

Before we go any further, it might be a good idea to define some terminology.

DTD (Document Type Definition)—a set of rules on how to apply SGML (see definition below) to a particular markup language.

HTML (Hyper Text Markup Language)—the basic subject of this book.

HTTP (Hyper Text Transfer Protocol)—this is the protocol used to transfer information between the client and server computer. Although vital for the operation of the web, it is not generally necessary to know any details of HTPP to provide information across the web.

MIME (Multimedia Internet Mail Extension)—this was originally intended as a way of embedding complex binary documents in mail messages, but is now used much more widely. When a server serves web information to a client browser, it first tells the client the type of information it is going to send using a MIME type and a subtype. The browser can then decide how it wishes to handle that document type. It may choose to process it internally, or invoke an external program to handle the information. MIME types consist of a main type and subtype. For example, plain text is `text/plain`, but `image/mpeg` specifies an image stored in `mpeg` format.

RFC (Request For Comments)—this is something of a misnomer, as almost all of the protocols and conventions that make the Internet function are defined in documents called RFCs. For example, RFC1725 defines POP3, the protocol often used for retrieving Internet mail, and HTML 2.0 can be found in RFC1866. All RFC documents can be found on the Internet.

SGML (Standard Generalized Markup Language)—a standard for defining markup languages.

URL (Uniform Resource Locator)—this is a way of specifying a resource. It consists of a protocol name, a colon (**:**), two forward slash characters (**//**), a machine name, and a path to a resource (using **/** as a separator). For example, the Wrox Press home page can be found at **http://www.wrox.com/**. URLs are the way that all resources are specified on the web. Note that URLs can specify more than just web pages. For example, to retrieve RFC1866 using FTP, we could specify **ftp://ds.internic.net/rfc/rfc1866.txt**. URLs are often embedded inside web pages, to provide links to other pages, as we shall see later.

Conventions

We have used a number of different styles of text and layout in the book to help differentiate between the different kinds of information. Here are examples of the styles we use and an explanation of what they mean:

Advice, hints, or background information comes in this type of font.

Important pieces of information come in boxes like this

 Important Words are in a bold type font

 Words that appear on the screen in menus like the File or Window are in a similar font to the one that you see on screen

 Keys that you press on the keyboard, like *Ctrl* and *Enter*, are in italics

 Code has several fonts. If it's a word that we're talking about in the text, for example, when discussing the **For...Next** loop, it's in a bold font. If it's a block of code that you can type in as a program and run, then it's also in a gray box:

```
<STYLE TYPE="text/javascript">
... Some Javascript ...
</STYLE>
```

 Sometimes you'll see code in a mixture of styles, like this:

```
<HTML>
<HEAD>
<TITLE>Javascript Style Sheet Example</TITLE>
<STYLE  TYPE="text/javascript">
tags.BODY.color="black"
classes.base.DIV.color="red"
</STYLE>
</HEAD>
```

 The code with a white background is code we've already looked at and that we don't wish to examine further.

These formats are designed to make sure that you know what it is you're looking at. I hope they make life easier.

Tell Us What You Think

We've worked hard on this book to make it useful. We've tried to understand what you're willing to exchange your hard-earned money for, and we've tried to make the book live up to your expectations.

Please let us know what you think about this book. Tell us what we did wrong, and what we did right. This isn't just marketing flannel: we really do huddle around the email to find out what you think. If you don't believe it, then send us a note. We'll answer, and we'll take whatever you say on board for future editions. The easiest way is to use email:

feedback@wrox.com

You can also find more details about Wrox Press on our web site. There, you'll find the code from our latest books, sneak previews of forthcoming titles, and information about the authors and editors. You can order Wrox titles directly from the site, or find out where your nearest local bookstore with Wrox titles is located. The address of our site is:

http://www.wrox.com

Customer Support

If you find a mistake, please have a look at the errata page for this book on our web site first. Section J outlines how can you can submit an errata in much greater detail, if you are unsure. The full URL for the errata page is:

http://www.wrox.com/Scripts/Errata.idc?Code=0685

If you can't find an answer there, tell us about the problem and we'll do everything we can to answer promptly!

Just send us an email to **support@wrox.com**.

or fill in the form on our web site: **http://www.wrox.com/Contact.stm**

Chapter

1

Introducing Dynamic HTML

It's always the same. You'd finally come to grips with all the new tags and attributes in HTML 3.2, and everything seemed to be settling down with the forthcoming ratification of this version of the language, when suddenly it's 'all-change time' once again. This has been precipitated by the release of Microsoft's browser, Internet Explorer 4 (IE4), and Netscape's new browser, Communicator 4. Both these browsers support many of the proposals made in the draft of the new version of HTML standard, HTML 4.0.

This is a departure from the way things have tended to happen in the past. Usually, each new browser release carried with it some new HTML tags and a few new attributes. However, with HTML 4.0, both Netscape and Microsoft have been very active in proposing new additions to the language as part of the forthcoming standard. Previously, Netscape and Microsoft have tended to support each others new tags in their last couple of releases (with some exceptions), but—as any hardened HTML author knows—trying to build pages that will work correctly on different browsers is not as easy as it should be. So this time they've both contributed to the standards set by the World Wide Web Consortium to produce a new version of HTML. Sadly, however, it is still not one with which they both totally comply. The full draft of HTML 4.0 can be found at `http://www.w3.org`.

HTML 4.0 isn't really that different from the previous versions of HTML. The key changes can be summed up by the word **dynamic**. HTML 4.0 will now allow the user to manipulate and access the text and image elements with a scripting language. The web page has become dynamically updateable meaning the screen display can now be altered and updated automatically without the user having to click on page refresh each time. This might seem like no big deal, as most operating systems have boasted this for years, but in web pages it's quite a major advance. However the adjustments required to the language aren't just in a few new tags and attributes. While most of the tags in 3.2 remain present in 4.0, it's this new ability to manipulate and access elements with a scripting language without requiring interaction with the server that forms the unique innovation for HTML. As a result, both Netscape and Microsoft have christened the set of features that allow dynamic updates and positioning as **Dynamic HTML**.

So, why do we need these new features—and will they actually help to reduce compatibility problems in the future? We'll answer these two questions for you, but to do this we first need to show you what Dynamic HTML actually is, what it can do and how you use it. We'll show you how it fits into the Web as a whole, and how it broadens existing concepts and techniques to let you achieve new kinds of effects in your web pages.

In this chapter, we'll aim to cover:

 The foundations of Dynamic HTML

 Its similarities to, and differences from, existing HTML

 What we can do with it, and what we need to learn

The Foundations of Dynamic HTML

Dynamic HTML is a development of the 'traditional' HTML we already use to create Web pages of all kinds. HTML stands for **HyperText Markup Language**, and is designed to be a standard way of representing information so that many different types of client browser can display it. Before we go too deeply into Dynamic HTML itself, we'll take a brief look at the background to HTML, and the other **document definition languages** from which it originated.

Document Definition Languages

The original documents that were used in the World Wide Web were in the format we call HTML—Hyper Text Markup Language. Perhaps the two most important features of this were that a basic HTML document was simple to create, and that HTML was almost totally platform and viewer independent.

HTML is a markup language that tells the client, in general terms, how the information should be presented. For example, to define a heading in an HTML document, you might write:

<H2>This is a heading</H2>

This tells the client that the text 'This is a heading' should be displayed as a level 2 heading, but leaves it up to the client to decide the most appropriate way of displaying it. As HTML has developed, this original concept is being diluted. More and more specific information, such as fonts, point size, and colors, can now be defined for the client.

> *An interesting side-effect of this way of defining documents is that it allows people with visual disabilities to use special browsers that render the documents in a form which is easier for them to comprehend.*

The first version of HTML was a fairly loosely defined standard. Version 2 of HTML was more rigorously defined in terms of another standard, known as SGML.

SGML

SGML is the abbreviation for **Standard Generalized Markup Language**. This language, or meta-language as it should be called, was defined by International Standards in 1986 as ISO 8879:1986.

The purpose of SGML is very simple. At the time it was developed, there were several 'markup languages', none of which were particularly portable between platforms or even software packages. The purpose of SGML is to allow a formal definition of markup languages that can then be used to give complete flexibility and portability of information display between applications and platforms.

It is tempting for the newcomer to SGML to view it as a markup language in its own right—defining a set of tags and so on, and providing meanings for them. This is not the case. What SGML *does* do is describe the relation of components within a document. As such, SGML is not a competitor with the likes of TeX or Postscript, which define such things as layout, but a way of describing what the document 'is' rather than how it should be 'rendered'.

A markup language consists of a set of conventions that can be used together to provide a way to encode text. A markup language must also specify what markup is allowed, what markup is required and how the markup is distinguished from the text of the document. SGML does all this—what it doesn't do is specify what the markups are, or what they mean.

DTD

DTD stands for **Document Type Definition**. Its purpose is to define the legal productions of a particular markup language. A simple DTD would do nothing more than, say, define a set of tags that can be used by a particular markup language.

The HTML 3.2 standard is a formally defined SGML DTD. In other words, the definition of HTML 3.2 is itself specified using the SGML meta-language. This allows HTML specifications to be rigorously defined.

To fully define HTML 3.2, two different specifications are required. The first is the relatively small SGML definition that defines general features, such as the character set and size limits. The main information is contained in the DTD, which defines the detail, such as the tags and attributes, which we will learn more about later.

The HTML 3.2 DTD can be found at the following address:

```
http://www.w3.org/pub/WWW/TR/WD-html32
```

Hypertext Markup Language

HTML 3.2 is the latest standard to be awaiting final ratification by the World Wide Web Consortium. This has led to some confusion over what is now standard and what isn't. HTML 3.0 was never an official standard, it was always only a working draft. The web developed so rapidly, with vendors implementing proprietary tags all the time, that the draft HTML 3.0 specification was left looking dated before it could even be issued. The consortium decided, probably wisely, that rather than continue work on HTML 3.0, they would move immediately to HTML 3.2. The HTML 3.2 standard incorporates all of HTML 2.0 (with some very minor changes) plus many of the proposals that were in the HTML 3.0 draft, and additional features such as tables and applets.

Since the 3.2 standard was proposed, more additions continue to be made to new browsers—over and above the requirements to meet the standard. In fact, the standard itself is now in danger of being completely overtaken before it ever reaches the stage of final ratification. Even though HTML 4.0 is not *that* different from HTML3.2, there are several subtle changes that require a new standard to be defined. These standards are likely to be accepted by W3C, but considering 3.2 is still to be ratified, it could take a little while.

Hopefully there should be less need for new tags and new attributes as a general framework has been established and changes might only need to be made to the scripting languages from now on. Therefore HTML 4.0 should see the standard settling down at long last. Only once there is a stable standard that the major companies adhere to, do we have any chance of achieving a fully standardized and platform-independent way of viewing information from across the planet.

You can download full specifications of Microsoft's proposals for Dynamic HTML from:

```
http://www.microsoft.com/sitebuilder/workshop/
author/dhtml
```

What's New in Dynamic HTML

Having considered the background to the development of Dynamic HTML, it's time to see what's different. What can it do that we can't already do with HTML, scripting languages, ActiveX controls and Java applets? This is the subject of the next section, and you'll be pleased to know that—from some viewpoints—not much seems to have actually changed.

Internet Explorer 4 looks very similar to its predecessors, and it will (of course) display existing pages that employ almost any of the techniques currently used to make Web pages more exciting. It hosts ActiveX controls and Java applets, runs code written in VBScript and JavaScript, and supports all the other features that are becoming accepted requirements—such as tables and frames.

What Hasn't Changed

So, Dynamic HTML isn't a radical departure from the version of HTML that's currently awaiting ratification by the World Wide Web Consortium. If it were, we would be looking at all kinds of problems when different browsers accessed pages that exploited its features. Two main points to consider are:

While HTML 4.0 does introduce several new tags, the Dynamic HTML part of it actually requires no new HTML tags and very little in the way of new attributes to go with them. More support is provided for Netscape-specific tags, such as **`<EMBED>`**, and plug-ins. The **`<BLINK>`** tag, however, is still not supported—probably a decision a lot of people will agree with.

 The same **object model** is available to scripting languages and components, but with extensions proprietary to Dynamic HTML. This means that existing scripts will still execute successfully.

An object model is just a method of using the scripting code in a page to access both the browser environment and the contents of the page itself – we'll look at the browser object model in detail in Chapter 3.

What's Actually New

Much of the outward appearance of the Internet Explorer browser remains very familiar. However, a lot of the structure of both the page and the browser has been exposed to the HTML author for the first time. This allows some very exciting new effects to be achieved. For example, we've provided a jigsaw page in the samples available for this book. You can drag and rotate the individual pieces to re-assemble the original picture:

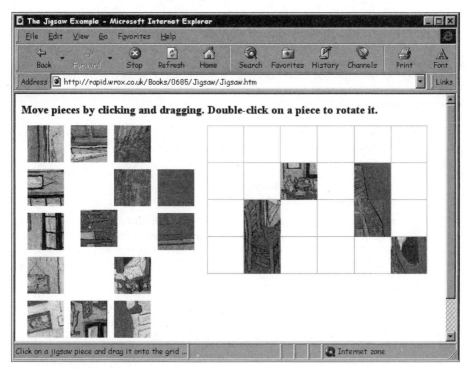

You can download, or just browse, all the samples for this book from our Web site at **http://rapid.wrox.co.uk/books/0685**

13

In particular, Dynamic HTML provides these new features:

 All of the elements in the page (tags, images, text, etc.) are now accessible to script written in the page (as opposed to only some of them in previous releases).

 An extension to the implementation of styles and style sheets provides more hooks to the page elements from scripting code

Extensions to the browser object model are included, which provide added functionality for the scripting languages used in the pages

Absolute positioning of elements, including a third dimensional coordinate known as the z-index, which allows a desktop publishing style of authoring, and a 2.5-D (i.e. fake 3-D) appearance

Dynamic re-drawing of any or all parts of the page allows changes to a loaded page to be made visible. Pages no longer need to be reloaded to show the updated version.

New event-handling techniques are supported, including bubbling events up through the object hierarchy

Graphic filters which allow the user to add multi-media effects to graphics and text such as flipping an image vertically or horizontally, making text appear to glow, adding motion blur to an image or even making it appear in x-ray form.

While these are new features of the Dynamic HTML language itself, they do, of course, depend upon the browser to display the results. You can't expect the Dynamic HTML-specific parts of a page to do much in Navigator 3 or Internet Explorer 3. Like all new developments in HTML, the browser must provide support before the page can perform as it should. The format of HTML 4.0 allows the old browsers to degrade gracefully though, without lots of errors caused by incompatibility.

There are also several new developments within Microsoft's Internet Explorer 4 browser, which interface with Dynamic HTML pages:

 Internet Explorer 4 supports an updated version 3 of Microsoft's scripting language, **VBScript**, which contains several new functions and methods. It also provides support for languages like **Perl** and **Rexx**.

 New **scripting components** are included with Internet Explorer. These are designed to make production of attractive and interactive pages a lot easier. For example, the Advanced Data Connector can provide dynamic and automatic updating between HTML-style controls in the page and a data file on the server.

In this book, we're focussing on Dynamic HTML as a language. You'll learn how to create pages that conform to the Microsoft proposals for Dynamic HTML. To learn more about the different methods you can use to program the browser and the Active Desktop, look out for Professional Dynamic HTML and IE4 Programming—from Wrox Press, of course.

In this chapter, we'll start by looking at the things we listed as being the new features, and seeing how they provide opportunities to do things we can't do in existing HTML pages. In later chapters we'll get down to examining exactly how we can implement these new features in our pages—and you'll see how the examples we're using in this chapter work.

Accessing the Elements in the Page

In traditional HTML, it's impossible to 'get at' most of the contents of a Web page once it's been rendered (i.e. displayed) by the browser. You can write scripts that read or change the values in HTML controls, such as text boxes and checkboxes. You can also include objects in the pages, such as ActiveX controls or Java applets, and access them through script code. And, of course, you can change the background color of the page, or the color of the links on the page, through script.

What you can't do is read or change anything else. You can't change the text on the page, either in headings, lists, tables, or body text. You can't change the font or style of the text, add or remove images, or change their position. In fact, you can't do much at all.

Of course, the Web—and therefore the browser that displays the pages—was originally designed as an information delivery system. The whole idea was that you got a page full of text and graphics to read. In those days, no-one expected you to want to *play* with it...

With Dynamic HTML, all this changes. Every part of the page that the browser displays can be accessed from a scripting language. You can change almost anything in the page, while it's being displayed. As an example, this page (named **ListChange.htm**) displays items in a list in a different color, size, and font style when the mouse pointer moves over them. Notice that they're not even hyperlinks, just a normal unordered list created with the **<UL>** tag. It's done using script code that detects the movements of the mouse, and then changes the style of the text.

15

Properties, Styles and Style Sheets

In the previous example, we saw that a scripting language like JavaScript or VBScript can change some relatively minor aspects of a loaded page by responding to the mouse moving over part of it. It's been possible in the last couple of versions of the mainstream browsers to control the size and font face of the text in a page, although it could only be set in a page as it was being designed, and not on-the-fly while it was being displayed.

This was done by using two HTML tags, **<FONT>** and **<STYLE>**. The simplest way was to enclose text in **<FONT> </FONT>** tags, and specify the font family, size, color, and other effects:

```
<FONT FACE="Arial Black" SIZE=4 COLOR=green>
    This is some text in big green letters
</FONT>
```

Instead of doing this every time, you could use the **<STYLE>** tag to define a set of named styles, then allocate them to different parts of the text. And using the standard formatting tag names avoided the need to specify which style applied to which part of the text. If you wanted all your **<H2>** text to be large and green you just defined this in a **<STYLE>** section at the start of the page:

```
<STYLE>
    .biggreen {font-family:"Arial Black"; font-size=18; color=green}
</STYLE>
<BODY>
    <P CLASS=biggreen>This is some text in big green letters</P>
    ...
```

An even better way, if you wanted a lot of pages to have the same style, was to put the **<STYLE>** definition into a separate file, called a **cascading style sheet** (CSS), and attach it via a URL in a special tag to each page. Then, you could change the styles in all the pages just by changing the entry in the style sheet file.

*Don't worry if you're not up to speed on using styles like this. We'll be
looking at how it's done in more depth in the next chapter, and we've included
full details in the reference section at the back of the book.*

But, why are we talking about existing methods? The point here is that
Dynamic HTML uses the characteristics you specify for the items in the page to
provide **properties** for each one. In other words, we now have to think of every
part of the page as an individual **element** or **object**, and not just as a tag. The
text between the `<H2>` and `</H2>` tags is now part of that heading element,
and it has a whole range of properties that are accessible from script code. The
`font-size` is no longer just a number in a `<STYLE>` or `<FONT>` tag, but the
`fontSize` property of an `H2` element object.

We'll be looking at style sheets in a lot more detail later. For the moment, you
just need to appreciate that they provide a link between the definition of all the
parts of the page in HTML, and that they can react to the script code within
the page in a new way—as properties of that element object.

The Extended Browser Object Model

So, all the pages we load into our shiny new browser are going to consist of
hundreds of different objects, rather than a static page full of text and graphics
with a few HTML controls, or ActiveX and Java objects. It sounds like trying to
program all this lot in scripting code will be a terrifying experience. As in most
other programming environments, the browser provides an object model which
organizes all the different objects and elements in a way that makes them
manageable. If you've programmed using VBScript or JavaScript before, you'll
have used this.

To cope with the flood of all kinds of new objects, Internet Explorer 4
introduces several additions to the browser object model. Bear in mind that this
object model is designed around HTML 4.0, the language, so it will be available
in all browsers that will host Dynamic HTML. This means that as long as we
write our pages and scripts to this model, they should work in all the other
browsers that support it.

We'll look in detail at the object model in later chapters, and it's fully
documented in the reference section at the back of this book. You'll see how it
becomes part of everything we do when we work with scripts in Dynamic
HTML.

Absolute Positioning and the Z-order

One of the biggest criticisms of existing HTML has been the difficulty of
accurately controlling the appearance of a page. Until the implementation of
styles, as we saw earlier, everything was displayed in a default font (usually
something like Times Roman), in default colors, and almost at random within
the browser window.

The most you could do was specify where a paragraph should start or end,
and whether graphics or other elements should align to the left, center, or right
of the page. The big problem was that, as the user resized the browser window,

17

everything moved about again. To some extent, using tables helped to solve this, and when frames became more universally supported they allowed even more control.

However, one other technique appeared in Internet Explorer 3, along with support for ActiveX controls. A special ActiveX control, called the Layout Control, provided an area of the page that behaved like a form in Visual Basic—you could place controls and other objects on it in fixed positions. It was rather like the screen window that fronts a normal Windows application.

One of the biggest advances in Dynamic HTML is the support for a system of achieving precise layout within the page, without having to use an ActiveX control. As you'll see when we come to look at positioning in the next chapter, this very useful feature has evolved from these earlier techniques.

This means that elements can be sized and positioned in the browser window exactly as the author requires. They can even be overlaid, something that could previously only be done by employing tricks with style sheets. The new concept of laying out pages is therefore very similar to desktop publishing techniques (unfortunately, however, the tools available to help still have some way to go). To see the difference it makes, here's one of the sample pages from this book as it appears in Internet Explorer 4, followed by the same page loaded into Internet Explorer 3:

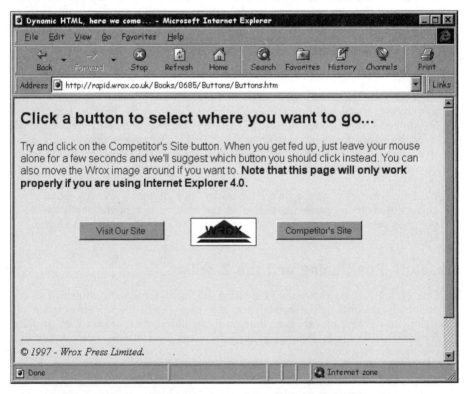

The Dancing Buttons page in Internet Explorer 4

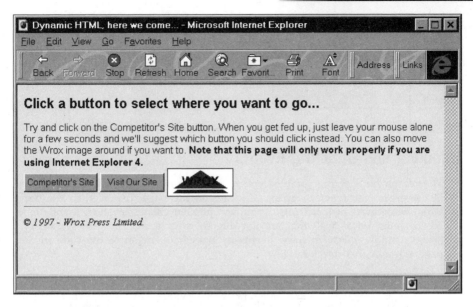

The Dancing Buttons Page in Internet Explorer 3

*You can download, or just browse, all the samples for this book from our Web
site at* **http://rapid.wrox.co.uk/books/0685**

Movement and Dynamic Page Re-drawing

The fact that we can accurately position elements on the page immediately
prompts the next question. If we can put them exactly where we want them,
can we move them around as well? This is probably the most visible advantage
that Dynamic HTML provides. It's linked to the fact that the browser will now
redraw all or part of the page using a stored representation of the contents,
rather than the original HTML source code stream.

This rather unusual effect can be seen if you load a Dynamic HTML page, then
carry out a task which changes the page—such as moving an element around.
The usual View Source option in the browser opens the original HTML code in
NotePad, but it doesn't reflect the currently displayed page. It's just the original
source that created the page in the first place. And, as you'd expect, clicking the
Reload button in the browser just reloads this original version of the page
again.

Of course, the browser always had the ability to redraw parts of the page. If
you changed the value in an HTML text box using script code, the new value
was visible on the page. The big difference now is that the entire stored page
representation, which can itself be manipulated by the code, will show these
changes on screen almost as soon as they happen.

You've already seen this in the two examples we've shown you earlier. In the
page with the two buttons, one of them jumps out of the way of your mouse,
while the other creeps under it when you stop moving the pointer around.

19

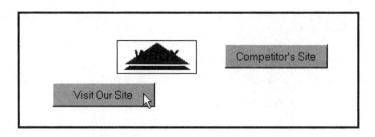

Handling and Bubbling Events

The reason both of the samples you've seen behave as they do is that the code in the pages can react to **events**. Clicking on the page displayed in the browser window, or even just moving the mouse pointer, creates an event—and there are others going on as well that are not directly your fault. The browser, being the active window, reacts to these events by passing them on to the code in the page through the object model.

OK, so this happens in most applications. It used to happen in Internet Explorer 3, Navigator 3, and other browsers. What's new is that there are now a whole heap of options when it comes to reacting to the events in our scripting code. These not only give us more choice about how we create pages, but can also make the job of writing the code easier. We can provide one routine to handle an event in several objects, or several different events for one object.

Probably the two most useful additions to Dynamic HTML are **event bubbling** and **source element identification**. We can allow (or prevent) an event from 'bubbling up' through the browsers' object hierarchy, and handle it at different levels. We can identify which element on the page actually caused the event (or to be more exact, which one was the 'topmost' element that received it). Finally, we can identify which element is being moved to, and which is being moved from, when we detect mouse movement events.

To see how useful event bubbling can be, try the buttons sample page again. You'll find that you can push the Competitor's Site button underneath the central Wrox logo, and it still responds to mouse movements even though the pointer is actually over the logo graphic. The button is still picking up the events caused by the mouse, even though it's moving over the graphic.

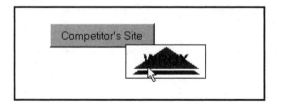

Filters

Finally one of the largest leaps in Internet Explorer 4 is the addition of multimedia effects which are fully programmable via style sheets and scripting properties. There are several multimedia controls that have been added to Internet Explorer 4, but the two which can be accessed with Cascading Style Sheet properties are the **Visual Filter** and the **Transitions Filter**. These allow the developer access to a multitude of effects. The Visual Filter makes it easy to manipulate the image or add simple effects previously the preserve of art packages such as Corel Draw or Paintshop Pro. It has 13 effects available, allowing anything from a simple image flip, horizontally or vertically to a motion blurring effect and even an x-ray filter! We have a simple program that demonstrates what all the filters can do to text and images:

The Transition Filter allows you to gradually reveal or hide objects using one of any 23 types of predefined pattern. For example, you can make an image fade away, in the form of a vertical blind, while at the same time making another one appear. This example also allows you to select any of the effects on offer.

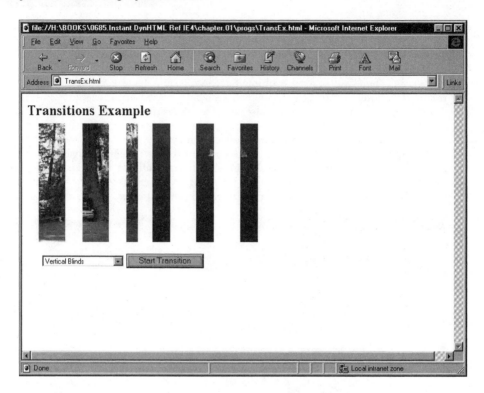

You can download, or just browse, all the samples for this book from our Web site at **http://rapid.wrox.co.uk/books/0685**. *These particular samples are taken from Chapter 4.*

The difference is that all of these effects, which would have taken quite some calculating in a normal programming language, are easily available through just one line property call together with parameters. Being a graphics whiz has never been easier.

We've skipped through the list of new and exciting features in Dynamic HTML very briskly here. This is intentional, both to let you see what's new (and hence, what you're going to learn about in this book), and to give you an understanding of the terminology and how it all fits together. In the remainder of this chapter, we'll look at what you'll need.

Getting Started with Dynamic HTML

By now, you should appreciate that Dynamic HTML is not exactly a revolution, more an evolution of existing techniques and technologies. You don't need to sit down and learn a whole new language, just develop and extend your existing knowledge of HTML and browser scripting.

The Background Knowledge You'll Need

In this book, we're assuming that you already have some background in both of these areas—in other words that you know how to create a traditional Web page using HTML tags, and that you have at least a rudimentary grasp of how scripts are used in Web pages. It doesn't matter if you know VBScript or JavaScript, because we're only using them to manipulate the elements and do basic number crunching. Both languages accomplish this in similar ways, although the actual syntax is different. The difference is that while VBScript is definitely easier for the newcomer to grasp, JavaScript has now been adopted by ECMA (the European Standards Organization) as the standard scripting language. As JavaScript is therefore very likely to remain the dominant scripting language (Communicator 4 doesn't support VBScript and future releases are unlikely to), it might be worth the extra work to learn it, if you don't know it already, although in this book we feature examples in both languages.

We've included a section on both VBScript and JavaScript in the reference section of this book to help you. Section H also includes a VBScript tutorial. We haven't included a JavaScript tutorial as it requires a greater in-depth explanation of its features than we have room for in this book. If you want to learn more about JavaScript, look out for Instant JavaScript, *ISBN 1-861001-274.* If you want to learn more about VBscript, look out for Instant VBScript *ISBN 1-861000-44-8* and finally if you want to know more about HTML up to version 3.2, look up Instant HTML Programmer's Reference *ISBN 1-861000-76-6*—all from Wrox Press.

The Tools You'll Need

When creating pages in HTML, many people use an authoring tool such as HotDog, HotMeTaL Pro, Microsoft FrontPage, or even Microsoft Word 97. This is fine for a static page, which just uses the normal HTML tags to create the appearance the user sees. FrontPage can also add WebBots, which provide some interactivity when HTML controls, such as text boxes and lists, are included.

However, these tools hide the actual structure of the page—the tags that do all the work—from the author. They are also unable to create much in the way of script. The bad news is that none of these are going to be much help when we come to use Dynamic HTML.

FrontPage 98

There is one very powerful tool that Microsoft have just upgraded to include Dynamic HTML usage and that is FrontPage 98. FrontPage is a very versatile application which allows you to create web pages graphically, and then does the generation of the HTML underneath itself.

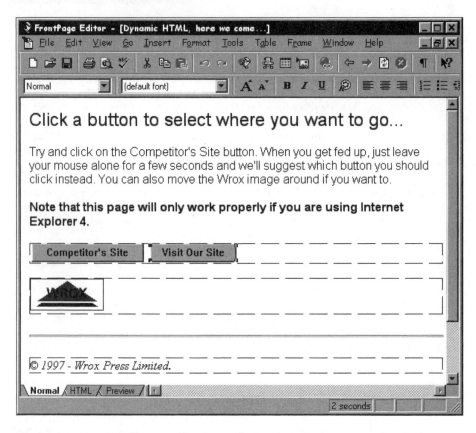

However, you get a lot more freedom when using any programming language (and that's very much what Dynamic HTML is about) if you actually understand what's going on under the hood. Getting a tool to generate your code for you isn't actually going to help you get to grips with the language underneath.

An Old Favorite, NotePad

So, in this book, we're going to be using the single most popular Web page development tool of all time, the NotePad text editor that comes with Windows. It doesn't add any frills or decorations, it won't design your pages for you, but it'll allow you to write the programs yourself.

If you prefer, there's no reason why you can't use any other text editor. One that can provide line numbers is particularly useful when you come to look at finding and fixing script errors. You can even use Microsoft Word for this, as long as you remember to save your files with a .txt extension in Word 97 (and then rename them as HTML files later). Otherwise, it will automatically convert them into HTML files, and, next time you open one, you'll see the results, rather than the actual source HTML tags and script which create the page.

Finally, of course, you'll need a browser that supports Dynamic HTML. We'll do a quick comparison of the relative merits of Internet Explorer 4 and Communicator 4 in the final chapter of this book.

So, now that we've assembled our tool kit, let's get on and look at how Dynamic HTML works in more detail. The first stop is to understand more fully how style sheets and style tags are used in Web pages, then see how this affects what we do in Dynamic HTML. This is the subject of the next chapter.

Summary

In this chapter we've taken a view of what it is that makes Dynamic HTML different from earlier versions of HTML, and explored some of the ways we can use the new features to create more dynamic Web pages. In the broadest terms, the major new features are:

 All the elements in the page (tags, images, text, etc.) are now accessible to script written in the page

 An extension to the implementation of styles and style sheets provides more hooks to the page elements from scripting code

 Extensions to the browser object model are included, thus providing more programmability for the scripting languages used in the pages

 Absolute positioning of elements, including control of the z-order, allows a desk-top publishing style of authoring, and '2.5-D' appearance

 Dynamic re-drawing of any or all parts of the page allows changes to a loaded page to be made visible. Pages no longer need to be reloaded to show the updated version

 New event-handling techniques are supported, including bubbling events up through the object hierarchy

In the rest of the book, we'll explore each of these concepts in depth, and see how we can use them in the pages we create.

Style Sheets, Absolute Positioning and Z-Order

In the previous chapter, we looked briefly at what is new in Dynamic HTML, saw some examples of dynamic pages, and discovered the things we have to learn to start working with it. We're now ready to delve a little deeper into the workings of Dynamic HTML. We'll begin with style sheets, which can be used to connect the elements in the page to the scripts. Previously, in standard HTML, styles were either specified in the attributes of tags or in style sheets and couldn't be changed without refreshing the whole page. One of the main innovations in Dynamic HTML is to allow the user to alter properties dynamically, which in turn allows elements on the page (such as text or graphics) to be changed or moved, without needing the page to be refreshed every time. Dynamic HTML also allows much greater control over positioning of elements on a page—to the nearest pixel, in fact—and allows you to place elements on top of each other, or move one in front of another.

The basis for all of this stems from style sheets and in case you've not really used them much before, we'll begin with a quick reminder of how they work and how they can be used to enhance the layout of your pages. Then we'll look at all the new properties that Dynamic HTML introduces and how they work. This chapter is concerned with how we build pages using a desktop-publishing metaphor- as stable, author-designed documents- rather than in the traditional, browser dependent, HTML way.

So we'll be covering:

- How styles and style sheets work in general
- How we can use style tags to achieve absolute positioning
- How we can control the z-order of elements in the page
- How we achieve a 'two-and-a-half-D' effect
- How to use style sheets to connect scripts to page elements

All this will reinforce our existing understanding of the way styles are used, and introduce a couple of new style attributes. We've supplied a full style reference at the back of this book to help you out.

Using Styles and Style Sheets

As we discussed in Chapter 1, style sheets are the major way in which we provide a link between the elements in our Dynamic Web pages and the code that manipulates them. In this chapter, we'll consider how this link works in more detail, but for the moment we'll concentrate on how style sheets are used in the traditional way. You need to be familiar with this concept before you can start to take advantage of the extensions to the technique that Dynamic HTML offers.

Thereare currently two main ways to implement style sheets, both of which have ugly acronyms. Internet Explorer 4 implements style sheets through the use of **Cascading Style Sheets Level One**, or **CSS1** (in case you were wondering: no, there isn't a Level Two yet). CSS1 is designed to be easy to use and implement, so it has something of a lead over the alternative, **DSSSL-Online.** This, although more comprehensive, is rather more difficult to use and is therefore not supported by IE4.

> **DSSSL-Online** *is the web version of **Document Style Semantics and Specification Language**, a remarkably large and complex standard supported by the ISO.*

CSS1 is well on the way to becoming the de facto standard for web style sheets, since the major browsers and W3C supported it in HTML version 3.2. Dynamic HTML, in the proposed HTML 4 standard, extends style sheets by adding some new attributes. It also continues to omit some style properties implemented by Netscape in their current browsers.

What are Style Sheets

There are three primary advantages of using style sheets. The first is their universality of application. This means that we can develop a style sheet and then apply it to any document or group of documents, by simply setting them so that they refer to the style sheet we have just created. This universality has an added benefit: we can change the appearance of all our pages by simply changing the style sheet.

The next advantage is that style sheets can convey greater typographic control than is normally possible. CSS provides a number of properties that can be used to create effects like drop-caps, overlapping text, shadowed text and so on.

The third benefit is that style sheets, unlike other methods of display control, retain the content/presentation split. This means that style sheet information is separate from the actual text information. This can result in smaller file sizes—five 10K documents can reference one 15K style sheet, instead of having five 25K documents that each contain their own style information. Furthermore, the split allows better skill management, because content can be altered without having to have the document re-formatted with the correct HTML tags

28

An Example

The following picture is actually all text, with no bitmaps (the giant 'we' appears in red type in the original).

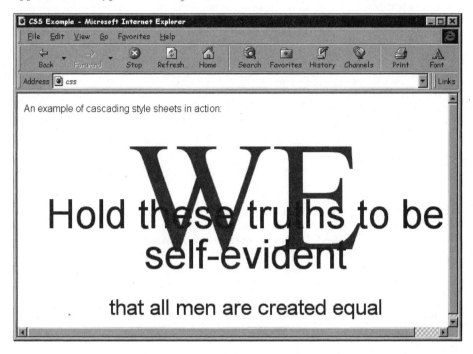

You can run this page from our web site at:
`http://rapid.wrox.co.uk/books/0685`

The actual HTML file that generates this page is:

```
<HTML>
<HEAD>
<TITLE>CSS Example</TITLE>
<STYLE TYPE="text/css">
<!--
BODY {     color: black;
 font-size: 16px;
 font-family: Arial }
 .base {    color: red;
 weight: medium;
 margin-top: 10px;
 font-size: 250px;
 line-height: 250px;
 font-family: Times }
 .layer1 { color: black;
 margin-top: -130px;
 weight: medium;
 font-size: 65px;
 line-height: 65px;
 font-family: Arial }
 .layer2 { color: black;
 margin-top: 30px;
```

```
       weight: medium;
       font-size: 35px;
       line-height: 45px;
       font-family: Arial }
     -->
     </STYLE>
     </HEAD>
     <BODY>
     An example of cascading style sheets in action:
     <CENTER>
     <TABLE WIDTH=730 CELLPADDING=0 CELLSPACING=0 BORDER=0>
     <TR>
     <TD ALIGN=CENTER VALIGN=TOP>
     <DIV CLASS=base>WE</DIV>
     <DIV CLASS=layer1>Hold these truths to be self-evident</DIV>
     <DIV CLASS=layer2>that all men are created equal</DIV>
     </TD></TR>
     </TABLE>
     </CENTER>
     </BODY>
     </HTML>
```

> Notice that this HTML file doesn't contain any images. This is an example of the sort of thing that we can do with style sheets, without resorting to special workarounds or tricks. Anyone viewing this page would only have to download a little over 1K, which is significantly smaller than the equivalent page constructed from images.

We'll start by looking at how you go about specifying the rules in this example that go to a make up a style sheet.

Creating Style Sheets

A style sheet is essentially a declaration of display rules, specifying the display attributes of particular HTML constructs. These rules are easy to write, consisting of combinations of tags, property names and values.

Syntax

All CSS declarations (they're officially termed 'selectors') follow the same format:

TAG { property: value }

For example, to set all level 1 headings to white, we could use either of the following statements:

```
H1 { color: white }
H1 { color: #FFFFFF }
```

As you can see, both of these lines declare that everything enclosed by an **<H1>** tag will have the color white (or hex **#FFFFFF**) applied to it.

There's a list of the color names and values in section F of the reference section of this book.

We can apply a single property to multiple tags by simply grouping those tags in the selector statement. In this example, we've just set all three headings to display in black:

```
H1, H2, H3 { color: #000000 }
```

As well as grouping tags, we can also group properties. We simply enclose our multiple property declarations inside the curly braces and separate them with semicolons:

```
H2 {
  color: #000000;
  font-size: 14pt;
  font-family: monaco
  }
```

This example will display all level 2 headings in 14 point Monaco, in black (unless the client doesn't have access to the Monaco font, in which case it will revert to the default font). Note the use of a semicolon after each declaration to divide one property from another. In our example, we've spread the selector across multiple lines to make the code easier to read. It has the same effect as placing it all on one line. In both cases, though, don't forget the closing brace.

In our example we've defined a style for the <BODY> tag:

```
BODY {    color: black;
    font-size: 16px;
    font-family: Arial }
```

This means that all text that appears between the opening and closing <BODY> tags will automatically default to the style specified, just as the An example of cascading style sheets in action: text on the page does.

Inheritance

One of the best features of CSS is the ability to have one tag inherit the properties of an enclosing tag. This means that we don't need to specify every possible tag; if we neglect to set a property for **<EM>** it will simply acquire the characteristics of whatever tag encloses it. Consider the following:

```
<H3>Section Four: <EM>Colossal</EM> Widgets</H3>
```

If our style sheet specified that all **<H3>** items were to be in green, but didn't say anything about **<EM>**, then Colossal would be green, just like the rest of the line. If, on the other hand, we carefully specified that **<EM>** was blue, it would appear as such. This system of inheritance follows through all of the possible properties, allowing us to set default values. We then only need to worry about the exceptions to our rules (the best way to do this is to set all default properties for **<BODY>**, and then change things for all of the usual tags where necessary).

Even better, we can specify that one property will have a value that is relative to its parent property:

```
P { font-size: 14pt }
P { line-height: 120% }
```

In this instance, line height is defined as a percentage of font size, which will ensure that the paragraph is easy to read. This is useful when we come to revise the styles later, since it automatically ensures that our line heights will instantly change whenever we change the font size. If we explicitly declared the line height, we would need to change it manually—easily forgotten in the heat of designing a site.

Contextual Selectors

Another useful feature of inheritance is that it can be used to apply styles contextually. For example, not only can we set `<H3>` to green and `<EM>` to blue, but we can also set all instances of `<EM>` that occur in `<H3>` as yellow, without affecting either of our other declarations. This is remarkably easy to achieve:

```
H3 EM { color: yellow }
```

Here the style sheet is specifying that any instance of `<EM>` that occurs inside `<H3>` will be shown as yellow. This does not affect any other instance of `<EM>`. You must be careful to omit the comma between the tags when using this method, or the declaration will be interpreted as meaning that both `<H3>` *and* `<EM>` should be yellow.

This technique can be applied in great detail. For example, it is possible to specify that all emphasized words are in red, in small print, but only when they appear in a listing that is itself enclosed by `<I>`. These types of declarations are termed **contextual selectors,** since they select values based on their context. It is also possible to specify values for several contextual selectors in a single statement, by dividing them with commas. For example:

```
H3 EM, H2 I { color: yellow }
```

has the same effect as:

```
H3 EM { color: yellow }
H2 I { color: yellow }
```

One of the first things budding CSS designers do is to go crazy with the control they've just acquired. Sure, you can make your links all appear in pink 24pt Times, but do you really want to? Changing properties, simply because you can, is a recipe for reader dissatisfaction. If visitors can't figure out 'what is a link' versus 'what is just an emphasis', or 'why all of the lines are in 6pt type', they probably won't bother visiting your site again. A full list of style sheet properties can be found in Section C.

Cascading Style Sheets

One of the niftiest, and most confusing, capabilities of CSS is the ability to have style sheets that **cascade**—hence the name **Cascading Style Sheets**. This means that compliant browsers are supposed to allow multiple style sheets to have control over the same document at the same time. It is possible, for example, to have three separate style sheets trying to format a document at once. This is actually more useful than it sounds.

The idea is this: when authors set up documents and refer to style sheets, they are expressing their preferred mode of display. Browsers have a 'default style' of their own that they prefer to use when displaying pages. As the browser interprets documents on the Web, it will display them in its default style. If, however, it runs across a document that uses CSS, it will give way to the preferences stated in that style sheet. The basic idea appears to be that 'normal' HTML documents have nothing to lose by being formatted according to browser preferences, but that documents using CSS ought to be displayed the way the author intended (or else they wouldn't have been formatted that way in the first place).

Which style sheet 'wins' is determined on a selector-by-selector basis, so that the browser can win sometimes, and the author others. The method that browsers use to determine which instructions will be used is basically as follows:

 Determine if the settings for any element actually conflict. If not, any inherited values (from 'parent' tags) are used instead. If there aren't any, the default values are used

 If there is a conflict, the values are sorted by origin (author values are higher than reader values)

 Sort by specificity: if two values conflict, and one applies only to the situation at hand, but the other applies in all cases, then the restricted value will win

Notice that this system allows for the possibility of having effects from multiple style sheets all appearing at once on the page. This is actually a benefit, since it allows you to create multiple focused style sheets, and then apply them in different combinations to different documents. Unfortunately, however, this is neither particularly easy to do nor very intuitive, and requires careful use of the correct **implementation tags** within the document

Implementing Style Sheets

So, the next question is how do we actually incorporate the style sheet functionality into our HTML document? There are several ways to do this and they each have slightly different effects. It is important to decide which method suits your purpose, since they're not functionally identical.

Using <LINK>

The first method is a special use of the `<LINK>` tag. This can be used to reference independent style sheets, which can then be applied to the document at will. To use the `<LINK>` method, we place the following in the `<HEAD>` of our document:

```
<LINK REL=STYLESHEET TYPE="text/css" HREF="http://foo.bar.com/style"
TITLE="Style">
```

33

Obviously, you would need to change the **HREF** to point to your own style sheet.

> *You should note that this means you can apply style sheets that reside on completely different servers. This can be particularly useful in an Intranet situation, where one department can set up several 'approved' styles for all documents to use. As a point of Internet etiquette, it is a good idea to ask the original style sheet author for permission before 'borrowing' their style sheet in this manner.*

Using <STYLE>

The next way to use style sheets is to use the **<STYLE>** element. The idea here is to enclose the style sheet data in the **<STYLE>** tag, so that it can be parsed and applied as the document is loaded. To this end, we use the following code, placed in the **<HEAD>** of our document:

```
<STYLE TYPE="text/css">...style info goes here... </STYLE>
```

This seems quick and easy (and it is) but there are a few things you should be aware of. The first problem is that older browsers will ignore the **<STYLE>** tag, and will try to handle the style data as if it were normal text. This can be avoided by enclosing the whole line in HTML comment tags as we did in our previous example, since style-aware browsers will still find the style information and handle it appropriately.

The second problem is that by using the **<STYLE>** tag in the manner described above, we need to include a complete style sheet in every document. This not only increases the time needed to create a document, but increases the file sizes and makes it more difficult to change a complete site's appearance as well. In effect, this method erases two of the three advantages conferred by style sheets, and should be avoided if possible.

Using @import

Fortunately, there is a way to automatically apply style sheets and still keep the file sizes down: you can use a special notation in CSS1 that was designed for this very purpose:

```
<HTML>
<HEAD>
<TITLE>CSS Example</TITLE>
<STYLE>
@import URL("http://rapid.wrox.co.uk/books/0685/style.css");
</STYLE>
</HEAD>
<BODY>
An example of cascading style sheets in action:
<CENTER>
<TABLE WIDTH=730 CELLPADDING=0 CELLSPACING=0 BORDER=0>
<TR>
<TD ALIGN=CENTER VALIGN=TOP>
<DIV CLASS=base>WE</DIV>
<DIV CLASS=layer1>Hold these truths to be self-evident</DIV>
```

```
<DIV CLASS=layer2>that all men are created equal</DIV>
</TD>
</TR>
</TABLE>
</CENTER>
</BODY>
</HTML>
```

This notation tells the browser to get the style sheet **style.css** from the server at **rapid.wrox.co.uk**. If we place the **@import** line between **<STYLE>** tags in the **<HEAD>** of our document, the style will be automatically retrieved and applied before our document is displayed.

All of these methods, used on their own without additional tags, apply their style sheets to the entire document, so we can't style just one paragraph unless we employ an extra technique.

Applying Style Sheets to Specific Text

If once you've linked the style sheets into the document and you don't want it to apply to the whole document, you'll need a way of identifying the text to which you wish to apply the style.

Using STYLE with Individual Tags

One way of doing this is to specify the CSS1 information as part of the tag that we want it to affect.

```
<P STYLE="color: green">This paragraph will be green</P>
```

This is extremely flexible and easy to use, but it does have the major drawback that we need to specify each tag individually. (This, of course, removes two of the major advantages of style sheets). In Dynamic HTML all text and graphics tags now support the **STYLE** attribute and the new properties that we will discuss shortly. To provide more control over how things are formatted, CSS utilizes the concept of a **'class'**.

Classes

A class can either be a defined as a property or as a subset of a previous declaration. We can specify properties on a class-wide basis, with any properties of that class applying to all instances of that class—even when used with different tags. Declaring the properties of a class is easy. In our example we define a class **base** as follows:

```
.base {   color: red;
weight: medium;
margin-top: 10px;
font-size: 250px;
line-height: 250px;
font-family: Times }
```

Notice the period that appears before **base**—this establishes that we are naming a class and defining its properties.

35

We then use the **CLASS** attribute of the **<DIV>** tag to apply it solely to the text WE:

```
<DIV CLASS=base>WE</DIV>
```

We can also create a subset of a previous declaration. For example if we specify that **<H3>** is blue, we can create a subset of **<H3>** that is white. This subset will retain any other properties we've given the parent, and must be referenced by name (in order to separate it from the parent.) The following code demonstrates this by creating a new class named **second** to apply to **<H3>** tags:

```
H3 { font-size:14pt, font-family: monaco, color: #0000FF }
H3.second { color: #FFFFFF }
```

To implement our newly created class, we must call it explicitly like this:

```
<H3 CLASS=second> This is in white fourteen-point monaco </H3>
<H3> This is in the default color and fourteen-point monaco </H3>
```

The advantage with defining a class as a property rather than as a subset is that if we define it as a property, as follows:

```
.second { color: #FFFFFF }
```

we can then apply the properties of **second** wherever we call it, without having to set up every conceivable combination of tag and class:

```
<H1 CLASS=second> Level One </H1>
<EM CLASS=second> Emphasis </EM>
```

In this example, both items of text will be in white, and each will have whatever characteristics were previously defined, without having to explicitly define the properties of **H1.second** and **EM.second**.

In our original example we also used a tag which didn't introduce any new styling but instead identified sections of text. This was the **<DIV>** tag.

The <DIV> Tag

This tag was introduced in the HTML 3.2 standard. It is used to define an area of the page, or **document division**. Anything between the opening and closing tag is referred as a single item. The **<DIV>** tag doesn't allocate any particular style to the text, just allocates an area. When used together with the **CLASS** attribute, you can apply sets of styles (such as colors and font sizes) to this 'area' or to any individual element.

This tag was used in our style sheets example to enclose each of the separate bits of text and to allow the different bits of text to be layered on top of one another. In HTML 3.2, the tag doesn't allow for any more direct manipulation of the individual 'layers'.

```
<DIV CLASS=base>WE</DIV>
<DIV CLASS=layer1>Hold these truths to be self-evident</DIV>
<DIV CLASS=layer2>that all men are created equal</DIV>
```

Look at the text which has the style `layer1`. It appears over the top of the text with the style `base`. However, rather than being able to specify which sheet should appear on top of another in the code, the order of the `<DIV>` tags is all that the browser has to go by. If we changed around the `<DIV>` tags attached to the `base` and `layer1` style classes, the text layering would also be reversed. This problem is addressed in Dynamic HTML by **2.5-D layering**, which we'll look at later in this chapter.

Also it isn't possible to define where, in x and y type co-ordinates, a division should appear on a page. It's possible to define the height, width and margin size of document divisions, and even where they can be positioned in relation to each other, but not much more. So while style sheets offer greater flexibility in these terms over standard HTML, they're still not the answer to everything.

New Dynamic HTML Style Properties

Having taken a refresher in how style sheets are used, let's now see exactly what advantages Dynamic HTML provides in page formatting. First, Dynamic HTML provides support for six completely new properties, and extends the existing properties available for formatting the background and setting margins (or borders) around elements.

The six all-new properties that we'll be looking at in particular are:

```
left            top             z-index
position        visibility      overflow
```

> You can find a list of all the properties available in Section A.

The extensions to existing border properties are:

```
border-color            border-style
border-right-width      border-left-width
border-top-width        border-bottom-width
```

The extensions to the background formatting properties are:

```
background-attachment   background-color
background-image        background-position
background-repeat
```

We won't be spending time on these last two sets of properties. They really only duplicate existing properties, although making them easier to use. You'll find a complete listing of all the style properties available in the reference section at the end of the book. So, instead, let's look at what is really new.

Displaying and Positioning Elements

The six new style properties allow us to create pages in a way more akin to desktop publishing than to existing web page authoring techniques. The reason is simple, and can be seen in the names of just three of the new properties: `left`, `top` and `z-index`. With HTML version 3.2, either we depended on the browser to place our elements in consecutive order as they were progressively rendered on the page or we used a style sheet with positive or negative margin settings. However, in Dynamic HTML, we can now simply specify the x, y and z coordinates (in pixels) of each element on the page.

This is just like the way we design the forms or dialogs for a normal Windows application, using a 'real' programming language. The new `top` and `left` properties of the **STYLE** attribute can be used to define—with pixel point accuracy—where on a page a tag should go.

- The `left` property (the X coordinate) is used to specify, in pixels, how far away from the left of the window (or a container) an element should be placed. Values are stored as strings, in the form **100px** (which would denote 100 pixels)

- The `top` property (the Y coordinate) specifies, in pixels, how far from the top of a window (or container), an element should be placed

- The `z-index` property adds a new dimension, or more accurately, a series of layers to the page. The higher the value that the `z-index` property of an element is set to, the 'closer' it appears on the page. By this we mean, elements with higher `z-index` properties will appear on top of elements with lower `z-index` properties

So you can see that we can work with Dynamic HTML to produce a 3-D style page layout. While it does provide a 'kind' of 3-D appearance, we can actually only specify the three standard x, y, and z co-ordinates—we can't achieve real 3-D. For this reason, it's often referred to as **two-and-a-half-D** layout.

Going 2.5-D in a Web Page

The first step in creating a 2.5-D layout using Dynamic HTML is to understand how document divisions work. For each division we want to create on a page, we can specify the `top`, `left`, `width` and `height` properties. We combine these with the `left`, `top` and `z-index` properties of the elements to get a display that looks as if it was created by using frames. This is the sample page `2point5d.htm`:

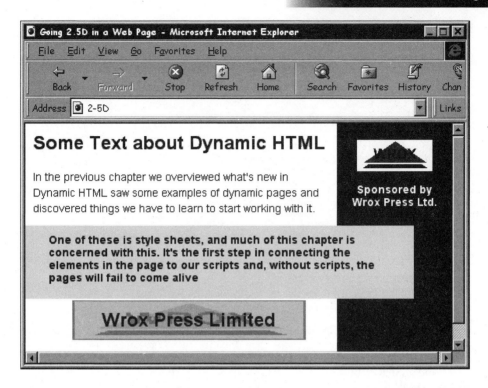

You can run this page from our web site at:
`http://rapid.wrox.co.uk/books/0685`

Notice how the central band of text overlaps the right-hand dark-colored column. This kind of layout would be just about impossible to achieve with tables. However, it's easy using Dynamic HTML. In fact, this page demonstrates several ways of using the new properties to build more free-form, desktop-publishing-like web pages. Here, so that you can see the overall contents, is the complete HTML source code for this page:

```
<HTML>
<HEAD><TITLE> Going 2.5D in a web Page </TITLE></HEAD>

<STYLE>
  P      { font-family:"Arial, sans-serif"; font-size:14 }
  P.bluetext { font-weight:Bold; color:darkblue }
  P.reverse { font-weight:Bold; color:white }
  H2     { font-family:"Arial, sans-serif"; font-size:24;
           font-weight:Bold; color:darkblue }
</STYLE>

<BODY>

<DIV STYLE="position:absolute; top:0; left:0; width:400; height:100;
          margin:10">
  <H2> Some Text about Dynamic HTML </H2>
  <P STYLE="line-height:140%"> In the previous chapter we overviewed what's new in
  Dynamic HTML saw some examples of dynamic pages and discovered things we have to learn
  to start working with it.</P>
  </DIV>
```

```
<DIV STYLE="position:absolute; top:0; left:400; width:150; height:300;
     background:darkblue">
 <IMG SRC="wrox0.gif" STYLE="position:relative; top:20; left:25">
 <CENTER>
  <P CLASS=reverse STYLE="margin-top:30">Sponsored by<BR>Wrox Press Ltd.</P>
 </CENTER>
</DIV>

<DIV STYLE="position:absolute; top:130; left:0; width:500; height:80;
     background:yellow; margin-top:10; margin-left:30; margin-right:30">
 <P CLASS=bluetext> One of these is style sheets, and much of this chapter is
concerned with this. It's the first step in connecting the
elements in the page to our scripts and, without scripts, the
pages will fail to come alive </P>
</DIV>

<DIV STYLE="position:absolute; top:225; width:400; left=:0">
 <CENTER>
  <H2 STYLE="color=darkred; line-height:200%">Wrox Press Limited</H2>
  <IMG SRC="wrox1.gif" STYLE="position:absolute; top:0; left:50; z-index:-1">
 </CENTER>
</DIV>

</BODY>
</HTML>
```

As you can see, there are five main sections to the code. The first is the **STYLE** tag that sets the font styles, sizes, colors, and so on for each kind of text style we are going to use in the page. You'll notice that it creates a style for the standard **<P>** paragraph tag, then two sub-class styles based on this. These have a bold font weight, and different colors. The fourth style is just used to create the headline **<H2>** style.

Of course, these style definitions could just as well be a separate style sheet, to permit easier updating of several pages in one go if required. However, what we're really interested in are the other four sections of the page—the 'working parts'. These are the four **<DIV>** tags.

Working with Document Divisions

One of the easiest ways to think of the **<DIV>** document division tag is that it creates a section within the page where we can place other elements and these sections can overlap each other. Each section becomes a **container**, and its contents can be placed accurately within this container using the Dynamic HTML **left** and **top** style attributes. This is how we've divided our page up into separate sections that overlap.

To present the page as separate divisions, we need to use another of the new style properties, **position**. This is used to specify where the browser will place the division, and can also be applied to any other elements that can be positioned using the **left** and **top** properties.

The Dynamic HTML Position Property

This new property allows us to position elements at fixed positions within the browser window, in conjunction with the **top** and **left** property. It can be set to one of three possible values: **absolute**, **relative**, or **static**.

40

absolute means that the element will be placed at an absolute position with respect to the top left hand corner of its container. This effectively removes it from the HTML source as far as its influence on following elements is concerned. For example, specifying left and top values will position the element at those x and y coordinates with respect to the division that contains it. If it is not within a division, it is placed in that position with respect to the top left corner of the page. Its actual position will not affect any elements that follow it in the HTML source

relative means that the element will be placed in a position relative to its position within the HTML source for the page. In other words, if an image follows three lines of text in the HTML source, has its position property set to relative, and the left and top set to zero, it will appear in the same position with respect to the text as if there were no positioning attributes included. If we specify relative, and set the left and top properties to non-zero figures (positive or negative), it will be placed at this horizontal and vertical offset from the normal position. Other elements in the HTML source that follow it will still be placed after this element in the usual way, and hence initially offset by the same amount

static means that the element will be placed in the usual position with respect to the HTML source for the page, and is the default value if position is not specified in the **STYLE** tag

The **position** property applies to the **<DIV>** tag, as well as to other elements, so we can use it to place our document divisions accurately in the page. In the example above, we used these four divisions to build up the basic structure of the page:

```
<DIV STYLE="position:absolute; top:0; left:0; width:400; height:100; ... ">
   ...
</DIV>
```

```
<DIV STYLE="position:absolute; top:0; left:400; width:150; height:300; ... ">
   ...
</DIV>
```

```
<DIV STYLE="position:absolute; top:130; left:0; width:500; height:80; ... ">
   ...
</DIV>
```

```
<DIV STYLE="position:absolute; top:225; width:400; left=:0">
   ...
</DIV>
```

Notice that there is no **height** property set for the last one. If we omit any properties like this, the division will assume default values. For example, if we omit the **width** property, it will span the width of the browser window by default.

Document divisions also act in a different way to the normal page. While text will flow across division boundaries, if it won't all fit within the division in which it has been declared, other elements such as images are cropped. When the browser window is resized, text in a division does not repaginate like text displayed directly on the page. With careful design, both of these properties can be used to advantage in our pages. In particular, it means that our designs are now independent of the size of the browser window, and the user must adjust the size, or scroll the page, to see it all.

Using Divisions in Specifying Dynamic HTML Layout

Having placed our document division containers on the page, we can now get on and fill them with our page elements. Anything enclosed in a <DIV> and </DIV> tag pair will appear within the area of the screen designated to that division. The first division is simple enough—it just displays the heading and some introductory text:

```
<DIV STYLE="position:absolute; top:0; left:0; width:400; height:100;
        margin:10">
 <H2> Some Text about Dynamic HTML </H2>
 <P STYLE="line-height:140%"> In the previous chapter we ... etc. </P>
 </DIV>
```

The next division is the dark colored section to the right of the page. In it, there's a logo and some text. Notice that we've specified the image element with a **position** property of **relative**. This effectively just offsets it while 'reserving' its place in the HTML source, so that the text that follows will appear below it:

```
<DIV STYLE="position:absolute; top:0; left:400; width:150; height:300;
        background:darkblue">
 <IMG SRC="wrox0.gif" STYLE="position:relative; top:20; left:25">
 <CENTER>
  <P CLASS=reverse STYLE="margin-top:30">Sponsored by<BR>Wrox Press Ltd.</P>
 </CENTER>
 </DIV>
```

If we had declared the **position** property as **absolute** for the image, instead of **relative**, it would appear in the same place, but the text would be displayed at the top of the division, overlaid by the image. The image would have 'disappeared' from the HTML source as far as its effect on the following text is concerned:

You'll also see that the usual formatting tags work normally within a division. We've used the <CENTER> tag to center the text in the division, and applied the **P.reverse** style we defined earlier, just as we would in a traditional web page.

The next division is very similar to the first. It uses some extra style properties to set variable margins around the text, so that it fits nicely into the One of these is style sheets... division (the bottom one in the previous screenshot):

```
<DIV STYLE="position:absolute; top:130; left:0; width:500; height:80;
        background:yellow; margin-top:10; margin-left:30; margin-right:30">
 <P CLASS=bluetext> One of these is style sheets, and ... etc. </P>
 </DIV>
```

Layer Control with the Z-index Property

The final division demonstrates one more technique. Here, we have an `<IMG>` tag overlaid by text. In traditional Web pages, this isn't possible. The text is wrapped around any images on the page, unless you arrange for it to be used in the `<BODY>` tag as the page background.

Dynamic HTML adds a new property `z-index`, which allows the web page author to specify at what level (or layer) an element is displayed. This can be in comparison to the body text or headings in the page, or any other elements. The body text and titles are displayed in level zero, or layer 0, and so have a `z-index` of zero.

Specifying the Z-index

By specifying positive numbers, we can arrange for our elements to appear above the text, and by specifying negative numbers, below it. And of course, we can layer individual non-text elements with respect to each other by using higher or lower `z-index` values.

In the fourth division of our example page, we have some text, and a logo inside an `<IMG>` tag. The text is defined first in the HTML, and uses the `line-height` style property to place it in the correct vertical position inside the division. Then the logo is specified, using absolute positioning to get it centered with respect to the text. (If the logo were relatively positioned, it would follow the previous text and, since it would no longer fit into the division, would simply be clipped.) Finally, to make it appear with the text rendered on top, we set its `z-index` property to `-1`:

```
<DIV STYLE="position:absolute; top:225; width:400; left=:0">
 <CENTER>
  <H2 STYLE="color=darkred; line-height:200%">Wrox Press Limited</H2>
  <IMG SRC="wrox1.gif" STYLE="position:absolute; top:0; left:50; z-index:-1">
 </CENTER>
</DIV>
```

The result isn't terribly pretty, but it serves to demonstrate the point.

Overlaying Document Divisions

No doubt you've realized that the browser sets the `z-index` of elements automatically as it renders the page. When two elements with an equivalent 'default level', such as two image tags, are defined in the HTML source for the page, the one that comes last will have the highest `z-index`. Therefore, if these two elements are made to overlap, using any of the positioning techniques, the second one will appear on top of the first one. If you look back at the previous example, you'll see that the third (yellow) document division overlays the second (dark blue) one, because it was declared later in the HTML.

By setting an element's `z-index` in a style tag—or, as you'll see later on, dynamically with script code—we can control this layering process to provide exactly the effect we want.

43

Controlling Overflow and Visibility

In this chapter, we've seen how four of the new Dynamic HTML style properties can be used to create pages in a fundamentally new way, by accurately positioning elements and controlling the layering. The new properties we've used are the **left**, **top** and **z-index** properties, which effectively define the x, y, and z coordinates, plus the **position** property which defines how the coordinates are used and what effect the positioning has on other elements that follow in the HTML source. The other two new properties are used to control the **overflow** and **visibility** of elements.

Using the Overflow Property

The **overflow** property is used to determine what should happen when an element's contents exceed the height or width of a window. It can be set to one of three values:

 A value of **none** indicates that no clipping is to be performed. For example, preformatted text that extends past the right edge of an element's boundaries would be rendered anyway

 A value of **clip** indicates that clipping should be performed with no scrolling mechanism

A **scroll** value causes a scrolling mechanism to be invoked

Using the Visibility Property

The last new style property in Dynamic HTML is **visibility**. As the name suggests, this controls whether the element will be visible on the page. When we create wholly static pages, using only absolute positioning, it isn't terribly useful. After all, if an element won't be seen, there's not a great deal of point in including it in the HTML source.

Where the **visibility** property is useful is when we come to add scripting code to our page. It can change the properties of the elements in the page, thereby making them visible or invisible as required, while the page is displayed.

However, there is one case where the **visibility** property can be useful when formatting a static page. Looking back at our 'two-and-a-half-D' example, we found that the text below the *Wrox* image in the right-hand division depended on the image tag having a **position** property value of **relative**. This prevents the text from appearing at the top of the division. If we remove the image tag, the text will not be in the same position, because there is no relative image to move it down the page.

If, for some reason, we wanted to 'remove' the image and not move the text, we can set its visibility property to **hidden** (the default is **visible**). The result is that everything else stays the same, but the image itself is not rendered on the page:

Sponsored by
Wrox Press Ltd.

Easy 3-D Text Effects

Next on our agenda is using Dynamic HTML properties to provide an easier
way of displaying 3-D style titles. By using document divisions and the absolute
positioning abilities of Dynamic HTML, we can achieve better results, faster.
Here's an example page, named **3dtitles.htm**:

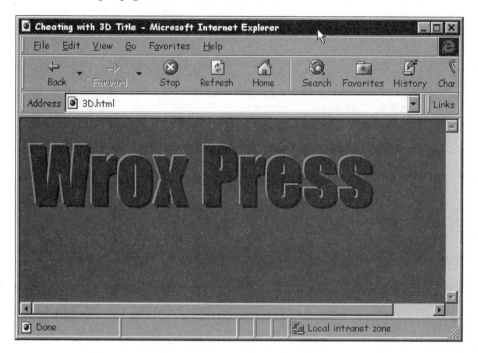

You can run this page from our web site at:
http://rapid.wrox.co.uk/books/0685

Here's the HTML that creates this page. It consists of a **<STYLE>** section that
defines the three text styles, and three document divisions denoted by the
<DIV> and **</DIV>** tags. The **<STYLE>** section defines a standard paragraph
format using a large red font, then two subclasses with the same font, but in
different colors:

```
<HTML>
<HEAD><TITLE> Cheating with 3D Title </TITLE></HEAD>

<STYLE>
  P { font-family: "Impact, sans-serif"; font-size:96; color:red }
  P.highlight { color:silver }
  P.shadow { color:darkred }
</STYLE>

<BODY BGCOLOR=408080>

<DIV STYLE="position:absolute; top:5; left:5; width:600; height:100; margin:10">
<P CLASS=shadow> Wrox Press </P>
</DIV>
```

45

```
<DIV STYLE="position:absolute; top:0; left:0; width:600; height:100; margin:10">
<P CLASS=highlight> Wrox Press </P>
</DIV>

<DIV STYLE="position:absolute; top:2; left:2; width:600; height:100; margin:10">
<P> Wrox Press </P>
</DIV>

</BODY>
</HTML>
```

The three divisions are identical except for their **top** and **left** properties, and—since they are all defined with a **position** property of **absolute**—they will appear at these slightly different positions, but display different colored text. The order that they are defined in the page controls the **z-index**, so we end up with the silver highlight overlaid by the dark red shadow, and then by the top-level bright red text.

Changing the appearance, shadow depth, or colors is simply a matter of changing the **top**, **left**, **z-index** and **color** properties, and this can create some very different appearances.

Adding Script to HTML Pages

So far, you might be forgiven for thinking that many of the effects we've demonstrated could have been achieved – albeit with a little more effort - with cascading style sheets and without any of the new Dynamic HTML properties. While this is true to some extent, it's because we've hidden the real power Dynamic HTML offers, which is the ability to dynamically manipulate properties with a **script** and therefore update the positions and styles of elements in the page.

At its most basic, a scripting language is just a way of making your pages reactive, enabling them to interact with the user so they are more than just code. Scripting has been present in both Internet Explorer and Netscape Navigator/Communicator since version 3. Internet Explorer 4 supports both JScript (Microsoft's implementation of JavaScript) and VBScript, while Communicator 4 only supports JavaScript (without the aid of a proprietary add-in). The focus of the book is Internet Explorer 4, and we'll be using examples in both VBScript and JScript. There is a full reference to the two languages at the back of the book, and a tutorial on VBScript is provided as part of Section H.

Rather than start off by talking about how to make your page react to events in too much detail, we've chosen to describe how to manipulate the new Dynamic HTML properties first and include only simple event code. In Chapter 5, Scripts and Event Handling, we'll look in more detail at how both VBScript and JScript are used with the object model.

However, there are a couple of things you will need to know before you start. We'll briefly show you how script code appears in a page, and how we create code routines. This will be enough to carry you through to Chapter 5.

Where to Place Your Script

Scripting code is placed in the page within the HTML `<SCRIPT>` and `</SCRIPT>` tags. These tell the browser that the code between the tags is to be interpreted and executed as the page is loaded. Inside the opening `<SCRIPT>` tag, we use a **LANGUAGE** attribute to tell the browser which interpreter to use. If omitted, the browser will assume it's JavaScript, and getting it wrong will provoke error messages as the page loads.

```
...
<SCRIPT LANGUAGE=VBSCRIPT>
    ... VBScript code goes here
</SCRIPT>
...
```

```
...
<SCRIPT LANGUAGE=JAVASCRIPT>
    ... JavaScript code goes here
</SCRIPT>
...
```

The script section can be placed almost anywhere in the page. The favorite position is often at the end, so that the rest of the page is loaded and rendered by the browser before the interpreter loads and runs the code. However, if we are using the code to insert something into the page, like the time and date, we need to place the `<SCRIPT>` section in the appropriate position within the HTML source.

```
...
The date and time is
<SCRIPT LANGUAGE=VBSCRIPT> document.write(Now) </SCRIPT>
<P>
...
```

This causes the browser to execute the VBScript **Now** function and pass the result to the **write** method of the **document** object. This method writes the information into that page at the point where it's called, so the result is something like this:

If this page is loaded into a browser that doesn't support VBScript, the code itself will simply be displayed as text on the page. The traditional way to prevent this is to enclose the contents of the `<SCRIPT>` section in a comment tag. Non-script enabled browsers will then ignore it, while browsers that do support scripting will still be able to interpret and execute it (unless of course they only support JavaScript, in which case the script will be ignored).

```
...
<SCRIPT LANGUAGE=VBSCRIPT>
<!-- hide from older browsers
    ... script code goes here
-->
</SCRIPT>
...
```

Of course, we're aiming our page at Dynamic HTML-enabled browsers, and support for a scripting language is a prerequisite for this anyway. However, it

47

doesn't hurt to hide the scripting in case the page is loaded by an older browser—even though it will probably still look odd because the browser won't support the other layout features of Dynamic HTML either.

Creating Script Routines in a Page

The other technique you need to be familiar with is how we create separate code routines in a page that are *not* executed as the page is loading. Much of the dynamic nature of modern web pages is down to script code that reacts to **events** occurring within the browser. Changing the contents of a page by executing script as it is loading does provide a dynamic page, but doesn't provide the true dynamic page refresh that we're seeking.

To prevent VBScript code being executed as the page loads, we place it inside a **subroutine** or a **function**. The only difference is the way they are defined in the script, and that a function produces a value that gets passed back to the code that called it. As far as this book is concerned, we'll mainly be using subroutines.

If you want to know more about VB Script and its applications than we cover in this book, try the Wrox Press book

Instant VB Script, ISBN 1-861000-44-8

```
<SCRIPT LANGUAGE=VBSCRIPT>

Sub MyNewRoutine()
 .. VBScript code goes here
End Sub

Sub window_onLoad()
 .. VBScript code to run when the window object gets an 'onLoad' event
End Sub

Function GetAnyNumber()
 .. VBScript code goes here, including setting the return value
 GetAnyNumber = 42
End Function

</SCRIPT>
```

These routines will only run when we call them from code elsewhere, or an event occurs in the browser that calls them automatically. In the second example, the code will run when the window has finished loading a new page, for example. In JavaScript, things are slightly different, because it doesn't support subroutines, only functions. We also have to write the code a little differently:

```
<SCRIPT LANGUAGE=JAVASCRIPT>

function MyNewRoutine()
{
 .. JavaScript code goes here;
}

function window_onLoad()
{
```

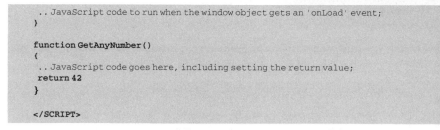

```
  ..JavaScript code to run when the window object gets an 'onLoad' event;
}

function GetAnyNumber()
{
  ..JavaScript code goes here, including setting the return value;
 return 42
}

</SCRIPT>
```

*JavaScript requires the code in a routine to be enclosed in curly braces, and
each line within a function to be separated by a semicolon.*

Using a Script to Manipulate the Dynamic HTML Properties

We're going to look at an example which shows how we can dynamically
update the properties of an element on the page with a script, to make it move
across the screen. However before we can do that, we need to understand how
we can update properties using code. This is all done via the **style** object.

The Style Attribute

The various style properties of elements are the most useful properties of all,
and the ones we'll use in most of our dynamic pages. They are decided by the
element's **STYLE** attribute, within the tag that creates the element. We can get at
any of the properties defined here—and best of all we can change most of them
within our code.

As an example, if we declare our heading tag like this:

```
<H2 ID=MyHeading STYLE="font-family:Arial; color:red; font-size:48">...
```

we can retrieve *and change* the font, size and color in our code. Remember that
styles can be inherited as well, so we can have properties that are set either by
a **<STYLE>** section in that page, or by a linked style sheet.

Using the Style Object

Every element that supports the HTML **STYLE** attribute has an equivalent
style object. This is how we can get at the style properties for that element.
It's important to realize that there are two different ways of setting the
properties for an element in the HTML source, and correspondingly two
different ways to access these properties in our code.

If we define an **<IMG>** tag like this:

```
<IMG ID=MyImage SRC="mypic.gif" WIDTH=100 HEIGHT=100>
```

we are controlling the width and height using traditional HTML attributes. The
width and **height** properties are then direct properties of the object, and we
can refer to them in our code using:

```
MyImage.width
MyImage.height
```

However, we can't define the **top** and **left** properties using normal HTML
attributes—we have to include them in a **STYLE** attribute like this:

```
<IMG ID=MyImage SRC="mypic.gif" STYLE="position:absoloute; top=50; left=200">
```

The values in the **STYLE** attribute are now properties of the image's **style**
object, not direct properties of the image element. We refer to these using:

```
MyImage.style.top
MyImage.style.left
```

Of course, we can also set the image's **width** and **height** properties in the
STYLE tag. (This over-rides the values in the traditional HTML attributes, if
they are set there as well):

```
<IMG ID=MyImage SRC="mypic.gif" STYLE="position:absolute; top:50;
left:200; width:150; height:75">
```

Now we can refer to the **width** and **height** through the **style** object, and
the 'direct' **width** and **height** properties will not be defined.

```
MyImage.style.top        'value is 50px
MyImage.style.left       'value is 200px
MyImage.style.width      'value is 150px
MyImage.style.height     'value is 75px

MyImage.width      'not defined
MyImage.height     'not defined
```

Just note that, while these properties have the same name as the various **STYLE**
attributes and HTML attributes defined in the HTML source, this isn't always
the case. For example the **font-size** and **font-family** attributes are
referenced by the **fontSize** and **fontFamily** properties.

*There's a full listing of the properties of the **style** object, and a list of
properties and the equivalent style attributes, in the reference section at the
end of this book.*

Coping with Missing Style Properties

One problem we may come across (as we briefly mentioned earlier) is that
unless a property is defined in the HTML **STYLE** attribute for an element, or
cascaded from a **<STYLE>** tag or a linked style sheet, it may not be available in
our code. If we don't define the **left** and **top** properties in the tag's **STYLE**
attribute, we may not be able to read them in code—although some elements
(like the image tag) provide a value based on the content. And remember that
many properties, such as **left** and **top**, aren't inherited, i.e. they don't
'cascade'.

The easy solution is just to define them in the HTML—and if we're using
relative or **absolute** positioning it's likely that we'll do this anyway.
However, we can add and remove properties, and retrieve their values, using

50

three methods supported by all visible elements; **setAttribute**,
removeAttribute and **getAttribute**.

```
MyImage.removeAttribute "top"
MyHeading.setAttribute "color", "blue"
MsgBox MyHeading.getAttribute("fontSize")
```

Moving Elements around a Page

Here's the bit you've been waiting for. Of course if we define an image tag like
this:

```
<IMG SRC="MyPic.gif" STYLE="position:absolute; left:200; top:100>
```

not only can we retrieve the image's **left** and **top** properties, we can also
change them—effectively moving it around the screen while the page is
displayed.

However, things aren't quite that simple. While we can freely set new values for
the **left** and **top** property (and the **width** and **height** if we want to), we
often want to know where the element is first. We might want to just move it
five pixels to the right, for example.

The problem is that the **left** and **top** properties, as we mentioned earlier, are
stored in pixels (the default unless we specify another unit such as **em** or **pc**).
If we retrieved these properties from the example above, we get the string
values **200px** and **100px**, rather than numbers. So we will have to use another
set of properties instead.

The posLeft, posTop, posWidth, and posHeight Properties

As the **left**, **top**, **width** and **height** properties are all stored as strings, we
can't do any calculations with them unless you strip off the **px** from the string
first. To save having to strip off the unit identifier and convert the property
values into numbers using code each time, we can use another set of properties;
posLeft, **posTop**, **posWidth** and **posHeight**. These are set by the browser
when it sizes and positions the element using the **STYLE** attributes, and return
the left, top, width and height as numeric values automatically:

```
MyImage.style.posTop       'value is 50
MyImage.style.posLeft      'value is 200
MyImage.style.posWidth     'value is 150
MyImage.style.posHeight    'value is 75
```

> *There's a list of the various measurement units that Dynamic HTML defines
> within the styles reference at the back of this book.*

Moving Elements around a page Example

Right, it's time to take a look at an example. We're going to 'move' an element
across the screen making it move behind one element and then in front of
another, by simply updating one property. The element will start its journey on
the far left of the screen and move gradually to the right:

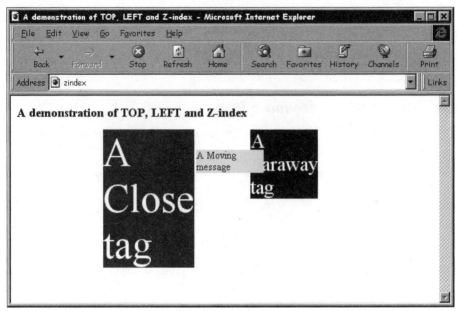

Scripting Dynamic Properties

You can run this page from our web site at:
`http://rapid.wrox.co.uk/books/0685`

The initial 'X 'and 'Y' co-ordinates of the tags are set out in the **STYLE** attributes of the **<DIV>** tags and each **<DIV>** tag is assigned a unique name, with an ID attribute so it can be identified in the script.

```
<!DOCTYPE HTML PUBLIC "-//IETF//DTD HTML//EN">
<HTML>
<HEAD>
<TITLE></TITLE>
</HEAD>

<BODY>
<H3>A demonstration of TOP, LEFT and Z-index</H3>

<DIV Id=CloseDiv STYLE="position:absolute; top: 50; left:140; height: 130;
width:100; background: red; font-size:60; z-index: 4">
A Close tag
</DIV>

<DIV Id=FarDiv STYLE="position:absolute; top: 50; left:360; height: 30; width:100;
background: blue; font-size:30; z-index: 2">
A Faraway tag
</DIV>

<DIV ID=MovingMessage STYLE="position:absolute; top: 80; left:0; height: 30;
width:100; background: yellow; font-size:15; z-index: 3">
A Moving message
</DIV>
<SCRIPT LANGUAGE=VBSCRIPT>
setTimeout "MoveLeft",10,"VBScript"
Sub MoveLeft
 MovingMessage.style.posLeft = MovingMessage.style.posLeft + 1
```

```
        If MovingMessage.style.posLeft <> 500 Then setTimeout "MoveLeft", 10, "VBScript"
        End Sub
        </SCRIPT>
        </BODY>
        </HTML>
```

The script is very simple: it just obtains the **posLeft** property of the
MovingMessage element and then increments it by one. This moves the
element rightwards by one pixel. The procedure is then executed again.

```
    MovingMessage.style.posLeft = MovingMessage.style.posLeft + 1
    If MovingMessage.style.posLeft <> 500 then...
```

So, after this procedure had
been executed 10 times the
message would be in this
position:

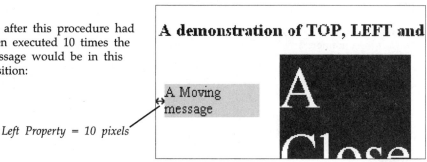

Left Property = 10 pixels

The script checks to see if it has reached 500 pixels across the screen, stops if it
has and runs the procedure again if it hasn't.

```
    If MovingMessage.style.posLeft <> 500 Then setTimeout "MoveLeft", 10, "VBScript"
```

There is one minor complication in the script. If you just go ahead and move
the block across the screen, and simply call the procedure again, the screen
won't have time to display the block as it moves. So we need to slow it down,
by using a timeout, which gives Dynamic HTML time to update the position of
the element on the screen.

This is a very simple example, but it demonstrates something that just wasn't
possible in HTML or style sheets previously, and shows that Dynamic HTML
opens up a lot of possibilities. What happens if you get the movement to be
triggered by the click of a mouse, for instance? However before we get carried
away, we need to look at the HTML object model and see how scripting makes
use of it. That is the subject of the next chapter.

Summary

In this chapter, we've seen how the formatting of pages in Dynamic HTML is far more dependent on **styles** than earlier versions of HTML. In particular, the six new style properties provide ways to control the positioning, layout, and z-order (or z-index) of the various elements in the page. Many HTML authors have shunned style sheets in the past, but now is the time to understand them better, because you are going to have to get used to them in the long term.

Dynamic HTML provides six new style properties that control the layout and appearance of pages:

 left and **top** define the x and y coordinates of the element within its container. This can be a document division, or the page itself

 z-index defines the z coordinate, or layer, in which the element will appear. It's set initially by the ordering of the elements in the HTML, if not specified directly

position defines how the left and top values are interpreted with respect to the element's position within the HTML source, and how it affects the elements that follow

overflow defines whether an element is allowed to flow beyond division boundaries, or if it is to be clipped with or without a scrolling mechanism

 visibility defines whether the element will be visible in the page when it is rendered. An element can be **hidden**, but still keep its place in the HTML source

And of course, we can still use the existing style properties from HTML 3.2 to control the other aspects of our design—as we did throughout this chapter. We also looked at how to manipulate some of these new properties with the aid of a script. We used the **style** object to access all of the new properties, and dynamically update the screen as they are changed. However, to understand how we can get the best out of scripting, we need to understand the **object model** on which the browser is built—and that is the subject of the next two chapters.

The Dynamic HTML Browser Object Model

Now that we've explored the new properties that are available in the Dynamic HTML implementation of style sheets, we can move on to look at the other major difference between traditional and Dynamic HTML. Since the advent of Netscape 2, the first browser to provide a documented **object model**, it has been possible to use the scripting code in a page to access both the browser environment, and the contents of the page itself. This access was severely limited when it came to the things other than controls in the page (such as text or graphics). While you could access such things as HTML text boxes and list boxes, and Java applets or ActiveX controls, you couldn't get at the real contents of the document. The text, images, headings, and other page contents remained temptingly out of reach.

This all changes in Dynamic HTML. Almost anything that's visible in the page, plus many things that aren't, can be accessed through the extensions to the object model. This is the subject of this chapter. We'll take an overview of the whole structure, then investigate the new and the most useful objects. In the next chapter, we'll continue this process, and look at the objects that are most useful for integrating our script into a web page.

In this chapter, we'll cover:

 The browser object model in outline, and compare it to older browsers

 A brief tour of the basic window objects, generally unchanged from earlier versions

A look at some of the more useful new objects and collections

We can't hope to give an in-depth explanation of the entire structure in this book, and there is no real need to do this anyway. Much of the structure is simple, and some is only used in very special cases. You will, however, find definitions and listings of the items which make up the structure in the reference section at the back of this book.

Introducing the Browser Object Model

If you haven't used scripting code in a web page before, you may not have realized that the browser is built around a structured set of **objects**. It's these objects that provide an interface between the HTML that creates the page, and the internal workings of the browser itself. To make the whole thing easier to visualize and work with, the various objects are organized into a structure called the **object model**.

Why Do We Need An Object Model?

When we just define a normal static web page with HTML, we don't need to know about the object model, or the structure of the browser itself. Even when we display several documents in different frames, we just give each frame a name, and target new pages to the appropriate one. For example, if we have defined a frameset which contains a frame named **mainwindow**, like this:

```
<FRAMESET>
  <FRAME NAME="mainwindow" SRC="http://www.wrox.com">
  ...
</FRAMESET>
```

we can load a different page into it using the **TARGET** attribute of the **<A>** tag:

```
<A HREF="http://rapid.wrox.co.uk" TARGET="mainwindow">The Wrox Rapid site</A>
```

So why do we need an object model?

The Object Model and Scripting

If you've used a scripting language like VBScript or JavaScript before, you'll know that this is an extremely simplified view. In reality, the browser stores the frames in the browser window as a **collection** (a structure, rather like an array, which we'll come back to later), and they become child objects of the main window. To refer to the main window in a scripting language, we have to reference it using the keywords **parent** or **top**. **parent** refers to the window immediately above the current window in the hierarchy, which may be the top window, while **top** always refers to the topmost window :

```
parent.frames("mainwindow").location.href = "http://rapid.wrox.co.uk"
```

> **Throughout this chapter we'll be using VBScript in our examples, unless we mention specifically otherwise. However, many of the properties and methods definitions in code are identical in JavaScript.**

*You'll no doubt have met the 'page targeting' keywords _top and _self before. In the **TARGET** attribute of an **<A>** tag, _top is used to load a page into the main browser window, instead of into a frame within the window — effectively replacing the frameset. _self can be used to load a page into the current window, though this is rarely used. The **top** and **self** keywords in scripting languages have the same meaning as these.*

So the concept of things belonging to collections, and having parents and children, implies that there is an underlying object model structure—even if you haven't actually seen it before. Don't worry about the code we've used here for the time being. In this chapter, we'll start to explore the object model, and see how to use it in Dynamic HTML.

The Object Model in Overview

The browser object model can be thought of as physically part of the software that forms the browser, while Dynamic HTML is (in theory at least) a universal browser-independent document definition language. This means that all browsers which host Dynamic HTML must provide the same object model. Otherwise, it would be impossible to create pages that performed properly on different browsers.

However, the object model is, in fact, simply an **interface** between the Dynamic HTML source code in the page, and the browser software routines that create the window and fill it with the elements defined in the page. How it does this filling of the window, or **rendering** of the page, is unimportant. Dynamic HTML simply defines what the results should be, not how the processes should be implemented.

So, we can think of the browser's object model as being a way of connecting our pages to the browser. The object model exposes a range of **objects**, **methods**, **properties** and **events**, which are present and active within the browser's software, to the HTML and scripting code in the page. We can use these to communicate our wishes back to the browser, and therefore to the viewer. The browser will carry out our commands, and update the page(s) it displays.

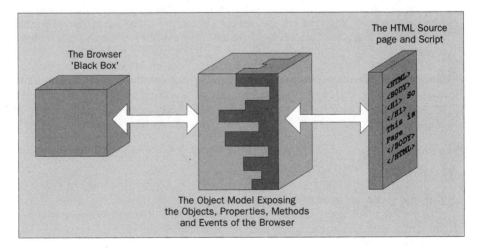

The HTML Source
page and Script

The Browser
'Black Box'

The Object Model Exposing
the Objects, Properties, Methods
and Events of the Browser

Objects, Methods, Properties and Events

So far we've talked about objects, methods, properties and events—and assumed that you are familiar with these terms. No doubt you've heard them used many times, but we'll recap briefly here before going on to look at the browser object model itself.

Objects

Modern software design is very much concerned with **objects**. You can think of these as being self-contained parts of a program such as the browser, which carry out specific functions. The key is that they will usually store their own data, in their own format, and contain the code routines called methods (see the definition below) that are required to manipulate that data.

You can think of an object as being rather like a video recorder, in that we put the tapes in and set the timer, but all the work of recording and playing back goes on inside the black box. We just tell it to record or play back, and we don't need to know what's actually going on inside. The video recorder stores its data (our TV program) itself, in its own format, without us having to worry about how it's doing it

Methods

Methods are an object's way of letting us do something with it. Our video recorder has methods built in that allow us to record or play back TV programs. The big advantage of having an object provide methods is that it takes away the worry of knowing what's going on inside the object. Rather than telling the video recorder the exact patterns of magnetism to lay down on the tape, and how to interpret the sound signal, we execute its Record method by pressing a couple of buttons.

Events

If methods are our way of telling an object what to do, **events** can be thought of as the object's way of telling us that something happened. It's likely that our trusty video recorder will have something we could term an **EndOfTape** event. This occurs when the end of the tape is reached, and will stop the motor to prevent it tearing the tape off the spool. This is the event being used internally to execute a **Stop** method of the tape-winding-motor object inside the video recorder.

However, at the same time it's likely that the video recorder will tell us that the end of the tape has been reached as well, by changing the display on the front or by rewinding and automatically ejecting the tape. This allows us to respond to the event, perhaps by putting the tape back in its library case.

Properties

Properties should be no problem to grasp by now. We regularly used the term in the last chapter when we were referring to the style properties of the elements in the page. All we really mean by a property is some setting, or stored value, that applies to an object. The object will usually expose a set of properties that affect the appearance or behavior of the object, and some that just provide information about it.

In our video recorder example there are read/write properties, where we can change the behavior or appearance. These might include the record speed setting, and the time setting on the clock. Read-only properties could be the age, the price, and the working condition. As you can see, there are often read-only properties that we would like to be able to change, but can't—and Dynamic HTML is no exception.

60

The Object Model Diagram

Being able to describe the object model of the browser is, as you've seen, a necessity if we are to understand how all the parts of the hierarchy fit together. The usual way to do this is to show a tree-style diagram, with the main objects at the top and the subsidiary ones below.

This is what we've done here. The top-level object in the browser hierarchy is the **window**. This is the parent object for every other object in the structure.

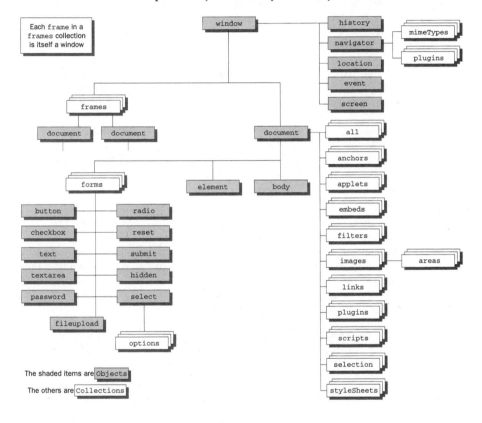

You'll notice that some of the 'things' in the object hierarchy are **objects**, and some are **collections**. In general, collections have a plural name, i.e. **anchors** rather than **anchor**. The one that breaks the rule is the **all** collection—we can only assume that calling it the **alls** collection would have sounded a little odd.

The diagram shows how each of the objects is related—and there are quite a few of them altogether. If you've used VBScript or JavaScript in any depth before, you'll recognize many of them. To maintain backwards compatibility with pages designed for older browsers, the object model for Dynamic HTML is a superset of that found in Internet Explorer 3 and Netscape Navigator 3.

Looking at the Structure

Looking at the diagram, you can see that although the **window** object is at the top of the tree, it's the **document** object that is really at the heart of things. This isn't surprising, because the bulk of our page and its contents are part of the **document** itself. The **window** is just the container that holds it.

If you are worried about remembering this structure, don't panic. A lot of it is of only minor importance when creating pages, and much of it is repeated. For example, a window can hold a selection of **frames**, but each frame is actually a **window** in its own right. Therefore, once you understand how to use the **window** object, you can use it in all the separate windows created by a frameset document.

Much the same happens with the **document** object. Each **window** object can contain a single **document** object. Every occurrence of a **document** object contains the same set of other objects and collections you see in the diagram.

In this chapter, we'll look at the **window** object and its subsidiary objects and collections. However, the **document** object, which is the other major object in the hierarchy, we'll leave until the next chapter where we'll have room to do it justice.

Understanding Collections

You can see from the diagram that many parts of the object model are implemented as **collections**. A collection is something like the arrays that you meet in programming languages, where each item is held in structure and related to its neighbors. A collection of **frames** is just a way of holding one or more frame objects together in such a way that they can be accessed in code. We can retrieve details of a frame in a browser window using either its name or its numerical position in the collection:

```
window.frames("mainframe")          'both of these refer to frames in a window
window.frames(0)                    'this is the first frame, with index zero
```

The browser assumes that the *active* **window** object (which may, of course, be a frame inside another window) is the default object for script in the page. Therefore, in most cases we don't need to specify it. The following code has the same meaning as that above:

```
frames("mainframe")
frames(0)
```

In the browser object model's collections, the first item is indexed zero. The actual ordering of the frames in a collection depends on their order in the HTML source. Frame zero will be the first frame defined in the **<FRAMESET>** tag. The same applies to other collections, such as the **form** or **image** collections in a document.

Understanding Parents and Children

The expression **window.frames(0)** we used above refers to the first frame in a window. However, this is the *current* window, which may not be the window at the top of the object tree. Imagine a case where there are three frames in a

62

window. As far as we are concerned, they are indexed **0**, **1** and **2** in the
frames collection.

```
┌─────────────────────────────────────────────────────┐
│ ┌─────────────────────────────────────────────────┐ │
│ │ window.frames(0)                                │ │
│ ├───────────────────────┬─────────────────────────┤ │
│ │ window.frames(1)      │ window.frames(2)        │ │
│ │                       │                         │ │
│ │                       │                         │ │
│ │                       │                         │ │
│ │                       │                         │ │
│ │                       │                         │ │
│ └───────────────────────┴─────────────────────────┘ │
└─────────────────────────────────────────────────────┘
```

However, this is the **frames** collection of the main (top) window. If we are
using scripting code in the page in the lower-left frame, **window** refers to our
own window and not the *top* main window. Our window is a **child** of the
main (top) window, and script running in it has to refer to other frames in
relation to the current frame. Remember, each frame is in effect a **window** in its
own right.

To refer to an object one step up the hierarchy, such as the **window** holding the
frames collection that created our frame, we use the **parent** keyword. To go
up the hierarchy two steps, we can refer to the **parent** of the **parent**, etc.:

```
parent.window.frames(0)        'this is the first frame in the parent window
parent.parent.window.frames(0)'and in the parent of this window if there is one
```

We can always refer to the topmost window in the object model (the browser
window itself, in effect) by using the keyword **top**, instead of having to specify
the correct number of **parent** keywords. This is useful in a complex page with
several layers of frames. However, remember that **top** may not refer to the
topmost frame in *your* layout. If the viewer loads your page into a frame
created by somebody else—for example by clicking a link to it on their site—it
could refer to that page. Therefore, if you load a new page into the **top**
window, you'll remove their frameset as well.

*Of course, now that we've discovered Dynamic HTML, we won't need all
those frames anyway!*

The Window Object

The **window** object is the 'top-of-the-tree' as far as the browser object model is
concerned, and everything else in the Dynamic HTML object model revolves
around it. Once we understand the **window** object, we'll have a pretty good
grasp of how we relate to the object model in our pages.

63

The `window` object refers to the current window. This may be the top-level window, but it might equally be a window that is within a frame created by a `<FRAMESET>` in another document. If the window is divided into frames (i.e. its document does contain a frameset) it will have a frames collection—as we saw earlier:

Collection	Description
frames	Collection of all the frames defined within a `<FRAMESET>` tag.

The window object also has a range of properties, methods and events. We'll look at these next, concentrating on the most useful ones.

The Properties of the Window Object

The following table shows all the properties of a `window` object. You'll see the `parent`, `self`, and `top` properties we mentioned earlier, which allow us to refer to objects elsewhere in the hierarchy, and the `name` property which reflects the name we give to a window in a `<FRAMESET>` tag.

Properties	Description
parent	Returns the parent window of the current window.
self	Returns a reference to the current window.
top	Returns a reference to the topmost window.
name	Name of the window.
opener	The window that created the current window.
closed	Indicates if a window is closed.
status	The text displayed in the browser's status bar.
defaultStatus	The default text from the browser's status bar.
returnValue	Allows a return value to be specified for the event or dialog window.
client	A reference that returns the navigator object for the browser.
document	Read-only reference to the window's document object.
event	Read-only reference to the global event object.
history	Read-only reference to the window's history object.
location	Read-only reference to the window's location object.
navigator	Read-only reference to the window's navigator object.
screen	Read-only reference to the global screen object.

The `opener` and `closed` properties are usually used when we create new browser windows, as you'll see later in the book. The `status` and `defaultStatus` properties refer to the text displayed in the status bar at the bottom of the browser window. **status** is useful when we want to display progress messages to the user, or for debugging script. We can display anything we like in the status bar while the script is running:

```
window.status = "The value of the variable 'MeaningOfLife' is usually 42"
```

The Methods of the Window Object

The **window** object's methods provide many ways of manipulating a window, and carrying out tasks within it.

New Browser Windows

If we want to create a new browser window from a web page, we can use the **open** and **close** methods. For example, the following code creates a new browser window containing the page **newpage.htm**:

```
window.open "newpage.htm"
```

We can also add other arguments to the method to get more control over how the new window is presented. The full syntax is: **window.open** *URL*, *features*, *name*, where *features* can be a string of instructions concerning the position, size and type of window, and whether it should contain scrollbars, a toolbar, etc.

Dynamic HTML also adds support for dialogs that can contain HTML code. This is effectively a new browser window that is displayed on top of the existing window, and the viewer has to close it before they can continue browsing. We'll look at modal and help dialogs, together with new browser windows generally, in more detail in Chapter 6 of the book.

```
window.showModalDialog "dialogpage.htm"
window.showHelp "helppage.chm"
```

Built-in Dialogs

There are built-in dialogs (originally designed for use with JavaScript, which doesn't have its own dialogs or message boxes) that we can display using **alert**, **prompt**, and **confirm**:

```
window.alert "You'll have to choose where to go next."
strLocation = window.prompt("Enter your preferred location", "Birmingham")
blnResult = window.confirm("Are you ready to load this page ?")
```

Here's an example that uses these dialogs to load a new page. The page **dialogs_vb.htm** consists of a single script section, containing this code:

```
<SCRIPT LANGUAGE=VBSCRIPT>
window.alert "You'll have to choose where to go next."
strLocation = window.prompt("Enter your preferred location", "Birmingham")
If strLocation <> "" Then
  If strLocation = "Birmingham" Then   'default text for the confirm dialog
    strAddress = "http://www.wrox.co.uk"
  Else
    strAddress = "http://www.wrox.com"
  End If
  window.status = "New location will be " & strAddress
```

```
        If window.confirm("Are you ready to load this page ?") Then
           window.navigate strAddress
        End If
     End If
     </SCRIPT>
```

You can run this example from our web site at
`http://rapid.wrox.co.uk/books/0685/`

The code in this page runs when it is loaded, and the first line displays an **alert** dialog with a simple message.

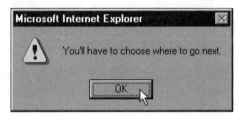

The second line uses the **window** object's **prompt** method to display a dialog where the user can enter some information. The first argument is the prompt itself, and the second is the default value for the text box in the dialog.

The value in the text box is returned to our code when the user clicks the OK button, and we assign it to a variable named **strLocation**. Now we can see what they actually entered—if anything. If they clicked the Cancel button in the dialog, or deleted all the text and didn't enter anything, we'll get an empty string back from the **prompt** method. We test for this first by comparing **strLocation** to an empty string (**""**), and only execute the following code if there actually is a value.

If the value is still Birmingham, the default, we set the value of another variable, **strAddress**, to the address of our UK web site. If not, we'll use the main US site address.

```
     ...
     If strLocation = "Birmingham" Then
        strAddress = "http://www.wrox.co.uk"
     Else
        strAddress = "http://www.wrox.com"
     End If
     ...
```

By now, we know we've got an address to go to, so we can display a message in the browser's status bar, by setting the **window** object's **status** property. We use some text and add the address string from the variable **strAddress** to the end of it like this:

```
window.status = "New location will be " & strAddress
```

Now we can perform a final check to see if they really want to do it. We use the window object's confirm method to display the OK or Cancel dialog. The string argument is the message displayed, and it returns **True** or **False** depending on which button the user clicks. Once they've clicked a button, we can check the result, and load the new page if it is **True**.

```
If window.confirm("Are you ready to load this page ?") Then
```

Notice the status bar displaying our message as well. Finally, the line that actually loads the new page uses the **navigate** method of the window object. We're supplying the address argument as the string variable **strAddress** we set earlier:

```
window.navigate strAddress      'strAddress is a string holding the page address
```

Using JavaScript Instead

In the previous example, we've used VBScript (despite the Explorer User Prompt displaying the contrary). This is generally easier to understand and work with than JavaScript, unless you are more used to Javascript—or have a background in C or C++. Here's the same routine in JavaScript, and it too can be found on our web site at **http://rapid.wrox.co.uk/books/0685/**:

```
<SCRIPT LANGUAGE=JAVASCRIPT>
window.alert("You'll have to choose where to go next.");
strLocation = window.prompt("Enter your preferred location", "Birmingham");
if (strLocation != "")
{
   if (strLocation == "Birmingham")
```

67

```
    {
        strAddress = "http://www.wrox.co.uk"
    }
    else
    {
        strAddress = "http://www.wrox.com"
    };
    window.status = "New location will be " + strAddress;
    if (window.confirm("Are you ready to load this page ?"))
    {
        window.navigate(strAddress)
    }
}
</SCRIPT>
```

You can see that the syntax of the methods and properties is exactly the same, but that JavaScript uses curly braces to define blocks of code like the `If {...}` section, rather than the VBScript method of using `If...End If`.

Focus, Scrolling and Timers

If there is more than one browser window open, we can switch the focus between them using the `blur` and `focus` methods. These effectively change which is the 'active' window. `blur` moves the focus from the window where the code is to the next window (like pressing *Tab*), while `focus` moves it to the window where the code is. We can also load a new document into a window using the `navigate` method. Again, you'll see an example of these methods, combined with new browser windows, in a later chapter.

When our page is larger than the browser window, the user has to scroll it around to see the contents. Instead, we can use another of the window object's methods, `scroll`, to move the page around for the user. For example, to scroll the page so that the point 250 pixels across and 150 pixels down is visible in the browser window, we could use:

```
window.scroll 250,150
```

Finally, we can set a timer that will cause part of our code to be executed after a certain number of milliseconds by using one of two methods. The first is the `setTimeout` method. In this example, we create a timer that will run for 5 seconds, and tell it to execute a routine named `MyTimer` that is written in VBScript (the language argument can be omitted if the routine is in the same script section and language):

```
TimeoutID = window.setTimeout("MyTimer", 5000, "VBSCRIPT")
```

We can react to the timer event by writing a subroutine that catches the `MyTimer` event:

```
Sub MyTimer()
    window.alert "Time's up!"
End Sub
```

However, once the timer has fired, we would need to reset it again if we wanted to repeat the process. There is another method, `setInterval` which functions in the same way as the `setTimeout` method. There is one main difference, which is that the **setInterval** method is called repeatedly every so many milliseconds.

```
TimeoutID = window.setInterval("MyTimer", 5000, "VBSCRIPT")
```

So if you ran the program now, the Time's up dialog would appear at 5000 millisecond intervals and not just once.

Here's a full list of the methods of the **window** object:

Methods	Description
open	Opens a new browser window.
close	Closes the current browser window.
showHelp	Displays an HTML Help window as a dialog.
showModalDialog	Displays a new browser window as a dialog.
alert	Displays an Alert dialog box with a message and an OK button.
prompt	Displays a Prompt dialog box with a message and an input field.
confirm	Displays a Confirm dialog box with a message, OK and Cancel buttons.
navigate	Loads another page, like changing the **location.href** property.
blur	Causes the page to lose focus, and fire its **onblur** event.
focus	Causes the page to receive the focus, and fire its **onfocus event.**
scroll	Scrolls the window to a specified x and y offset in the document.
setInterval	Denotes a code routine to execute repeatedly every specified number of milliseconds.
setTimeout	The code to execute a specified number of ms after loading the page.
clearInterval	Cancels an interval timer that was set with the **setInterval** method.
clearTimeout	Cancels a timeout that was set with the **setTimeout** method.
execScript	Executes a script. The default language is JScript.

The Events of the Window Object

The **window** object has nine events. Three of these occur when the user carries out some action. If there is more than one browser window open, the user can switch between them and this initiates the **onblur** and **onfocus** events. Notice that these can also be fired when the **window** object's **blur** and **focus** *methods* are called by our code:

69

```
Sub window_onfocus()
  window.alert "I've now got the focus."
End Sub

Sub window_onblur()
  window.alert "Oh no, I've lost it again."
End Sub
```

If the user presses the *F1* (or Help) key, the window receives an **onhelp** event:

```
Sub window_onhelp()
  window.alert "Tell me your problems..."
End Sub
```

If the user drags the edges of the window making it either bigger or smaller, the window receives an **onresize** event:

```
Sub window_onresize()
  window.alert "Metamorphosizing..."
End Sub
```

If not all of the display is visible and the user has to scroll the display to view it, then when the display is scrolled, the window receives an **onscroll** event.

```
Sub window_onscroll()
  window.alert "Scrolling..."
End Sub
```

There's a very useful event that occurs if an error occurs during the download of an image or element. It logs whether an error occurred or whether the transfer was aborted, which can allow the program to try and download the image again or take appropriate action. This is the **onerror** event.

```
Sub window_onerror()
  window.alert "Error occurred during download, please try again!"
End Sub
```

Finally, there are three events that occur when:

 the window loads a page.

just before the page is unloaded, allowing the user to stop the **onunload** event. This is done by returning a string to the event, which displays a dialog, giving the user the option to stay on the page.

 the page is unloaded —either before opening a new page or when the browser is closing down.

```
Sub window_onload()
  window.alert "Finished loading the page."
End Sub

Sub window_onbeforeunload()
  window.alert "About to unload the page"
End Sub

Sub window_onunload()
  window.alert "Unloading the page."
End Sub
```

Events	Description
onblur	Occurs when the window loses the focus.
onfocus	Occurs when the window receives the focus.
onhelp	Occurs when the user presses the F1 or help key.
onresize	Occurs when the element or object is resized by the user.
onscroll	Occurs when the user scrolls a page or element.
onerror	Occurs when an error loading a document or image arises.
onbeforeunload	Occurs just before the page is unloaded, allowing the databound controls to store their data.
onload	Occurs when the page has completed loading.
onunload	Occurs immediately prior to the page being unloaded.

The Window's Subsidiary Objects

The **window** object has several subsidiary objects, which are referenced through it. Three of these, the **history, navigator** and **location** objects, are all basically unchanged from earlier versions of the object model—with just a couple of new properties and methods added. There are two completely new objects, **event** and **screen**, that are added in Dynamic HTML.

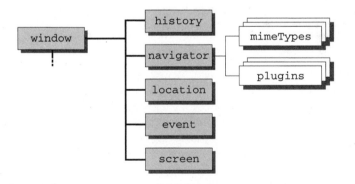

The History Object

The **history** object contains information about the URLs that the browser has visited in this session, as stored in the History list. It also allows us to move through the list using script code, loading the pages it contains. There is one property, the **length** of the list, and three methods.

71

Properties	Description
`length`	Returns the number of items in the browser's History list.

Methods	Description
`back`	Loads the previous URL in the browser's History list.
`forward`	Loads the next URL in the browser's History list. ·
`go` *n*	Loads the page at position *n* in the browser's History list.

To move through the list, we can use these properties and methods. Here, we'll go to the first entry in the list, then jump to the sixth one after checking that there are enough available. Notice that we have omitted the default **window** object from the code:

```
history.go 1
If history.length > 5 Then history.forward 5
```

The Navigator Object

The **navigator** object represents the browser application itself, providing information about its manufacturer, version, and capabilities. It has five properties, two collections and two methods:

Properties	Description
`appCodeName`	The code name of the browser.
`appName`	The product name of the browser.
`appVersion`	The version of the browser.
`cookieEnabled`	Denotes if client-side cookies are enabled in the browser.
`userAgent`	The user-agent (browser name) header sent as part of the HTTP protocol.

Collections	Description
`mimeTypes`	Collection of all the document and file types supported by the browser
`plugins`	An alias for the collection of all the `<embed>` objects in the page.

Methods	Description
`taintEnabled`	Returns False, included for compatibility with Netscape Navigator.
`javaEnabled`	Indicates if execution of Java code is enabled by the browser.

The Location Object

The `location` object contains information about the URL of the current page. It also provides methods that will reload the current or a new page. The properties consist of one that holds the complete URL string, `href`, and several which hold various parts of the URL string:

Properties	Description
`href`	The entire URL as a string.
`hash`	The string following the # symbol in the URL.
`host`	The `hostname:port` part of the location or URL.
`hostname`	The `hostname` part of the location or URL.
`pathname`	The file or object path name following the third slash in a URL.
`port`	The `port` number in a URL.
`protocol`	The initial sub-string indicating the URL's access method.
`search`	The query string or data following the `?` in the complete URL.

We can use these properties to change the page that is being displayed. The usual way is to reset the `href` property to a new value, which has the same effect as calling the window object's **navigate** method:

```
window.location.href = "http://rapid.wrox.co.uk"
```

The three methods provided by the `location` object can be used to either load another page, reload the current page or replace it in the browser's history list:

Methods	Description
`assign`	Loads another page. Equivalent to changing the `window.location.href` property.
`reload`	Reloads the current page.
`replace`	Loads a page replacing the current page's history entry with its URL.

The Event Object

The final new object is the **event** object. This allows the scripting language to get more information about any event that occurs in the browser—in effect it is global to all the objects. The **event** object provides a range of properties, a full list of which can be found in Section E, but for the moment we will be concentrating on the following:

Properties	Description
x	Horizontal position of the mouse pointer on the screen in pixels.
y	Vertical position of the mouse pointer on the screen in pixels.
clientX	Returns the x coordinate of the element, excluding borders, margins, padding, scrollbars, etc.
clientY	Returns the y coordinate of the element, excluding borders, margins, padding, scrollbars, etc.
offsetX	Returns the x coordinate of the mouse pointer when an event occurs, relative to the containing element.
offsetY	Returns the y coordinate position of the mouse pointer when an event occurs, relative to the containing element.
screenX	Returns the x coordinate of the mouse pointer when an event occurs, in relation to the screen.
screenY	Returns the y coordinate of the mouse pointer when an event occurs, in relation to the screen.
button	The mouse button, if any, that was pressed to fire the event.
altKey	Returns the state of the *ALT* key.
ctrlKey	Returns the state of the *CTRL* key.
shiftKey	Returns the state of the *SHIFT* key.
keyCode	ASCII code of key pressed. Can be changed to send a different character.
reason	Indicates whether data transfer to an element was successful, or why it failed.
type	Returns the name of the event as a string, without the 'on' prefix, such as 'click' instead of 'onclick'.
fromElement	Element being moved from in an onmouseover or onmouseout event.
toElement	Element being moved to in an onmouseover or onmouseout event.
returnValue	Specifies a return value for the event.
srcElement	Element deepest in the hierarchy that a specified event occurred over.
cancelBubble	Can be set to prevent the current event from bubbling up the hierarchy.

The first thirteen properties return values that indicate what was going on when the event occurred. If it was a mouse event, these include the **x** and **y** position of the mouse pointer on the screen, and the mouse **button** that was pressed. If it was a key-press event, the **keyCode** property returns the ASCII code of the key combination that was pressed. The next properties indicate if the *Alt, Ctrl* and/or *Shift* keys were being held down at the time. The **reason** property indicates whether a data transfer was successful and returns an integer indicating either success, aborted transfer or error, while the **type** property just creates a string of the event name which can be used within your program.

Next come two properties that are set if the event is **onmouseover** or **onmouseout**. These events occur when the mouse is moving over, or is at the point of leaving, an element (or the page itself). The properties indicate which element the mouse pointer was moving *onto* (**toElement**) and which element it was moving *off* (**fromElement**). These can be used to change the way an object is displayed when the mouse is over it, like the 'coolbar' you see in the latest windows programs (including Internet Explorer).

Read-Write Event Object Properties

The properties of the event object are set when an event occurs, and most of them are read-only. For example, we can't really expect to be able to change the **button** property, as it reflects the mouse button that was clicked. However, a couple of the properties are read/write. The **keyCode** property reflects the key that was pressed, but we can change this in code to cause a different value to be used when the event is actually handled. As an example:

```
...
If (event.keyCode < 48) Or (event.keyCode > 57) Then event.keyCode = 0
...
```

.This code simply checks if the key is a number key (**0** to **9**) by looking at the ASCII code. If it isn't, it changes it to the value ASCII zero (not **"0"** which has an ASCII code of **48**). When this code is received by an element on the page like a text box, it will be ignored.

The event object also supports the **returnValue** property that indicates if the event, or a modal HTML dialog, can return a value to be used by the code in the page. Setting it to **False** prevents the code receiving a return value—you'll see more when we come to look at events and modal dialogs later on.

Event Bubbling Properties

The final two events are concerned with a new aspect of scripting supported by Dynamic HTML, called **event bubbling**. We mentioned this in Chapter 1, and—briefly—the **srcElement** property indicates which element in the page or other container such as a division was 'topmost' when the event occurred. It could be the element under the mouse pointer for a **mousemove** event, or the textbox with the focus for a key-press event.

Depending on how we decide to handle the event, we can set the **cancelBubble** property of the event object to **True** to prevent the event being 'bubbled up' the object hierarchy to objects higher up.

75

We'll be looking into the whole subject of event handling in depth in Chapter 5—for the mean time, you just need to appreciate that the **event** object contains the two properties **srcElement** and **cancelBubble**, which are used in conjunction with event bubbling.

The Screen Object

The **screen** object is new in Dynamic HTML, and provides information about the viewer's screen resolution and rendering abilities. There are five properties:

Properties	Description
width	Returns the width of the user's display screen in pixels.
height	Returns the height of the user's display screen in pixels.
bufferDepth	Specifies an off-screen bitmap buffer.
colorDepth	Returns information to assist in deciding how to use colors in the page.
updateInterval	Sets or returns the interval between screen updates on the client.

The first two, **width** and **height**, are useful when we want to create new browser windows, or change the size of the existing one, in code. For example, we can use them to decide where to put a new window:

```
If screen.width > 800 Then
   open "newpage.htm", "top:100;left:600;width:200"
End If
```

The next two properties, **bufferDepth** and **colorDepth**, are useful for deciding which images to display, and instructing the browser how to display them. Without going into a discussion of how colors are represented, just accept that the browser can display images in a variety of color depths—2 colors for a monochrome display, 16 colors, or upwards in steps to 16 million colors ('True Color'). This read-only property value describes the color depth in terms of the number of bits per pixel, so **8** means 256 colors and **32** is 'True Color'.

If we display an image containing 256 colors, but the color depth of the user's system is only set to 16 colors, they will see a degraded version of the image. If we query the **colorDepth** property first, we can use the result to decide which of a series of images we display:

```
If screen.colorDepth < 8 Then
   'display monochrome image
Else
   'display 256 color image
End If
```

This can help to minimize download times as well. There's no point downloading a 'true-color' image if the user is working in 256 colors—we might as well send them a 256 color version instead. We can also instruct the browser to buffer the image and display it with a different color depth by setting the **bufferDepth** property.

The **updateInterval** property can be used to set or retrieve the update rate for the screen. This means that any 'invalidations' to the window are buffered and then can be drawn at intervals. The aim of this is to prevent glitches impairing the overall painting performance, such as when rapid animations are taking place. This is a powerful property and extreme values will adversely affect the page rendering response, so take care when using it.

A Window Object Example Page

To finish up this chapter, here's another page, **DocObject.htm**, that we've provided on our web site at **http://rapid.wrox.co.uk/books/0685/** for you to try out. It simply retrieves the values of properties from several of the objects we've looked at in this chapter, and displays them in a table:

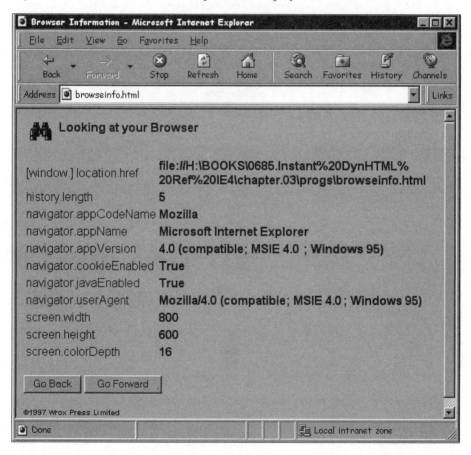

How It Works

The code that creates the page looks like this:

```
<HTML>
<HEAD><TITLE> Browser Information </TITLE></HEAD>
<STYLE>
<!--
   H1 {font-family:"Arial"; font-size:16; color:blue}
   H2 {font-family:"Arial"; font-size:10}
   {font-family:"Arial"; font-size:14}
-->
</STYLE>
<BODY BGCOLOR=#FFC0A0>
<H1><IMG SRC="binocs.gif" HSPACE=5 ALIGN=MIDDLE>
Looking at your Browser </H1>

<SCRIPT LANGUAGE="VBSCRIPT">
<!--
Dim strInfo
strInfo = "<CENTER><TABLE WIDTH=100%>" _
          & "<TR><TD>[window.] location.href</TD>" _
          & "<TD><B>" & window.location.href & "</TD></TR>" _
          & "<TR><TD>history.length</TD>" _
          & "<TD><B>" & history.length & "</TD></TR>" _
          & "<TR><TD>navigator.appCodeName</TD>" _
          & "<TD><B>" & navigator.appCodeName & "</TD></TR>" _
          & "<TR><TD>navigator.appName</TD>" _
          & "<TD><B>" & navigator.appName & "</TD></TR>" _
          & "<TR><TD>navigator.appVersion</TD>" _
          & "<TD><B>" & navigator.appVersion & "</TD></TR>" _
          & "<TR><TD>navigator.cookieEnabled</TD>" _
          & "<TD><B>" & navigator.cookieEnabled & "</TD></TR>" _
          & "<TR><TD>navigator.javaEnabled</TD>" _
          & "<TD><B>" & navigator.javaEnabled & "</TD></TR>" _
          & "<TR><TD>navigator.userAgent</TD>" _
          & "<TD><B>" & navigator.userAgent & "</TD></TR>" _
          & "<TR><TD>screen.width</TD>" _
          & "<TD><B>" & screen.width & "</TD></TR>" _
          & "<TR><TD>screen.height</TD>" _
          & "<TD><B>" & screen.height & "</TD></TR>" _
          & "<TR><TD>screen.colorDepth</TD>" _
          & "<TD><B>" & screen.colorDepth & "</TD></TR>" _
          & "</TABLE></CENTER><P>"
document.write strInfo

Sub cmdBack_OnClick()
  Dim intPlaces
  Randomize
  intPlaces = CInt((Rnd() * 3) + 1)
  MsgBox "Trying to go back " & intPlaces & " places."
  history.back intPlaces
End Sub

Sub cmdForward_OnClick()
  Dim intPlaces
  Randomize
  intPlaces = CInt((Rnd() * 3) + 1)
  MsgBox "Trying to go forward " & intPlaces & " places."
  history.forward intPlaces
End Sub
-->
</SCRIPT>
<INPUT TYPE=button VALUE="Go Back" NAME="cmdBack">
<INPUT TYPE=button VALUE="Go Forward" NAME="cmdForward">
<H2>&copy;1997 Wrox Press Limited</H2>
```

```
</BODY>
</HTML>
```

The first section, up to the opening **<SCRIPT>** tag, just provides the title and heading for the page, and defines the styles for the text. Inside the script section, we've defined a string variable named **strInfo**, and then filled it with a set of **<TABLE>**, **<TR>** and **<TD>** tags to create a two-column table.

```
Dim strInfo
strInfo = "<CENTER><TABLE WIDTH=100%>" _
        & "<TR><TD>[window.] location.href</TD>" _
        & "<TD><B>" & window.location.href & "</TD></TR>" _
        & "<TR><TD>history.length</TD>" _
        & "<TD><B>" & history.length & "</TD></TR>" _
        ...
```

The first column contains the text of the object and property we are querying, and the second column, the actual value. The underscores at the end of each line are VBScript's way of indicating that the statement continues on the next line—remember to leave a space between the underscore and the previous text, or an error will be generated. These two lines are repeated for each property we want to query.

Once we've got the table into our string variable, we can print it into the page. The browser doesn't know that the information is coming from our code, it just accepts it as though it were part of the HTML source stream coming from the server in the usual way. To put it into the page, we use the **write** method of the **document** object (you'll see more about this in the next chapter):

```
document.write strInfo
```

Jumping to Another Page in the History List

At the end of the page are two push buttons, created with the usual **<INPUT>** tag. These are named **cmdBack** and **cmdForward**:

```
<INPUT TYPE=button VALUE="Go Back" NAME="cmdBack">
<INPUT TYPE=button VALUE="Go Forward" NAME="cmdForward">
```

When one is clicked, the browser looks for a subroutine in the **<SCRIPT>** section that is a combination of the event, and the name of the element that caused it—in our case either **cmdBack_onClick()** or **cmdForward_onClick()**. We've provided both of these in our page. They simply create a random number and use the **back** and **forward** methods of the **navigator** object to load the relevant page. Here's the **cmdBack** routine again:

```
Sub cmdBack_OnClick()
   Dim intPlaces
   Randomize
   intPlaces = CInt((Rnd() * 3) + 1)
   MsgBox "Trying to go back " & intPlaces & " places."
   history.back intPlaces
End Sub
```

This VBScript code declares a variable named **intPlaces**, uses the **Randomize** statement to seed the random number generator, and then the **Rnd** function to

79

produce a pseudo-random number between zero and one. This is converted into an integer (whole) number between 1 and 3 with the VBScript **CInt** (convert to integer) function. Finally, it displays a message, and executes the **back** method of the **history** object specifying the number of places to jump.

Notice that this code uses the VBScript **MsgBox** statement, rather than the built-in **alert** method dialog. **MsgBox** offers more control over the dialog title and the buttons and icons that appear in it—it's just like a normal *Windows* message box.

> The VBScript reference at the end of this book contains information about using **MsgBox**, and all the other VBScript functions and statements.

Summary

In this chapter, we've begun our tour of the Dynamic HTML **object model**. If you have used scripting languages before, you'll be familiar with much of this—and so we've tried to concentrate on the new objects, properties, methods and events. However, we've included some examples of the existing ones to help you if you've previously only ever used HTML, and not tried scripting. Reference Section H also has a VBScript tutorial to help you out.

We started with the main browser object, the **window**, and looked at its properties, methods and events. Then we covered its subsidiary objects and collections, consisting of:

 The **frames** collection, which holds details of all the windows in a frameset within the current window

 The **history** object, which represents the browser's History list

 The **navigator** object, which represents the browser application itself

 The **location** object, which represents the URL of the page being displayed in the browser

 The **event** object, which represents the events that occur in the browser

 The **screen** object, which represents the browser's color rendering abilities

However, the main object we use in much of our code is actually the **document** object, and its subsidiary objects and collections. These are the subjects of the next chapter.

The Dynamic HTML Document Object

In the previous chapter, we discovered why we need an **object model** to use Dynamic HTML, and saw what it looks like. We also examined the top-level **window** object and its subsidiary objects. By now, you should be familiar with some of the techniques for using scripting code, like VBScript and JavaScript, in your web pages.

Of course, there is still a lot to learn. We're continuing our exploration of the browser object model by moving on to the central object in the hierarchy, the **document** object. We've isolated this object because it merits particular attention. The **document** object represents the HTML document in the browser window. You can use this object to get all sorts of information about the document, via its properties and methods, but you can also use it to modify the HTML elements and text on the page. And, using textrange object, you can even do things such as look for a particular word on the page and replace it with another word. No great shakes for Word 97, but for an HTML page, without using a page refresh, it's an entirely new trick. The **document** object, as you might expect, can also be used to process events.

So in this chapter, we'll be looking at:

- The properties, methods and events supported by the **document** object
- The collections it provides to organize all the other items that are part of the page
- The subsidiary **selection** object that allows us to work with the user's selections
- The visual and transition filters, which are scriptable via Cascading Style Sheet properties and the properties of elements that form part of the document object

There are other objects available to our code in Dynamic HTML, but these are not strictly part of the object model. We'll look at these in this and subsequent chapters, when we come to explore event handling and dynamic scripting in more depth. Here, we'll start with the **document** object itself.

The Document Object

The whole reason for using Dynamic HTML, or any other version of HTML, is to produce pages that we can display in a browser. The page itself is technically referred to as the **document**, and the object model provides a **document** object, plus subsidiary objects and collections, to organize the document itself and all the contents.

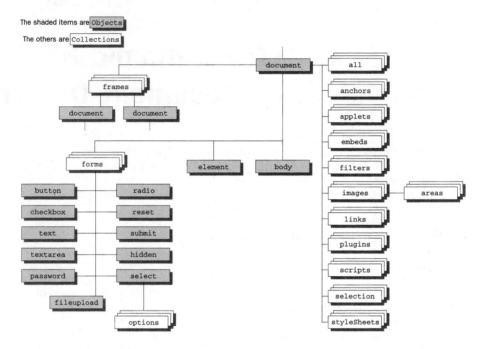

We'll start with a look at the properties, methods and events of the **document** object, then move on to look at the collections and subsidiary objects it supports. As the document has more properties, methods and events than the other objects in the hierarchy, we've divided them up into categories to make it easier to understand them. Reference Section **E**, at the back of the book, lists them all in alphabetical order, and provides a full list of their properties, methods and events.

The Properties of the Document Object

The document object's properties can be grouped in the following way:

 General properties which hold information about the document and the disk file that it is stored as

 Color properties that define the color of various parts of the document

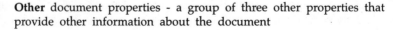 **Other** document properties - a group of three other properties that provide other information about the document

84

The General Document Properties

The general properties are mainly concerned with the document and its disk file, and provide information that can help the HTML author decide how to handle it. Most of them are self-explanatory, but we will look at the **domain** property in more detail. You'll find an example that demonstrates some of these properties later in this chapter.

General Properties	Description
title	The title of the document as defined in the **<TITLE>** tag.
body	Read-only reference to the document's implicit body object, as defined by the **<BODY>** tag.
selection	Read-only reference to the document's selection object.
URL	The Uniform Resource Locator (address) of the page.
location	A reference to the document's location (given as a URL).
domain	The security domain of the document.
cookie	The value of a cookie stored by the browser.
lastModified	Date the document was last modified.
parentWindow	Returns the parent window that contains the document.

Secure Domains

Dynamic HTML allows pages to have a **domain** property, initially the domain part of the document's URL. Imagine a situation where a frameset is displaying pages from two different sites (or domains). Normally, code in one page would be able to access the other page, even if it was loaded from a secure domain. In Dynamic HTML, you can't access or read the contents of a page from another domain. This helps to prevent suspect pages accessing secure information in others. You'll see an example of this in the examples later in this chapter. The **domain** property returns the domain of the document, and can be used to check that access is available, and prevent code errors.

The Document Color Properties

These properties provide read-write access to the colors of various parts of the page. In particular, they allow the code to read and change the color of the page background, the default color of the text, and the color of the unvisited hyperlinks, visited hyperlinks and active hyperlinks (i.e. while the mouse button is held down over the link).

Color Properties	Description
bgColor	Background color of the page.
fgColor	Default color of the document foreground text.
linkColor	The color for unvisited links in the page.

Table continued on following page

Color Properties	Description
aLinkColor	The color for active links in the page, i.e. while the mouse button is held down.
vlinkColor	The color for visited links in the page.

These properties are really leftovers from earlier versions of the object model, and we would normally use style properties to change the colors, as you saw in Chapter 2.

Other Document Properties

The final three properties of the **document** object are **activeElement**, **readyState** and **referrer**.

Other Properties	Description
activeElement	The element that has the focus.
readyState	Current state of an object being downloaded.
referrer	URL of the page that referenced the current page.

The last of these, **referrer**, survives from the object model of previous browser versions, although it never worked properly in Internet Explorer 3. The good news is that it does work in Internet Explorer 4, and is fully supported in Dynamic HTML. We'll show you this in an example we'll be using a little later in this chapter.

The new **activeElement** property provides a reference to the element on the page that currently has the input focus. We can use this to display messages in the status bar, or just track where the focus is going in the document.

The property, **readyState**, provides a value that indicates the current download 'state' of the document. Other objects that are embedded in the page, such as ActiveX controls, Java Applets, images or scripts, each have their own **readyState** properties as well, and this can be useful to discover if they are ready to accept instructions from our code. This solves a problem encountered previously, when the code in the page attempted to execute a method of an object that was not fully downloaded. The possible values are shown as follows:

Value	Description
1	Un-initialized, probably still downloading
2	Loading
3	Interactive
4	Complete

The Methods of the Document Object

The **document** object's methods fall neatly into two groups, **general** methods and **command** methods. We'll look at the general methods first, because they will be the ones most familiar to you.

Writing Text and HTML to the Document

As you've seen in the previous chapter, we can write text and HTML into a page using the **write** method of the **document** object. This is often used to create pages where the content is only decided by the browser's environment, such as the current date and time, or the properties of the browser itself.

There is a second related method, **writeln**, which acts in the same way, but appends a carriage return to the string it writes into the page. Of course, this has no effect most of the time, unless the string is being placed inside HTML tags such as **<PRE>**, which preserve line formatting.

Connected with the **write** and **writeln** methods are three others; **open**, **close** and **clear**. These allow the code to open an existing page, after the browser has finished rendering it, and then replace the text and HTML. Once complete, the **close** method is used to update the browser display. To remove the complete HTML source of the page, we can use the **clear** method – this will only work if **open** has been called first. The **open** method accepts a mime type, indicating the type of contents that will be displayed:

```
document.open("text/html")              'open the document
document.write "Some text and HTML"     'write some text
document.close                          'close it again
document.clear                          'and then clear the contents
```

You'll see many more ways of using these methods in Chapter 6, and we've also included a simple example later in this chapter, which uses them to create a listing of the contents of the document in a new browser window.

Creating and Referencing Elements

Dynamic HTML provides two methods for the **document** object that are connected with the new features of the language. We can create instances of certain types of new elements using the **createElement** method. This is limited to **IMG** image tags, list-box **OPTION** tags, and image-map **AREA** tags, and allows us to create a new element in code, and set its properties.
The element itself isn't displayed until it's added to the appropriate collection—you'll see an example of this in Chapter 7:

```
set objImage = document.createElement("IMG")
objImage.src="element.gif"    'set the image element's src property
MsgBox objImage.src           'and then display element.gif's src in a
                              message box
```

We can also get a reference to an element by specifying the x and y coordinates in relation to the top-left of the browser window, using the **elementFromPoint** method. The following line of code will show this message box if and only if the **element.gif** graphic is displayed at the location **100,70**:

87

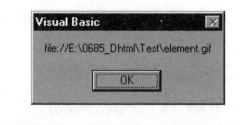

```
MsgBox document.elementFromPoint(100, 70).tagName
```

You can see this at work in the Document Object and Collections example later in the chapter.

General Methods	Description
open	Opens a stream to collect output, or a new browser window.
write	Writes text and HTML to a document in the specified window.
writeln	Writes text and HTML followed by a carriage return.
close	Closes an output stream.
clear	Clears the contents of the selection.
createElement	Creates an instance of the element object for the specified tag.
elementFromPoint	Returns the element at the specified x and y coordinates.

The Document Command Methods

The document also provides a set of **Command** methods that are used to manipulate ranges, such as that of a **TextRange** object. We're not ready to look at any of the range methods in depth here, although you will see a little more in a later example in this chapter. In Chapter 6, we'll be devoting a lot more attention to this whole subject.

Command Methods	Description
execCommand	Executes a command over the selection or range.
queryCommandEnabled	Denotes if the specified command is available.
queryCommandIndeterm	Denotes if the specified command is in the indeterminate state.
queryCommandState	Returns the current state of the command.
queryCommandSupported	Denotes if the specified command is supported
queryCommandText	Returns the string associated with a command.

The Events of the Document Object

The **document** object provides us with a wide range of events, which we can use to react to almost any action taken by the user. We've divided them up into three groups: **mouse** events, **key-press** events and **other** events. Remember that, unlike many other languages, Dynamic HTML bubbles events up through the object hierarchy—so these events can occur for the **document** even when the user targets their actions to an element on the page. Don't worry if this seems a strange concept, remember that we'll be covering event bubbling and event handling in more detail the next chapter.

Mouse Events in the Document

As you would expect, these events occur when the user performs some action using the mouse. Two new events, **onmouseover** and **onmouseout**, are very useful for providing effects such as the latest 'coolbar' toolbars. These events occur when the mouse pointer first enters, and just before it leaves, an element—allowing the code to change the way that element appears while the mouse pointer is over it. Here's a list of all of the mouse events.

Mouse Events	Description
onclick	Occurs when the mouse button is clicked on the document.
ondblclick	Occurs when the user double-clicks on the document.
onmousedown	Occurs when the user presses a mouse button.
onmousemove	Occurs when the user moves the mouse pointer.
onmouseout	Occurs when the mouse pointer leaves the element.
onmouseover	Occurs when the mouse pointer first enters the element.
onmouseup	Occurs when the user releases a mouse button.
ondragstart	Occurs when the user first starts to drag an element or selection.
onselectstart	Occurs when the user first starts to select contents of an element.

The **onmousedown, onmousemove** and **onmouseup** events provide information regarding the position of the mouse pointer, the button pressed, and the state of the *Shift, Ctrl* and *Alt* keys. The **ondragstart** event is needed to determine when the user presses down a mouse button, as the pointer is positioned over a particular element, and then starts moving the mouse pointer while holding the button down. We'll be looking at how we handle all the document mouse and key-press events in detail in the next and subsequent chapters, and we'll show you a simple example towards the end of this chapter.

> Note that the **onclick** event can also occur when the user presses the return key or space bar while some elements, such as buttons, have the focus. This shouldn't be surprising: in most Windows applications you can 'click' on the active button by pressing the Return key or space bar.

As well as providing information on the events created by the mouse, the document object also provides a set of key-press events.

Key-press Events	Description
onkeydown	Occurs when the user presses a key.
onkeypress	Occurs when the user presses a key and that keyboard input is translated. i.e. multiple onkeypress events occur if the key is held down, unlike onkeydown.
onkeyup	Occurs when the user releases a key.
onhelp	Occurs when the user presses the *F1* or 'help' key.

The onkeydown and onkeyup events provide information on the state of the *Shift, Ctrl* and *Alt* keys. The onkeypress event occurs when a key is pressed (and continues to occur if the key is held down) and then returns an ASCII code modified to take account of the state of the *Shift, Ctrl* and *Alt* keys. The onhelp event occurs in Windows when the user presses the *F1* key, the appropriate 'help' key in other environments or when they click on the What's This? (question mark) button and then click on a control or object.

Other Events in the Document

Four other events are provided for the document object. The first of these is linked to the readyState property we met earlier. Rather than having to monitor the readyState property to see if the page has finished loading, we can just react to the onreadystatechange event. This occurs each time the value of readyState changes, and we can read the new state each time.

Other Events	Description
onreadystatechange	Occurs when the readyState for the document has changed.
onbeforeupdate	Occurs before a page containing data-bound controls is unloaded.
onafterupdate	Occurs when data transfer to the data provider is complete.
onload	Occurs when the element has completed loading.

Microsoft's implementation of Dynamic HTML supports **data-binding**, where control elements on the page are linked (or **bound**) to individual fields in a data source. This source is normally a database on the server, although you may start seeing local data in comma delimited files being downloaded to the client to reduce server load. We'll come to this topic in the final chapter, although it is not the core subject of this book. When the data in a bound control is changed, and the user indicates that they are ready to update the source, two events—onbeforeupdate and onafterupdate—occur for that control. If the user attempts to unload the page before the changed data is saved, the events occur for the document itself. The user may just move the focus to another control on the page, load another page, or close the browser. In each case the `onbeforeupdate` event occurs before the new data is sent to the source, allowing the script code to validate it and cancel the update action if appropriate. Once the source has been updated, the `onafterupdate` event occurs. While the concepts of data binding are under consideration by W3C, these events and properties will probably not be available in browsers other than Internet Explorer, as this is currently the only browser to support data binding.

The Document Collections

Having covered the properties, methods and events of the document, it's now time to look at the range of **collections** that the document object provides. A web page contains a vast amount of information, and to allow us to access it using Dynamic HTML, it has to be organized in a sensible and usable way. This organization is achieved through nine collections:

Collection	Description
`all`	Collection of all the tags and elements in the body of the document.
`anchors`	Collection of all the anchors in the document.
`applets`	Collection of all the objects in the document, including intrinsic HTML controls, images, applets, embeds, and other objects.
`embeds`	Collection of all the `<EMBED>` tags in the document.
`filters`	Collection of all the filter objects for an element in the document. (It is not strictly a document collection.)
`frames`	Collection of all the frames defined within a `<FRAMESET>` tag.
`forms`	Collection of all the forms in the page.
`images`	Collection of all the images in the page.
`links`	Collection of all the links and image-map `<AREA>` blocks in the page.
`plugins`	An alias for collection of all the plugins available in the page.
`scripts`	Collection of all the `<SCRIPT>` sections in the page.
`styleSheets`	Collection of all the individual style property objects defined for a document.

We'll look at how we can work with these collections next, although some are intrinsically more useful that others. We'll be concentrating on those you are likely to come across most often.

Working with Document Collections

We looked briefly at collections in the previous chapter, where we saw how we can access other frames in a window using the `window` object's `frames` collection. We considered two ways of accessing the members of the `frames` collection:

```
window.frames(1)              'the index of a frame in the collection
window.frames("mainframe")    'the name of a frame in the collection
```

The **document** object supports a range of collections, and we can use the same techniques to access the members of all of them. For example, to access the second image on a page, we can use:

```
document.images(1)            'the index of an image in the collection
```

*You should remember that **images(1)** references the second image in a collection because all collections are zero indexed.*

If we have named the image, using the **NAME** attribute in the HTML **<IMG>** tag, we can even access it like this:

```
document.images("MyImage")    'the name of an image in the collection
```

As an example, here's part of a page that includes a single image:

```
<IMG SRC=element.gif NAME="MyImage">

<SCRIPT LANGUAGE=VBSCRIPT>
  Sub document_onClick()
    MsgBox document.images("MyImage").src
  End Sub
</SCRIPT>
```

Clicking on the page runs the **document_onClick()** routine, which uses the **images** collection to get a reference to the image named **MyImage**. It then displays the value of the image's **src** property, which is the Dynamic HTML equivalent of the value of the **SRC** attribute in the **<IMG>** tag.

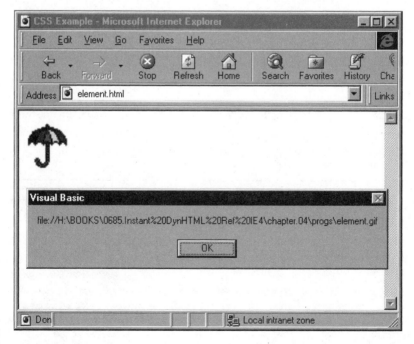

Collection Length and Filtering

We've talked about collections, and how we can access them, in several places in this and previous chapters. As we work with collections, we'll often want to retrieve a list of the objects that are available in that collection. For example we might need to know how many items there are in the collection. The easy answer is to use the collection's `length` property, which returns the number of items in the collection.

```
For objItem = 0 to document.all.length-1   'all the elements in the document
   MsgBox document.all(objItem).tagName     'display the text of the tag
Next
```

Iterating a Collection with For Each

Another solution is a special construct that works with collections in VBScript—
`For Each...Next`. This automatically executes the code for each object in the collection, and provides for more compact and neater code:

```
For Each objItem In document.all
   MsgBox objItem.tagName
Next
```

Filtering a Collection

There may also be occasions when we want to select only certain members of a collection. We can do this by **filtering** the collection, using its `tags` method. This returns a new collection, which contains only the members of the original collection which have that particular `tagName`. To create a collection which only contains the text paragraphs, i.e. the elements with a `<P>` tag, we can use:

```
Set NewCollection = OldCollection.tags("P")
```

Here's a simple example. It contains six paragraphs and four images. The code in the script section uses the `length` property and the `tags` method to display information about the page, and create a collection of the images only. Of course, we could have used the `images` collection directly, but this demonstrates the technique we've been discussing:

```
...
<P ID=para1>paragraph 1</P>      <IMG ID=img1 SRC="image1.gif">
<P ID=para2>paragraph 2</P>      <P ID=para3>paragraph 3</P>
<IMG ID=img2 SRC="image2.gif">  <P ID=para4>paragraph 4</P>
<P ID=para5>paragraph 5</P>      <IMG ID=img3 SRC="image3.gif">
<P ID=para6>paragraph 6</P>      <IMG ID=img4 SRC="image4.gif">

<SCRIPT LANGUAGE=VBSCRIPT>
   MsgBox document.all.length                'displays 15 (elements)
   Set colImages = document.all.tags("IMG")  'creates a new collection
   MsgBox colImages.length                   'displays 4 (images)
   MsgBox colImages("img4").src              'displays file://..\image4.gif
</SCRIPT>
...
```

All the collections work in this same way, providing easy access to any element on the page. However, one collection is slightly different from the others—the `forms` collection.

Using the Forms Collection

Web page authors can create pages that contain one or more sections defined as **forms**, by enclosing them in the `<FORM>` and `</FORM>` tags. Forms have special abilities, in that they can contain the `SUBMIT` and `RESET` types of `<INPUT>` tag, which either send the contents of the other controls (not ActiveX ones) in that form to the server for processing, or reset them to their default values.

This means that the forms in a document can themselves act as containers to hold other elements and objects. To manage this, each member of the `forms` collection (i.e. each `form` object) has its own sub-collection of `elements`:

elements   A collection of all the controls and other elements in the form.

This collection can be accessed in the same way as the **document** collections, this time with the collection name added to the end of the statement:

```
'access the third element in the first form on the page
document.forms(0).elements(2)

'access the element named MyTextBox in the second form on the page
document.forms(1).elements("MyTextBox")

'access the element named MyTextBox in a form named MyForm
document.forms("MyForm").elements("MyTextBox")
```

Accessing Properties and Methods

Of course, like all collections, the items in it are themselves objects. Therefore, we need to specify which property or method of the object we are referring to—as we did earlier to retrieve the source file from an image element. Here are some property retrievals:

```
strFileName  = document.images("MyImage").src        'image source
strTheValue  = document.forms(0).elements(2).value   'control value
strElementId = document.forms(3).elements(0).id      'element identifier
strAddress   = document.links("MyLink").href         'URL of a hyperlink
strPlugin    = document.plugins(0).name              'name of a plugin
```

And here's how we can call a method of an object in a collection. Here we're calling the **focus** method of the third element in the first form, and the **scrollIntoView** method of the fourth image in the page:

```
document.forms(0).elements(2).focus   'set the focus to this control
document.images(3).scrollIntoView     'bring this image into view
```

*The **scrollIntoView** method is provided for all visible elements, and simply brings that element into view in the browser window. You'll see it used in Chapter 6.*

A Document and Collections Example

The one collection we haven't mentioned is the `all` collection, although we
have already used it. This collection contains all the elements in the document,
including the **BODY**, **TITLE**, **HEAD** etc.. To show you how we can use this
collection, and demonstrate several of the properties of the **document** object at
the same time, we've provided a simple example page called The Document
Object and Collections (`DocObject.htm`) on our web site at
`http://rapid.wrox.co.uk/books/0685/`:

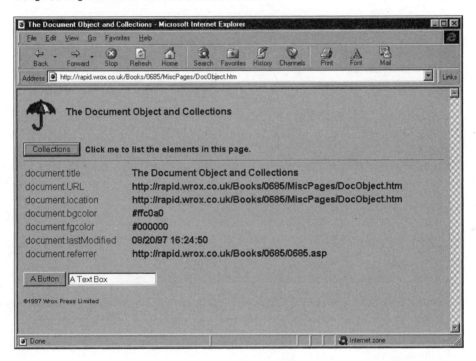

The page uses the same techniques as the similar example in the previous
chapter to display the values of several properties from the **document** object.
The text box and button are included simply so that you can see how their tags
and attributes appear within the `all` collection.

Using the All Collection

Go on then, click the Collections button at the top of the page. This opens a
new browser window, which lists all the elements in the original document:

95

```
http://rapid.wrox.co.uk/Books/0685/MiscPages/blank.htm - Microsoft Internet Explorer   _ □ X
File   Edit   View   Go   Favorites   Help

 ←  .   →  .    ⊗       ⬚      ⌂         ⬛       ⬚         ⬛        ⬛        ⬛       ⬛      ⬛
Back    Forward     Stop   Refresh   Home    Search   Favorites   History   Channels       Print     Font     M

Address    http://rapid.wrox.co.uk/Books/0685/MiscPages/blank.htm                    ▼    Links
```

The all Collection

HTML
HEAD
TITLE
STYLE
BODY
H1 - id=TopHeading
IMG - id=imgElement - src=http://rapid.wrox.co.uk/Books/0685/MiscPages/element.gif - name=
INPUT - name=cmdCollect
B
HR - id=HRule1
SCRIPT - src=
CENTER
TABLE
TBODY
TR
TD
TD
B
TR
TD

```
 Done                                              Internet zone
```

Some of them include extra information, such as an **id**, **name** or **src**. The code iterates (or loops) through the entire **all** collection, and places properties of each member into the page. In our case we've used the **tagName** property (the text of the actual tag, a property that every element has), and the **id**, **name** and **src** properties where they are available.

Ignoring Scripting Errors

One problem is that different types of elements have different properties. If we try to list the **src** property of every element, we'll get an error when we come to the first element, **HTML**, as it doesn't have a **src** property.

The answer to this problem is the VBScript statement **On Error Resume Next** (there doesn't seem to be a JavaScript equivalent). It simply tells the code to ignore any errors that occur, and carry on processing from the next line. By including this in our code, we can query properties that don't exist without the whole thing collapsing in a heap.

The Collections Button Code

Here's the complete code of the **cmdCollect_onClick()** routine, which runs when the Collections button is clicked:

```
Sub cmdCollect_OnClick()
  On Error Resume Next
  Set NewWindow = window.open("blank.htm")    'assuming that blank.htm exists
  NewWindow.document.write "<HTML><HEAD><TITLE>" _
                        & "The all Collection </TITLE></HEAD><BODY>" _
                        & "<H3>The all Collection</H3>"
  For Each objItem In document.all
    NewWindow.document.write objItem.tagName
    if objItem.id <> "" Then NewWindow.document.write " - id="  & objItem.id
    NewWindow.document.write " - src="  & objItem.src
    NewWindow.document.write " - name="  & objItem.name
    NewWindow.document.write "<BR>"
  Next
  NewWindow.document.write "<HR></BODY></HTML>"
  NewWindow.document.close
End Sub
```

Having 'turned off' error handling with **On Error Resume Next**, we open a
new browser window using the **window** object's **open** method. The source is a
file called **blank.htm**, which should have been placed on your system when
you installed the browser (and the program will error if it isn't present). Notice
that we have to use the **Set** keyword, because we are assigning an object to
our variable, and not just a simple value. The expression assigns the new
window object to a variable **NewWindow**, and we can then access it in our code.

Once we've got our new window, we can start to write to it with the **write**
method of the **document** object. At present it's empty, because we loaded a
blank page (**blank.htm**) into it. We're going to create the content in the
original page, and write it to the new page. Of course, this page is in the new
browser window, not our existing (current) one, so we need to call the write
method of the **NewWindow.document** object.

> *This page also demonstrates the **document** object's **elementFromPoint**
> method that we looked at earlier. Right-click on any part of the page to see the
> **tagName** of the element under the mouse pointer.*

Listing the Contents of the Collection

The next step is to list the members of the collection, and add some property
values where appropriate. The **For Each...Next** construct will step through
the complete collection automatically, and for each iteration it sets the variable
objItem to that member of the collection.

```
For Each objItem In document.all
  ...
  'write the property values to the new window
  ...
Next
```

All we have to do in the loop is **write** the **tagName** and other properties to
the new page. Every element has an **id** property, but it is blank (empty) if we
don't go to the trouble of setting it in the HTML source. For this reason, we
examine the value, and only include the **id** property in the new page if it is
not empty (**""**).

We haven't bothered with this for the other properties, though you could soon
implement this if it was important. And apart from this, the other properties

97

look after themselves. If we reference a property that doesn't exist the script will raise an error. Our code then ignores this line, and goes on to the next one.

Coming Back to Secure Domains

One interesting point arises from this example, and is connected with our earlier discussion of the document object's **domain** property. When we create a new window, but don't specify a file name of a page to display in it, the browser will load a default page named **blank.htm** from your **Windows/System** folder, if it exists, or create an empty blank document itself if it doesn't.

If it loads **blank.htm** from a directory or site that differs from the page where the main document was loaded, i.e. from a different **domain**, the code will fail with a security breach error. It won't be able to access the page in the new browser window. This is why we've had to include a blank file in the same directory as the example page.

The Selection Object

The only subsidiary object for the **document** is the **selection** object. This provides information about the current selection made by the user, when they drag over the page with the mouse. The **selection** object allows us to access all the selected elements, including the plain text, within the page.

Property	Description
type	The type of the selection, i.e. a control, text, a table or none.

The single property, **type**, returns a value depending on the type of elements selected. It can be:

Value	HTML Constant	Description
0 - None	htmlSelectionNone	No selection.
1 - Text	htmlSelectionText	Body text and text in any type of formatting tag.
2 - Control	htmlSelectionControl	A control element.
3 - Table	htmlSelectionTable	All or part of a table.

The **selection** object's methods provide us with a way to retrieve the selection into a **TextRange** object, delete the selected items from the page, and remove the highlighting when we have finished using it:

Method	Description
clear	Clears the contents of the selection.

Method	Description
createRange	Returns a copy of the currently selected range.
empty	Deselects the current selection and sets selection type to None.

You'll see a lot more about how we can work with text and selections in Chapter 6, where we explore the whole concept of working with the contents of a document. In the meantime, here's a simple example that uses the **selection** object, and introduces the concept of a **TextRange**.

Selections and Text Ranges

A **TextRange** is an object in its own right, and you'll meet it again in Chapter 6. For the time being, just accept that it is a way of storing a 'chunk' of a document in such a way that we can access different things within that 'chunk'.

Although the document is created by an HTML source stream—basically a string of text—we often want to retrieve it in other formats. The **TextRange** object allows us to work with our document chunk as either an HTML stream or the text as it is displayed on the screen. It also provides information on the start and end positions of the 'chunk' within the original page, plus a whole heap of methods that we can use to work with it.

A Selection Object Example

In our example, we're using a **TextRange** object to store the selection in the document, so that we can examine it later. Here's the page, **select.htm**, which you can run from our web site at: **http://rapid.wrox.co.uk/books/0685/**.

The code in the page's **<SCRIPT>** section is remarkably compact, when you consider what it is doing. The one thing we have to remember is that, to work with a selection, we have to respond to an event that occurs when the selection is made. If we put a button on the page for the user to click with the mouse in order to get information about the selection, the result will always be **None**—because clicking the button removes the selection from the page.

So we're responding to the **onmouseup** event for the document, which occurs when the mouse button is released. This event also provides four arguments that indicate which button was pressed, which other keys were held down and the coordinates of the mouse pointer:

```
Sub document_onmouseup()
    Set MyRange = document.selection.createRange
    strMsg = "Selection Type is: " & document.selection.type & Chr(10) _
           & "Content is: " & MyRange.text
    MsgBox strMsg
    If (window.event.button And 2) And (document.selection.type <> "None") Then
    document.selection.clear
    document.selection.empty
End Sub
```

The first step is to capture the selection into a new **TextRange** object, which we've called **MyRange**. Again, we have to use the **Set** keyword, because we are assigning an object to the variable **MyRange**, and not just a simple value. The expression **document.selection.createRange** calls the **createRange** method of the **document** object's **selection** object, which returns the **TextRange** object we need.

Now we can examine the user's selection. The kind of selection is retrieved using the **selection** object's **type** property, and the contents of the selection from our new **TextRange** object's **text** property. The **selection** object doesn't expose the text contents of the selection, which is why we had to assign it to a **TextRange** object in the first place.

Now we can display the results in a VBScript message box, then decide if we need to delete it from the document. The **button** argument supplied by the

onmouseup event will be **2** if the user clicked the right mouse button. We check this, and make sure that the selection type is not **None** before we remove the selection using the **selection** object's **clear** method. To clean up afterwards, we use the **selection** object's **empty** method which un-highlights the selection on the screen ready for the user to select some more of the page.

displayed in a message box. If you dra
as well.

. Almost anything that's visible in the page,
object model. This is the subject of this cha
and the most useful objects. In the next cha
for integrating our script into the page.

You'll see more about the way we react to events like **onmouseup**, and use the arguments it provides, in the next chapter. We'll be looking at the whole subject of manipulating the text of the document in more detail in Chapter 6.

Visual and Transition Filters

The filters collection isn't really a collection of the **document** object at all, so you might wonder why we're even talking about it here. That's because it's a collection of many of the elements that go to make up the **document** object. Filters had to be created with an ActiveX control in the first public platform preview release of Internet Explorer 4—they formed part of the multimedia controls suite—so it was a bit of a surprise to find that they were suddenly made part of Cascading Style Sheets in Platform Preview Release Two. A filters collection is now available on every element to allow script to access individual filters specific to an element. They are also available as properties within cascading style sheets.

So What is a Filter?

Filters are effects for enhancing the look of the graphics and text within your web pages. Internet Explorer 4.0 supports visual filter and transition filter effects through its Cascading Style Sheets. These filters can be applied to text, images, and groups of **<DIV>** text and images. They can do anything from flipping your text or images upside down to making them disappear in a random checkerboard pattern. There are two distinct kinds of filters available to the programmer in Internet Explorer. The first are the visual filters. These alter the appearance of an object, like a block of text or a graphic, and are static: once we apply a visual filter the result persists. There are 14 visual filter effects, which allow you to manipulate and alter your elements by applying various effects, from merely reversing your image to creating an 'x-ray' of your image. The second set of filters are known as transition filters. These cause a change to an image over some user configurable length of time. For example, one of the transition filters included with IE fades one image into another. This means that instead of an immediate transformation being applied to your element (as with the visual filter), the element is gradually dissolved or made to emerge. There are 23 transition effects available. However we'll start by looking at the visual filter effects and demonstrating all 14 of them.

The Visual Filter Effects

As previously stated, there are 14 effects in all, which can either be applied by the means of a Cascading Style Sheet or by setting properties in the browser object model. We'll look at how they're done in Cascading Style Sheets first.

filter: *filtername (fparameter1, fparameter2, etc)*

There's really no difference between programming filters and programming any other Cascading Style Sheet attribute. The following code applies the **flipH** filter effect to an image which flips the image horizontally:

```
<STYLE>
.effect {filter: fliph}
</STYLE>
...
<IMG CLASS=effect SRC=wrox0.gif>
...
```

This would have the following effect on the Wrox logo:

You can achieve the same effect through script by setting up an ID attribute of the image, then calling the filter method of the image through the style object. You must encase the filter name in quotes for it to work correctly, otherwise nothing will happen.

```
<SCRIPT LANGUAGE=VBSCRIPT>
Image1.style.filter = "fliph"
</SCRIPT>
...
<IMG ID=Image1 SRC=wrox0.gif>
...
```

Here's a complete list of all of the visual filters, what parameters they take and what they do.

Filter effect	Parameters Needed	Description
alpha	opacity, finish opacity, style, startx, starty, finishx, finishy	Sets a uniform transparency level.
blur	add, direction, strength	Creates a movement effect.
chroma	color	Makes one color transparent.
dropshadow	color, offx, offy, positive	Makes a silhouette of an object.
fliph	none	Creates a horizontal mirror image.
flipv	none	Creates a vertical mirror image.
glow	color, strength	Creates the effect that an object is glowing.
grayscale	none	Changes an object to monochromatic colors.
invert	none	Reverses all hue, saturation and brightness values.
light	none	Shines a light source onto an object.
mask	color	Creates a transparent mask from an object.
shadow	color, direction	Creates a silhouette of an object offset from the object.

Filter effect	Parameters Needed	Description
wave	add, freq, lightstrength, phase, strength	Creates a sine wave distortion of an object along the x axis.
xray	none	Shows just the outline of an object.

Visual Filters Example

However you really need to see many of them working to understand what the effects do. We've provided an example which allows you to apply each of the filters, or several of them altogether, to some text and graphics. Here's the page, **FilterEx.htm**, which you can run from our web site at:
http://rapid.wrox.co.uk/books/0685/.

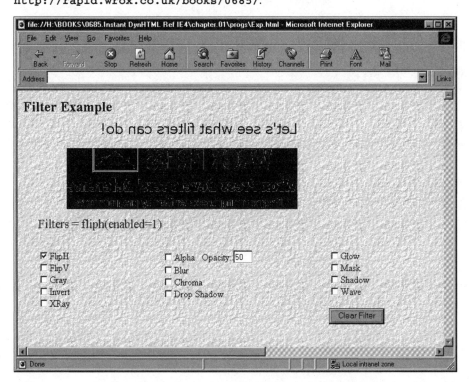

As you can see the filter is able to effect both the image and the text at the same time. By selecting more than one filter, you can apply several at the same time, if you wish. Once you've applied a set of filters, you have to clear them before you can apply any more. Let's take a look at some of the code behind the example.

How It Works

The first part of our script declares one global variable **bFilterApplied**. This is a boolean value which we use to determine whether or not a set of filters has been applied to our text and image.

103

```
<SCRIPT LANGUAGE="VBScript">
dim bFilterApplied
```

Next we need some code to execute when the browser first loads, triggered by the **Window_onLoad** event. When this is done, we initialize the value of **bFilterApplied** to false.

```
Sub Window_onLoad()
bFilterApplied = False
End Sub
```

The subprocedure **ApplyFilter()** is the one where all the interesting things happen:

```
Sub ApplyFilter() 'Update the text display
if bFilterApplied then
        divAB.style.filter=""
        bFilterApplied = False
        startFilter.Value = "Apply Filter"
        filterString.InnerText = ""
```

The first part of this procedure checks to see if the **bFilterApplied** value is true. If a filter has been applied, then we need to reset the display, set the value of **bFilterApplied** to false, change the button name to Apply Filter, and clear the name of the filter string. **FilterString** is an element on the page that is used to display the filter string that is currently in effect. Since the filter is in effect, then we set the **InnerText** of this element to " ". It's stored in a variable **strFilters**. So, if **bFilterApplied** is false, then the text and image is ready for us to apply a visual filter(s):

```
    else
            dim strFilters
            strFilters = ""
            if FlipH.checked then strFilters = strFilters + "fliph(enabled=1) "
            if FlipV.checked then strFilters = strFilters + "flipv(enabled=1) "
            if Gray.checked then strFilters = strFilters + "gray(enabled=1) "
            if Invert.checked then strFilters = strFilters + "invert(enabled=1) "
            if XRay.checked then strFilters = strFilters + "xray(enabled=1) "
            if Alpha.checked then
                    dim tmpOpacity
                    tmpOpacity = opacity.Value
                    if tmpOpacity = "" then tmpOpacity = 50
                    strFilters =strFilters +
"alpha(opacity="+tmpOpacity+",enabled=1)"
            end if
            if fltBlur.checked then strFilters = strFilters
            +"blur(direction=45,strength=15, add=0, enabled=1) "
            if Chroma.checked then strFilters = strFilters +"chroma(color=#FF0000
            ,enabled=1) "
            if DropShadow.checked then strFilters = strFilters
+"dropshadow(offx=5,
            offy=9, color=#008fff,enabled=1) "
            if Glow.checked then strFilters = strFilters +"glow(strength=5,
            color=#ffff00,enabled=1) "
            if Mask.checked then strFilters = strFilters +"mask(color=#FF0000
            ,enabled=1) "
            if Shadow.checked then strFilters = strFilters
            +"shadow(color=#FF0088,direction=315,enabled=1) "
            if Wave.checked then strFilters = strFilters +"wave(freq=2,
strength=6,
            phase=0, lightstrength=0, add=0, enabled=1) "
```

StrFilters is a string that is made up of all of the filters that will be applied. It is gradually built up one selection at a time by the script. When the user presses the Apply Filter button, the script looks at all of the check boxes to see which are selected and then adds an instruction to the end of the string **strFilters** for each one that is. By the end **strFilters** can be very large indeed. We actually display the contents of **strFilters** on the screen above the check boxes:

Filters = fliph(enabled=1) flipv(enabled=1) gray
(enabled=1) invert(enabled=1) xray(enabled=1)

☑ FlipH
☑ FlipV
☑ Gray
☑ Invert
☑ XRay

Once we have a set of instructions for the browser to execute we then can get around to the business of applying the filters.

```
        filterString.InnerText = "Filters = "+ strFilters
        divAB.style.filter = strFilters
        startFilter.Value = "Clear Filter"
        bFilterApplied = True
    end if
End Sub
</SCRIPT>
```

We apply the filter method of the **style** object of the **DIV** element **divAB**, which contains both our target text and image, by setting it to **strFilter**. The string that you see displayed on the page, below the image and text, is the actual text we assign to the style property. The string sets the parameters needed for each filter as well as setting the different filter types. Next, we change the name of the button to Clear Filter as we don't want to reapply filters to our **DIV** element. Finally we change the value of **bFilterApplied** to indicate this. And finally in this example somebody has to clear all of the filters before they can select any more.

This short script deals with all the possible outcomes in the program within one short subprocedure and demonstrates all of the different filter effects in action. If you're unsure of what any of them does or how they work, then go ahead and try them out. If not, we can now move on to transition filters.

The Transition Filters Effects

The transition filters are divided into two types: blend and reveal. Blend makes the element gradually blend in or out of the surroundings, while reveal makes the element gradually appear or disappear in one of 23 predefined patterns. You can set these effects either with Cascading Style Sheet properties or via script. At the time of writing, the transition filter effects didn't work in the method indicated by the Microsoft documentation. The documentation indicated that they should work in much the same way as the visual filters effects, and indeed in the final release they probably will. However, following these

105

instructions in the prerelease version of IE4 that we were using led to nothing happening. After much investigation we did find a method of making transitions work. We'll look at how the documentation recommends you do it first and then at how we actually did it.

As mentioned previously, you should be able to set transitions by setting style sheet properties and by scripting properties. The one main difference between transitions and visual filters is that a transition takes place between two states, such as a visible image and an invisible one. Therefore you will have to set the state of the image somewhere in the code and then, when you change it, the transition will come into effect. The length of the transition, and its type are specified in parameters. The syntax is as follows:

```
filter: blendtrans{duration = duration}
 revealtrans{duration = duration, transitionshape = transition}
```

You'd expect a working example where we blend the Wrox logo slowly in over a 10 second duration from a previously blank background to look something like this:

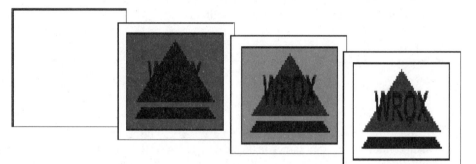

And the code necessary to achieve this should look like this, according to the Cascading Style Sheet documentation in the SDK (Software Development Kit):

```
<STYLE>
.effect {visibility: hidden; filter: blendtrans(duration = 10)}
</STYLE>
...
<SCRIPT>
Sub document_onclick()
 Image1.style.visibility = "visible"
End Sub
</SCRIPT>
...
<IMG ID=Image1 CLASS=effect SRC=wrox0.gif>
...
```

However when we tried this, while we didn't receive any error messages, we also didn't see any transitions. You'll experience this if you try and execute this code in the Platform Preview Release 2. To get the desired effect, what you can do is set the **filter** type within a **style** property and then set the duration parameter within a scripting language. At the beginning of the transition you have to freeze the image, then you have to make it visible, then finally supply the number of seconds you wish the transition to take in the **play** method. This final line of script effectively starts the transition:

```
<SCRIPT LANGUAGE=VBSCRIPT>
Sub document_onClick()
  call Image1.filters.item(0).Apply()   // Freeze the image
  I1.style.visibility = "visible"       // Make the image visible
  Image1.filters(0).play(2)             // Start the transition
End Sub
</SCRIPT>
...
<BODY>
<DIV ID = Image1 CLASS = effect STYLE="position: absolute; height: 100; width:
100; left:10; top:10; filter: blendtrans" >
<IMG ID=I1   STYLE="position: absolute; height: 100; width: 100; visibility:
hidden" SRC=wrox0.gif>
</DIV>
</BODY>
```

There is only one type of blend transition. To change a blend transition to a reveal transition requires only one extra line of script and an amendment to the style property setting. The extra line of script selects one of the 23 transition filter effects available:

```
<SCRIPT LANGUAGE=VBSCRIPT>
Sub document_onClick()
  call Image1.filters.item(0).Apply()// Freeze the image
  I1.style.visibility = "visible"            // Make the image visible
  Image1.filters.item(0).Transition = 2      // Selects the type of transition
  Image1.filters(0).play(2)                  // Start the transition
End Sub
</SCRIPT>
...
<BODY>
<DIV ID = Image1 CLASS = effect STYLE="position: absolute; height: 100; width:
100; left:10; top:10; filter: revealtrans" >
<IMG ID=I1   STYLE="position: absolute; height: 100; width: 100; visibility:
hidden" SRC=wrox0.gif>
</DIV>
</BODY>
```

We've set it to 2, which is a "circle in" transition. This would have the following effect:

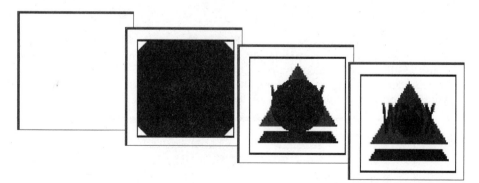

You can alter the type to any of the 23 transition effects. A full list of them can be found later in this chapter and in Section C of the reference section. In the next example you can try out any of the transition effects for yourself.

107

Reveal Transition Filters Example

In this example we've put two pictures together side by side, although one of the two is always hidden using the style sheet property **visibility**. The user can select the type of transition desired and then when he/she presses the button, one picture will appear as the other disappears. This is achieved by using a transition filter affect on the **<DIV>** that holds both images. The page, **TransEx.htm** can be run from our web site at: **http://rapid.wrox.co.uk/ books/0685/**. Here we're using the vertical blinds effect:

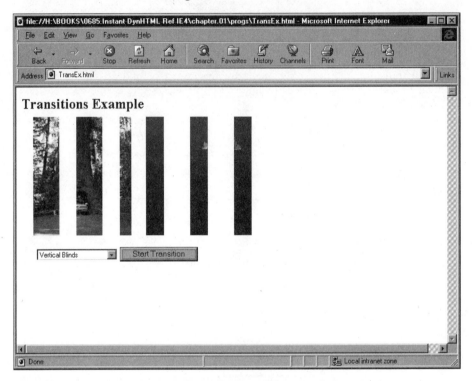

Each time a transition is begun, the chosen effect reverses the visibility of two the pictures, to reveal the previously hidden image and hide the visible. Here's a list of all of the different types of transition that are available. Most of them will be fairly self-explanatory from the name, but you can try them all out, if you're uncertain about what any of them do.

Transition Type	Number
Box in	0
Box out	1
Circle in	2
Circle out	3
Wipe up	4
Wipe down	5

108

Transition Type	Number
Wipe right	6
Wipe left	7
Vertical blinds	8
Horizontal blinds	9
Checkerboard across	10
Checkerboard down	11
Random dissolve	12
Split vertical in	13
Split vertical out	14
Split horizontal in	15
Split horizontal out	16
Strips left down	17
Strips left up	18
Strips right down	19
Strips right up	20
Random bars horizontal	21
Random bars vertical	22
Random selection of (0-22)	23

How It Works

We've already hinted at how this one works. The only differences to our earlier example using the Wrox logo is that we need to pass the user's choice of transition from the list box to the script code, and that we need to prevent the user from choosing another transition while one transition is already executing. The first part of our script declares some global variables:

```
<SCRIPT LANGUAGE="VBScript">
dim transDuration
dim TransDirection
dim bTransInProgress

transDuration=2.5
TransDirection = 0
```

The first **transDuration** is used to store the duration of the transition which has been preset by us at 2.5 seconds. The second **transDirection** is merely a way to track which image is currently visible, so that after the **Apply** they can switch visibility. A value of 1 indicates the right image is visible, a value of 2 indicates that the left image is visible. Finally, a boolean value **bTransInProgress** is set to true if the transition is currently in progress.

In the next section of code, we use two events to help set the global variable **bTransInProgress**, the first Window_onLoad event sets its value to false when the window is first loaded, as it isn't possible for there to be a transition currently in progress. The second event **OnFilterChange** is triggered when a transition has completed. It can be used with both visual and transition filters, it fires when a visual filter changes state or when a transition filter completes a transition. In this case when transition completes and the event is triggered, the **bTransInProgress** value is set to false.

```
Sub Window_onLoad()
bTransInProgress = False
End Sub

sub divAB_OnFilterChange()
bTransInProgress = False
End Sub
```

However, it's the **TransImage()** subprocedure that does the real work...

```
Sub TransImage()    'Update the text display
if bTransInProgress then Exit Sub
     call divAB.filters.item(0).Apply()      'Freeze the image

if TransDirection = 1 then
        TransDirection = 2
        Image3.Style.Visibility = ""
        Image2.Style.Visibility = "hidden"
else
        TransDirection = 1
        Image2.Style.Visibility = ""
        Image3.Style.Visibility = "hidden"
end if
divAB.filters.item(0).Transition = TransChoice.selectedIndex
divAB.filters(0).play(transDuration)
bTransInProgress = True
End Sub
</SCRIPT>
```

The script first checks to see if the transition is in progress and immediately exits if it is. After that we basically follow the routine we learned earlier. We freeze the image, and then we check the direction of the transition. Depending on the direction we make one of the images visible and hide the other one. Then we set the transition type to the choice selected in the user list box. Finally we set the duration of the transition to our preset global variable. One last thing is that we set the boolean variable **bTransInProgress** to indicate that we can't start another transition for the duration of this one. That's all there is to it.

> While the visual filters seemed pretty much complete at the time of writing, the transition filters didn't function in the way the documentation indicated. If there are any changes to them in the final release, then we will update this chapter and the examples in html format and you will be able to retrieve the chapter from our web site, http://rapid.wrox.co.uk.

Summary

In this chapter, we've completed our tour of the Dynamic HTML **object model**, by looking at the central character it provides—the **document** object. We've also looked at the other subsidiary objects and collections that it supports, and seen some ways we can use them in our pages. We looked at:

 How the entire content of the page being displayed by the browser is accessible through the **document** object and various other objects and collections

 How we can use the **document** object's properties, methods and events to manipulate the document, or just get information about it

 How we can access the various elements on the page, using the **document** object's collections

 How we can interact with the user through the **selection** object, and by reacting to events

 How we can access visual and transition filters using Cascading Style Sheet properties and scripting properties

You've probably also seen some new ways of using scripting in this chapter. We're actually going to be concentrating on scripting in the next chapter, and in the remainder of the book. Now you know what's inside the browser, it's just waiting for you to play with it through scripting code. OK, there are a few more things to learn—so turn the page, and let's get started.

Scripts and Event Handling

So far, we've covered a lot of the basics of Dynamic HTML. We've studied style sheets and style tags, looked at the new design opportunities they offer for static pages, discovered the object model that lurks inside the browser and how to get at it. We've also seen some ways of taking advantage of all these features. What we still haven't done is create any really wild dynamic pages.

Well, the time has now come. We know enough about the way Dynamic HTML interfaces with the browser and the pages it displays to start getting into script code in a big way. As we saw back in Chapter 1, most of what happens in script is in response to an event. This can be initiated by the viewer of our page, by the browser they are using, by a component within the page, or even by Windows itself.

When an event occurs, the browser passes it to our script code through the object model we've been exploring, and we can then choose to react to it if we wish to. To do this, we need to know more about how we hook our scripts up to the event, and how we use the exposed methods and properties that this same object model provides to actually manipulate the page contents and other 'non-page' items exposed by the browser.

In this chapter, you'll see:

 What events are, and where they come from

 How we connect our script to an event

 How we can decide which events to react to

 The kinds of things we can do when reacting to an event

Understanding the nature of events, and how we create the link between an event and our code, are the crucial steps. It's these that we'll look at first.

What are Events?

Most people have heard the term **event-driven programming**, and connect this with the way Windows works. But what does this actually mean? Why should a program be driven by events, rather than by any other method? And what other alternatives are there anyway?

These are questions that don't normally concern the Web page author, but you need to know a little about how Windows works to use Dynamic HTML to anything like its full potential. We'll take a brief overview of the subject, then see how we can use events in our pages.

What is Event-Driven Programming?

Before Windows in particular and graphical user interfaces in general, users usually worked with one application at a time—rather than having several open as we do these days. Within that application, the user carried out tasks by navigating from one 'menu' screen to another, and had only a finite set of choices available at any one time.

In a graphical user interface like Windows, users can run several applications at the same time, change the size of the screen windows as they go along, and switch from one to another. More importantly, the applications have no fixed 'route' through them. The user can click different buttons or select from any of the menus, to decide for themselves which course they want to take in the program.

As an example, consider a program that carries out technical calculations. In the years BW (Before Windows), on starting the application we would have been presented with a main menu, from which there were a fixed number of choices. Selecting an option would display more screens collecting information, then display the result. We would have followed this same course every time we wanted to carry out the query.

In the equivalent Windows program, or the equivalent in other graphical user environments, we can generally choose which windows to open, and open several at once. We can fill in text boxes, make selections from lists, set other controls, and click a range of buttons—in almost any order we like. To keep control of all this, the operating system has to work in a fundamentally different way.

Where Do Events Come From?

When you carry out some action in Windows, say clicking on a window with the mouse, the operating system raises an **event**. This is simply a signal that something has happened. Windows examines the event to decide what caused it, and what to do about it. This isn't always as simple as it may seem. For example, the user may have clicked on a window that was not currently active (i.e. not part of the application they were working with).

In this case, Windows has to work out where the mouse pointer is on the screen and which application is under the pointer, bring this application's window to the front, and tell the other application that it is no longer the active one. And this is only a simplified view. In reality there will be a lot more happening 'under the hood'—a stream of messages is being sent to all the applications by the operating system. Each application can choose to either do something about the message, or simply ignore it.

However, some events may not be aimed at any application in particular. For example pressing a key when Microsoft Word is active will normally cause that character to appear in the page. But if there is another application running at the same time, and the key-press is *Alt-Tab*, Windows brings up its own task-switching window instead of passing the event onto Word.

Events in Dynamic HTML

In the case of the browser and Dynamic HTML, this constant barrage of messages provides a way for us to react to things that are going on in the browser. We can link code in our pages to the events that are occurring, and use them to interact with the viewer of our pages.

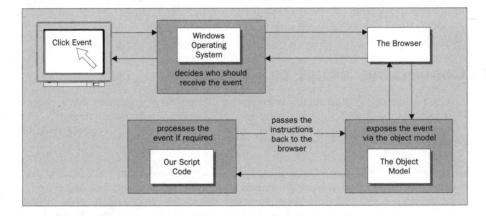

For example, just clicking the mouse button creates several events—descriptively named **onmousedown**, **onmouseup**, and **onclick**. Each message is collected by the Windows operating system, which then decides what to do with it. If the user pressed the mouse button while the pointer was on the screen over the browser window, Windows sends a message to the browser. It includes information on which button was pressed, what other keys were held down, and where the pointer was on the screen.

The browser then decides if it is going to handle the event. If they clicked on one of the browser toolbar buttons, it just gets on and does whatever is required—perhaps printing the page, refreshing it, or loading the user's Home page. If, however, the click was over the page itself, the browser then **exposes** it, by passing it on to our script code via the browser's object model. At this point, we can react to the event ourselves if we want.

The reverse path is taken if we actually do decide to respond. The instructions in our code are passed back to the browser via the object model. It decides what effect this will have on the page and tells Windows. Windows then updates the screen to show the new page. The great thing is that, as Dynamic HTML programmers, all we have to do is decide which events to respond to, and what instructions to give the browser. Everything else is looked after automatically.

Reacting to Browser Events

To be able to react to an event, we have to be able to detect it happening. If we don't react to it, the browser will just carry on regardless—perhaps carrying out some action of its own. And even if we do decide to react, we can still let the browser carry out the original task as well. If this sounds confusing, think about the following example.

When we have a Submit button on a page, and the user clicks it, the browser sends the information from all the HTML control elements on the form to the server. However, it also provides an event that we can react to, called `onsubmit`. If we want to, we can react to this event, have a look at what the user entered, and decide if we want to submit the form or not. If we don't, we can instruct the browser to ignore the event, as though it never happened. We'll explore this in more detail later in the chapter.

Connecting Script to Events

So, we're now getting to the crux of the matter. All we have to do is capture the event, by connecting our code to it, and then decide how to react to it ourselves. The first step, then, is to understand how we can connect code to an event.

There are 39 different events that the browser exposes to our script—but for any one element in the page, only a limited number of these are available. For example a heading in the page, such as `<H2>Some Text</H2>`, only provides 14 events, while an image tag `<IMG>` provides 25 different ones. In Section A of this book's reference pages, you'll find a description of all the events, and, in Section B, a list of those available for each HTML element tag.

We took a brief look at event-handling routines in Chapter 3, using several there to demonstrate the object model in action. Here, we'll summarize the way event handlers are written, and show you the other ways you can link your code to events.

Event Handling in VBScript

In VBScript, we have four ways of connecting our code to an event. The main one we've used so far is to create a subroutine or function whose name is a combination of the *element* name and the *event* name. To react to a click on some heading text, we can use:

```
<H2 ID=MyHeading> Some Text </H2>
...
<SCRIPT LANGUAGE=VBSCRIPT>
  Sub MyHeading_onClick()
    MsgBox "You clicked me!"
  End Sub
</SCRIPT>
```

Alternatively, we can create a routine with almost any name, and link it to the event and the element by declaring the name of the routine in the element tag. And we don't need an **ID** in this case:

```
<H2 LANGUAGE=VBSCRIPT ONCLICK="MyClickCode"> Some Text </H2>
...
<SCRIPT LANGUAGE=VBSCRIPT>
  Sub MyClickCode()
    MsgBox "You clicked me!"
  End Sub
</SCRIPT>
```

Another way is to use 'inline' script code, which does away with the need for a separate code routine. We simply write the code inside the tag, as the value of the event name attribute. Notice how we have to use single quotes inside the **ONCLICK** attribute, because this itself is a string:

```
<H2 LANGUAGE=VBSCRIPT ONCLICK="MsgBox 'You clicked me!'"> Some Text </H2>
```

The final method is to use a different script section for each event. This is done by identifying the element and the event in the **<SCRIPT>** tag:

```
<H2 ID=MyHeading> Some Text </H2>
...
<SCRIPT LANGUAGE=VBSCRIPT FOR=MyHeading EVENT=ONCLICK>
  MsgBox "You clicked me!"
</SCRIPT>
```

Event Handling in JavaScript

In JavaScript (or Microsoft's implementation of JavaScript, called **JScript**), we don't have as many options for connecting events to our code. And the two things we have to watch out for are that JavaScript only supports functions, and the language interpreter is case-sensitive in all browsers.

The most usual way of making the connection between the function and the element is by defining the name of the function in the element tag itself. Notice that we need **MyClickCode()**, not just **MyClickCode**, to satisfy the JavaScript syntax requirements. We also have to use the browser's built-in **alert** dialog, rather than **MsgBox**, which is part of VBScript:

```
<H2 ONCLICK="MyClickCode()"> Some Text </H2>
...
<SCRIPT LANGUAGE=JAVASCRIPT>
function MyClickCode()
  {
    alert("You clicked me!");
  }
</SCRIPT>
```

117

This is fine for connecting script to specific elements in the page, but what about when we want to connect event handlers to the document itself? In this case, we simply put them all in the **<BODY>** tag:

```
<BODY ONMOUSEMOVE="MyMouseMoveCode()" ONCLICK="MyClickCode()">
```

We can also use inline code, within the element tag. This time, we're using the alternative **LANGUAGE** description of **JSCRIPT**:

```
<H2 LANGUAGE=JSCRIPT ONCLICK="alert('You clicked me!');">Some Text</H2>
```

And because JavaScript is the default language in the browser, we can omit the **LANGUAGE** attribute if we want to, making our code more compact:

```
<H2 ONCLICK="alert('You clicked me!');"> Some Text </H2>
```

Finally, we can create the separate **<SCRIPT>** sections for each event, just as we did for VBScript. However, this time, we have to make sure that the name of the event is all lower-case:

```
<H2 ID=MyHeading> Some Text </H2>
...
<SCRIPT LANGUAGE=JAVASCRIPT FOR=MyHeading EVENT=onclick>
  alert("You clicked me!");
</ SCRIPT>
```

Handling Window Events in JavaScript

We've seen how we can place event handler declarations, such as **onmousemove**, in the **<BODY>** tag of the document to cause them to occur at **document** level. The other situation is how we handle events at **window** level. In Internet Explorer, we can place the event handler declarations on the opening **<HTML>** tag:

```
<HTML ONMOUSEMOVE="MyMouseMoveCode()" ONCLICK="MyClickCode()">
...
</HTML>
```

Alternatively, we can use a technique similar to the VBScript method of naming an event handler in line with the ID of the element and the event name. This time, we separate the two with a period (full stop) rather than an underscore. For example, the following are both supported in Internet Explorer 4—but bear in mind that this is not the generally accepted method for connecting events and their code. (It works because the functions are themselves actually stored as properties of the **element** object.)

```
<H2 ID=MHyeading > Some Text </H2>
...
<SCRIPT LANGUAGE=JAVASCRIPT>
function MyHeading.onclick()
  {
    alert("You clicked me!");
  }
</SCRIPT>
```

The same works for the main browser objects as well, such as the **document** and **window**:

```
<SCRIPT LANGUAGE=JAVASCRIPT>
function window.onload()
  {
    alert("I've just loaded!");
  }
</SCRIPT>
```

*The **LANGUAGE** attribute in a script or element tag can take one of four values. **VBSCRIPT** and **VBS** both instruct the browser to pass the script to its VBScript interpreter, while **JAVASCRIPT** or **JSCRIPT** pass it to the Internet Explorer JScript interpreter. Omitting the attribute altogether sends the script to the JScript interpreter as well.*

Canceling an Event Action

Some events, such as **onsubmit**, allow us to provide a return value that controls how the browser behaves. As you'll recall from Chapter 2, to return a value in VBScript we have to use a **function** rather than a **subroutine**. In JavaScript, everything is a function anyway. This example uses JavaScript, and defines a form section with a single text box named **Email**, and a Submit button:

```
<FORM ID=MyForm ONSUBMIT="return CheckAddress()"
     ACTION="http://www.somesite.com/scripts/doit.asp">
  <INPUT TYPE=TEXT ID=Email>
  <INPUT TYPE=SUBMIT>
</FORM>

<SCRIPT LANGUAGE=JAVASCRIPT>
function CheckAddress()
{
  strAddress = document.forms["MyForm"].elements["Email"].value;
  if (strAddress.indexOf("@") != -1)   // contains @ somewhere
    return true
  else
  {
    alert("You must supply a valid email address.");
    return false
  }
}
</SCRIPT>
```

This code uses the **indexOf()** function to find the position of the first **@** character in the string the user enters into a textbox named **Email** on the form. If there isn't a **@** character in the string the function returns **-1**. In this case, we can assume it's not a valid email address, display a message, and cancel the submission of the form by returning **false**. Notice that we have to use the **return** keyword in the element's **ONSUBMIT** attribute as well, so that the result is fed back to the browser's own form submission code:

```
<FORM ID=MyForm ONSUBMIT="return CheckAddress()"
     ...
```

You can also see how we have to use the browser's object model to get at the text in the text box. The string we want is the **value** property of the element object named **Email**. This form is a member of the **elements** collection of the form named **MyForm**, which is stored in the **forms** collection of the **document** object. (We could have started with **window.document**, but—as you'll recall—the **window** object is the default anyway.)

119

Instead of returning a value from the function directly, we can also cancel the default action for any event by setting the `returnValue` property of the `event` object. You'll see this technique used in an example later in the chapter.

Responding to Events

Now that we've found ways of connecting our code to an event, we can start to write the code that instructs the browser—and tells it what we want to do. In general, this involves three tasks—getting information about the event, finding out about the element the event occurred for, and carrying out the task. This is where the links between our code and the elements in the page (as exposed by the object model) come into play.

Getting Information about an Event

All the ways you've seen here of connecting code to an event were equally valid in earlier releases of browsers that supported scripting (though the heading element didn't expose its events—only a very limited subset of controls did this previously). Dynamic HTML also adds another way of getting information about an event.

In Chapter 3, we briefly mentioned the `event` object, which is part of the new object model and a subsidiary object to the top-level `window` object. The `event` object is constantly being updated to include information about each event that occurs in our page—it is global to all events in this sense. So, when an event occurs we can query the `event` object's properties to learn more about the event.

Mouse Information and the Event Object

As you've seen in Chapter 3, the `event` object provides a whole range of properties that tell us about an event that has just occurred. We simply query these properties inside our event handler to find the information we need to make a decision on what to do. Here's how we can query the properties of the `event` object to get information about the mouse button that was pressed, and the position of the mouse pointer when the event occurred:

```
<H2 ID=MyHeading> Some Text </H2>
<SCRIPT LANGUAGE=VBS>
Sub MyHeading_onmousedown()
    strMesg = "You clicked the "
    If window.event.button = 1 Then strMesg = strMesg & "left "
    If window.event.button = 2 Then strMesg = strMesg & "right "
    If window.event.button = 4 Then strMesg = strMesg & "middle "
    strMesg = strMesg & "button, at position x = " & window.event.x _
        & ", y = " & window.event.y
    strMesg = strMesg & Chr(10) & "and you held down the "
    If window.event.shiftKey Then strMesg = strMesg & "Shift key "
    If window.event.ctrlKey Then strMesg = strMesg & "Ctrl key "
    If window.event.altKey Then strMesg = strMesg & "Alt key "
    MsgBox strMesg
End Sub
</SCRIPT>
```

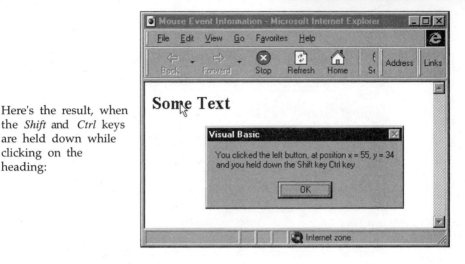

Here's the result, when the *Shift* and *Ctrl* keys are held down while clicking on the heading:

> Notice that in this example, we've preceded the event object with the default window object. This is not necessary in JavaScript (or JScript), but must be done in VBScript to prevent a clash between the event object and the VBScript event keyword.

Key-press Information and the Event Object

If we query the **event** object for a key-press event, we can use the same techniques as we did for a mouse event to find out where the mouse pointer is, and use the **shiftKey**, **ctrlKey** and **altKey** properties. However, more than that, we can use the **keyCode** property to find out which key was pressed. In this example, we're reacting to the **onkeypress** event of the **document**:

```
Sub document_onkeypress()
    strMesg = "You pressed the " & Chr(window.event.keyCode) & " key, " _
            & "which has an ASCII value of " & window.event.keyCode
    strMesg = strMesg & Chr(10) & "while holding down the "
    If window.event.shiftKey Then strMesg = strMesg & "Shift key "
    If window.event.ctrlKey Then strMesg = strMesg & "Ctrl key "
    If window.event.altKey Then strMesg = strMesg & "Alt key "
    strMesg = strMesg & Chr(10) & "The mouse pointer is at position " _
            & "x = " & window.event.x & ", y = " & window.event.y
    MsgBox strMesg, vbInformation, "The Event object parameters"
End Sub
```

Here's the result. Look where the mouse pointer is in the screenshot, and at the values of the mouse position retrieved from the **event** object. It still works if the pointer isn't over the page:

*Both of the pages demonstrating the **event** object, **mdown.htm** and **kpress.htm**, can be run directly from our Web site at:*
http://rapid.wrox.co.uk/books/0685

Examining the Source of an Event

Often the first step in reacting to an event is to find more out about the event itself, and the element it occurred for. We've seen how we can find out more about the actual event from the **event** object. The next question is how do we find out more about the element that originally raised the event?

Examining an Element's Properties

Every element in a page has a set of **properties**, and you'll find a complete list of these in the reference section at the back of the book. For example, this **<H2>** heading has an **align** property, which indicates how we aligned the text when we created the page in HTML:

```
<H2 ALIGN=CENTER> Some Text </H2>
```

We can query the element's **align** property in code using the **Me** keyword (which provides a reference to the element to which the event is bound) like this:

```
Sub MyHeading_onclick()
   MsgBox Me.align
End Sub
```

*In JavaScript or JScript, the equivalent to **Me** is the keyword **this**.*

In this case, our heading will have the value **center** for its **align** property. (Notice that the value is returned in lower case.) This is one useful way in which Dynamic HTML exposes the properties of the elements within the page, and allows them to be changed in our code. There is a whole range of different properties available for different element tags, depending on which HTML attributes are valid for that tag.

An `<IMG>` tag has (amongst many others) the `width`, `height` and `src` properties—while the `<BODY>` tag can have `aLink`, `bgColor` and `scroll` properties. Updating the properties, as you would expect, causes the change to appear dynamically on the page where appropriate.

> *One point you need to watch out for is that many elements return an empty string as the value of a property that has not been set explicitly. For example, the default alignment of a <H2> tag, if no ALIGN attribute is included, is left. However the align property in this case returns an empty string.*

Amongst the standard properties of all elements is the `id`. As you've seen, we use the `id` property, which we define in the `ID` attribute of the tag, to give an element a unique name that we can use to refer to in our script code:

```
<H2 ID=MyHeading> Some Text </H2>
```

We can always retrieve this value using `Me.id`, though you'll see other ways of identifying elements later on.

Element Properties vs Style Properties

While setting the attributes of an element is an accepted way to control its alignment, appearance, etc., there is another way. All the visible elements on a page also have a `style` object, and this can be used to control the way the element appears—as well as, or instead of, the traditional attributes of its HTML tag.

We met the `style` object in Chapter 2 and you should remember that we can use it to set, retrieve and change style properties for elements in our code, from the font size and font color, to the positioning of the text and graphics on the page.

```
<H2 ID=MyHeading STYLE="font-family:Arial; color:red; font-size:48">
   Some Text
</H2>
```

We can align our text heading in the same way, and in fact this is the technique recommended by W3C for the upcoming version 4.0 of the HTML standards:

```
<H2 ID=MyHeading STYLE="text-align:center"> Some Text </H2>
```

Once we've applied a style property like this, we have to remember to query the element's `style` object to get the value—in this case the `textAlign` property:

```
Sub MyHeading_onmousedown()
   MsgBox Me.style.textAlign
End Sub
```

Here's the equivalent in JavaScript:

```
<SCRIPT LANGUAGE=JAVASCRIPT>
function MyHeading.onmousedown()
   {
      alert(this.style.textAlign);
   }
</SCRIPT>
```

Remember that when we align text using a **STYLE** attribute like this, the **align** property of the element returns an empty string unless it's also been set to a specific value.

Generating Our Own Pseudo-Events

As well as setting the values of properties, and calling the methods of various objects within the browser's object model, our code can also generate its own pseudo-events. Because all the event routines we write are available to our code, we can call them directly. They will run just that same way as if that event had occurred, though of course the browser and Windows itself won't behave as if they had received the event.

As an example, imagine we have a page with a button named **cmdUpdate**, which updates some part of the page. We can call this code directly from elsewhere in the page like this:

```
Sub cmdUpdate_onClick()
   '.. some code to update the page
End Sub

Sub cmdOther_onClick()
   '.. do something else to change the page
   cmdUpdate_onClick   'run the cmdUpdate routine
End Sub
```

Bubbling and Canceling Events

One major topic that makes Dynamic HTML different from scripting in earlier versions, either with VBScript, JavaScript or any other language, is the way that the browser manages the events that are occurring in the page. We've already seen this to some extent when we looked at the **event** object earlier.

However, the **event** object plays another major role in the way we create script routines in Dynamic HTML. It not only stores the values of the environment as each event comes along, it also plays a part in controlling how these events are propagated to our code. It does this through two properties, **cancelBubble** and **srcElement**.

The Event Object's Control System

When an event occurs in a page, the **event** object gets the first look at it, and decides which element should receive it. Take the situation shown below where we have a **<H3>** heading inside a **<DIV>** document division on the page:

```
<DIV ID=MyDiv STYLE="background-color=aqua">
<H3 ID=MyTitle> Click Here To Fire An Event </H3>
</DIV>
```

When the **event** object receives an **onclick** event, it looks to see which element the mouse pointer was over at the time. (If two elements are overlapped, it uses the one with the higher z-index). If it was the heading line (which has the **ID** of **MyTitle**), it looks for a routine connected to this event, and—if it finds one—executes it:

```
Sub MyTitle_onclick()
   ...
End Sub
```

Bubbling Events to the Container Element

However, it doesn't stop there. It now looks to see which element is the **container** of the heading tag. In our case, it's the **<DIV>** tag named **MyDiv**, so it runs the **onclick** event code for this as well:

```
Sub MyDiv_onclick()
   ...
End Sub
```

This process continues while there are containers available. In our case, the only remaining one is the document itself, so it looks for the equivalent event code for this and executes it:

```
Sub document_onclick()
   ...
End Sub
```

This probably isn't what you were expecting, and perhaps it's difficult to see why it should work this way. After all, if the viewer clicks on a heading, surely we just want to know about that heading? In fact **event bubbling**, as this process is called, is very useful. For one thing, it helps to minimize the code we have to write, by letting one routine handle an event for several elements. Now that all the elements support events, this is particularly helpful.

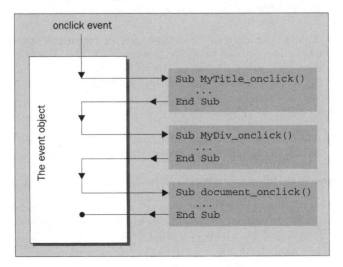

125

Using a Single Event Handler

To see why event bubbling can help to minimize the code we write, think about what happens when we have a lot of similar elements on the page. This is the case with the Jigsaw example you saw in Chapter 1. There are 24 image elements holding the different pieces of the puzzle.

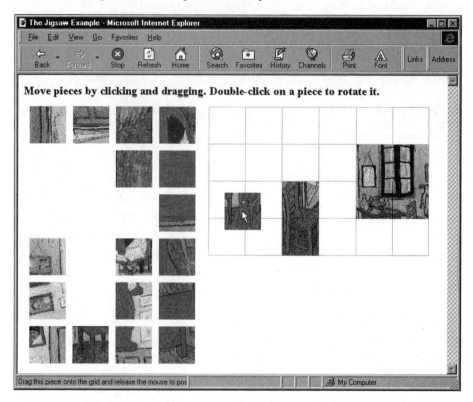

This page can be loaded from our Web site at
http://rapid.wrox.co.uk/books/0685/

However, one event-handling routine takes care of rotating all the pieces when the user double-clicks on one of them. It responds to the **ondblclick** event at document level, and stores the unique id of the image that was clicked. Then it can apply the rotation code to just that image, using the id. If we didn't have event bubbling, we would have to attach every one of the images to an event handler that rotated the piece separately.

We'll be looking at how we identify the correct image in a while, for the moment let's consider another way that event bubbling is useful.

Using Containers in Dynamic HTML

The second advantage event bubbling offers is that it allows us to work with the concept of **containers**. In HTML, when we create a list of items in the page, we group them together in **<UL>** or **<OL>** tags:

```
<STYLE>
.notover    {font-family=Arial; font-weight:normal; font-size:12;
             color:blue; visibility: show}
.color      {font-family="Arial Narrow"; color:red; font-size:12}
.sizechange {font-family=courier; font-size:26; color:blue}
.disappear  {font-family=Arial; font-weight:normal; font-size:12;
             visibility: hidden}
</STYLE>
...
<DIV ID=DivTag STYLE="position:absolute; top:50; left:30;
                      height:200; width:400; cursor:default">
  <UL ID=MyList>
    <LI ID=Item1 CLASS=notover> Change the font and size of text
    <LI ID=Item2 CLASS=notover >Change the position of elements
    <LI ID=Item3 CLASS=notover> Change the color and style of things
    <LI ID=Item4 CLASS=notover> Make elements appear and disappear
  </UL>
</DIV>
```

Notice that we've given the list and each item in it an **ID** here, and used style classes to create the styles for the list. We've also wrapped the whole list in a **<DIV>** tag, so that we can position it absolutely and move it around in our code.

This time we want to react to the **onmouseover** event for all the items in the list, by creating one single event handler for the list itself—the **container** of the list items:

```
Sub MyList_onmouseover
  ...
End Sub
```

Finding the Source Element

OK, so we can react to an event by using a handler that collects the event when it gets down to the **document**, or down as far as the element's container. The only thing is that we generally need to know where it actually came from—either to move the correct piece of the jigsaw or do something with the items in our list. This is where the **srcElement** property of the **event** object comes in.

The srcElement Property in Action

Inside any event routine, we can retrieve the object that was 'topmost' and active when the user clicked the page, or when the event occurred, from the event object's **srcElement** property. For example, if they click on a heading tag inside a document division on the page, the topmost element is the heading tag. If they click on the division, but not the heading, the topmost element is the division. If they click on the blank page, there is no topmost element, and the event goes straight to the document.

In the **ListChange** example page, which we first saw in Chapter 1, we use the **srcElement** property to discover which element the mouse is over. We're reacting to two events, **onmouseover** which occurs when the mouse first moves onto an element, and **onmouseout** which occurs when it moves off it again:

127

```
Sub MyList_onmouseover 'occurs when the mouse enters any item in the list
  'get a reference to the source of the event
  Set objItem = window.event.srcElement
  'change its style class as required, depending on the item
  If objItem.id = "Item1" Then objItem.classname = "sizechange"
  If objItem.id = "Item2" Then DivTag.style.pixelLeft = 100
  If objItem.id = "Item3" Then
    objItem.classname="color"
    'we also make the last item re-appear here
    document.all("Item4").classname = "notover"
  End If
  If objItem.id = "Item4" Then objItem.classname = "disappear"
End Sub
```

```
Sub MyList_onmouseout  'occurs when the mouse leaves any item in the list
  'again, get a reference to the source of the event
  Set objItem = window.event.srcElement
  'if it's not the last item, change its style class back to normal
  If objItem.id <> Item4" Then objItem.classname = "notover"
  'move the division back to the normal position, in case it got
  '.. moved by the onmoueover event changing its style
  DivTag.style.pixelLeft = 30
End Sub
```

In each case, we get a reference to the list item that was topmost, i.e. the one that received the event first, using `Set objItem = window.event.srcElement`. We have to use the `Set` keyword in Visual Basic, because we are assigning an *object* (the list item element) to the variable here.

Although the code looks more complex that this, it's just a matter of changing the `classname` property of that element to the appropriate class (except for the positioning of elements, which requires the `style` property to be updated). When the mouse pointer enters the element, we set it to the appropriate value:

```
If objItem.id = "Item1" Then objItem.classname = "sizechange"
...
```

When the mouse pointer moves out of the element, we return the `classname` to `notover` (except for the fourth item where hiding the element actually causes an `onmouseout` event, so we only reset this one when the mouse returns to the third item in the list):

```
If objItem.id <> "Item4" Then objItem.classname = "notover"
```

You can run the ListChange example from our Web site at
`http://rapid.wrox.co.uk/books/0685/`

The cancelBubble Property in Action

The other situation is that sometimes we want to be a little more selective about the way we react to an event. For example, we may want most of the elements on a page to react to an event, but for one or two particular ones not to. In cases like this, we can use the **event** object's **cancelBubble** property to give us that extra control.

All we do is create an event handler that reacts to the event for just this element. Normally, once the code in this event handler has finished executing, the event will be bubbled up the object hierarchy to the next container, or to the top-level document object. To prevent this, all we have to do is set the **event** object's **cancelBubble** property to **True**.

For example, if we wanted to do this for an element with the **ID** of **picture**, we just need to add the **cancelBubble** property assignment to the **onclick** event handler of that element:

```
Sub picture_onclick()
   'some code to react to the onclick event
   'now stop the event being bubbled to any other event handlers
   window.event.cancelBubble = True
End Sub
```

This breaks the chain of events, and the **document** object will not receive this **onclick** event. Of course, we can set the **cancelBubble** property in any of the events in the chain, and stop the processing at any point we choose. There's not much point in doing it in the **document** event handler, which is at end of the chain, and we can't stop the first event handler from running because this is our first chance to set the **cancelBubble** property.

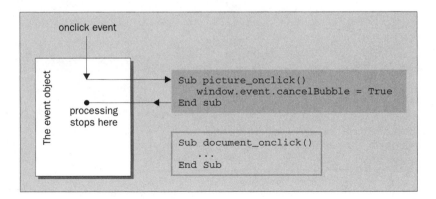

To see the **cancelBubble** property in action, run the sample **Bubbling.htm,** which you'll find on our Web site at `http://rapid.wrox.co.uk/books/0685`. It provides a **<H3>** heading within a **<DIV>** document division on the page, plus a checkbox where you can choose to cancel event bubbling in the `onclick()` event for the heading, instead of letting it bubble up through the hierarchy:

```
<DIV ID=MyDiv STYLE="text-align:center; position:relative; left:5; width:500;
                     height:25; top:5; background-color:aqua">
  <H3 ID=MyTitle> Click Here To Fire An Event </H3>
</DIV>
<INPUT TYPE=CHECKBOX ID=chkBubble> Cancel Bubble
```

The script section is all JavaScript this time, just for a change. It contains event handlers for each element on the page, and in each one it uses the `srcElement` property of the `event` object to reference the element that the event originally fired for. In an `alert` dialog, it provides this element's `tagName` and `id` properties, so that you can trace the event bubbling up through the hierarchy:

```
function HeadingClickCode()
{
  strMesg = "MyTitle onclick event fired.\n"
          + "Source tag name is " + event.srcElement.tagName + "\n"
          + "srcElement is " + event.srcElement.id;
  alert(strMesg);
  if (document.all["chkBubble"].checked) event.cancelBubble = true
}


function DivClickCode()
{
  strMesg = "MyDiv onclick event fired.\n"
          + "Source tag name is " + event.srcElement.tagName + "\n"
          + "srcElement is " + event.srcElement.id;
  alert(strMesg);
}

function DocClickCode()
{
  strMesg = "document onclick event fired.\n"
          + "Source tag name is " + event.srcElement.tagName + "\n"
          + "srcElement is " + event.srcElement.id;
  alert(strMesg);
}

function CheckClickCode()
{
  event.cancelBubble = true
}
```

Notice that we've included code to cancel event bubbling for the checkbox element `chkBubble`. If we didn't do this, the message box from the `document_onclick()` event would appear when you changed the checkbox setting, because the event would bubble up to the document. Here's a compounded screen shot showing the result when we do allow event bubbling to take place:

Now, if we set the Cancel Bubble checkbox and click the heading again, we only get the first message box.

The fromElement and toElement Properties

Before we leave the **event** object, there are two other properties that are useful for finding out what's going on in a Dynamic HTML page. As the mouse moves into and out of elements, it fires the **onmouseover** and **onmouseout** events, as we've seen in the ListChange example. These are useful for updating the object that the event is fired for, but not much use in telling us about what's going on in other elements.

By adding a line to the **onmouseover** code, we can display the value of the **event** object's **fromElement** or **toElement** property as an event is received. The useful one here is **fromElement**, which returns a reference to the element that the mouse was leaving when the event was fired:

```
Sub MyList_onmouseover
    ...
    window.status = window.event.fromElement.id
End Sub
```

Here, you can see that it was previously over the **Item3** element—the last but one item in the list—and is now over **Item2**:

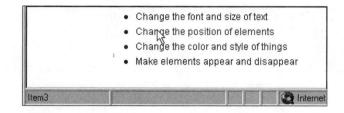

The returnValue Property

Earlier in this chapter, we saw how some events allow us to handle them with a **Function** rather than a **Subroutine**, and prevent the browser's default action taking place by setting the return value of the function to **True**. The example we looked at was a form submission, and we found that we could use this method to prevent the browser's default action of sending the data in the form to the server.

The **event** object in Dynamic HTML allows us to use another technique. All we have to do is set the **returnValue** property of the **event** object to **False.** This cancels the default action. For example, here's a page containing an **<A>** tag, which jumps to our home page when clicked:

```
...
<A ID=MyLink HREF="http://www.wrox.com">Wrox Press Limited</A>

<SCRIPT LANGUAGE=VBSCRIPT>
Sub MyLink_onclick()
  If MsgBox("Go to our site?", vbYesNo + vbQuestion, "Jump?") = vbNo Then
    window.event.returnValue=False
  End If
End Sub
</SCRIPT>
...
```

Clicking on the link in the page runs the **MyLink_onclick()** event handler code, which displays a message box asking the viewer to confirm their action. If they select **No**, we just have to set the **returnValue** property to **False**, and the browser ignores the jump, as though they hadn't clicked it in the first place.

*Notice how we've used the built in VBScript constants to define the **MsgBox** function parameters. You'll find a list of these in Reference Section H, at the back of this book.*

132

Dynamic Element Positioning

In a couple of the examples, we've used the various 'position' properties of the event object to find out where the mouse pointer was when the event occurred. In fact, as you may recall from Chapter 3, there are several 'sets' of these properties. The event object provides four pairs of position properties: **offsetX** and **offestY**, **clientX** and **clientY**, **screenX** and **screenY**, and plain **x** and **y**.

The Event Object's Position Properties

The **screenX** and **screenY** properties return the mouse pointer position in absolute terms, with respect to the screen. So the bottom-right corner in vanilla VGA mode will be **screenX = 800** and **screenY = 600**. The other sets of properties return values that are based on the mouse pointer position with respect to the browser window and document.

In many cases, such as our earlier examples using mouse and key-press events, all except **screenX** and **screenY** return the same values. This is because we didn't have any containers in the page, so the **offsetX** and **offsetY**, and **clientX** and **clientY** properties all reverted to being based on the document itself. However, once we add containers like document divisions, all this changes.

- **clientX** and **clientY** return the position of the mouse pointer in relation to the 'client area' of the browser window. This is the part of the browser that displays the page itself, excluding the window frame, scrollbars, menus, etc.

- **offsetX** and **offsetY** return the position of the mouse pointer in relation to the top-left corner of the element that actually received the event. In some cases, the values reflect the position of the top left corner of the content with respect to the top left corner of the container. An example of this is when the element is a container itself and the contents of the container are not all visible and have been scrolled within it. Where there is no container, the values returned are with respect to the document itself.

- **x** and **y** return the position of the mouse pointer in relation to the top-left corner of the first absolutely- or relatively-positioned container which holds the element that received the event. If none of the containers is positioned (i.e. does not have **position:relative** or **position:absolute** in its **STYLE** attribute) then the values returned are in relation to the main document and are the same as the **clientX** and **clientY** properties. This was the situation with our earlier examples.

Some Event Position Property Examples

To help you understand these different sets of properties we've provided a simple page that contains two nested containers. These are both **<DIV>** tags, with the inner one relatively positioned within the absolutely-positioned outer one. Here's the HTML that creates the page:

```
<BODY ID=MyBody>
    <DIV ID=OuterDiv STYLE="position:absolute; left:50; top:50; width:300;
                            height:100; background-color:blue">
        <DIV ID=InnerDiv STYLE="position:relative; left:50; top:25; width:200;
                                height:50; background-color:yellow">
        </DIV>
    </DIV>
</BODY>
```

The code itself is simple. It just retrieves the values of the various properties, and displays them in a message box. Notice here how we've created a reference to the event object, to save having to keep using the full **window.event.**_property_ syntax:

```
<SCRIPT LANGUAGE=VBSCRIPT>
Sub document_onclick()
  Set e = window.event
  strMesg = "srcElement is " & e.srcElement.id & chr(10) _
          & "clientX = " & e.clientX _
          & ", clientY=" & e.clientY & chr(10) _
          & "offsetX = " & e.offsetX _
          & ", offsetY = " & e.offsetY & chr(10) _
          & "screenX = " & e.screenX _
          & ", screenY = " & e.screenY & chr(10) _
          & "x = " & e.x & ", y = " & e.y & chr(10)
  MsgBox strMesg
End Sub
</SCRIPT>
```

Clicking outside either of the divisions produces the following result, with all except the 'screen' properties producing the same values:

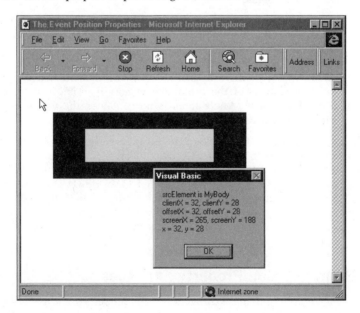

When we click inside the outer division, the `clientX` and `clientY`, and the `x` and `y` properties, are still the same as each other. However, the `offsetX` and `offsetY` properties now reflect the position of the mouse pointer within the outer division:

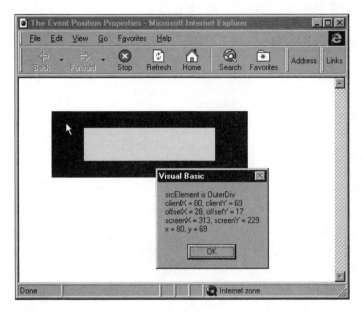

Finally, clicking inside the inner division produces different values for each set of properties. Now, the `x` and `y` properties reflect the position with respect to the outer (parent) division, while the `offsetX` and `offsetY` reflect the position with respect to the inner division. The `clientX` and `clientY` properties still show the position with respect to the document—i.e. the client area of the browser:

You can run this page, Position.htm, from our Web site at
`http://rapid.wrox.co.uk/books/0685`

The Dancing Buttons Page

To finish off this chapter, we'll take a brief look at another sample that uses events and style properties to provide a dynamic page—which includes moving button elements around, as well as moving images. We saw what this page does in Chapter 1, and here we'll see how some of the effects are achieved with techniques we've learned in this chapter.

The HTML that creates the Dancing Buttons page is simple enough. The events are connected to the appropriate handlers at the end of the script section. After the introductory text for the page comes an absolutely-positioned division named **divDoc**, which contains two buttons and an image. These, again, are absolutely positioned within the division. Finally, a second division contains the horizontal rule and the copyright text for the bottom of the page:

```
<BODY BACKGROUND="bg.gif">
<FONT FACE="Arial">
<H2>Click a button to select where you want to go...</H2>
Try and click on the Competitor's Site button. When you get ...
</FONT>
<DIV ID="divDoc" STYLE="position:absolute; top:0; left:0;
                        width:600; height:350">
  <INPUT ID="btnTheirs" TYPE=BUTTON VALUE="Competitor's Site"
    ONCLICK="cmdTheirsClick()"
    STYLE="position:absolute; top:185; left:400; width:130; height:28">
  <INPUT ID="btnOurs" TYPE=BUTTON VALUE="Visit Our Site"
    ONCLICK="cmdOursClick()"
    STYLE="position:absolute; top:185; left:100; width:130; height:28">
  <IMG ID="imgWrox" SRC="wrox0.gif" NAME="imgWrox" WIDTH=100 HEIGHT=42
    STYLE="position:absolute; top:180; left:270">
</DIV>
<DIV STYLE="position:absolute; top:355; left:10; width:600; height:100">
  <HR><CITE>&copy; 1997 - Wrox Press Limited.</CITE>
</DIV>
...
</BODY>
```

Here's how the page appears when you first load it:

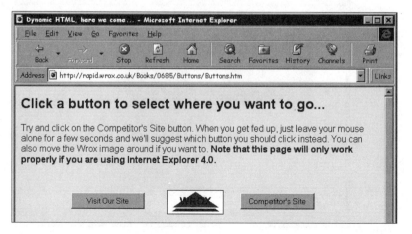

How It Works

Inside the `<SCRIPT>` section of the page, a subroutine is used to respond to the `onmousemove` event. We've switched back to JavaScript for this example, so that you can see how it is used to reference the various items in the page:

```
function MouseMoveEvent()
{
   ...
   objDiv = document.all["divDoc"].style;
   dw = objDiv.pixelWidth;          // main layer width
   dh = objDiv.pixelHeight;         // main layer height
   ...
   if (event.srcElement.id == "imgWrox" && event.button == 1)
   {
      // move the Wrox image element around
      ...
   }
   else
   {
      // move the Competitor's Site button away from the mouse pointer
      ...
   }
};
```

Storing References to Objects

Notice how, in the first few lines of the code, we use the browser object model to get at the style properties that we are going to need for our page. We're using the `all` collection of the `document` object, which contains all the elements in the page. We refer to the document division we want, which we've given an `ID` of `divDoc` in the HTML, using `document.all.divDoc`. Remember that the window is the default object, so we don't need `window.document.all.divDoc` in this case.

However, the properties we want aren't *direct* element properties, but those stored in the element's `style` object. To get at this, we just add it to the end of the statement:

```
objDiv = document.all["divDoc"].style;
```

Now we have a reference to the division's `style` object, and we can use it to make our code more compact and easier to read. Instead of using `document.all.divDoc.style.pixelWidth` to get the width of the division, we can simply use `objDiv.pixelWidth`.

Checking the Source Element

We want to allow the user to drag the Wrox logo around the page by holding down the left mouse button, but allow the mouse to 'chase' the Competitors Site button underneath the logo if they are not holding down the mouse button. To do this, we need to know two things: which element was the source of the `onmousemove` event, and was the left mouse button pressed at the time?

We've seen how to discover both of these things in this chapter. In our example, we use the `event` object's `srcElement` property to get a reference to the element that first received the event (the one the mouse pointer was over),

137

and compare its **id** to that of our Wrox logo tag. At the same time, we check if the button parameter of the **onmousemove** event is **1**, indicating that the left button is pressed. If both are **true**, we move the logo. If not, we move the Competitors Site button away from the mouse pointer:

```
if (event.srcElement.id == "imgWrox" && event.button == 1)
   {
      // move the Wrox image element around
      ...
   }
   else
   {
      // move the Competitor's Site button away from the mouse pointer
      ...
   }
```

Moving the Elements

Moving the Wrox logo is easy enough. Here's the code we use—it simply places some text in the window's status bar, then calculates the new horizontal and vertical positions for the image using the **pixelWidth** and **pixelHeight** properties and the **x** and **y** mouse coordinates. Below, we've reprinted the whole of the first part of the **MouseMoveEvent** function, so that you can see how we find out about the position of the image before we move it. We've set the values of three variables **dh**, **dw** and **db** previously, to refer to the height and width of the document division, and the minimum distance we want to get to the edge of it. Once we've calculated the new position, we just assign it back to the image element's **pixelLeft** and **pixelTop** properties:

```
function MouseMoveEvent()
{
   db = 15;                        // how close to the edge
   objDiv = document.all["divDoc"].style;
   dw = objDiv.pixelWidth;         // main layer width
   dh = objDiv.pixelHeight;        // main layer height
   blnCreeping = false;            // and reset the global flag
   x = event.x;                    // get x and y position of
   y = event.y;                    // mouse pointer as of now
   lastX = x;                      // store x and y position of
   lastY = y;                      // mouse for timer routine
   if (event.srcElement.id == "imgWrox" && event.button == 1)
   {
      // move the Wrox image element around
      window.status = "Drag me to a new position";
      window.clearInterval(timMoveID);  // reset the creep interval
      timMoveID = window.setInterval('timMove()', 4000);
      objImage = document.all["imgWrox"].style;
      iw = objImage.pixelWidth;       // width of the image
      ih = objImage.pixelHeight;      // height of the image
      nx = x - (iw / 2);              // new horizontal position
      if (nx < db) nx = db;           // stop at left and right edges
      if (nx > (dw - db - iw)) nx = (dw - db - iw);
      ny = y - (ih / 2);              // new vertical position
      if (ny < db) ny = db;           // stop at left and right edges
      if (ny > (dh - db - ih)) ny = (dh - db - ih);
      objImage.pixelLeft = nx;
      objImage.pixelTop = ny
   }
   else
   ...
```

Moving the Competitors Site Button

Moving the Competitors Site button follows the same process, but is complicated by the fact that we need to find out the position of the sides of the button in relation to the mouse pointer, and decide which direction to move it. In fact, there are around fifty lines of code to do all this, though the principle is no different to that of moving the image.

We just retrieve the current position, calculate the new position and assign it back to the buttons' `pixelTop` and `pixelLeft` properties. You can open and view the source code for the page to see it in detail, and we've commented it throughout to help you.

Reacting to Button Clicks

The only other code in this page that we want to consider is that for the two buttons. The Visit Our Site one is obvious—it just changes the `window` object's `location` object's `href` property, which loads the new page:

```
function cmdOursClick()
{
  location.href = "http://www.wrox.com"
};
```

The Competitors Site button shouldn't need any code, because the whole idea is that the user won't be able to get the mouse pointer over it. However, we're going to cover the occasion where they load the page into a non Dynamic HTML-savvy browser:

```
function cmdTheirsClick()
{
  strMsg = "You aren't using InternetExplorer 4 then ?\n" +
           "If you were, you wouldn't have been able to " +
           "click the button.\nTo see why you'll have to" +
           "install it and come back again...";
  alert(strMsg);
  location.href = "http://www.wrox.com"
};
```

For example, here it is running in Internet Explorer 3.02:

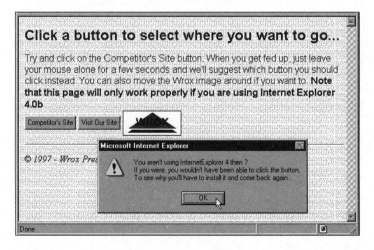

Moving the Visit Our Site Button

Of course, we haven't yet considered how the other dynamic effect of the page is achieved. If you stop moving your mouse for a few seconds, the Visit Our Site button creeps towards the mouse pointer. It's obviously not responding to an event that we are causing, because it happens when we aren't doing anything.

In fact, this event is powered by the browser's built-in interval timer—the `setInterval` and `clearInterval` methods that are part of the `window` object. If you look at the code for the page, you'll see that we have done a few extra things that aren't part of moving the Competitors Site button on the *Wrox* image.

At the start of the `<SCRIPT>` section, we declare three variables that will be global. We can store values in these that will be available all the time the page is loaded. The first is a flag to show if we are currently moving the Visit Our Site button, and the other two are the last known x and y positions of the mouse pointer as it passed over the page division:

```
<SCRIPT LANGUAGE=JAVASCRIPT>
var blnCreeping;   // our button is creeping
var lastX;         // last known X position
var lastY;         // last know Y position
var timMoveID = window.setInterval("timMove()", 10000);
```

Working with Interval Timers

The last line of the code above declares and initializes an interval timer using the new `setInterval` method of the window object. This is very similar to the `setTimeout` method that was available in Internet Explorer 3 and other browsers, but fires repeatedly until cleared, rather than just firing once. The first parameter is the name of the function we want to execute when it fires, and the second is the time in milliseconds between firings.

In the `MouseMoveEvent` code, which runs when the user moves the mouse over our page, we have a few things to do. First, we set the global 'creeping' flag to `false` to indicate that our Visit Our Site button should not be moving while the user is moving the mouse. Secondly, we store the current position of the mouse pointer, ready for when they stop moving it. Thirdly, we clear our current interval timer, and reset it with a value of four seconds:

```
function MouseMoveEvent()
{
    ...
    dh = objDiv.pixelHeight;        // main layer height
    blnCreeping = false;            // and reset the global flag
    x = event.x;                    // get x and y position of
    y = event.y;                    // mouse pointer as of now
    lastX = x;                      // store x and y position of
    lastY = y;                      // mouse for timer routine
    if (event.srcElement.id == "imgWrox" && event.button == 1)
    {
        // move the Wrox image element around
        window.status = "Drag me to a new position";
        window.clearInterval(timMoveID);  // reset the creep interval
        timMoveID = window.setInterval("timMove()", 4000);
        ...
```

Now, four seconds after the user stops moving the mouse, the interval timer will fire and run our `timMove()` event code. This checks to see if the button is already moving (i.e. if `blnCreeping` is already `true`). Of course, it won't be the first time, because we set it to `false` in every `mousemove` event. Instead, our `timMove()` function sets it to `true`, and changes the interval from four seconds to one of less that a second:

```
function timMove()
{
    if (blnCreeping == true)
    {
        // Move the Visit Our Site button towards the mouse pointer
        ...
    }
    else
    {
        // Set the interval timer to a short interval
        blnCreeping = true;
        window.clearInterval(timMoveID);
        timMoveID = window.setInterval("timMove()", 200);
        window.status= "Please click me ...";
    };
};
```

After the interval has expired, the `timMove()` code runs again. This time `blnCreeping` is `true`, and so the first part of the function is executed instead. This simply mirrors the code used to move the Competitors Site button. You can open the page and view the source yourself to see it in detail.

```
if (blnCreeping == true)
{
    ...
    objDiv = document.all["divDoc"].style;
    dw = objDiv.pixelWidth;          // main layer width
    dh = objDiv.pixelHeight;         // main layer height
    objOurs = document.all["btnOurs"].style;
    hw = objOurs.pixelWidth / 2;     // half button width
    hh = objOurs.pixelHeight / 2;    // half button height
    nx = objOurs.pixelLeft;          // left of button
    ny = objOurs.pixelTop;           // top of button
    ...
    // calculate the new coordinates, nx and ny
    ...
    objOurs.pixelLeft = nx;          // move the button to
    objOurs.pixelTop = ny;           // the new position
}
```

The process of moving the Visit Our Site button continues every 200 milliseconds until the user moves the mouse pointer again. This sets the interval back to four seconds, and clears the `blnCreeping` flag so that the whole cycle can be repeated.

*Remember that you can try the ListChange, Jigsaw and Buttons pages —
and the other samples from this chapter — yourself. Visit our Web site at*
`http://rapid.wrox.co.uk/books/0685.`

141

Summary

In this chapter, we've spent a lot of time studying the basics we need to know to work with script code in Dynamic HTML. As you'll appreciate, scripting is at the heart of any Dynamic HTML page where we want to make it interactive, and responsive to the user. Only pages that use the positioning abilities of Dynamic HTML, and are not truly *dynamic*, can manage without some code. Thankfully, the changes to the object model and workings of Dynamic HTML, from earlier versions of browsers that supported scripting, means that we can often create these exciting pages using very little actual script code. In particular, the new **event** object makes it easier to get information about the elements in the page, and manipulate them, than ever before.

We've seen how:

 Events are Windows' way of telling applications that something has happened

 The browser exposes many events to our script code through its **object model**

We can respond to these events if we want to, or just ignore them

Each element maintains a set of **properties**—either directly or through a **style** object—whose values we can access, and often change to make the page dynamic

 By default, all events bubble up through the browser object hierarchy, from the source element to the document

We can use the **event** object to get information about an event, and prevent event bubbling taking place

With this chapter, we've completed our tour of the main parts of Dynamic HTML. It's now time to see some other techniques in action, and learn more about some of the other objects we haven't covered in depth so far. The next chapter begins this process, by discovering how we can use the various properties of the elements in the page, and the **TextRange** object, to retrieve and manipulate the text and the page's contents.

Manipulating the Contents of the Page

With our coverage of how scripts and events worked in the previous chapter, we completed our overview of the basics needed to create attractive and dynamic web pages with Dynamic HTML. In this and the next chapter of the book, we'll be exploring some more advanced techniques, such as manipulating the text and other content in a page, using separate browser windows, and working with tables, forms and databases.

In this chapter we'll be exploring the final major change from 'traditional' HTML to Dynamic HTML. As you'll already have discovered, Dynamic HTML makes almost all the elements in the page available to our scripting code—meaning that we can achieve all kinds of effects that just weren't possible before. However, the one thing that we often want to get at is the normal text displayed in the page, either in the **BODY** of the document, or in things like lists and tables.

In fact, one of our examples focuses directly on tables, and shows you just some of the things that are possible. Dynamic HTML is a language that offers so much freedom to work with the page that it's probably only the limits of your imagination that will hold you back.

In this chapter, we'll look at how we can:

 Reference and retrieve the text from a loaded page

Change the text displayed in a document dynamically

Search for text in a document that is displayed in the browser

Manipulate the contents of HTML tables using scripting code

There are two basic methods for manipulating the actual contents of a document, and we'll be covering both in this chapter.

Changing the Elements in a Page

The ability to change the appearance of a web page by altering its content while it's displayed is a huge advance on existing HTML technologies, where very little of what was displayed in the page was available to our script code. Now, we can actually get at almost anything that is displayed there—including the plain body text.

Up to now, almost everything we've done in Dynamic HTML has involved changing the properties of elements on the fly—either their direct properties such as the `src` of an image, or the style properties, such as `pixelTop`.

Neither of these techniques really changes the element itself, though. They simply change the appearance by altering the way that the element is displayed, or the source data that is used when it is rendered. But now, with Dynamic HTML, we can change the actual contents of the elements—even to the extent that they 'become' a different element. For example we can change the text displayed in a normal paragraph on the page, or even replace a text heading with a graphic.

The two different methods we can use to achieve these kinds of effects are:

 Working with the **content manipulation properties and methods**, such as `innerText`, `outerHTML`, and `InsertAdjacentHTML`

 Working with `TextRange` objects that we create to refer to particular parts of the page

Content Manipulation Properties and Methods

The easiest way to manipulate the contents of a page is to use the special properties that are supported by the majority of visible elements. They expose to the page author the contents of each part of the document, almost as it appears in the source code. By assigning new values to these properties, we can change the contents of the page that is being displayed.

By **document**, we mean a stream of characters that consists of both text and HTML and which represents the current page. Don't confuse the document with the *actual* HTML source code though. This is why we said 'almost as it appears in the source code'. The browser translates the source code into its own representation of the page before displaying it, and changing the contents of an element on the page does not update the original HTML source—just the browser's internal representation of it.

In fact, the examples later in this chapter show how the browser's internal representation of the page does in fact differ from the original HTML source.

The Element 'Content' Properties

There are four properties that are supported by most of the visual elements in the page:

Property	Description
innerText	The complete text content of the element, including the content of any enclosed element, but excluding any HTML tags. Assigning a new string to it replaces only the content of the element, and any new HTML tags are rendered as text, and not interpreted.
outerText	The complete text content of the element, including the content of any enclosed element, but excluding any HTML tags. It returns the same string as innerText, but assigning a new string to it replaces the entire element.
innerHTML	The complete text and HTML content of the element, including the content of any enclosed element. Assigning a new string to it replaces only the content of the element, and HTML tags within it are rendered correctly.
outerHTML	The complete text and HTML content of the element, including the start and end tags of the element and the entire text and HTML content of any enclosed element. Assigning a new string to it replaces the entire element, and the HTML content of the new string is rendered correctly.

You can see that there are two 'classes' of property, those that preserve the HTML tags within the element and those that ignore it. Which we use depends on the task we want to accomplish. We'll use JScript in our following examples to illustrate what the different properties do.

The innerText Property

For example, if the element is a simple heading, such as:

```
<H3 ID=Heading1>This is my Heading</H3>
```

The innerText property can easily be used to change this to And this is my NEW Heading:

```
objHead1 = document.all["Heading1"];
objHead1.innerText = "And this is my NEW Heading";
```

This preserves the original <H3> tags, and only replaces their content. However, if we had some formatting within the heading to contend with, we need to consider using the innerHTML property instead. If this is the original HTML source:

```
<H3 ID=Heading1>This is <I>my</I> Heading</H3>
```

and we apply the same action to it:

147

```
objHead1.innerText = "And this is my NEW Heading";
```

we'll lose the formatting of `<I>` and `</I>` tags, because the `innerText` (and `outerText`) properties don't preserve it. Conceptually, the resulting HTML source will be:

```
<H3 ID=Heading1>And this is my NEW Heading</H3>
```

If we change the assignment to include the HTML tags we want, like this;

```
objHead1.innerText = "And this is <I>my</I> NEW Heading";
```

we still get the wrong result. In the page, the heading will be This is <I>my</I> NEW Heading—in other words the `<I>` and `</I>` tags will be visible as text, and the word my will not be italic. Remember that `innerText` and `outerText` do not interpret any HTML within the strings, it's just rendered as text.

The innerHTML Property

However, if we use the `innerHTML` property, we'll get the result we want:

```
objHead1.innerHTML = "And this is <I>my</I> NEW Heading";
```

This is because the 'HTML' content properties cause the browser to interpret any HTML within the strings correctly. In fact, they are even clever enough to force the new content to be structurally correct—although we might not get quite the result we want. For example if we only provide an opening `<I>` tag in our new content, the browser will add the closing `</I>` tag automatically to prevent the rest of the page being affected. Using:

```
objHead1.innerHTML = "And this is <I>my NEW Heading";
```

will actually produce the conceptual HTML source:

```
<H3 ID=Heading1>And this is <I>my NEW Heading</I></H3>
```

Of course, this time the words NEW Heading will also be rendered as italic—probably not what we wanted to happen. Later in this chapter we'll be using a simple example page to show you more about how these properties work. You can also use this example page to experiment with the properties yourself.

> Not every visible element supports all four 'content' properties. Some only support the 'text' properties, and others may only support a single property—for example the `<TD>` tag (as you'll see later) only provides the `innerText` property. The reference section at the end of this book lists the properties and methods available for each element.

The Element InsertAdjacent Methods

As well as using the four properties to change an element's contents, we can use two methods that are supported by many of the visible elements:

148

Method	Description
`InsertAdjacentText`	Inserts text into or adjacent to the element. Any HTML tags are ignored. Text can be inserted at the start or end of an element within the element's tags, or immediately before or after the element—outside its opening and closing tags.
`InsertAdjacentHTML`	Inserts text and HTML into or adjacent to the element. HTML within the string is correctly rendered after insertion. Text and HTML can be inserted at the start or end of an element within the element's tags, or immediately before or after the element—outside its opening and closing tags.

You can immediately see that these two methods mirror in some respects the workings of the content properties we looked at in the previous section. The first disregards an HTML content (rendering it as plain text), while the second causes the browser to render it correctly.

The syntax of the methods is:

```
insertAdjacentText(where, text_to_insert)
insertAdjacentText(where, HTML_and_text_to_insert)
```

The *where* argument controls where the new content is inserted. It is a string that can be one of

`"BeforeBegin"`	Immediately before the element's opening tag.
`"AfterBegin"`	Immediately after the element's opening tag.
`"BeforeEnd"`	Immediately before the element's closing tag.
`"AfterEnd"`	Immediately after the element's closing tag.

Again, these methods will preserve the structure of the document, by adding a closing tag if it is omitted in the new string. However, this may again not behave exactly as you would expect. For example, if we use the `insertAdjacentHTML` method to insert a `<FONT>` tag before the beginning of an element, with the intention of inserting the `</FONT>` tag after the end, we don't actually get any formatting of the element's content:

```
objHead.insertAdjacentHTML('BeforeBegin', '<FONT FACE="Arial">');
```

This results in the conceptual HTML source of:

```
<FONT FACE="Arial"></FONT><H3 ID=Heading1>And this is <I>my NEW Heading
   </I></H3>
```

149

A Content Manipulation Sample Page

So that you can experiment with the various document manipulation techniques, and see their results, we've provided a sample page for you to try out. It's named **DocChange.htm**, and you can run it or download it from our web site at **http://rapid.wrox.co.uk/books/0685**

When you first load it, you see a single line of formatted text, and a selection of text boxes, lists, and buttons:

The first four controls show the content properties of the line of text at the top of the page. You can see that the **innerText** and **outerText** properties are the same. This is what we would expect because they only return the *text* content, and ignore any HTML. Therefore, even though the **outerText** property 'includes' the opening and closing tags, these don't appear in the value of the property. However, there is a reason for providing both, as you'll see in a while.

The HTML Part of the Page

The page is created using tables and traditional HTML controls. We've defined an event handler for the **ONLOAD** event of the page by placing its name, **DisplayProperties()** in the **<BODY>** tag. It is used to fill the text boxes with the current property values when the page is first loaded. After it, you can see the text and HTML with a **<P>** and **</P>** tag pair that creates the line of formatted text at the top of the page:

```
<BODY ONLOAD="DisplayProperties()">

<P ID=MyText>Things you <I>can</I> change
<B>while the document is loaded</B>!</P>

<TABLE>
<TR>
   <TD ALIGN=RIGHT><B>InnerText:</B></TD>
   <TD><INPUT ID=txtIText TYPE=TEXT SIZE=70></TD>
```

```
          <TD><INPUT ID=cmdIText TYPE=BUTTON VALUE="Change"
                 ONCLICK="UpdateProperties(this)"></TD>
     </TR>
     ...
       HTML for other content properties controls repeated here
     ...
     </TABLE>
```

Each of the four content properties has a text box and a button which runs the
UpdateProperties() code when clicked. We'll look at this code later on. The
rest of the HTML part of the page consists of the code to create the
insertAdjacentText and **insertAdjacentHTML** controls. In these two cases,
the buttons are connected to two code routines named **InsAdjText()** and
InsAdjHTML() (not shown):

```
     <TABLE>
     <TR>
       <TD ALIGN=RIGHT><B>InsertAdjacentText</B></TD>
       <TD> - Where:
         <SELECT ID=1stTPosn SIZE=1>
           <OPTION SELECTED>BeforeBegin
           <OPTION>AfterBegin
           <OPTION>BeforeEnd
           <OPTION>AfterEnd
           </SELECT>
       </TD>
       <TD> - What: <INPUT ID=txtInsText TYPE=TEXT SIZE=38></TD>
       <TD><INPUT TYPE=BUTTON VALUE="Insert" ONCLICK="InsAdjText()"></TD>
     </TR>
     ...
       HTML for insertAdjacentHTML controls repeated here
     ...
     </TABLE>
```

The remainder of the page is the **<SCRIPT>** section that does all the work.

Displaying the Property Values

The first thing our code has to do is retrieve the values of the four content
properties when the page first loads. This is done in the
DisplayProperties() function, which is attached to the **ONLOAD** event of the
document as we saw earlier. Here's the complete function:

```
     function DisplayProperties()
     {
       objSampleText = document.all["MyText"];
       if (objSampleText == null)
       {
         document.all["txtIText"].value = null;
         document.all["txtOText"].value = null;
         document.all["txtIHTML"].value = null;
         document.all["txtOHTML"].value = null
       }
       else
       {
         document.all["txtIText"].value = objSampleText.innerText;
         document.all["txtOText"].value = objSampleText.outerText;
         document.all["txtIHTML"].value = objSampleText.innerHTML;
         document.all["txtOHTML"].value = objSampleText.outerHTML
       }
     }
```

All we do is create a reference to the `<P>` element named **MyText** at the top of the page, then check that it actually exists. Yes, this seems odd, because we know it's there. We wrote it in the original HTML. But remember, this is a dynamic page and, like your waist-line, it might not be there forever. If it has disappeared, we place the value **null** in each text box. Otherwise, we can look up the relevant property for each one and drop it in instead.

Updating the Property Values

So, let's see what happens when we update a property—starting with the simplest one.

Changing the innerText Property

In the next screen shot, you can see that we've changed the **innerText** property:

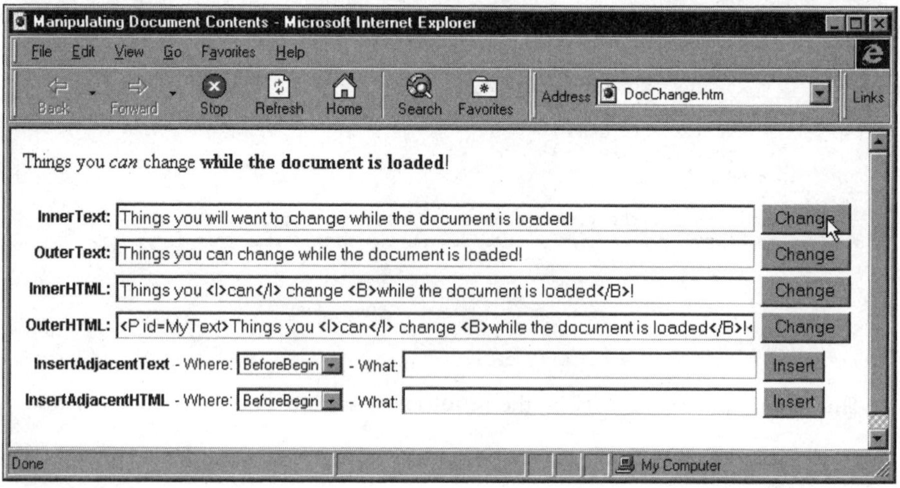

Clicking the Change button then updates the property of the `<P>` element named **MyText** and then updates all four property text boxes to reflect the new values:

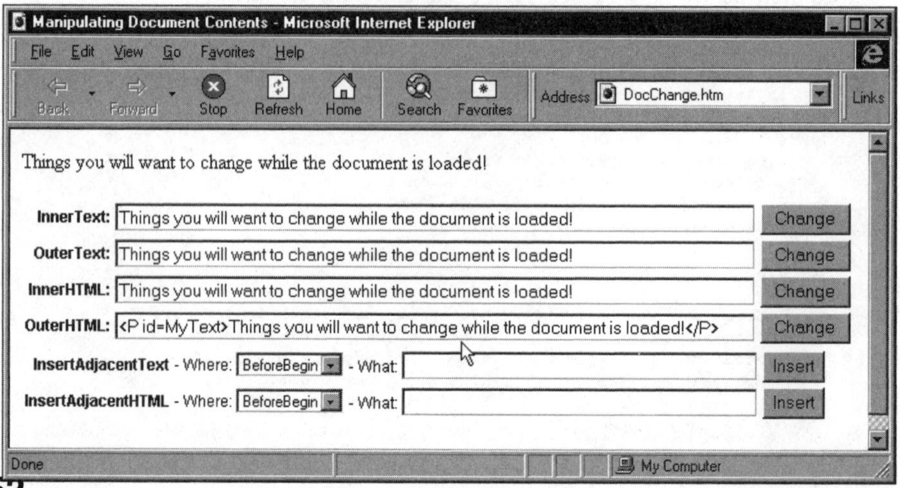

The first thing to notice is that, as we'd expect, all four properties have changed. However, the text itself has lost its formatting, and in the `outerHTML` property you can actually see that the `<I>` and `<B>` tags have disappeared. This is, of course, because we've assigned only text to the contents of the element—replacing the original text and HTML. Also, because the text is now unformatted, there is no inner HTML to display, and so the `innerHTML` property has also lost its tags.

The UpdateProperties() Function

The function that updates the properties is simple enough, following the same pattern as the `DisplayProperties()` function we looked at earlier. The major difference is that each Change button provides a reference to itself as a parameter to our function, using the `this` keyword:

```
<INPUT ID=cmdIText TYPE=BUTTON VALUE="Change"
       ONCLICK="UpdateProperties(this)">
```

In the function, we use this parameter to find the `ID` of the button, and we can then use this `ID` to decide which text property to update. Once we've done that, we call the `DisplayProperties()` function to update all four text boxes again:

```
function UpdateProperties(objButton)
{
  strButtonID = objButton.id;
  objNewSample = document.all["MyText"];
  if (strButtonID == "cmdIText")
    objNewSample.innerText = document.all["txtIText"].value;
  if (strButtonID == "cmdOText")
    objNewSample.outerText = document.all["txtOText"].value;
  if (strButtonID == "cmdIHTML")
    objNewSample.innerHTML = document.all["txtIHTML"].value;
  if (strButtonID == "cmdOHTML")
    objNewSample.outerHTML = document.all["txtOHTML"].value;
  DisplayProperties()
}
```

Changing the outerText Property

So now let's try changing the `outerText` property. Here, we've edited it in the text box, and we are ready to click the Change button:

The result may come as a bit of a shock—all the properties are now **null**:

What's happened is that we've replaced the entire element with just text, removing the start **<P>** and end **</P>** tags. The element has been removed from the document, although the new text we assigned to the property remains. This is why we had to test for the existence of the element in our **DisplayProperties()** function. So the **outerText** property is useful when we want to remove elements from the page altogether.

Changing the innerHTML Property

OK, it's time to get to the really clever stuff. This time, we'll add some new HTML to the page, within the existing tag. When we change the **innerHTML** property, the new value is interpreted by the browser as HTML. Therefore, we can do almost anything we like, as long as it doesn't contravene the structure rules of HTML (for example, we can't place a **<P>** tag within another **<P>..</P>** element). If you reload the page from the Wrox web site, just hit Refresh— the original HTML source is reloaded and you get back to the original page, which we need to start from for the next example.

In the screen shot, you can see that we've edited the **innerHTML** text box to insert an **<IMG>** tag within the property:

Clicking **Change** updates the property, and displays the new `<P>` element with our graphic included. It also, of course, displays the values of all four content properties as they now stand:

Notice how the **innerHTML** and **outerHTML** properties now include the new `<IMG>` tag, but not in the same format as that we entered—the ordering of the attributes is different and they are now all lower-case. Internet Explorer 4 is interpreting the HTML and placing it in its own internal representation of the page in its own format.

Changing the outerHTML Property

The final property we can change is `outerHTML`. In the following screen shot, we've simply changed the `<P>` and `</P>` tags into `<H3>` and `</H3>` tags:

In our screen shot, `</H3>` is just off the screen, but clicking the Change button produces the result that you will be expecting:

Of course, we can't change the `ID` of the element in our example, because the `DisplayProperties()` function would then fail. The `MyText` element it was looking for would not exist. However, there is no reason why we can't change the `ID` in other pages we create, allowing us complete freedom to redesign the page dynamically while it is loaded.

Using the insertAdjacent Methods

The sample page also allows us to experiment with the `insertAdjacentText` and `insertAdjacentHTML` methods. For each one, we can select where we want to insert the new values from a drop-down list.

Using the insertAdjacentText Method

In the screen shot below, we're adding some text after the beginning of our **MyText** element with the `insertAdjacentText` method:

Here's the result. You can see that the four content properties are also updated, as you'd expect:

The InsAdjText() Function

The execution of the `insertAdjacentText` method is done by a simple function in the `<SCRIPT>` section of our page, which runs when the appropriate Insert button is clicked:

```
<INPUT TYPE=BUTTON VALUE="Insert" ONCLICK="InsAdjText()">
```

The function itself is simple enough. We create a reference to the `MyText` element first using the all collection of the document object as before. Then we retrieve the `selectedIndex` property of the drop-down Where list to find out the index of the currently selected option. Using this index with the list element's `options` collection gives us the value of the selection as a text string—in our case `"AfterBegin"`. Then we can retrieve the value of the What text box and call the `insertAdjacentText` method of the `MyText` heading object:

```
function InsAdjText()
{
  objNewSample = document.all["MyText"];
  intPosn = document.all["lstTPosn"].selectedIndex;
  strPosn = document.all["lstTPosn"].options[intPosn].text;
  strText = document.all["txtInsText"].value;
  objNewSample.insertAdjacentText(strPosn, strText)
  DisplayProperties()
}
```

The function for the `insertAdjacentHTML` method is almost identical, but uses the other set of controls on the page to provide the arguments to the method.

Using the insertAdjacentHTML Method

When we want to add HTML as well as text, or create a new element in the page, the `insertAdjacentHTML` method is very useful. In the next screen shot, we've used it to add a new `<H2>` heading line above our existing `<P>` element:

The **InsertAdjacentHTML** method is useful if we need to add new elements to our pages, and generally works more reliably that the **outerHTML** property for this. The big advantage of the **insertAdjacent** methods is that we don't have to read the existing property and add the new text or HTML to it first. However, if we want to just change part of the content of the element, it's often easier to read the **innerHTML** or **outerHTML** properties and manipulate them in code, then write them back to the element.

> *One thing to watch out for when you add or remove elements in a page is that all the element collections are updated at the same time. So, if you remove the third image from a page, the images collection will shrink by one, and what was previously* **document.images[3]** *will become* **document.images[2]**. *If you have stored the collection index in a variable, you'll get the wrong element when you access it later in your code.*

Working with TextRanges

The second way of manipulating the contents of the page dynamically is to use TextRange objects. We very briefly mentioned text ranges back in Chapter 4. They provide another method of adding and removing elements from a page, and changing the contents of a document. We'll be using them throughout the remainder of this chapter.

What is the TextRange Object?

The **TextRange** object is really just a set of internal references (properties and methods) that point to specific parts of the document. It's very important to remember that the **TextRange** object doesn't actually hold the text and elements—it just allows us to reference the text or other elements in the page displayed in the browser. By using its properties and methods, we can manipulate the text and elements that are encompassed by these references .

As a simple graphical example, consider the diagram below. It shows conceptually how the **TextRange** object keeps track of the contents of the document, and can therefore retrieve or change them as required:

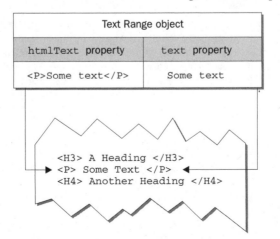

Text Range object	
`htmlText` property	`text` property
`<P>Some text</P>`	`Some text`

```
<H3> A Heading </H3>
<P> Some Text </P>
<H4> Another Heading </H4>
```

Creating a TextRange

We can create a **TextRange** object in two different ways:

 Use the **createTextRange** method on the document's **BODY** element to create a range covering the entire body of the document, or on an individual **TEXTAREA**, **BUTTON** or **INPUT TYPE=TEXT** element in the page.

These are the only elements that support the **createTextRange** method:

```
objMyBodyRange = document.body.createTextRange();
objMyTextAreaRange = document.all["MyTextArea"].createTextRange();
objMyButtonRange = document.all["MyButton"].createTextRange();
objMyTextInputRange = document.all["MyInput"].createTextRange();
```

Every visible element has an **isTextEdit** property, which is **true** only for the elements that support the **createTextRange** method.

 Create a copy of an existing **TextRange** using the **duplicate** method:

```
objCopyOfRange = objMyRange.duplicate;
```

This is what we did to create a **TextRange** from the contents of the document's selection object in Chapter 4.

Moving a TextRange

We can change the contents of a **TextRange** by moving the start and end positions. This means that we are effectively changing the text and elements that the **TextRange** refers to, but *not* changing the actual text itself. We can do this with the following techniques:

 Using the **expand, collapse, move, moveStart, moveEnd,** or **setEndPoint** methods to change either the start position, end position, or both together

The Expand and Move Methods

The **expand** method accepts a string parameter indicating the unit we want to move the start or end position by. The three **move** methods accept an optional string parameter indicating the unit we want to move the start or end position by, and the number of these units that we want to move. The values for the units are **"character"**, **"word"**, **"sentence"**, and **"textedit"**. The last of these, **"textedit"**, resets the range to its original position, when it was first created:

```
blnSuccess = objMyRange.expand("sentence");
lngNumberMoved = objMyRange.move("word");
lngNumberMoved = objMyRange.move("sentence, 3");
lngNumberMoved = objMyRange.moveStart("character", -10);
lngNumberMoved = objMyRange.moveEnd("textedit");
```

The **move** methods return a number indicating how many units they actually succeeded in moving. Notice that we can use negative numbers to move backwards in the document, and if we omit the optional second argument the value **1** is assumed. When the unit is **"textedit"**, the second argument is never required.

The setEndPoint Method

If we have another **TextRange**, which has start or end positions where we want to move the start or end of our range to, we can use the **setEndPoint** method instead. The first argument is one of the four strings shown here, and indicates which end of the other range to use, and which end of our range to move to it:

```
objMyRange.setEndPoint("StartToStart", objOtherRange);
objMyRange.setEndPoint("EndToEnd", objOtherRange);
objMyRange.setEndPoint("StartToEnd", objOtherRange);
objMyRange.setEndPoint("EndToStart", objOtherRange);
```

The Collapse Method

We can shrink a **TextRange** to a single point, either at the start or end of the current range, with the **collapse** method. The **start** and **end** properties then refer to the same point. We specify **true** or **false** for the *start* parameter, to decide which end to collapse it to:

```
objMyRange.collapse(true);  // to start of the current range
objMyRange.collapse(false); // to end of the current range
```

 Using the **moveToBookmark**, **moveToElementText** or **moveToPoint** methods to change the **TextRange** to cover a different part of the document.

Using Bookmarks

We can create a **bookmark** in a document, so that this refers to the text that is currently referenced by a **TextRange** object. Then, later on in our code, we can move this or another existing **TextRange** object to reference the same parts of the document:

```
strMyBookmark = objMyRange.getBookmark();
blnSuccess = objMyRange.moveToBookmark(strMyBookmark);
```

Moving to an Element or a Point

Alternatively, we can move an existing **TextRange** object to reference a particular element within our page. This element must already be within an existing **TextRange**, which we effectively shrink to cover just the element. The easiest way to do this is to create a **TextRange** covering the entire **BODY** of the page first:

```
objMyBodyRange = document.body.createTextRange();
objMyBodyRange.moveToElementText("MyElement");
```

If we want to pick out the word or part of a document that is at a particular point in the page, such as under the mouse pointer, we can use the

moveToPoint method. This shrinks a **TextRange** object to a single point (the start and end positions are the same) at the x and y positions we provide as argument—but only as long as it is within the existing text range. Again, the easiest way to use this method is to create a **TextRange** covering the entire **BODY** of the page first:

```
objMyBodyRange = document.body.createTextRange();
objMyBodyRange.moveToPoint(event.x, event.y);
objMyBodyRange.expand("sentence");
```

This code uses the mouse pointer position, as stored in the **x** and **y** properties of the **event** object, and then expands the **TextRange** to cover the word under the mouse pointer.

Finding Text in a Range

 Using the **findText** method to move the **TextRange** to cover some text that we've searched for in the page

The **findText** method takes a single string argument—the text to search for—and positions the range to cover that text. If it doesn't find a match, it returns false and doesn't move the range:

```
blnSuccess = objMyRange.findText("Find This Text");
```

Getting Information About a TextRange

Once we've created our **TextRange** object, or moved it to a new position, we can get information about the current text and elements it refers to by:

 Querying the **text** or **htmlText** properties to get the contents of the range as a string

 Using the **parentElement** method to retrieve the element that completely contains all of the text range

 Using the **compareEndPoints**, **isEqual** and **inRange** methods to see if the current range is equal to, or contains, another range

Comparing Ranges

The **compareEndPoints** method accepts a string parameter, rather like the **setEndPoint** method, that defines which ends of the two **TextRange** objects to compare. It returns **-1** if the existing **TextRange** end point is before the other one in the document, **0** if it is the same, and **1** if it is after the other one:

```
objMyRange.compareEndPoints("StartToStart", objOtherRange);
objMyRange.compareEndPoints("EndToEnd", objOtherRange);
objMyRange.compareEndPoints("StartToEnd", objOtherRange);
objMyRange.compareEndPoints("EndToStart", objOtherRange);
```

If two **TextRange** objects cover exactly the same part of a document, the **isEqual** and **inRange** methods both return **true**:

```
objMyRange.isEqual(objOtherRange);
objMyRange.inRange(objOtherRange);
```

If the first range is smaller than, and completely within, the second range, only the **inRange** method will return **true**.

Manipulating the Contents of a TextRange

We can also use three other of the **TextRange** object's methods. We can:

 Bring the range into view in the browser, if it is outside the visible area of the window, using the **scrollIntoView** method

 Highlight the contents of the range on the screen, as though the user had dragged over it with the mouse, with the **select** method

 Replace the contents of the range with our own text and HTML using the **pasteHTML** method, or by assigning a new string to the **text** property

Using Range Commands

One feature of text ranges that we won't be covering in detail is the ability to carry out a command on the text. This is designed for situations where the browser is being used as an embedded object, or control, within another application—and allows the application to edit the text in the page without worrying about the HTML format.

For example, the application could make the text within a **TextRange** object bold by executing the **execCommand** method of the **TextRange** object. There are also matching methods that determine if a command is supported and enabled, what state it is in, and the text representation and value of the command.

```
if (objMyRange.queryCommandEnabled)
  objMyRange.execCommand("Italic")
```

TextRange Object Summary

Here's a list of the properties and methods of the **TextRange** object that we use most often. You'll find a full alphabetical listing of them all in Reference Section **E** at the back of this book.

Property	Description
htmlText	Returns the contents of a text range as text and HTML source.
text	Returns the plain text contained within the text range.

Method	Description
collapse	Shrinks a text range to either the start or end of the current range.
compareEndPoints	Compares two text ranges and returns a value indicating the result.
duplicate	Returns a duplicate of a text range object.
expand	Expands a text range by a character, word, sentence or story so that partial units are completely contained.
findText	Sets the start and end points of a text range to cover the text, if found within the current document.
getBookmark	Returns a unique bookmark value to identify that position in the document.
inRange	Denotes if the specified text range is within or equal to the current text range.
isEqual	Denotes if the specified text range is equal to the current text range.
move	Changes the start and end points of a text range to cover different text.
moveEnd	Causes the text range to grow or shrink from the end of the range.
moveStart	Causes the text range to grow or shrink from the beginning of the range.
moveToBookmark	Moves a text range to encompass the range referenced a bookmark value previously defined with **getBookmark**.
moveToElementText	Moves a text range to encompass the text in the element specified.
moveToPoint	Moves and collapses a text range to the point specified in x and y relative to the document.
parentElement	Returns the parent element that completely encloses the current text range.
pasteHTML	Pastes HTML and/or plain text into the current text range.
scrollIntoView	Scrolls the text range into view in the browser, optionally at the top of the window.
select	Makes the active highlighted selection in the page equal to the current text range.
setEndPoint	Sets the start or end point of the text range based on the start or end point of another range.

A TextRange Example Page

To give you a better idea of how we use the `TextRange` object, try this example which is available from our web site at **http://rapid.wrox.co.uk/ books/0685**. It displays some text about an exciting new authoring language, while demonstrating some of the things the `TextRange` object can easily achieve :

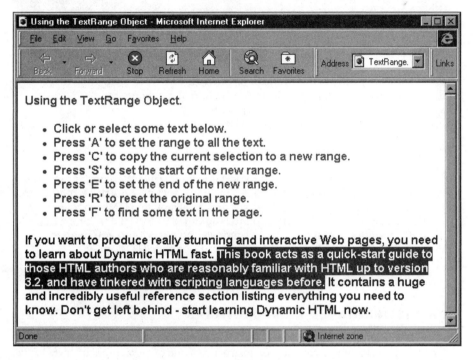

What the TextRange Example Does

In the screenshot, we've selected a text block (or text range) by clicking on the paragraph and pressing the *S* key, then clicking again and finally pressing the *E* key. The code in the page turns this text white with a red background. We can get the same effect by dragging over the text to select part of it in the usual way, then pressing *C*. We can also change the selection by changing the start and end points afterwards. Pressing the *R* key resets all the text back to normal, while pressing *A* selects all the text in the paragraph. Finally, we can search for text in the whole page by pressing the *F* key.

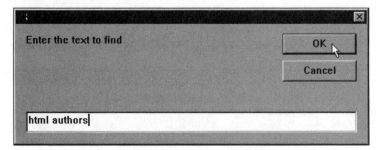

165

This brings up an input box, where we enter the text to find. Clicking OK selects the found text (this time in green) and displays it in the window's status bar:

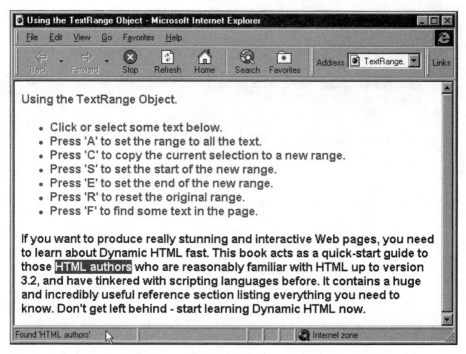

How the TextRange Example Works

The visible part of the page itself is simple, consisting of an `<H3>` heading section, a `<UL>` unordered list of instructions and a paragraph of text. We've used a `<STYLE>` tag to define the style of the text here—and in the single `<P>` paragraph tag that holds the text we're going to be working with :

```
<P ID=MyText STYLE="font-family:Arial, sans-serif; font-weight:bold">
If you want to produce really stunning and interactive web pages, you
need to learn about Dynamic HTML fast. .. etc. </P>

<SCRIPT LANGUAGE=VBSCRIPT>

Dim objMyRange        'the current 'active' range on screen
Dim objSavedRange     'the original text as a TextRange object
Dim strOriginalText   'the saved version of the original text as a string

Set objSavedRange = document.body.createTextRange()
objSavedRange.moveToElementText(MyText)
strOriginalText = objSavedRange.HTMLtext
...
```

Inside the `<SCRIPT>` section, we've defined three variables that will be **global**, and retain their values while the page is displayed. The last three lines of this part of the script are also outside any subroutine or function, and so will be executed as the page is loaded. The first two create a new `TextRange` object from the body element and then shrink it to cover just the `MyText` paragraph element. This **TextRange** object is assigned to the global variable **objSavedRange**. The final line here retrieves the HTML and text from that range—the original text in the page once it has loaded—using the **HTMLtext** property. This is stored in the global variable **strOriginalText**.

Responding to a Key Press

Our page works by responding to a key-press from the user, so we need to create a routine to handle the **onkeypress** event for either the **<P>** element or the **document** object. We've chosen to react to the document's event, so that we can show you how the **parentElement** method works. Here's the main event handler routine, with the code for each key-press removed for clarity:

```
...
Sub document_onkeydown(shift)
   Set objSelRange = document.selection.createRange
   strTagName = objSelRange.parentElement.tagName
   If strTagName <> "P" And strTagName <> "FONT" Then Exit Sub
   If IsEmpty(objMyRange) Then
      Set objMyRange = objSelRange.duplicate
   End If
   Select Case window.event.keyCode
      Case 65 ' "A" - set range to all text
         ...
      Case 67 ' "C" - copy all selection to range
         ...
      Case 83 ' "S" - set start of range
         ...
      Case 69 ' "E" - set end of range
         ...
      Case 82 ' "R" - reset text to original style
         ...
      Case 70 ' "F" - find text in the document
         ...
   End Select
End Sub
```

Each time we detect a key-press, we start by saving the current user's selection from the page into a **TextRange** object named **objSelRange**, by calling the **createRange** method of the **selection** object. We saw this done back in Chapter 4, where we examined the **selection** object in some depth. It gives us a reference to where the text cursor is on the screen, even if the user hasn't dragged to highlight any text—but they must have clicked on the paragraph first.

Tracking Down the parentElement

Next, we need to check if the selection we've retrieved is within our **MyText** paragraph element. The **parentElement** method   returns the highest (or innermost) element for the current selection, and we use the **tagName** property to get the text name of the tag. It will be **P** when we start off, but might at some point—as you'll see in a while—be **FONT**. We check both, and if it isn't either of these, we can exit from the subroutine without doing anything:

```
strTagName = objSelRange.parentElement.tagName
If strTagName <> "P" And strTagName <> "FONT" Then Exit Sub
```

167

> *Notice that the `tagName` property always returns the tag as upper case, even if it's lower-case in the HTML source of the page.*

Checking for an Empty Object Variable

If our code is still running at this point, we know we have something to do—so we can check if we've got an existing `TextRange` set up from the last time the user pressed a key. Because we're saving the `TextRange` between key-presses in a global variable, we have to see if this is the first key-press since the page was loaded. If it is, we need to initialize our `TextRange` this time only, and we do this by checking if the global variable is storing an object reference or is 'empty'. The VBScript `IsEmpty` function returns `true` if the variable we specify as its argument does not refer to an object. In this case, we assign a copy of the current contents of the `objSelRange` (the current selection) to it:

```
If IsEmpty(objMyRange) Then
   Set objMyRange = objSelRange.duplicate
End If
```

The final section of the code is just the `Select Case` construct that determines which code will be executed, depending on the ASCII value of the key-press. This is retrieved from the **event** object's **keyCode** property, as you saw in the previous chapter.

Setting the Start or End Position

If the user pressed *S* (start of range) or *E* (end of range), we need to change the start or end position of the current `TextRange` object `objMyRange`. This is done using the **setEndPoint** method of the `TextRange` object, which means that we need an existing range that has the correct start or end point already. The answer, as before, is the **selection** object. At the start of the event routine we set it to the current selection on the page, so we know where the text cursor is within our paragraph:

```
Set objSelRange = document.selection.createRange
```

To change the start of the current range in `objMyRange`, we simply execute the **setEndPoint** method with the value `"StartToStart"` or `"EndToEnd"`, depending on which end we want to set:

```
Case 83          ' "S" - set start of range
   objMyRange.setEndPoint "StartToStart", objSelRange
   strNewText = "<FONT STYLE=""color:white; background:red"">" _
            & objMyRange.text & "</FONT>"
   objMyRange.pasteHTML strNewText

Case 69          ' "E" - set end of range
   objMyRange.setEndPoint "EndToEnd", objSelRange
   strNewText = "<FONT STYLE=""color:white; background:red"">" _
            & objMyRange.text & "</FONT>"
   objMyRange.pasteHTML strNewText
```

Displaying the Selection

Now that we've got our `TextRange` object pointing to the correct text, we can create the string that will produce the white-on-red text to indicate the current range. We simply enclose the current text, retrieved from the **objMyRange** object's **text** property, in a **<FONT>** tag—specifying the style we want for it. Then we replace the current text with the new string using the **pasteHTML** method.

> In fact this doesn't always work, because it leaves existing <FONT> and </FONT> tags in the HTML—before and after the new range. This means that after a few operations, the page stops responding correctly, as you may have discovered. Also, if you set the end of a range to the end of a word, then the space gets dropped because it is ignored by the HTML parser. However, it serves to demonstrate the techniques without clouding the issue with extra complexity.

Selecting All the Text

If the user presses the *A* key, we need to change our current range to include the whole paragraph. We've done this by simply re-creating the **TextRange** object to point to the complete paragraph **MyText**, then pasting into it the **<FONT>** tags and the existing text and HTML from the **text** property. This removes any leftover **<FONT>** and **</FONT>** tags that might have been embedded into the page previously. Because the user is selecting all the range, and some of it might be off-screen if they have resized the browser window, we finish up by using the **scrollIntoView** method to bring it into view:

```
Case 65        ' "A" - set range to all text
   Set objMyRange = document.body.createTextRange()
   objMyRange.moveToElementText(MyText)
   strNewText = "<FONT STYLE=""color:white; background:red"">" _
               & objMyRange.text & "</FONT>"
   objMyRange.pasteHTML strNewText
   objMyRange.scrollIntoView
```

Copying the Current Selection

Pressing *C* makes the current range equal to the users on-screen selection. All we have to do is to **duplicate** the copy of the user's screen selection from **objSelRange**, and add the **<FONT>** tags and paste it into the page:

```
Case 67        ' "C" - copy all selection to range
   Set objMyRange = objSelRange.duplicate
   strNewText = "<FONT STYLE=""color:white; background:red"">" _
               & objMyRange.text & "</FONT>"
   objMyRange.pasteHTML strNewText
```

Resetting and Removing the Highlighted Range

Pressing *R* removes all the highlighting from the page, and sets the current range to a single point in the paragraph. We do it by creating a new range in **objMyRange** from the **MyText** paragraph element, then paste into it the text we originally saved in **strOriginalText** when the page was loaded. Then we shrink our range to the start of the paragraph using the **collapse** method:

```
Case 82        ' "R" - reset text to original style  Set objMyRange =
document.body.createTextRange()
   objMyRange.moveToElementText(MyText)
```

169

```
objMyRange.pasteHTML strOriginalText
objMyRange.collapse True      'go to start of text
```

Finding Text in the Document

The final user option is to search for text in the whole document by pressing the *F* key. In this case, we first reset the current range using the same techniques as above, then display an input box to collect the string to search for. Providing the user doesn't leave it empty ("") we can look for it in the document.

To actually find the string, we create a new **TextRange** object that covers our **<P>** paragraph element, as before. This time we've named it **objFoundRange**. Then we can display the **InputBox**, and check if we got any input. If the user clicks Cancel, or doesn't enter any text, the result will be an empty string.

```
Case 70        ' "F" - find text in the document
  Set objFoundRange = document.body.createTextRange()
  objFoundRange.moveToElementText(MyText)
  strFind = InputBox("Enter the text to find", "")
  If strFind <> "" Then
    If objFoundRange.findText(strFind) Then
      strNewText = "<FONT STYLE=""color:white; background:green"">" _
                   & objFoundRange.text & "</FONT>" _
      objFoundRange.pasteHTML strNewText
      window.status = "Found '" & objFoundRange.text & "'"
      objFoundRange.scrollIntoView
    End If
  End If
```

Providing we've got a string to search for, we just have to call the **findText** method of the **TextRange** object. It returns true if the text was found, and we can go on to surround it in the **<FONT>** tag we want this time, and paste it into the page. The final task is to update the status bar, and scroll the found text into view in the browser.

Creating Dynamic Tables

Working with HTML tables and their contents isn't a whole lot different from working with the plain text in the page. This shouldn't be surprising, because tables are just a heap of HTML **<TABLE>**, **<TH>** and **<TD>** tags anyway. We can use the techniques we've seen in this chapter to manipulate them as easily as we manipulate text.

The Rows and Cells Collections

What makes tables interesting, however, is that Dynamic HTML finally brings the concept of rows and columns to a table created with HTML tags. We can use the **rows** and **cells** collections to access individual rows and cells in a table whenever we like:

rows	Collection of all the rows in the table, including those in the <THEAD>, <TBODY>, and <TFOOT> sections.
cells	Collection of all the <TH> and <TD> cells in the row of a table.

Using the Collections

These collections work in the same way as the collections we've met throughout the book. We can access individual rows in the **rows** collection using the **ID** of the <TR> element for that row, or an index number starting at zero for the first row. We can loop through the rows using the **For Next** construct. Each row in the **rows** collection is an element representing that <TR> tag, and has its own **cells** collection representing the cells in that row.

The **cells** collection is accessed in the same way, using the **ID** of the <TD> or <TH> tag, or an index number representing that cell's position in the row—where the left-most cell is indexed zero. Each object in the **cells** collection is an element representing the <TD> or <TH> tag.

A Dynamic Table Sample Page

We've provided a sample page named **Table.htm** that demonstrates how we can use the **rows** and **cells** collections, and follows up on the techniques we've seen earlier in this chapter. You can run it directly from our web site at **http://rapid.wrox.co.uk/books/0685/**.

171

The Initial Page

As you can see, the page consists of a simple table containing five numbered rows. Each row contains a whole number between **0** and **100**, plus the value of its square and square root. Each time you refresh the page, the numbers are different, so we've got a dynamic page that is obviously not created by ordinary HTML. In fact, it uses techniques that have been possible with scripting code in earlier versions of HTML.

Writing a Dynamic Page

To create the table, we used script code plus VBScript's random number generator. Here's the HTML for the first part of the page, starting with the normal HTML **<TABLE>** tag and the **<TH>** tags for the heading row:

```
...
<TABLE ID=MyTable WIDTH=90% ALIGN=CENTER BORDER=1>
<TR><TH>Row</TH><TH>Number</TH><TH>Square</TH><TH>Sq.Root</TH></TR>

<SCRIPT LANGUAGE=VBSCRIPT>
'Create the initial table using random numbers
Randomize
For intRow = 1 To 5
  intNumber = CInt(Rnd * 100) + 1
  strTableRow = "<TR ALIGN=CENTER><TD ID=MyRow" & CStr(intRow) _
              & "><I><B>" & FormatNumber(intRow, 0) _
              & "</B></I></TD>" _
              & "<TD ID=MyNumber" & CStr(intRow) & ">" _
              & FormatNumber(intNumber, 0) & "</TD>" _
              & "<TD ID=MyNumber" & CStr(intRow) & ">" _
              & FormatNumber(intNumber * intNumber, 0) & "</TD>" _
              & "<TD ID=MyNumber" & CStr(intRow) & ">" _
              & FormatNumber(Sqr(intNumber), 4) & "</TD></TR>"
  document.write strTableRow
Next
</SCRIPT>
</TABLE>
...
```

After the heading row you'll see there is a script section containing a **For..Next** loop, which is executed as the page is being rendered. With each iteration, the code in the loop creates a string **strTableRow**, which contains the complete HTML code for one row in the table. Then it just has to display it in the page using the **write** method of the **document** object.

Creating the Initial Table Rows

Before starting the loop, we use **Randomize** to seed the random number generator, and prevent the same results appearing every time. Then the code in our **For...Next** loop is repeated five times to get the five numbered rows.

First it calls the **Rnd** function, which returns a random number greater than or equal to zero and less than one. We convert this into a whole number by multiplying by **100**, taking the integer result, and adding one.

Now we can create the table row. First there's a center-aligned `<TR>` tag, and then a `<TD>` tag with the `ID` set to `MyRowx`—where *x* is the row number. Then we insert the row number itself, formatting it as a string with the `FormatNumber` function. We're using a simple form of this function here, supplying just the numeric value to convert and a parameter indicating the number of decimal places we require.

> *The new version of VBScript (3.0), as supported by Dynamic HTML and Active Server Pages, provides several new functions.* `FormatNumber` *is a very useful addition, and allows us to specify the number of decimal places to include, whether to include leading zeros, how negative numbers should be represented, and how to group the digits. There are also new functions to format dates, percentages and currency values.*

We continue adding the `<TD>` tags for each cell to the string, including an `ID` for each one. As we go along, we use the random number calculated for that row, and the calculated square and square root values. In the final cell, we format the value to four decimal places.

Adding the Row Selector

Once the table is complete, we add a document division containing the HTML drop-down list element. This contains the row numbers, plus an empty option so that no number is displayed when the page is first loaded. As we are going to respond to the list's **onchange** event, we need the user to make a choice in the list to start our code running:

```
...
<DIV ID=MyDiv STYLE="position:absolute;top:220;left:150;
                     width:300;height:100">
Select a row to change:
<SELECT ID=1stSelect STYLE="width=40">
  <OPTION VALUE=0>
  <OPTION VALUE=1>1
  <OPTION VALUE=2>2
  <OPTION VALUE=3>3
  <OPTION VALUE=4>4
  <OPTION VALUE=5>5
</SELECT>
</DIV>
...
```

Updating the Table Contents

That's the original page complete, and now we need to consider how we update a row. Making a choice in the row selector drop-down displays an input box. This shows the row number, the current value, and allows a new value to be entered. The current value is also highlighted in the original table:

Retrieving the Current Value

Here's the code that runs when a selection is made in the drop-down list. First we collect the user's row selection from this list, which is a string, and convert it into a number. If they have selected the empty entry at the top of the list, we just exit from the routine. Otherwise, the value is stored in the variable `intRow`. Then, we can start the process of retrieving the current value from the table:

```
...
<SCRIPT LANGUAGE=VBSCRIPT>
Sub lstSelect_onchange()
   intRow = CInt(lstSelect.value)
   If intRow = 0 Then Exit Sub    'selected the blank entry
   Set colTheRow = document.all.MyTable.rows(intRow)
   Set objTheCell = colTheRow.cells(1)
   Set rngExisting = document.body.createTextRange()
   rngExisting.moveToElementText(objTheCell)
   rngExisting.select
   ...
```

The `all` collection of the `document` object holds all the elements in the page. One of these is the table we created, and named `MyTable` in the `ID` attribute of the `<TABLE>` tag. This table element is the parent of all the rows in the table, and has a `rows` collection. We use this to get an object reference to the selected row into a variable `colTheRow`. Once we've got the row, we can reference the members of the `cells` collection for that row. We want the cell indexed `1`, which is in the second column, and we've assigned it to the object variable `objTheCell`.

174

The next part of the code should look familiar. Once we've got a reference to an element, we can create a **TextRange** for it like we did in our earlier examples. Once this is done, we highlight it on screen using the **select** method of our new **rngExisting** object.

Why Don't We Use the 'Content' Properties?

You may be wondering why we've used **TextRanges** again here to get at the contents of a table cell. There are two reasons for this. One is that we want to be able to select the cell contents, so that they are highlighted on screen. This can only be done using the **select** method of a **TextRange** object.

Secondly, we intend to change the text that makes up the contents of the cell. For most visible elements, we would do this by assigning a new string to the **innerHTML** property. However, the **<TD>** tag, and most other parts of a table, don't support this property—only the **innerText** property. This is fine if we just want to change the text, but as you'll recall, this property doesn't interpret any HTML we include in it.

In our case, we're going to make the updated row of the table display in bold, so we need to be able to include HTML tags and have them interpreted. Again, this forces us down the route of using a **TextRange** object.

Collecting and Validating the New Value

Now it's time to get the new value from our user. We display an **InputBox**, and check that they didn't leave it blank, or press the Cancel key. If they did, the **If..Then** statement skips the rest of the routine.

Next we check if the text they entered can be converted to a valid number— and if it can, that it's between **1** and **99**. If either of these tests fail, a suitable message box is displayed. If all is still OK, we can get on and update the table:

```
    ...
    strPrompt = "The existing number in row " & intRow _
              & " is " & rngExisting.text & ". Enter a new whole" _
              & " number to use in this row:"
    strNewNumber = InputBox(strPrompt, "")
    If strNewNumber <> "" Then
      If IsNumeric(strNewNumber) Then
        intNewNumber = CInt(strNewNumber)
        If (intNewNumber > 0) And (intNewNumber < 100) Then
          ...
          'code to update the table cell in the page
          ...
        Else
          MsgBox "Number must be between 1 and 99.", _
                 vbOKOnly + vbExclamation
        End If
      Else
        MsgBox "'" & strNewNumber & "' is not a number!", _
               vbOKOnly + vbExclamation
      End If
    End If
  End Sub
  </SCRIPT>
```

Creating the New Value in the Table

The chunk of code missing from the routine above is what does all the work of creating the new values for the table row, and putting them into the table. Here's how it works. We just need to format our new value into a string, and paste it onto the **TextRange** object **rngExisting** together with the new **<B>** and **</B>** tags that will make it bold:

```
...
'code to update the table in the page
strNewNumber = FormatNumber(intNewNumber, 0)
rngExisting.pasteHTML "<B>" & strNewNumber & "</B>"
For intCell = 2 To 3
  Set objTheCell = colTheRow.Cells(intCell)
  Set rngExisting = document.body.createTextRange()
  rngExisting.moveToElementText(objTheCell)
  If intCell = 2 Then
    strNewNumber = FormatNumber(intNewNumber * intNewNumber, 0)
  Else
    strNewNumber = FormatNumber(Sqr(intNewNumber), 4)
  End If
  rngExisting.pasteHTML "<B>" & strNewNumber & "</B>"
Next
...
```

Now we can update the other two columns. As you'll see from the code, the technique is much the same as when we retrieved the value from the second column earlier on. We've used a **For..Next** loop, because the code for each of the two cells we're interested in is very similar. This also allows us to use the loop index variable, **intCell**, in the line that references the **cells** collection. We've already got a reference to the **cells** collection in **colTheRow**, so we can just **Set** the **objTheCell** variable to refer to it.

With the reference to the cell, we can then re-create the **TextRange** object **rngExisting** and move it to reference that cell. Then we only have to paste in the new value. We've used the value of the loop variable again here to decide how to calculate the new value—it's the square in column 3 and the square root in column 4. The next screen shot shows the result:

Dynamic HTML Tables - Microsoft Internet Explorer

File Edit View Go Favorites Help

Back | Forward | Stop | Refresh | Home | Search | Favorites | Address | Links

Select a row and change the contents of the table.

Row	Number	Square	Sq.Root
1	60	3,600	7.7460
2	27	729	5.1962
3	30	900	5.4772
4	42	1,764	6.4807
5	43	1,849	6.5574

Select a row to change: 4

Done | My Computer

Mathematical Error Prevention

When we come to play with mathematical functions like this, there's an increased chance of errors arising in our code. Users can type any text into an **InputBox**, so it's always a good plan to check it's valid before trying to do arithmetic with it. This is where the **IsNumeric** function, and a timely message box, come in.

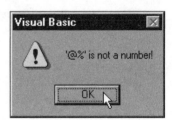

In our example page, we've also limited the user's entry to positive numbers less than **99** on purpose. Anything much larger that around **180** would have caused an error message to appear, because we are using integer numbers and the **CInt** function—which only accepts positive values up to **32767**. And if you're a mathematician, you might like to ponder on the result of calculating the square root of a negative number.

Summary

In this chapter, we've looked at the different ways that we can actually modify the contents of the page while it is displayed, rather than just playing with the properties or styles of the elements. We've seen how we can remove elements, add new ones, or modify the contents of existing ones. All in all, we now have the techniques available to completely rewrite a loaded HTML page within the browser if we wish.

We've seen how we can:

 Read and assign values to the 'content' properties of the elements, such as **innerText**, **outerText**, **innerHTML** and **outerHTML**, to change the contents, or the entire elements

 Use the **insertAdjacentText** and **insertAdjacentHTML** properties of elements to add text and HTML before or after the element, or at the beginning or end of the existing content

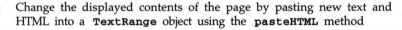 Reference the elements and their contents in a page with a **TextRange** object, and retrieve the contents using this object's text and HTML text properties

 Change the displayed contents of the page by pasting new text and HTML into a **TextRange** object using the **pasteHTML** method

 Use a **TextRange** object to search for text in a page, through its **findText** method

 Use **TextRange** objects to retrieve and manipulate the contents of all kinds of elements, including cells in tables

Reference the contents of tables using the **<TABLE>** element's **rows** and **cells** collections

In the next chapter, we'll be looking at a mixture of other techniques that add even more power to our pages. We'll see how Dynamic HTML provides new opportunities to work with windows, dialogs, forms and data.

Dialogs, Forms and Data Binding

With the increasing availability of Java applets and ActiveX controls for the third-generation browsers like Internet Explorer 3 and Netscape Navigator 3, web pages have become a mixture of HTML and external **objects**. These objects provide the browser with abilities that were unavailable using only HTML and scripting code. But, in Dynamic HTML, the extensions of the language itself mean that some of the reasons for using these objects are no longer valid.

In this chapter, we'll look at why this is a good thing and how we use these new features in our pages—in particular how we can now build interactive forms far more easily. We'll also see how we can use the new features of Dynamic HTML that allow us to display modal dialogs, as well as the traditional new browser windows.

However, there will always be tasks to perform that *can't* be achieved using Dynamic HTML alone, so we'll also look at some of the ways that objects can be used as well. Some of these tasks are those that involve databases and multimedia. We won't be looking at the multitude of Java applets and ActiveX controls that are available, but we will cover the generic way that these and other objects can be added to make your pages more usable and exciting. We'll also briefly outline the new techniques for data binding, where the controls in an HTML form can be dynamically linked to a data source on the server.

So, we'll be covering:

- How we create separate windows and dialogs to display individual pages
- Ways of getting the most from Dynamic HTML when creating forms
- The new tags and attributes that make building interactive forms easier
- How we use embedded Java applets and ActiveX controls in our pages
- An introduction to the proposed data-binding abilities of Dynamic HTML

To start, we'll look at how we can create new browser windows and dialog windows.

Creating New Windows and Dialogs

One way to make your web site appear different from the rest is to display some of the pages in a new browser window, instead of in the current one. For example, you may open a new window to display details of a product that the viewer has selected in the main browser window's page. This means that they can still see the original page and the new page opens separately.

This is already possible using traditional HTML methods and with scripting code in older browsers. However, not only does Dynamic HTML support and expand on these methods, it adds some new ones as well. You can now display a different page either as a **modal dialog window**, or in a special help dialog.

While the last of these options is some way down the road in terms of development—the new HTML Help system is still undergoing changes at the time of writing—you may wish to take advantage of modal dialogs. We'll look at an example in this chapter, and show you the differences between dialogs and new browser windows.

New Browser Windows

To open a new browser window we have two choices. We can do it using a normal HTML **<A>** tag, and specify a name for the new window—not the name of an existing frame—as the **TARGET** attribute in the tag. (If we use a name that is the same as an existing frame in the current window, the page will be loaded there instead of into a new window.) As an example, this code creates a new window named **MyNewWindow**, and loads the *Wrox* home page into it:

```
<A HREF="http://www.wrox.com" TARGET="MyNewWindow">
  Wrox Press Limited
</A>
```

We can do the same kind of thing using script code, by executing the **window** object's **open** method. We supply the address of the page to load into the new window, the name for the new window, and a string containing the settings, or **features**, that we want the new window to have. The **open** method returns a reference to the new window, which we can use later in our code if we wish by assigning it to a variable. For example:

```
strFeatures = "top=100,left=100,width=450,height=265,"
    + "toolbar=no,menubar=no,location=no,directories=no";
objNewWindow = window.open("mypage.htm", "MyWin", strFeatures);
```

This code is JavaScript. If you use VBScript, remember that you have to include the Set keyword when you assign an object to a variable, for example:

```
Set objNewWindow = window.open("mypage.htm", "MyWin",
strFeatures)
```

As you can see from the code, we get a lot more control over what the new window looks like, and where it appears on the screen, when we use this method. In our example, we've positioned the new window 100 pixels from the top and left of the screen, set the size to 450 by 265 pixels, and turned off display of the toolbar, menus, address text box (**location**) and the directory buttons.

The second argument, **MyWin** in our example, acts like the **TARGET** attribute in an **<A>** tag, in that it allows us to target an existing window instead of creating a new one. We can also add the optional **replace** argument to the method call. Setting it to **true** causes the document being loaded to replace the current entry in the window's history list, if there is a document already displayed in that window. In this case, we don't need to specify the 'features' for the existing window:

```
objNewWindow = window.open("mypage.htm", "MyWin", "", true);
```

The Open Method Features Summary

Here's a full list of all the available 'feature' arguments for use with the **window** object's **open** method:

Attribute	Values	Description
channelmode	yes | no | 1 | 0	Show the Channel controls
directories	yes | no | 1 | 0	Include directory buttons
fullscreen	yes | no | 1 | 0	Maximize the new window
height	number	Height of window in pixels
left	number	Left position in pixels on desktop
location	yes | no | 1 | 0	The URL Address text box
menubar	yes | no | 1 | 0	The default browser menus
resizeable	yes | no | 1 | 0	Window can be resized by user
scrollbars	yes | no | 1 | 0	Horizontal and vertical scrollbars
status	yes | no | 1 | 0	The default status bar
toolbar	yes | no | 1 | 0	Include the browser toolbars.
Top	number	Top position in pixels on desktop
Width	number	Width of window in pixels

Modal Dialog Windows

In Dynamic HTML, we can also open a new window using the **showModalDialog** method of the **window** object. This uses a 'features' string like the **open** method, but the attributes we use in it are different and the format of the string is also more specific. On top of this, the **showModalDialog** method accepts an **arguments** argument (if you see what we mean) instead of the window name, and does not provide the optional **replace** argument.

What are Modal Dialog Windows?

The big difference between opening a window with the `open` and `showModalDialog` methods is the way the new window behaves with respect to the existing one. Using `open` creates an independent window, as a new instance of the browser. If the user closes the original window, the new window remains.

When we create a window using `showModalDialog`, however, the behavior is totally different. As the name of the method suggests, the new window becomes **modal** with respect to the original window. The user cannot activate the original window until they close the new modal one. This is similar to the way that application dialogs and message boxes operate. It provides a window that is more like a form in Visual Basic, VBA as found in Office 97, or other traditional programming languages. Here's an example—notice that in this case we have a simple value returned from the method, which we've just assigned to a normal variable, rather than a reference to the new window as in the `open` method. You'll see how we use this value later on:

```
strFeatures = "dialogWidth=500px;dialogHeight=320px;"
    + "scrollbars=no;center=yes;border=thin;help=no;status=no";
Result = window.showModalDialog("mydlg.htm", "MyDialog", strFeatures);
```

The first argument is again the name (which can be a full HTTP URL) of the page we want to open. The second argument is a value that will be passed to the new dialog window once it's opened. The third argument is the 'features' string—notice that the format requires semi-colons rather than commas between entries. You can also use colons instead of 'equals' signs, in the same format as a style sheet entry:

```
... "dialogWidth:500px;dialogHeight:320px;scrollbars:no; ..."
```

We can use this dialog window in any number of ways. We can place controls on it to prompt for information, allow the user to make selections, or even create a Wizard, like the ones we see in many modern applications. We've used it as a book selector in our example, which you'll see at the end of this section.

The ShowModalDialog Features Summary

The options available in the 'features' string for the `showModalDialog` method are subtly different to those for the open method. The following table lists them all:

Attribute	Values	Description
`border`	`thick` | `thin`	Size of border around window
`center`	`yes` | `no` | `1` | `0`	Center window on browser
`dialogHeight`	*number + units*	Height of the dialog window

Attribute	Values	Description
dialogLeft	*number + units*	Left position of window on desktop
dialogTop	*number + units*	Top position of window on desktop
dialogWidth	*number + units*	Width of the dialog window
font	*CSS string*	Default font and style for window
font-family	*CSS string*	Default font family for window
font-size	*CSS string*	Default font size for window
font-style	*CSS string*	Default font style for window
font-variant	*CSS string*	Default font variant for window
font-weight	*CSS string*	Default font weight for window
help	yes | no | 1 | 0	Include Help button in title bar
maximize	yes | no | 1 | 0	Include Maximize button in title bar
minimize	yes | no | 1 | 0	Include Minimize button in title bar

The inclusion of the CSS font attributes shows why the features string needs to be formatted in the same way as in a normal **STYLE** attribute. We can use the **font** attribute to set several features of the default font, or use the individual **font-*xxxx*** attributes instead.

```
strFeatures = "center:yes;font-size:10;font-family:Arial"
```

Notice that the dialog window size and position attributes require a CSS unit to be specified. This is why our example features string included: `"dialogWidth:500px;"`.

A Windows and Dialogs Example

So that you can see how we use new windows and modal dialogs, we've provided a sample page **NewWin.htm** on our web site at **http://rapid.wrox.co.uk/books/0685**. It displays a normal HTML page containing two links. They both open the same new page, but one as a new browser window and the other as a dialog:

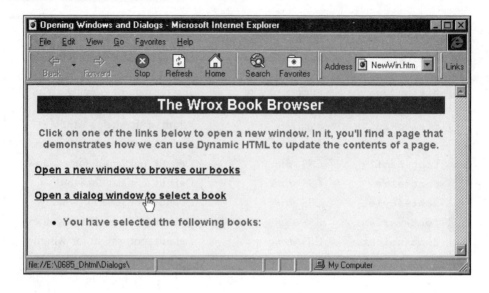

The Initial Book Browser Page

This page uses two `<A>` tags to create the links. Each one has the `HREF` set to an empty string, because we're going to look after the opening of the new window ourselves in code—rather than letting the browser open a default new window. Of course, we could just have easily used buttons rather than links:

```
<A HREF="" ONCLICK="return OpenWindow()">
   Open a new window to browse our books</A>
<A HREF="" ONCLICK="return OpenDialog()">
   Open a dialog window to select a book</A>
```

Within each `<A>` tag is the connection to an event handler that will execute when the link is clicked. In fact, using `<A>` tags like this creates an extra problem. When the user clicks on a link, and after our own code has executed, the browser will attempt to load the page referenced in the `HREF`. To prevent this, we need to use the syntax you see above to return the value `false` to the browser after our function has run— that way, the browser won't follow the link. All we need to do now is ensure that our functions return `false`—and this will be passed on to the browser automatically.

Opening the New Browser Window

The first link in the page opens a new browser window in the traditional way, using the following code. You can see that the routine contains a line that displays the message Opened a new browser window in the status bar of the main window. You'll see why as we go along:

```
function OpenWindow()
{
  window.status = "";
  strFeatures = "top=100,left=100,width=450,height=265,"
    + "toolbar=no,menubar=no,location=no,directories=no";
  objNewWindow = window.open("dialog.htm", "MyNewWindow",
                             strFeatures);
```

186

```
    window.status = "Opened a new browser window.";
    window.event.cancelBubble = true;
    window.event.returnValue = false;
}
```

Notice that we have set the **cancelBubble** property of the event object to
true to prevent the event being passed back up through the document object
hierarchy. However, and more important, is that we set the event object's
returnValue property to **false**. This will return the **false** value we want to
the **<A>** tag in the page, and prevent the browser trying to load another page.

> *Alternatively, we could have used the line **return false** in the function.
> Either technique will work in this situation, though we prefer to use the
> **event** object's **returnValue** property.*

Clicking the Open a new window to browse our books link displays a small
new window, with the features (or lack of them) that we specified in our code:

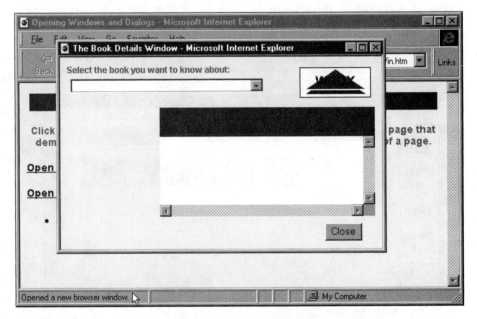

OK, so the new window doesn't look much at the moment, but it is another
Dynamic HTML page—we'll look at its code in a moment. Notice that the
status bar of the main window shows the message Opened a new browser
window. You can switch between the two windows and even load a different
page into the main window without changing the new window. They act
independently.

Opening the Modal Dialog Window

Before we go any further, click the Close button to close the new window, then
click the Open a dialog window to select a book link. The same new page is
displayed (with an extra button), but this time it's a modal dialog window, and
you can't go back to the original window. Clicking on it doesn't bring it to the
front like a normal browser window.

187

This is the code that opens the new dialog window in response to the click on the second link:

```
function OpenDialog()
{
  window.status = "";
  strFeatures = "dialogWidth=500px;dialogHeight=320px;"
    + "scrollbars=no;center=yes;border=thin;help=no;status=no";
  strTitle = window.showModalDialog("dialog.htm", "MyDialog",
                                    strFeatures);
  window.status = "Opened a modal dialog window.";
  // code here to handle the returned value
  ...
}
```

Code Execution and Modal Windows

You'll be expecting the second difference between new windows and modal windows if you're used to programming in other languages, but it may come as a surprise if you've only used VBScript or JavaScript before. When we open the dialog window, the code in the main page stops at the **showModalDialog** method. If you look at status bar in the main page while the dialog window is open, there is no message:

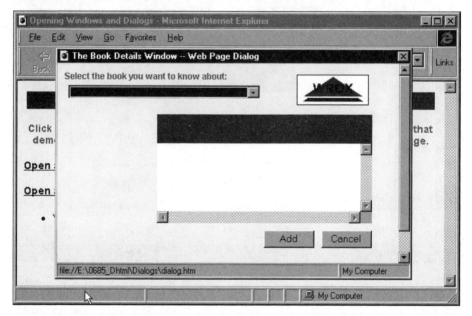

The reason is that the code line **window.status = "Opened a modal dialog window."** is not executed until *after* the modal dialog is closed. At this point you see the message appear. This means that we will be able to use values that the user selects or enters in the dialog in the *original* window's code. You can see from the comment in the code above that this is what our example does.

The Dynamic New Window Page

The page you see in both the new browser window and the modal dialog is a Dynamic HTML document. We've designed it using absolute positioning, as demonstrated back in Chapter 2, and incorporated some effects that were either difficult, or even impossible, to achieve in traditional HTML—even using ActiveX controls. Here's the first part of the HTML for this page:

```
...
<DIV ID=divMain STYLE="position:absolute; top:10;
                       left:10; width:450; height:300">
  <P>Select the book you want to know about:</P>
  <SELECT ID=lstBooks ONCHANGE="BookListChange()"
          STYLE="position:absolute; font-weight:bold;
                 width:270; top:20; left:5">
  <OPTION VALUE=0>
  <OPTION VALUE=0723>Professional Active Server Pages
  <OPTION VALUE=0464>ActiveX Web Database Programming
  <OPTION VALUE=0448>Instant VBScript Programming
  <OPTION VALUE=0685>Instant Dynamic HTML Reference
  <OPTION VALUE=0707>Professional IE4 Programming
  </SELECT>
  <IMG SRC="wrox0.gif"
       STYLE="position:absolute; top:5; left:325">
  <IMG SRC="" ID=imgCover
       STYLE="position:absolute; top:60; left:5; visibility:hidden">
  <DIV ID=divTitle
       STYLE="position:absolute; margin:5; top:60;
              left:130; width:300; height:30;
              background-color:red; overflow:clip">
    <P ID=pTitle CLASS="main"
       TITLE="Visit our Web site for more information"></P>
  </DIV>
  <DIV ID=divText
       STYLE="position:absolute; margin:5; top:100;
              left:130; width:300; height:110;
              background-color:white; overflow:scroll">
    <P ID=pText CLASS="text"
       TITLE="Visit our Web site for more information"></P>
  </DIV>
  ...
  // code here for the buttons at the bottom of the page
  ...
</DIV>
</BODY>
```

The page consists of a main document division, placed 10 pixels in from the top and left of the window and filling the rest of it. Inside this are two more divisions. The first, with a red background, will display the title of the book selected in the list, and the other the descriptive text for that book. In both cases, there is an empty paragraph section within the division that sets the style **class** for that text. These style attributes for the classes, shown below, are defined at the top of the page.

```
<P ID=pTitle CLASS="main" TITLE="Visit our Web site ... etc."></P>
...
<P ID=pText CLASS="text"  TITLE="Visit our Web site ... etc."></P>
```

It's into these **<P>** elements that we'll be placing the title and description of each book as the user selects it from the drop-down list at the top of the page.

The Add, Cancel and Close Buttons

At the bottom of the page that's displayed in our new window or dialog are buttons that allow you to close the window (or dialog) and return to the original window. You may have noticed that different buttons appear, depending on whether you've opened a new window or a dialog:

Dialog Window Buttons

New Browser Window Button

This raises two questions. How do we know which buttons to display in the new windows, and how do we actually display different ones anyway?

The answer is some script within the new document that is executed as the page is being rendered. To tell which buttons we want, we use the **arguments** argument that is available in the **showModalDialog** method. You may recall from our earlier discussion that we set this to the string value **"MyDialog"** in the function that opened the dialog window:

```
window.showModalDialog("dialog.htm", "MyDialog", strFeatures);
```

*This value is passed across to the new window, and we can access it within the new page. While we've only used a simple string, there is no reason why you can't use a different type of value, such as an array or a series of values in delimited format. Remember that this is very different from the way the **open** method works, because its second argument is used to provide a name for the window so that we can target pages to it using an **<A>** tag or script. In a modal dialog, the second parameter is passed to the window as a value for use in our script.*

Using the window.dialogArguments Property

So, we can tell if we are displaying our new page in a dialog or a separate browser window by examining this value. It becomes available in the new page as the **dialogArguments** property of the new **window** object. Here's how we've used it to create the **appropriate** buttons in the page—if we are opening the page in a new browser window the **window.dialogArguments** property will be **null**:

```
. . .
<SCRIPT LANGUAGE=JAVASCRIPT>
// add the buttons we want to the bottom of the page
if (window.dialogArguments == "MyDialog")
{
  strButtons = '<INPUT TITLE="Add book to order '
             + 'and return to main window" '
             + 'ID=cmdOK TYPE=BUTTON VALUE="Add" '
             + 'ONCLICK="AddClicked()" '
             + 'STYLE="position:absolute; top:220; '
             + 'left:280; width:70">'
             + '<INPUT TITLE="Return to main window '
             + 'without adding book to order" '
             + 'ID=cmdClose TYPE=BUTTON VALUE="Cancel" '
             + 'ONCLICK="CloseClicked()" '
             + 'STYLE="position:absolute; top:220; '
             + 'left:360; width:70">';
}
else
{
```

```
            strButtons = '<INPUT TITLE="Return to main window" '
                  + 'ID=cmdClose TYPE=BUTTON VALUE="Close" '
                  + 'ONCLICK="CloseClicked()" '
                  + 'STYLE="position:absolute; top:220; left:360">';
      }
      document.write(strButtons);
    </SCRIPT>
  </DIV>
</BODY>
```

The Title Selector List

Now that we've got our new page displayed, we'll look at some of its features. Near the top of the page is a `<SELECT>` tag that creates a normal HTML drop-down list box, and fills it with book titles. For each one, it sets the `VALUE` to the book's code number, and it includes a blank entry at the top of the list. One extra trick here is to use the `STYLE` attribute to set the `width` of the element—something we couldn't do in HTML, and which often resulted in the end of the selected entry being cut off by the 'drop' button.

```
<SELECT ID=1stBooks STYLE="position:absolute; font-weight:bold;
                           width:270; top:20; left:5">
  <OPTION VALUE=0>
  <OPTION VALUE=0723>Professional Active Server Pages
  <OPTION VALUE=0464>ActiveX Web Database Programming
  <OPTION VALUE=0448>Instant VBScript Programming
  <OPTION VALUE=0685>Instant Dynamic HTML Reference
  <OPTION VALUE=0707>Professional IE4 Programming
</SELECT>
```

The drop-down list looks like this:

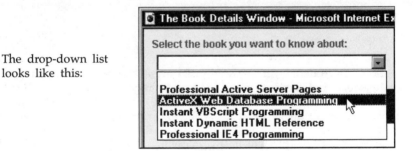

An Invisible Image Control

The page also contains an `<IMG>` tag with an `ID` of `imgCover`, and a `SRC` that is an empty string. This is where we'll display a picture of the book's cover, but we want it to be blank when the page is first opened. If we don't supply an `SRC` for the element, we'll get a 'missing picture' frame displayed in the page. To get round this, we can use the `visibility` style property. In the HTML source, we set it to `hidden` so that the image element is not visible when the page is first displayed:

```
<IMG SRC="" ID=imgCover
  STYLE="position:absolute; top:60; left:5; visibility:hidden">
```

191

Displaying the Selected Book Details

All we have to do now is respond to the user selecting a book title in the drop-down list, and display the details and cover picture on the page. Here's the first part of the script section in the page. In it, we define two variables **strTitle** and **strText**, which will hold the title and description of the selected book. Declaring them first like this, outside any of the subroutines or functions in the page, means that they are **in scope** (i.e. available and will retain their values) the whole time the page is displayed:

```
<SCRIPT LANGUAGE=JAVASCRIPT>

var strTitle = "";  // the book title
var strText = "";   // the text description

function BookListChange()
{
  objCoverImage = document.all["imgCover"];
  // get the selected book
  strBookID = document.all["lstBooks"].value;
  if (strBookID == "0")
    // hide the imgCover element
    objCoverImage.style.visibility = "hidden"
  else
  {
    // put picture in imgCover and make it visible
    objCoverImage.src = strBookID + ".gif";
    objCoverImage.style.visibility = "visible";
  }
  //set the new text and title
  SetBookText(strBookID);
  // put title and text into <P> tags
  document.all["pTitle"].innerText = strTitle
  document.all["pText"].innerText = strText
}
...
```

The rest of the code shown above is in an event handler that responds to the **onchange** event of the drop-down list box **lstBooks**. It will run when the user selects a book from the list. In it, we first create a reference to our invisible **imgCover** image element in **objCoverImage**, so that we can access it easily afterwards. Then we retrieve the user's selection from the list into a variable **strBookID**. This will be the currently selected **VALUE**—in other words, the books code number. We've been clever enough to name the cover image files using this book code, so we can retrieve the correct one easily.

Next, we check that the selection isn't **0** (the blank entry at the top of the list). If it isn't we can then create the filename of the image, assign it to the **imgCover** element's **src** property to load it into the **<IMG>** element, and finally make it visible by setting the element's visibility property to **visible**. If the user did select the blank entry, however, we just have to set the visibility property back to **hidden**.

Getting the Book Title and Description

The next line in our event handler calls another function, which we've named **SetBookText**. It takes as a parameter the book code number **strBookID**, as selected in the drop-down list. This function simply sets the value of the **strTitle** and **strText** variables to the appropriate ones—we've omitted the text and some of the **if** statements here to save repetition:

```
...
function SetBookText(strBookID)
{
  // fills up the text and title strings
  if (strBookID == "0723")
  {
    strTitle = "Professional Active Server Pages";
    strText = "Active Server Pages is simply .... etc."
  }
  if (strBookID == "0685")
  {
    strTitle ="Instant Dynamic HTML Reference";
    strText = "If you want to produce really stunning .... etc."
  }
  ...
  // 'if' statements for the other books here
  ...
}
```

Inserting Text into the Page

Up until now, much of this has been stuff you could easily do in earlier
versions of browsers that supported VBScript or JavaScript. The next part,
however, is one of the things that make Dynamic HTML special. We need to
insert the book title and description, currently held in two string variables, into
the page. We've previously set aside two empty **<P>** elements in the HTML
source ready to receive them. But how do we get the text into them?

As you saw in the previous chapter, it's easy. We just assign the text we want
to the **innerText** property of the appropriate element:

```
// put title and text into <P> tags
document.all["pTitle"].innerText = strTitle
document.all["pText"].innerText = strText
```

And here's the result, with the page opened as a new browser window. Notice
the effect of setting the **overflow** property to **scroll** for the **<DIV>** element
that contains the book description:

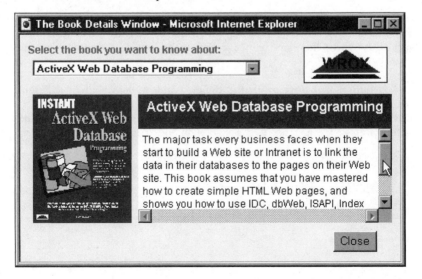

Displaying Tooltips for Elements

You'll see from the next screenshot that we have also arranged for the various elements to display 'tool-tips' when the mouse pointer pauses over them—including the <P> element that holds our book description. This is easily done for any element by simply specifying the text of the tooltip in the tag's **TITLE** property. We have set it in the HTML source, but it could just as easily be set and changed in code, like any other property:

```
<P ID=pText CLASS="text" TITLE="Visit our Web site for more information">
```

It also works for the buttons at the bottom of the window, which we created using script when the page was loaded:

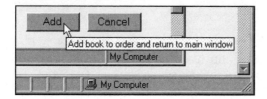

Closing the New Window

The final section of code in this page is used to close the new window or dialog when the appropriate button is clicked. This could be either the Close button in the new browser window page, or the Add or Cancel buttons in the dialog window page. In fact, the Close and Cancel buttons both use the same function, named **CloseClicked()**:

```
function CloseClicked()
{
  window.returnValue = "";
  window.close()
}
```

It simply sets the **returnValue** property of the **window** object (not the **event** object this time) to an empty string, and calls the **close** method of the **window** object. This works the same way for both new browser windows and modal dialogs.

The Add button that appears in the dialog window uses slightly different code. Here, we want to return the title of the currently selected book, so that we can use it in our original page. The string **strTitle** holds the last book title selected, and so we just need to assign it to the **returnValue** property:

```
function AddClicked()
{
  window.returnValue = strTitle;
  window.close()
}
```

Take care to use the correct object when returning values from a dialog window. Both the `window` object itself, and the global `event` object, have a `returnValue` property. For the `event` object, it is a `true`/`false` value that the event returns to the browser, and is used to cancel the default action for that event. For a `window` object, it is a string or numeric value that is passed back to the object as the return value of the `showModalDialog` method.

Using the Returned Value

Our new dialog page returns a value to the original window that opened it, by assigning that value to the **window.returnValue** property. As we saw earlier, the code in the original page stops executing at the call to the **showModalDialog** method, and only resumes when the dialog is closed. At this point, the **returnValue** becomes available as the value that is returned by the **showModalDialog** method.

So, we can use this value in our code. In the Book List example page we've been working with, we add it to the original page—inside an unordered list. Each time the dialog is closed, the current book title is added:

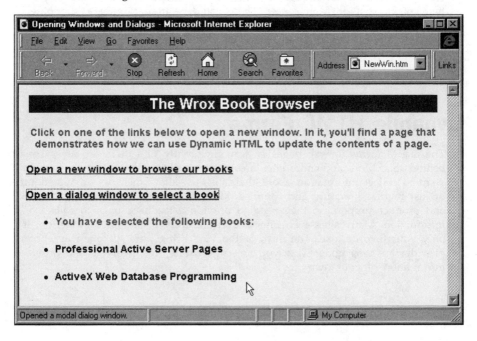

Inserting the Titles into the Page

Back in the original **NewWin.htm** page, where we opened the dialog window in the first place, the code that adds the title to the list is simple enough. Here, we've highlighted it within the complete function. It simply adds a new **<LI>** element containing the book title into the **<UL>** element we have provided in the page, using the **insertAdjacentHTML** method:

```
function OpenDialog()
{
  window.status = "";
  strFeatures = "dialogWidth=500px;dialogHeight=320px;"
    + scrollbars=no;center=yes;border=thin;help=no;status=no"
  strTitle = window.showModalDialog("dialog.htm", "MyDialog",
                                    strFeatures);
  window.status = "Opened a modal dialog window.";
  // examine the returned value
  if (strTitle != null && strTitle != "")
  {
    objList = document.all["ListTag"];
    objList.insertAdjacentHTML("AfterEnd","<LI>"+strTitle+"</LI>");
  }
  window.event.cancelBubble = true;
  window.event.returnValue = false;
}
```

Now we have the techniques we need to build pages that offer separate dialogs that get information from a user. These could be used to offer a 'shopping cart' facility, or a pop-up options dialog, or almost any kind of task where we need to collect information from a user. Because the original page remains loaded and active in the background, we can keep updating it as we go along, or use it to store intermediate values. It is also useful when we come to use forms in our pages, as you'll see in the next section.

Dynamic HTML Forms

The use of forms in web pages is growing rapidly, and there are several reasons behind this. More and more sites are commercially oriented, and the owners want to collect information about their visitors, allow them to submit enquiries, or just request literature and samples. More companies are offering technical and product support, so they need to provide a feedback page to collect information. Many sites even offer the opportunity to submit information, if only your favorite joke. The days of the Web being purely a one-way content provider are long gone. Now you are expected to 'get involved' and provide information of your own:

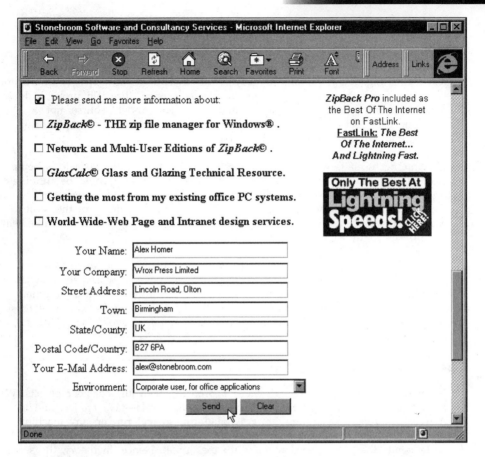

However, there is a stronger underlying trend that makes web-based forms a requirement in a web site, rather than just an add-on. More and more web-based client/server applications are being written to use a Web browser as the front end, or **interface**. This means that a few text boxes and option buttons are no longer enough. We need to provide the kind of rich, attractive and responsive interface that users have become accustomed to in traditional Windows applications.

These rich user interfaces have already started to appear, especially in the world of the Intranet where bandwidth is generally not a problem, and everyone is using the same browser. On the Internet as a whole, however, there are some problems with previous versions of HTML. While using the latest features of HTML and adding applets and controls to pages is a great way to produce a richer experience, there is a considerable down-side.

197

Balancing the Needs of Compatibility

Web page authors have always faced the problem of which version of HTML to write to. Early versions couldn't offer anything like the control of layout and text formatting that is possible in HTML 3.2—there were no tables or frames for example. If you created a page using the latest version, it would probably look a mess, or not even be viewable, on older browsers. And of course, not everyone uses Netscape Navigator, which supports HTML 3.2 cross-platform, never mind Windows with Internet Explorer.

The Internet itself is mainly a Unix-based system underneath, as well as being cross-platform as far as the client is concerned. The browser could be running on anything from a green-on-black text-only terminal, to a Macintosh, to a Cray—with Windows nowhere in sight. It's likely that, in many of the more esoteric environments, your carefully crafted HTML 3.2 pages will look like they were designed by a gorilla.

Of course, Dynamic HTML won't prevent this happening, and for a time is only likely to make the situation worse—now you have to worry about what your page will look like on earlier Windows-based browser, such as Internet Explorer 3 or Netscape Navigator 3, as well. The redeeming factor is that it's likely we'll see an accepted and more universal standard evolve as HTML 4.0, based on Dynamic HTML.

The Embedded Object Dilemma

If you think HTML versions can cause a problem, then just consider objects. We already encounter two different types on a regular basis—Java applets and ActiveX controls. Java applets are **cross-platform**, so will run on any machine that implements the correct environment. This is simply an interpreter that understands the bytecodes that make up the applet. Hence, in theory, the same Java applet works on any machine with an appropriate interpreter.

ActiveX controls are not cross-platform, but instead are **cross-language objects**. They can be written in any one of several different programming languages, but are specific to a particular operating system. You have to provide a different one for each platform where you want your page to be available. Worse than that, they'll only work on browsers that have a suitable environment, which means at least Internet Explorer 3 or Netscape Navigator 3 with the correct plug-ins installed.

In both cases, the browser has to download the object and install it on the user's system, unless it is already available there. This reduces response times in the page, often annoys users, and may not work at all depending on the settings in their browser or the proxy server on their network. While technologically a wonderful system, it doesn't score well in usability terms generally unless you stick to using the common objects that are likely to be installed on the user's system by default. Instead, it would be nice if we could do without them altogether.

Creating Dynamic Forms

So, let's see how Dynamic HTML can help to limit our requirements for non-HTML controls. It still implements the same set of intrinsic HTML controls as earlier versions: `<INPUT>`, `<SELECT>`, `<OPTION>` and `<TEXTAREA>`. On top of this, it proposes the new `<BUTTON>`, `<FIELDSET>`, `<LEGEND>` and `<LABEL>` tags, plus some new features which extend the capabilities of existing controls. And of course, these are useful not only in forms on a normal Web page, but in the new dialog windows we saw in the previous section.

Absolute Positioning in Forms

If you were creating forms in Internet Explorer 3, you could take advantage of an ActiveX control called the **Layout Control**. This was designed to provide an absolute positioning feature in HTML for third-generation browsers. Embedding a Layout Control in a page effectively creates a document division, in which other controls can be accurately positioned and overlapped. However, to work, it requires a separate file containing the definition of the division, and then a whole series of other ActiveX controls.

In Dynamic HTML, we can do without any of this. As you've seen in earlier chapters, we can create a document division using the `<DIV>` tag, and then position almost any other elements inside the division using the `top`, `left` and `z-index` style properties. And more than that, we can get a lot more control over the size of the elements by using the `width` and `height` properties—as you saw in the previous chapter.

New Tags and Properties

If you've been experimenting, however, you'll have discovered that some elements don't respond to absolute positioning (at least in the platform preview they didn't). This includes the body text inside the division, and other elements like heading tags, which you can only position by setting the margins within the division. This is obviously a problem in a page that hosts several controls, such as a web-based application. To get round this, we can use `<DIV>` tags to position the text in a small document division.

We can also create generic command (push) buttons using the new `<BUTTON>` tag, as well as with the existing `<INPUT>` tag, and group controls like option buttons together with the `<FIELDSET>` and `<LEGEND>` tags. You'll see examples of all these shortly.

And to add to the list of ingredients for more usable forms, all the HTML controls have gained some new attributes (and therefore properties). We can set the `tabIndex` of all the controls, which means we no longer depend on the order of the controls in the page to determine the way the focus (or text cursor) moves between them. We can also create a 'hot-key' to activate a control, using its `accessKey` property, and make it read-only by setting its `readOnly` property. We can include a text `title` for the elements, as you saw earlier in this chapter, to provide a pop-up tool-tip, and use the `disabled` property to enable and disable controls as required.

More Events Supported

The final new ingredient for building application interface-type pages is the extended number of events that the HTML controls respond to. The original list was limited to `onclick`, `onblur`, `onfocus`, `onchange`, and `onselect` (depending on the type of control), but now we have twelve new events to react to in our code. These include keyboard events like `onkeypress` and `onhelp`, update events `onbeforeupdate` and `onafterupdate`, and a range of mouse events—including `onmousemove`, `ondblclick`, and `onmousedown`.

If you have programmed in a traditional language like Visual Basic, Delphi, or C++, you'll be used to using all these in your interface code. Now, you can do much the same in a web page using VBScript, JavaScript, or other scripting languages. In the example coming up later in the chapter, you'll see many of these new events used—and all of it without an applet or ActiveX control is sight. But first, we'll look at the proposed new tags and attributes that make it possible.

The <BUTTON> Tag

When we create buttons using the `<INPUT>` tag, we have little real control over the appearance of the button itself. The proposed `<BUTTON>` element allows us to create buttons which more closely resemble those seen in normal Windows or other GUI-based operating system applications. We can include other elements, such as images, as well as text on the button itself.

To make it possible, the `<BUTTON>` tag has a closing tag, `</BUTTON>`, and anything between the opening and closing tags is rendered on the button face. For example, we can create a button that contains a picture instead of text like this:

```
<BUTTON>
  <IMG SRC="mypic.gif">
</BUTTON>
```

The button tag also provides absolute positioning through a `STYLE` attribute, so we can size and place it accurately on the page. If the content doesn't fit on the button, the button is sized to contain it all automatically:

```
<BUTTON STYLE="position:absolute; top=200; width:80; left=325">
  <IMG SRC="mypic.gif">
</BUTTON>
```

And we can include more than one element on the button. Here, we're adding a text caption. Normally (as in an HTML page) the contents are laid out next to each other. To get the text onto the next line we include a `<BR>` tag. Each 'line' of elements is automatically centered on the button face:

```
<BUTTON STYLE="position:absolute; top=200; width:80; left=325">
  <IMG SRC="mypic.gif" WIDTH=25 HEIGHT=30><BR>Stop
</BUTTON>
```

Notice that we've also included the **WIDTH** and **HEIGHT** attributes. These allow us to force the picture to a new size, and therefore prevent it making the button expand to fit the original image if it is larger that the button size we want. On top of that, they prevent the button being resized as the image loads, by informing the browser what the actual size will be—as when placing an image in the page in the usual way.

Finally, we'll generally also include an **ID** attribute, so that we can refer to the button in our code. And by including an **ID** for the **<IMG>** tag as well, we can access the image element at run-time, and change the picture it displays. This is what we've done in the example you'll see later on:

```
<BUTTON ID=cmdStop STYLE="position:absolute; top=200; width:80; left=325">
   <IMG ID=imgbtnStop SRC="stop.gif" WIDTH=25 HEIGHT=30><BR>Stop
</BUTTON>
```

The <FIELDSET> and <LEGEND> Tags

When we create groups of controls, especially things like a set of related option buttons or checkboxes, we would often like to enclose them in a 'box' of some type, in the same way as most standard Windows applications do. This can be done using document divisions, with the **border** properties set to provide a border around the controls, but the new **<FIELDSET>** and **<LEGEND>** tags provide a much neater solution.

The new **<FIELDSET>** tag works in a similar way to a **<DIV>** tag, in that it can create a container to hold the controls. The **<FIELDSET>** will generally include a **<LEGEND>** element for the group, which defines the text to be placed at the top of the 'box':

```
<FIELDSET ID=fldFruit>
   <LEGEND>Select a fruit</LEGEND>
   <INPUT TYPE=RADIO NAME=Fruit VALUE=Orange> Oranges <BR>
   <INPUT TYPE=RADIO NAME=Fruit VALUE=Banana> Bananas <BR>
   <INPUT TYPE=RADIO NAME=Fruit VALUE=Mango> Mango, my favorite <BR>
</FIELDSET>
```

Here's what it looks like in the browser:

The <LABEL> Tag

The usual way to add a text caption to other control elements is to place text before or after it in the HTML source, or position it using a table. When we come to place controls using absolute positioning, this is a lot more difficult. We can create a separate <DIV> for each caption, and position it as required.

To get round this, W3C is considering proposals for the <LABEL> tag. This will place any text (or other elements contained in the <LABEL> tag) next to a control automatically. The label effectively acts as a container for the control element:

```
<LABEL>
   Enter your name:
   <INPUT TYPE=TEXT ID=txtYourName>
</LABEL>
```

At the time of writing, this tag is supported, but not fully working. In particular, the positioning features are unreliable. For this reason, you'll see that we use the <DIV> method in our example page.

The ACCESSKEY and TABINDEX Attributes

One of the things that users appreciate in an application is the ability to press a 'hot-key', or short-cut key to place the focus on a particular control. This saves tabbing to it, or reaching for the mouse each time. While we can create this effect by reacting to the **onkeydown** event of the document—as suggested in earlier chapters—a better way is proposed. This involves the **ACCESSKEY** attribute.

Adding an **ACCESSKEY** attribute to a <BUTTON>, <LABEL> or <CAPTION> tag will render the text in the label or caption with one of the letters underlined, or highlighted in a way appropriate for the operating system the browser is running on. Here's the Stop button we looked at earlier, with the access key set to T:

```
<BUTTON ACCESSKEY="T" ID=cmdStop TABINDEX=13
        STYLE="position:absolute; top=200; width:80; left=325">
  <IMG ID=imgbtnStop SRC="stop.gif" WIDTH=25 HEIGHT=30><BR>Stop
</BUTTON>
```

You can also see that the **TABINDEX** attribute has been added, setting this control to be the thirteenth in the tab order of the form. This useful technique allows us to control the tab order when the page is created, and change it dynamically while the page is open if required.

*In our example page, you'll see that the **ACCESSKEY** and **TABINDEX** attributes are included, and work properly with just one exception. Setting the access key for labels and buttons does not currently underline the relevant letter.*

A Dynamic Form Example

This example page is simplified mock-up of an interface for a web-based client/ server application that controls the cutting plant in a factory. It demonstrates just how much more we can achieve using the integral controls that are part of Dynamic HTML. It's called the Cutting List Controller (`CutList.htm`), and you can run or download it from our web site at **http://rapid.wrox.co.uk/ books/0685**. This is how it looks when you first open it

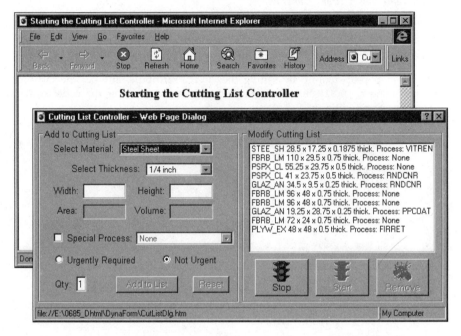

The original page, `CutList.htm`, uses the `showModalDialog` method we looked at in the previous section to open the form in a dialog window. This allows us to control which parts of the browser window will be visible, so we can make it look more like an application's form by omitting the toolbars, location bar, etc. This time, we've also included the 'Help' button in the title bar, by including the attribute `help:yes` in the 'features' string:

```
<BODY ONLOAD="OpenCutListPage()">
...
<SCRIPT LANGUAGE=JAVASCRIPT>
function OpenCutListPage()
{
  showModalDialog("CutListDlg.htm", "MyDialog",
                  "dialogWidth=620px;dialogHeight=310px;"
                + "center=yes;border=thin;help=yes");
  event.cancelBubble = true
}
</SCRIPT>
```

203

New Properties and Control Settings

As you can see from the screen shot, the form in the dialog window looks more like a 'real' compiled application than a web page. Many of the techniques it demonstrates are just not possible in earlier versions of HTML without resorting to external embedded controls, such as those from the Microsoft Forms ActiveX controls range.

The Left-hand 'Input Area' Controls

When creating the controls themselves, we've used absolute positioning. We also placed those in the left-hand area on a **<FORM>**, so that we can use a **RESET** button to clear the values. Here's part of the HTML that creates the controls—notice how we assign a hot-key to them using the **ACCESSKEY** attribute, provide a pop-up tool-tip by setting the **TITLE** attribute, and set the tab order by providing a **TABINDEX** attribute (we've removed some of the code to avoid unnecessary repetition):

```
<! The Input controls section >
<FIELDSET ID=Input STYLE="position:absolute; width:300;
                          height:255; top:5; left:5">
  <LEGEND> Add to Cutting List </LEGEND>
  <FORM ID=frmInput>
    <SELECT ID=cboMaterial ACCESSKEY="M" TABINDEX=1
            TITLE="Select the type material you require"
            STYLE="position:absolute; width=140; top=20; left=120">
      <OPTION VALUE="PSPX_CL">Clear Perspex
      ...
      <OPTION VALUE="PLYW_EX">Exterior Plywood
    </SELECT>
    <SELECT ID=cboThickness ACCESSKEY="T" TABINDEX=2
            TITLE="Select the thickness of the material you require"
            STYLE="position:absolute; width=100; top=50; left=160">
      <OPTION VALUE=0.1875>3/16 inch
      ...
      <OPTION VALUE=0.75>3/4 inch
    </SELECT>
    <INPUT TYPE=TEXT ID=txtWidth ACCESSKEY="W" TABINDEX=3
            TITLE="Enter the width of the material"
            STYLE="position:absolute; width=65; top=80; left=65">
    <INPUT TYPE=TEXT ID=txtHeight ACCESSKEY="H" TABINDEX=4
            TITLE="Enter the height of the material"
            STYLE="position:absolute; width=65; top=80; left=195">
    ...
```

We also make some of the controls read-only, and change the background color to indicate this to the user:

```
    ...
    <INPUT TYPE=TEXT ID=txtArea READONLY
            STYLE="position:absolute; width=65; top=110; left=65;
                   background-color:silver">
    ...
```

The buttons at the bottom of the left-hand control area are created using the traditional **<INPUT>** tag, with a type of **BUTTON**. This emphasizes the differences between this and the new **<BUTTON>** tag that we're using in the right-hand area. To make the buttons disabled when the page loads, we just have to include the **DISABLED** attribute:

204

```
        . . .
        <INPUT TYPE=BUTTON ID=cmdAdd VALUE="Add to List"
              ACCESSKEY="A" TABINDEX=10 DISABLED
              TITLE="Add the current cutting entry to the cutting list"
              STYLE="position:absolute; top=215; left=115">
        <INPUT TYPE=RESET ID=cmdReset ACCESSKEY="E" TABINDEX=11
              TITLE="Clear the current cutting entry details" DISABLED
              STYLE="position:absolute; top=215; left=230">
      </FORM>
    </FIELDSET>
```

The Right-hand 'Cutting List' Control Area

The right-hand control area contains a list and three buttons. To make the
<SELECT> tag show as an open list, instead of a drop-down combo box, we
just need to set the SIZE attribute. We've also provided some entries in the list
when the page is first loaded, so that you can see it working:

```
    <! The Cutting List controls>
    <FIELDSET ID=Output STYLE="position:absolute; width:300;
                                height:255; top:5; left:310">
      <LEGEND> Modify Cutting List </LEGEND>
      <SELECT ID=1stCutting SIZE=12 TABINDEX=12
             TITLE="Select an item in the list and click 'Remove'"
             STYLE="position:absolute; width:280; top=20; left:7">
        <OPTION>STEE_SH 28.5 x 17.25 x 0.1875 thick. Process: VITREN
        . . .
        <OPTION>PLYW_EX 48 x 48 x 0.5 thick. Process: FIRRET
      </SELECT>
      . . .
```

You can also see the code to create our three picture buttons here. The last two
are disabled when the form first loads. We've defined the access key for each
one, the tab index, and the text for the pop-up tool-tip that appears when the
mouse pointer pauses over the control:

```
      . . .
      <BUTTON ID=cmdStop ACCESSKEY="T" TABINDEX=13
             TITLE="Stop the cutting process"
             STYLE="position:absolute; top=190; width:80; left=17">
        <IMG ID=imgbtnStop SRC="stop.gif" WIDTH=25 HEIGHT=30>
        <BR>Stop
      </BUTTON>
      <BUTTON ID=cmdStart DISABLED ACCESSKEY="S" TABINDEX=14
             TITLE="Restart the cutting process"
             STYLE="position:absolute; top=190; width:80; left=108">
        <IMG ID=imgbtnStart SRC="lightoff.gif" WIDTH=25 HEIGHT=30>
        <BR>Start
      </BUTTON>
      <BUTTON ID=cmdRemove DISABLED ACCESSKEY="A" TABINDEX=15
             TITLE="Remove an item from cutting list"
             STYLE="position:absolute; top=190; left=199">
        <IMG ID=imgbtnRemove SRC="remgray.gif" WIDTH=28 HEIGHT=30>
        <BR>Remove
      </BUTTON>
    </FIELDSET>
```

Pre-Loading and Caching Images

As well as the pictures that are visible on the buttons as the page loads, we'll
be using others when the button state changes—i.e. when the disabled ones

become enabled and vice versa. To prevent a delay while the new picture is loaded the first time, we force the browser to cache them by loading them into hidden **<IMG>** controls on the page:

```
<! Pre-load the other button pictures in hidden image controls >
<IMG SRC="remove.gif" STYLE="visibility:hidden">
<IMG SRC="lightoff.gif" STYLE="visibility:hidden">
```

The Control Labels

Finally, we place all the labels for the controls in the two control areas. As explained earlier, we've done this using **<DIV>** tags, because text positioning with the **<LABEL>** control was still a little unreliable in the version of Dynamic HTML we were using. Again, we set the hot-key using the **ACCESSKEY** attribute—although this doesn't yet provide a way to graphically indicate which letter is being used in the final page:

```
<! The Labels for the Input controls>
<DIV STYLE="position:absolute; width:100; height:20; top:35; left:25">
  <LABEL ACCESSKEY="M" FOR="cboMaterial">Select Material:</LABEL>
</DIV>
<DIV STYLE="position:absolute; width:150; height:20; top:65; left:30">
  <LABEL ACCESSKEY="T" FOR="cboThickness">Select Thickness:</LABEL>
</DIV>
...
```

The Script That Makes It Work

As you may have guessed, the page contains quite a lot of script code. We'll look at the important routines here to show you how it works, but we aren't printing it all. Many of the techniques are duplicated across controls, and the whole thing is fully commented. You can view the source of the page, or download it with the rest of the samples to run and examine on your own system. We've implemented this example in VBScript, so that you get the chance see both languages in action throughout the book and the example pages.

Referring to the Form

Because all the controls in the right-hand area are in a **<FORM>**, we've created a global variable to reference it, and we set this when the page first loads—in the **window_onload ()** event. At the same time, we place the text cursor in the top Select Material list and start the cutting timer running. Like the Dancing Buttons page we looked at in Chapter 5, this page uses a timer created with the **setInterval** method:

```
<SCRIPT LANGUAGE=VBSCRIPT>

Dim gInputForm   'global reference to the Input form
Dim gCutTimer    'global interval timer reference

Sub window_onLoad()
  Set gInputForm = Document.Forms("frmInput") 'set form reference
  gInputForm.cboMaterial.focus                'set text cursor focus
  'start the cutting timer running to remove items from the list
  gCutTimer = window.setInterval("CutTimer_Interval()", 5000)
End Sub
```

From this point on, we can refer to any control on the form by using the **gInputForm** variable.

Calculating the Area and Volume

When you enter values for a new entry, the Area and Volume controls are filled in as soon as the cursor leaves the appropriate control. The four controls that contribute to this are Width, Height, Thickness and Quantity, and the calculation is only done when they all have legitimate values. At the same time, the Add to List and Reset buttons become available:

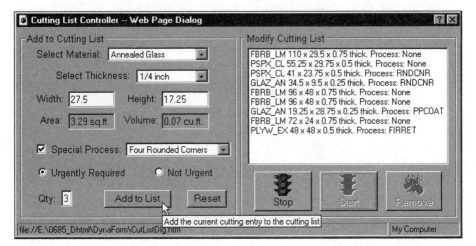

To do this, we have to react to the **onchange** event for the four controls that supply the values for the calculation. In each one, **txtWidth**, **txtHeight**, and **cboThickness**, we call a separate subroutine named **UpdateAreaVol**, which performs the calculation and updates the page once you tab or move to the next control:

```
Sub txtWidth_onchange()      'occurs when Width changed in text box  UpdateAreaVol
'call the UpdateAreaVol subroutineEnd Sub...'same code for txtHeight_onchange()
'cboThickness_onchange()
'and txtQty_onChange()
...
```

Here's the **UpdateAreaVol** subroutine in full—to simplify the code we've omitted any checking for out-of-range result values:

```
Sub UpdateAreaVol() 'runs when the height, width or thickness change
   If IsNumeric(gInputForm.txtWidth.Value) _
   And IsNumeric(gInputForm.txtHeight.Value) _
   And IsNumeric(gInputForm.txtQty.Value) Then
      'set the values of the Area and Volume text boxes
      sngResult = gInputForm.txtWidth.Value
                * gInputForm.txtHeight.Value / 144
      gInputForm.txtArea.Value = FormatNumber(sngResult, 2) & " sq.ft."
      sngresult = sngResult * gInputForm.cboThickness.Value  / 12
      gInputForm.txtVolume.Value = FormatNumber(sngResult, 2) & " cu.ft."
      'enable the Add and Reset buttons
      gInputForm.cmdAdd.Disabled = False
      gInputForm.cmdReset.Disabled = False
   Else
      'disable the Add and Reset buttons
      gInputForm.cmdAdd.Disabled = True
      gInputForm.cmdReset.Disabled = True
```

```
        'clear the Area and Volume text boxes
      gInputForm.txtArea.Value = ""
      gInputForm.txtVolume.Value = ""
   End If
End Sub
```

Using the VALUE property of a <SELECT> Element

You can see that the **UpdateAreaVol** code first checks that the Width and Height controls contain valid numbers. Notice that we don't check the Thickness list for a valid number. When we created it in the HTML, we used decimal numbers for the **VALUE** attribute of each **<OPTION>** tag, and the text equivalent for the entry the user sees:

```
<SELECT ID=cboThickness ...>
   <OPTION VALUE=0.1875>3/16 inch
   <OPTION VALUE=0.25 SELECTED>1/4 inch
   <OPTION VALUE=0.3125>5/16 inch
   <OPTION VALUE=0.5>1/2 inch
   <OPTION VALUE=0.75>3/4 inch
</SELECT>
```

Now, because it's a drop-down list, we know we'll always get a valid number for the **value** property.

Enabling and Disabling Buttons and Controls

The final part of the **UpdateAreaVol** routine enables or disables the buttons at the bottom of the left-hand control area, depending on the outcome of the update process. If the calculation is possible, the results are placed in the Area and Volume controls, then the two buttons have their **disabled** property set to **false**. If we don't have enough information, we set the **disabled** property to **true**, and clear the contents of the Area and Volume controls.

A similar technique is used to set the **disabled** state of the Special Process drop-down list. Here, we react to the user clicking on the checkbox **chkSpecial**, and examine its **checked** property to decide if we need to enable or disable the drop-down list **cboProcess**:

```
Sub chkSpecial_onclick()  'Special Process' checkbox clicked
   If gInputForm.chkSpecial.checked Then
      gInputForm.cboProcess.disabled = False    'enable the combo list
   Else
      gInputForm.cboProcess.disabled = True     'disable the combo
      gInputForm.cboProcess.selectedIndex = 0   'and set it to 'None'
   End If
End Sub
```

If we are disabling it, we can also change the setting to None simply by assigning a new value to the control's **selectedIndex** property. The entry we want is the first in the list, so it has an **index** of zero. Of course, we can set it to any appropriate value using this technique.

208

Adding the Entry to the Cutting List

The next task we need to consider is how we add an item to the list. If you've been watching the right-hand list, you'll see that it keeps shrinking. Items are removed automatically every five seconds or so, to simulate the processing in the factory. This is something new. We couldn't change the contents of a `<SELECT>` list while a page was loaded in HTML 3.2 without using an embedded control.

To understand how it works, we need to look at how the list stores its entries. When we create the control in HTML, we use a series of `<OPTION>` tags to define the contents. Like all other elements in Dynamic HTML, we can change the contents of the HTML source dynamically while the page is displayed. The clever bit is that this includes adding `<OPTION>` tags to, and removing then from, a `<SELECT>` list.

The Options Collection

The `<SELECT>` tag stores its entries in a collection called `options`, which represents the `<OPTIONS>` tags within the HTML source. All we need to do is add new members to the collection, or remove existing ones. We can also tell how many members there are at any time by querying the collection's `length` property. We'll come to removing members in a while, but for the mean time let's consider how we go about adding them. Here's the code that runs when the Add to List button is clicked:

```
Sub cmdAdd_onclick()                        'Add to List' button pressed
  gInputForm.cmdAdd.Disabled = True     'disable the button
   'create the new string for the cutting list
   strEntry = gInputForm.cboMaterial.Value & " " _
           & gInputForm.txtWidth.Value & """ x " _
           & gInputForm.txtHeight.Value & """ x " _
           & gInputForm.cboThickness.Value & """ thick. " _
           & "Process " & gInputForm.cboProcess.Value
  intQty = gInputForm.txtQty.Value        'get the quantity
  For intLoop = 1 To intQty               'loop for the quantity required
    'create a new element of type OPTION for the cutting list
    Set objEntry = document.createElement("OPTION")
    objEntry.text = strEntry              'set text string to show in the list
    If gInputForm.optUrgent.checked Then
      lstCutting.add objEntry, 1          'add it to the top of the list
    Else
      lstCutting.add objEntry            'add it to the end of the list
    End If
  Next
End Sub
```

The first thing it does is disable the Add to List button so that the user can't accidentally add the same item twice. Then it builds up the text for the new entry in a string `strEntry`. Now we have to consider how we add it to the options collection. Each member of the collection is an `OPTION` element object, not just a string. It has an `index` and a `value` (as set by the `VALUE` attribute), as well as the `text` property that we see in the list.

Creating New Elements in a Collection

We can create an instance of an HTML element object using the `createObject` method of the `document`—here we're creating a new `OPTION` element object:

```
Set objEntry = document.createElement("OPTION")
```

Then we can assign the values we want for its properties. In our case, we don't need the **value** property, but we do need the **text** property to be shown in the list. This, of course, is **strEntry**:

```
objEntry.text = strEntry          'set the text string to show in the list
```

Now we can add the new element to the **options** collection using the **add** method. In our example, we'll add it at the top of the list if it's urgent, by using the optional second **index** parameter:

```
lstCutting.add objEntry, 1        'add it to the top of the list
```

Otherwise, we add it to the end by omitting this parameter.

Removing Cutting List Entries

The entries in the cutting list are removed every five seconds or so automatically, but the user can also select and remove them using the **Remove** button in the right-hand area of the page. This button is disabled until they click on the list to select an entry.

So, we need to respond to a click on the list, and enable the **Remove** button. This is easy enough—we use the **onclick** event of the list, and set the button's **disabled** property as appropriate. But how do we know which one they selected? We use the **selectedIndex** property of the list—this is **-1** if nothing is selected, or the **index** of the selected item (starting from zero for the first one).

Of course, the task is more than just setting the **disabled** property, like we did with the buttons in the left-hand control area. Here, we also have to change the picture they display. We've provided the pictures for each button as both a color image and a grayed-out version. When we disable the button, we just have to change the **src** property of the **<IMG>** tag as appropriate as well:

```
Sub lstCutting_onclick()                    'a click in the cutting list
    If lstCutting.SelectedIndex >= 0 Then   'existing entry selected
        cmdremove.Disabled = False          'enable the 'Remove' button
        document.all("imgbtnRemove").src = "remove.gif" 'load the new picture
    Else
        cmdremove.Disabled = True           'disable the 'Remove' button
        document.all("imgbtnRemove").src = "remgray.gif" 'load the new picture
    End If
End Sub
```

Removing Elements from a Collection

Once we've enabled the button, we can respond to it being clicked by removing the item and disabling the button again. Removing an item from a collection is done with the **remove** method. It takes the **index** of the item to remove, and again we get this from the list's **selectedIndex** property:

```
Sub cmdRemove_onclick()                          'Remove' button pressed
   lstCutting.remove lstCutting.SelectedIndex    'remove the selected entry
   lstCutting_onclick                            'and update the buttons
End Sub
```

Then we can update the enabled states of the buttons by simply calling the **lstCutting_onclick** routine ourselves.

Stopping and Starting the Cutting Process

The other two buttons in the right-hand section of the page allow the user to stop and restart the cutting process as required. To stop it, all we have to do is clear the interval timer that we started running when we loaded the page. Of course, we have to change the enabled state of the Stop and Start buttons as appropriate as well:

```
Sub cmdStop_onclick()                            'Stop' button pressed
   window.clearInterval gCutTimer                'stop the timer running
   cmdStop.Disabled = True                       'disable the 'Stop' button
   document.all("imgbtnStop").src = "lightoff.gif"
   cmdStart.Disabled = False                     'enable the 'Start' button
   document.all("imgbtnStart").src = "go.gif"
End Sub
```

To re-start the process, we just reverse the actions we took to stop it. However, we also need to make sure that there are some items in the list first, and we'll remove the first one straight away to indicate that cutting has restarted:

```
Sub cmdStart_onclick()                           'Start' button pressed
   If lstCutting.length > 0 Then                 'if there are items in the list
      lstCutting.remove 0                        'remove top one, then start timer
      gCutTimer = window.setInterval("CutTimer_Interval()", 5000)
      cmdStop.Disabled = False                   'enable the 'Stop' button
      document.all("imgbtnStop").src = "stop.gif"
      cmdStart.Disabled = True                   'disable the 'Start' button
      document.all("imgbtnStart").src = "lightoff.gif"
   End If
End Sub
```

The Interval Timer Code

While the cutting process is running, the **setInterval** method calls our **CutTimer_Interval** routine every 5 seconds. Here, we simply remove the top item from the cutting list, and if it's now empty we call the **cmdStop** button routine. This looks after changing the enabled state of the buttons for us:

```
Sub CutTimer_Interval()                          'timer interval over
   lstCutting.remove 0                           'remove top entry from cutting list
   lstCutting_onclick                            'update the buttons
   'if list is empty then stop the timer
   If lstCutting.length = 0 Then cmdStop_onclick
End Sub
```

You'll notice in several of these routines that we've created our own 'pseudo-events' by running other event handler routines directly. This technique often saves us from having to write so much code, and makes maintenance much easier. What you have to watch out for, however, is not to create a loop where an event handler calls another one, which itself calls the first one. This is a good way to lock up the browser and prevent your pages working at all!

Providing Context Sensitive Help

The final technique we want to look at in the Cutting List Controller page is the new support for context-sensitive help in a web page. If we are going to build interactive applications that use a browser as the front end, we need to be able to mirror as much of the functionality of a normal Windows application as possible.

One thing that makes any application easier to use, especially for newcomers, is the provision of easy-to-access help— plus tips on the way that the application works. We've already seen how to implement the pop up tool-tips that are used in almost all new applications, by setting the **TITLE** attribute for the element within the HTML.

Another way that we can provide help is by using the 'What's This?' button at the top of a dialog window. Clicking this in a normal application, then clicking somewhere in the dialog, provides a pop-up window containing more information about the dialog and its contents. Placing the text cursor in a control and pressing the *F1* key usually has the same effect.

Reacting to the onhelp Event

We can respond to the 'What's This?' button and the *F1* key in our web pages by using the new **onhelp** event that is supported for nearly all visible elements. Our page displays some specific help in a message box when you click the 'What's This?' button and click on a control or its label, or press the *F1* key when a control has the input focus:

![Screenshot of the Cutting List Controller Web Page Dialog]

How it Works

When the `onhelp` event occurs, we can look for the source element using the
`event` object's `scrElement` property. However, in our example, we're being a
bit cleverer than that. We want a click on a control's label to display the help
message as well, so we've made sure that each control and label have `ID`
properties that vary only in the first three characters.

For example, the Quantity text box has the `ID` property `txtQty`, while its label
has the `ID` property `lblQty`. By chopping off the first three characters, we can
use a `Select Case` statement that gives the same result for each control and
its label:

```
Sub document_onhelp()       'Window's help event occurred
   'This may be with the ? button at the top of the window, or by
   'pressing F1. First we set the default help message
   strHelpMesg = "No more information is available for this item."
   'find source element ID and remove first three letters. This means (for
   'example) that lblMaterial and cboMaterial will show the same message.
   strSourceID = Mid(window.event.srcElement.id, 4)
   Select Case strSourceID
     Case "Material"
       strHelpMesg = "Click on the down arrow button ... etc."
     Case "Width"
       strHelpMesg = "Type in here the width you want ... etc."
     ...
     ...
     Case "Remove"
       strHelpMesg = "Use this button to remove an item ... etc."
   End Select
   'display the help message
   MsgBox strHelpMesg, vbInformation, "Cutting List Controller Help"
   window.event.cancelBubble = true
End Sub
```

Using Objects and Controls

Of course, there are times when we want to achieve effects that aren't possible
using just the HTML controls. In these cases, we still end up needing to use an
ActiveX control or a Java applet to carry a particular task that even Dynamic
HTML can't manage on its own. Although there are lots of improvements to the
way forms work, and extra properties, methods and events exposed that we can
use in our code, they may not be able to give us exactly what we need.

It's at this point that we have to make a decision as to how we implement an
'outside' object in our page. We've discussed the merits and shortcomings of
applets and ActiveX controls, and this is the point where you decide which
route to take. We'll look briefly at the possibilities here.

Using Java Applets

We can embed Java applets into a page using the `<APPLET>` tag. This accepts a
special set of attributes and parameters that define what the object is, where it
comes from, and how it should be used. On top of that are the more usual
attributes that control the size of the applet's visible representation on the page,
and the positioning with respect to the surrounding elements.

The <APPLET> Tag

To use the <APPLET> tag, we add the attributes that define the location of the applet's code and its appearance within the page, inside the opening tag. Between this and the closing </APPLET> tag, we can provide parameters which define the custom properties for that applet:

```
<APPLET WIDTH=100 HEIGHT=50 ALIGN=CENTER NAME=MyApplet ALT="Wrox Applet"
        CODEBASE="http://www.wrox.com/java/" CODE="WroxApp.class">
   <PARAM NAME="STARTCOLOR" VALUE="green">
   <PARAM NAME="RATINGLEVEL" VALUE=24>
   <PARAM NAME="FAILUREMSG" VALUE="Whoops">
</APPLET>
```

In this example, we're using a fictitious object whose code file **WroxApp.class** is stored in the server directory **http://www.wrox.com/java**. It provides three properties that we need to set when we start the object running in the page: **STARTCOLOR**, **RATINGLEVEL**, and **FAILUREMSG**. We use <PARAM> tags to set the values of these within the <APPLET> tag.

Once the page is downloaded, the browser fetches the applet code from our server, creates an instance of the object that the code defines, sets the properties using the <PARAM> tag values, and starts it executing.

The <APPLET> Attributes

Here's a full list of the attributes that the <APPLET> tag supports in Dynamic HTML:

Attribute	Description
ALIGN	The alignment of the object horizontally and vertically on the page.
ALT	The text to display while the object loads, or if it is not available.
CLASS	The style class to associate with the element to control its appearance.
CODE	The name of the Java class file to be executed, such as Animator.class.
CODEBASE	The URL where the class file can be downloaded from if required.
DATAFLD	Defines the field in the data source for data-bound controls.
DATASRC	Defines the data source for data-bound controls.
DISABLED	When set to true prevents the object code from executing.
HEIGHT	Sets the height of the object on the page.
HSPACE	Sets the horizontal distance between the object and surrounding elements.
ID	Provides an ID string to refer to the object by.
NAME	Provides a name to refer to the object by.

Attribute	Description
SRC	Defines the URL of file that provides the applet's data.
STYLE	The CSS style properties for the object's container.
TITLE	The text for the tool-tip displayed when the mouse pointer is over the object.
VSPACE	Sets the vertical distance between the object and surrounding elements.
WIDTH	Sets the height of the object on the page.

While some applets may be simply decorative animations, the more recent are aimed at achieving something more useful. The common ones are things like stock tickers and graphic manipulation objects, but the range of available applets is huge. To see more, visit the home of Java at **http://www.gamelan.com** or **http://www.jars.com**

Object and Container Properties, Methods and Events

To be of real use in a dynamic page, an object needs to provide properties, methods, and events. However, when an object is embedded into the page, you have to remember that there are two distinct sets of properties, methods, and events available:

 The HTML page provides a **container** which holds the object, and this container has properties, methods, and events that are the same in all cases—irrespective of the object it contains

 The object that runs inside this container may also expose its own properties, methods, and events. These are separate from those of the container, and can be different for each object

The **properties** of the **<APPLET>** tag (the container), as listed above, are set by the attributes of the tag—and can be manipulated in code like any other properties. However, the two mainline browsers, Internet Explorer and Netscape's Navigator/Communicator, implement the connection between the object and the script in the page in different ways.

Working with Applets in Internet Explorer

In Microsoft's Internet Explorer browser, Java applets are 'wrapped' in an ActiveX/COM interface when they are instantiated in the page. This makes them appear to the browser like any other integral object, which has a set of properties, methods and events that mirror those in the control and those of the container.

For example, the applet adopts the standard Dynamic HTML set of **methods** such as **scrollIntoView**, **getAttribute**, etc. through its container element (the **<APPLET>** tag), but this does not support any events directly. The object may also provide its own properties, methods—and events—for use in our code. For example we might want to change the **RATINGLEVEL** property while our page is displayed, or react to the object's **ratinglevelchange** event:

215

```
MyApplet.ratinglevel = 36  'change the rating level

Sub MyApplet_ratinglevelchange()
  'runs when the user changes the rating level in the applet
  ...
  'code to respond to the event goes here
  ...
End Sub
```

Working with Applets in Netscape Browsers

In Netscape's Navigator and Communicator browsers, communication between a Java applet and the JavaScript code in the page is handled by a mechanism called **LiveConnect**. We won't be going into this in depth, but in outline it allows a Java applet that is defined in the page to be added to the **applets** object array of the **document** object. To refer to the applet, we use the **document.applet** array. For example, we can execute a method named **verifylevel** using:

```
document.MyApplet.verifylevel()   //execute the applet's verifylevel method
```

And we can access the applet's parameters (i.e. properties) in a similar way as we do in Internet Explorer, remembering to include the base **document** object:

```
document.MyApplet.ratinglevel = 36    //change the rating level
```

Using ActiveX Controls

To insert an ActiveX control into our page, we use an **<OBJECT>** tag. Internet Explorer supported ActiveX controls from version 3 onwards, and it's likely that other new browsers will do so as well. Because the ActiveX standard is a development of the existing Microsoft OLE technology, there are hundreds of ActiveX controls available for use in our pages—and many are provided as standard with Internet Explorer. A gallery showing some of those that are available is at **http://www.microsoft.com/activeplatform/default.asp**

The <OBJECT> Tag

The basic principles of using ActiveX controls and the **<OBJECT>** tag are similar to the **<APPLET>** tag we looked at earlier. We use the normal HTML attributes to set the size and relative position of the visible portion of the object in the page, and a series of **<PARAM>** tags to set its properties. Notice that, this time, we use the **ID** attribute rather than the **NAME** attribute to set the object's 'identity', so that we can refer to it in our code:

```
<OBJECT ID="timMove" WIDTH=39 HEIGHT=39
   CLASSID="CLSID:59CCB4A0-727D-11CF-AC36-00AA00A47DD2"
   CODEBASE="http://activex.microsoft.com/controls/iexplorer/timer.ocx">
   <PARAM NAME="Interval" VALUE="4000">
   <PARAM NAME="Enabled" VALUE="False">
</OBJECT>
```

The **CODEBASE** attribute defines the URL or location of the object's code, in case it is not already available on the client and has to be downloaded—just like a Java class file. This time, there is no **CODE** attribute, however. As objects are downloaded, they are registered on the client in Windows registry so that the system can find and use them the next time, without having to download them again.

To ensure that each one has a unique registered identity, it contains a `CLASSID` string—created inside the object when it is built and guaranteed to be unique. Using just a name would provide too many opportunities for clashes when two designers used the same name for their different controls.

Here is a full list of the current and proposed attributes for the `<OBJECT>` tag. The valid values for each one, where applicable, are given in reference section **B**. We'll be coming back to the data-binding attributes, `DATA`, `DATAFLD` and `DATASRC` later in this chapter:

Attribute	Description
ACCESSKEY	Defines the 'hot-key' that can be used to activate the control.
ALIGN	The alignment of the object horizontally and vertically on the page.
ALT *	The text to display if the object is not available.
CLASS	The style class to associate with the element to control its appearance.
CLASSID	The unique registry value to identify the control.
CODE	The class name of a Java applet, if this is the object source.
CODEBASE	The URL or location where the class file can be downloaded from.
CODETYPE	Defines the type of the object, and the way the operating system handles it
DATA	Defines the URL of the data source for data-bound controls.
DATAFLD	Defines the field in the data source for data-bound controls.
DATASRC	Defines the data source for data-bound controls.
DECLARE *	Indicates that the object should be downloaded but not instantiated.
HEIGHT	Sets the height of the object on the page.
HSPACE *	Sets the horizontal distance between the object and surrounding elements.
ID	Provides an ID string to refer to the object by.
LANG	Defines the language type for the object container events, such as `"script/javascript"`.
LANGUAGE	Defines the language name for the object container events, either `"VBSCRIPT"` or `"JAVASCRIPT"`.
NAME	Provides a name to refer to the object by.
SHAPES *	Indicates that the object is an image containing defined areas.
STYLE	The CSS style properties for the object's container.

Table continued in following page

Attribute	Description
TABINDEX	The tab index for the object's container.
TITLE	The text for the tooltip displayed when the mouse pointer is over the object.
TYPE	Defines the Mime type for the object, as defined in the registry.
USEMAP *	The name of a client-side image map to use with the object.
VSPACE *	Sets the vertical distance between the object and surrounding elements.
WIDTH	Sets the height of the object on the page.

An asterisk indicates those that are part of the W3C Cougar (HTML 4.0) discussion document, and not yet supported in Internet Explorer 4.

Object and Container Properties, Methods and Events

The <OBJECT> tag provides a set of properties, methods and events for the container, and the object can provide its own set of properties, methods and events as well. The container properties are the attributes you've seen above, and the methods are the standard Dynamic HTML methods such as **scrollIntoView**, **getAttribute**, etc.

The <OBJECT> tag also provides a wide range of events for the container. There are 21 in all, and for visible controls we can react to them in code in the same way as we would for an ordinary HTML element. However, they will not all be available for non-visible controls:

The <OBJECT> Container Events

onafterupdate	onbeforeupdate	onblur	onclick
ondblclick	ondragstart	onfocus	onhelp
onkeydown	onkeypress	onkeyup	onmousedown
onmousemove	onmouseout	onmouseover	onmouseup
onreadystatechange	onresize	onrowenter	onrowexit
onselectstart			

And, of course, the object itself will usually provide us with its own events. The <OBJECT> tag example we used earlier inserts a Microsoft **Timer** ActiveX control into the page. It has just one event of its own, and two properties, that we can use in our code:

```
timMove.Interval = 5000   'set the Interval to 5 seconds
timMove.Enabled = True    'and set the timer running

Sub timMove_Timer()
   'occurs regularly every 'Interval' number of milliseconds
End Sub
```

218

If an object exposes properties, methods or events that have the same name as the its container (i.e. the **<OBJECT>** element) we have a problem. By default, accessing the object through the **ID** of the **<OBJECT>** tag will provide a reference to the container's property method or event if one exists with that name. To get round this, we use the **object** syntax:

```
MyObject.width = 100;        // sets the object container's width property
MyObject.object.width = 75;  // sets the object's width property
```

There are two ActiveX controls that you will no doubt meet in Internet Explorer 4 as you start to develop your own site. These provide us with a way of connecting our pages to a database, and are the subject of the next section.

Data Binding in Dynamic HTML

A great deal of browser use, especially on a corporate Intranet or web-based client/server application interface, is to do with viewing and manipulating the contents of databases. These may be databases in the traditional sense, systems like Oracle, SQL Server, Access, or other specialist implementations. To achieve this task, the traditional route has been through some type of server-side programming—perhaps CGI, scripting languages like Perl, or more specialist methods like Active Server Pages.

The Downside of Server-side Processing

This is an excellent solution in most situations, because the server executes the code at its end, and sends the client the final HTML-only page. However, when the user wants to interact with the database, perhaps updating information or just scrolling through the records, it involves repeated server-side processing and the regular transfer of data and instructions between the server and the browser.

This isn't usually a problem on a local network or Intranet, unless the demands on the server are so high as to absorb all its processing capacity. Out on the Web, however, the repeated connections and data transfer demand a more elegant approach.

Caching Data Client-side

One obvious solution is to cache the data at the client (browser), rather than only sending extracts each time, and allow the browser to extract what it wants and display it. This adds another advantage in that the user can update several rows of a data set (i.e. several records), then send back the complete package of changes in one go.

We're not going to be concerned with the internal workings of all this here, as you can appreciate it's a very involved subject. Instead, we'll show you with a simple example how the proposed extensions to the Dynamic HTML language provide the 'hooks' that allow it to be implemented. The current specification, as implemented in Internet Explorer 4.0, is still very much a draft and will change over time. But it is such an important concept that you should be aware of how it's developing.

219

Providing a Data Source

To achieve data binding in a Dynamic HTML page, there has to be a way of connecting the controls on the page with a data source. In our example, we're using a very simple source—a small text file containing nutritional information. In fact, the next screen shot shows our 'database':

```
food.txt - Notepad
File  Edit  Search  Help
Food,Calories,Group
Hamburger,3000,Junk
Apple,250,Fruit
Milk,500,Dairy
Orange,300,Fruit
Cheese,350,Dairy
Scones,300,Junk
```

So the first step is to connect this database to our page, so that the controls in the page can access the data. This requires a connector component that can read the data and access our page, and currently this means either the Microsoft **Remote Data Service** (RDS) control or the **Simple Tabular Data** (STD) control. The RDS control is designed to access ODBC-equipped data sources, and offers the ability to update the data from within the browser. As we only have simple tabular data, however, we'll use the STD control instead.

Inserting the Simple Tabular Data Control

We insert the data connector control, in our case the Simple Tabular Data control, using a normal `<OBJECT>` tag. We've given it an `ID` of `food`, specified our database `food.txt` (in the same directory as the page) for the `DataURL` property, and set the `FieldDelim` property to a comma—this is the field delimiter within our file's 'records'. The final `<PARAM>` tag sets the `UseHeader` property to `True`, because our database has the field names in the first record (or row):

```
<OBJECT ID="food" WIDTH=100 HEIGHT=51
  CLASSID="CLSID:333C7BC4-460F-11D0-BC04-0080C7055A83">
  <PARAM NAME="FieldDelim" VALUE=",">
  <PARAM NAME="DataURL" VALUE="food.txt">
  <PARAM NAME="UseHeader" VALUE=True>
</OBJECT>
```

Once the page is loaded, the browser will fetch the data from the `DataURL` and create a connection to it.

Data Binding Attributes

To connect the fields in the database with controls on our page, we use the new tag attributes `DATASRC`, `DATAFLD`, and `DATAFORMATAS`. These are available for a range of tags, as shown in reference section **B**. To understand why they apply to some tags and not others, we need to delve a little deeper.

220

The concept behind data binding is that, once a connection is made to a data source, the browser has two options. It can either show individual values from this source in separate controls (called **single-valued data binding**), or display lists of whole or partial records in a set of table controls (called **tabular data binding**). We'll look at single-value data binding first.

Single-Value Data Binding

To bind individual controls to a data source, we have to provide two items of information: a reference to the connector object for that data source, and the name of a field within the data source for this control. For example, we can bind an **<INPUT>** tag to the **Calories** field in our **food** data source like this. Notice that **food** is the **ID** of the STD control we inserted into our page, not the name of the database file. It is preceded by a hash sign (**#**) to indicate this:

```
<INPUT TYPE="TEXT" DATASRC="#food" DATAFLD="Calories">
```

When the page is loaded, the control will display the value of that field for the first record in our database. We'll see how to display other records in a while.

This method works for different kinds of controls, depending on the type of data the data source contains. We can display text or numeric data in **TEXT**-type **INPUT** controls, **SELECT** lists, **TEXTAREA** and **MARQUEE** controls, plus ordinary document **SPAN** and **DIV** controls. We can also use it as a **PARAM** to an object tag, if the control is an ActiveX control or Java applet. And if the text is the name of an image file, we can use it in an IMG tag as well. **True/False** values can be displayed in **CHECKBOX**- and **RADIO**-type **INPUT** controls, as well as in the **PARAM** tag of an object.

This example page— which is available from **http://rapid.wrox.co.uk/books/0685**— shows how we can display the contents of a record from our **food** database. It also contains buttons to move around the recordset created by the STD control:

Here's an extract of the HTML source for the page. It uses two tables. The first holds the heading and the three text **<INPUT>** tags. The second holds the four navigation buttons:

```
    <TABLE WIDTH=100%><TR><TH COLSPAN=2> Food Browser </TH></TR>
    <TR>
      <TD ALIGN=RIGHT> Food Item: </TD>
      <TD> <INPUT TYPE="TEXT" DATASRC="#food" DATAFLD="Food"> </TD>
    </TR>
    <TR>
      <TD ALIGN=RIGHT> Calories: </TD>
      <TD> <INPUT TYPE="TEXT" DATASRC="#food" DATAFLD="Calories"> </TD>
    </TR>
    <TR>
      <TD ALIGN=RIGHT> Group: </TD>
      <TD> <INPUT TYPE="TEXT" DATASRC="#food" DATAFLD="Group"> </TD>
    </TR>
  </TABLE><P>
  <TABLE WIDTH=100%>
    <TR >
      <TD ALIGN=CENTER>
        <INPUT NAME="cmdFirst" TYPE="BUTTON" VALUE="First">
        <INPUT NAME="cmdPrevious" TYPE="BUTTON" VALUE=" < ">
        <INPUT NAME="cmdNext" TYPE="BUTTON" VALUE=" > ">
        <INPUT NAME="cmdLast" TYPE="BUTTON" VALUE="Last">
      </TD>
    </TR>
  </TABLE>
```

Navigating the Recordset

To move through the records, we use objects and methods exposed by the STD control. These are similar to those provided by most Microsoft (and other) database technologies. The control provides a **recordset** object that represents our data, and this has methods that allow us to manipulate it:

```
Sub cmdPrevious_onclick()
  If Not food.recordset.bof Then food.recordset.movePrevious
End Sub

Sub cmdNext_onclick()
  If Not food.recordset.eof Then food.recordset.moveNext
End Sub

Sub cmdFirst_onclick()
  food.recordset.moveFirst
End Sub

Sub cmdLast_onclick()
  food.recordset.moveLast
End Sub
```

Notice here that we check the **bof** (beginning of file) and **eof** (end of file) properties before we move to the previous or next record. When we are at the first record in the recordset, we can still **movePrevious** without an error, and the controls display an 'empty' record. At this point the **bof** property becomes **True**, and any further attempt to **movePrevious** produces as error. The same kind of process works at the end of the file, with **eof**.

Tabular Data Binding

When we want to display the contents of several records, in a tabular view, we need to repeat certain parts of our page once for each record. This can be done in different ways. The most usual is to create a document division and use a table with the special tags that define the heading and body sections of the table.

Here's an example. We use a `<DIV>` tag to denote an area of the page as a division, and inside it build a table. This time, we use the `DATASRC` attribute in the `<TABLE>` tag, to indicate that the whole table is bound to the data connector control we named `food`:

```
<DIV ALIGN=CENTER>
<TABLE ID=Data WIDTH=75% DATASRC=#food>
  <THEAD>
    <TH> Group </TH> <TH> Food </TH> <TH> Calories </TH>
  </THEAD>
  <TBODY>
    <TR>
      <TD ALIGN=CENTER> <SPAN DATAFLD="Group"> </SPAN> </TD>
      <TD ALIGN=CENTER> <SPAN DATAFLD="Food"> </SPAN> </TD>
      <TD ALIGN=CENTER> <SPAN DATAFLD="Calories"> </SPAN> </TD>
    </TR>
  </TBODY>
</TABLE>
</DIV>
```

Inside the table, we want to display the field names (the headings of the columns) then repeat the data from the records—one per table row. To indicate to the browser which section of the table is which, we use `<THEAD>` and `<TBODY>` tags. The `<THEAD>` section will only appear once, but the `<TBODY>` section will be repeated for each record in our recordset.

However, we can't provide the field value to the `<TD>` tag, like we did earlier with the `<INPUT>` tag—it doesn't accept 'values' as such. Instead, we just place a `<SPAN>` (or `<DIV>`) tag in the appropriate position and set *its* `DATAFLD` attribute to the field name.

Sorting and Filtering

Sometimes, we don't want to display all the records in the data source, or we may want to display them in a different order from the order they exist in the data source. In our earlier single-value data binding example, it would be easier to find a particular food if the records appeared in alphabetical order. If we are listing records in tabular format, it would be handy if we could just list records that matched certain criteria—calorie values below `250`, for example.

We can do both of these things, and more, by setting other properties of our data connector control. Here, we're filtering on the field (or column) named `Group`, and selecting only values where it is equal to `"Dairy"`. We're also sorting the resulting recordset by the value in the field named `Food`:

```
<OBJECT ID="food" WIDTH=100 HEIGHT=51
  CLASSID="CLSID:333C7BC4-460F-11D0-BC04-0080C7055A83">
  <PARAM NAME="FieldDelim" VALUE=",">
```

223

```
        <PARAM NAME="DataURL" VALUE="food.txt">
        <PARAM NAME="UseHeader" VALUE=True>
        <PARAM NAME="FilterColumn" VALUE="Group">
        <PARAM NAME="FilterCriterion" VALUE="=">
        <PARAM NAME="FilterValue" VALUE="Dairy">
        <PARAM NAME="SortColumn" VALUE="Food">
    </OBJECT>
```

When combined with the earlier code to create a tabular format, this is what we get:

Of course, this is only a taster of what data binding can achieve. For example, it's possible to arrange for the data source to be updated—the cached 'local' data is returned to the server. To find out more about data binding, and client/server programming with data binding, look out for **Professional Dynamic HTML and IE4 Programming, ISBN 1-861000-70-7**, from Wrox Press.

Summary

In this chapter, we began by looking at how we can create new browser windows, and started to think about working with HTML controls such as the `<SELECT>` drop-down list control. We also started looking at how Dynamic HTML makes it possible to build more interactive web-based pages—including forms—without having to resort to using embedded ActiveX controls or Java applets.

The new properties, methods and events provided for the intrinsic HTML form controls gives us a lot more freedom in building really dynamic forms, and we used these to build a sample client/server front end using Dynamic HTML in the browser.

However, as we discovered, there are times when the standard HTML controls just can't cut it. At this point, you have to know how to take advantage of the hundreds of pre-built objects that are now available. We looked briefly at the issues of compatibility between browsers that affect their use, and how the two tags `<APPLET>` and `<OBJECT>` can be used to insert them into our pages.

Finally, we ended the chapter by using a special ActiveX control that provides data-binding capabilities to Dynamic HTML. We briefly introduced the way that this new technology can be used to make working with databases in the browser much more responsive and user-friendly.

In all, the main points of this chapter are that we can:

 Create new windows and dialogs to display individual pages, using the `open` and `showModalDialog` methods of the current `window` object

 Build interactive forms using just HTML controls and standard tags, within a dialog window if required

 Use the new HTML tags, and the new properties and events of the existing HTML controls, to make our forms more usable and dynamic

 We can now easily provide context-sensitive help in web pages, using the new `onhelp` event

 Insert ActiveX controls and Java applets into our pages, to cope with the inevitable situations where Dynamic HTML alone cannot provide what we need

 Bind a server or client-based data source to our web pages using the new technology of data binding, providing different ways to display information in the browser

Browser compatibility is becoming an increasingly more difficult problem than ever before. It affects not only objects that are inserted into the pages, but the whole area of Dynamic HTML—as we considered in the introduction to this book. To finish up, we'll use the final chapter to look at some of the problems that web page authors now face, and the new issues that Dynamic HTML raises.

Browser Compatibility and the Future of HTML

In the introduction to this book, we talked about the World Wide Web Consortium (W3C) Project Cougar proposals, which were ultimately paving the way for HTML 4.0. At the time of writing, W3C had just published the first working drafts of HTML 4.0, to cover the tags and attributes that they expect to be part of the final ratification. However, what we haven't done is to look at what Project Cougar actually encompasses. We avoided a dry, technical discussion of the current proposals in favor of showing you what Dynamic HTML can do, and how you can use it to make your web pages more interactive—and more dynamic.

We also mentioned the problems that always arise when HTML standards change or are updated. At the time of writing, both the major players in the game (Microsoft and Netscape) have released versions of their browser with support for Dynamic HTML. In this final chapter, we'll look at how each of them compares to the current proposals.

We also need to consider the issue of compatibility between these two browsers, not only how they compare in support for Dynamic HTML, but also how compatible they are with existing standards as well. Unless you are working in the confined environment of an Intranet, where you can control which browser is used and which pages are available for viewing, you must consider how you go about supporting existing pages out there on the Internet as a whole.

So, this chapter will cover:

    The outline proposals for Project Cougar (or Dynamic HTML as it has become known)

    The compatibility of the two main browsers with the proposals, and with each other

    The compatibility of the two new browsers with existing pages

    How we can create pages that are compatible with both of the new browsers

We'll start with a look at what W3C are currently discussing as the new version of HTML.

Project Cougar - HTML for the Future

Some would say that HTML standards are a mess. Different browsers support different feature sets, and we still await the final ratification of the most recently agreed standard—HTML 3.2. However, W3C have a huge task to accomplish, and progress in the software industry doesn't take time off to wait for them. As fast as W3C agree on new standards for one generation of HTML, the mainline manufacturers bring out new browsers with even more new and product-specific features.

However, none of this is the reason for the upheaval Project Cougar (or HTML 4.0) will bring to the whole game. The problem is that in other areas of development, such as word processing, document management, presentation systems and desktop publishing, the ability to produce ever more complex and dynamic results means that the Web browser is being left behind. On top of this, as we saw in Chapter 7, the Web browser is fast becoming a tool for running application interfaces for Web-based client/server programs—a task that sorely stretches its current abilities to provide a visually appealing and interactive front end for this kind of task.

The Evolution of HTML Standards

Of course, the explosive growth in the use of the Internet for all kinds of activities has taken most people by surprise. Because the fundamental way that HTML and the Web work hasn't really changed since the introduction of HTML, the web page is still constructed with a very basic structure. Essentially, the HTML source and any other content is flowed into a single column window—although it is possible to control the position of elements to some extent through the use of alignment attributes, tables and relative spacing between elements. In more complex pages, the window may be divided up into frames, but each of these is, again, just a simple single-column page.

As we explained in Chapter 1, the way that the HTML tags and attributes actually define the elements of this single-column page is laid down in a series of Document Type Definitions (DTD), written using a language called Standard Generalized Markup Language (SGML). These lay down the syntax requirements and provide browser manufacturers with a detailed guide to how the elements should behave. As we've seen, however, it's often the browser manufacturers who add the tag to their products first, leaving W3C to decide if, and how, to adopt it as part of the HTML standards.

The Traditional Structure of the Document

The inclusion of scripting in the browser also produces a new set of compatibility problems. As long as the appearance of the page is mainly due to the elements it contains, the browser just has to accept them in the HTML stream coming from the server and render them visibly on screen. Provided that everything is in the right place, in theory at least, you've done the job.

228

All this falls apart when you add programmability to the browser, where scripts written in the page—or within an external plug-in component—can access the page elements and change their contents. To do this, the browser has to organize the elements into a structural hierarchy that provides the scripting language with clearly defined access to them. And for pages to be compatible between different browsers, they must all implement this structure in exactly the same way.

W3C refers to this structure as the **Document Object Model**, though—as you've seen in this book—this isn't the whole story. The browser will actually implement an object model which contains another layer of objects 'above' the document itself, the window object and associated objects and collections (or object arrays). These allow the script to access the browser itself, as well as the document(s) it is displaying. Project Cougar aims to define the Document Object Model as well as the tags and attributes that are available.

> *The current documentation, proposals and working drafts for Project Cougar and HTML 4.0 are available from the W3C web site at*
> **http://www.w3.org/pub/www/TR**. *At the time this book was being written, the first working draft of HTML 4.0 had just been released. The manufacturers who are listed as part of the Cougar development team are Adobe, Hewlett Packard, IBM, Microsoft, Netscape Communications, Novell, SoftQuad and Sun Microsystems.*

Project Cougar in Outline

Back in Chapter 1, we listed the new features of Dynamic HTML that this book concentrated on. They were:

 All the elements in the page **(tags, images, text, etc.) are now accessible to scripts written in the page**

 An extension to the implementation of **styles and style sheets** that provides more hooks to the page elements from scripting code

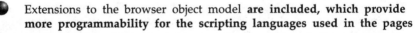 Extensions to the browser object model **are included, which provide more programmability for the scripting languages used in the pages**

 Absolute positioning of elements, including control of the z-order, **allows a desktop publishing style of authoring, and 'two-and-a-half-D' appearance**

 Dynamic re-drawing **of any or all parts of the page allows changes to a loaded page to be made visible. Pages no longer need to be reloaded to show the updated version**

New event-handling techniques **are supported, including the ability to bubble events up through the object hierarchy**

While these are part of a whole raft of the Project Cougar proposals, they are by no means the only new features. It's just that these are the ones that represent the real advances as far as the web page author is concerned. We'll go back a little, and see where the initial proposals for Cougar came from.

The Background to Project Cougar

The main motivation behind the search for a new approach to web page design is the problem of keeping up with both the changing methods of document production and the continual evolution of document appearance. The challenge is to provide a language that can produce these ever more complex and dynamic pages, while maintaining backward compatibility with existing HTML standards.

All the changes to HTML are controlled by the **HTML Working Group** at W3C. This is made up of the leading software and hardware manufacturers in the industry, and individuals who have helped to develop the technology of the Web so far. Their target is to provide a language that supports:

 Interactive Documents and Rich Forms

 Dynamic Pages Driven by Script Code

 More Flexible Frames and Subsidiary Windows

 Better Multimedia Object Handling

Improved Access for People with Disabilities

We've seen how many of these aims are being met in earlier chapters. The complete proposal will also go on to tackle tasks such as:

 Support for different fonts and other internationalization issues

 Security in scripts through digital signatures

 An improved mechanism for providing information about the page to both web search engines and 'viewing control programs' that monitor pages for the type of content

The New Document Object Model

The current 'work in progress' documentation describes the overall structure of a document object model that is language neutral and platform independent. It includes the proposal that *all* elements, their attributes, their style properties and their contents will be:

Part of a defined object structure within the user agent (i.e. the browser). This will include 'implied' elements, such as `<HTML>`, `<HEAD>` and `<BODY>`

Accessible from within the document by scripting code embedded there, and by external agents (such as components, plug-ins, or embedded controls)

Able to generate events that bubble up through the document structure

In essence, these three statements describe the kinds of things we've been looking at throughout the book. It's clear that either the browser manufacturers have worked quickly to implement the proposals, or that (and of course this is the most likely) the proposals were drawn up based on original developments by the browser manufacturers themselves. Whichever is the case, the outline drafts of the project already provide a good guide to what the language will have to offer in the long term.

Browser Compatibility with Cougar

As we've suggested earlier, the two mainline browsers aren't completely in line with all the current proposals being discussed as part of Project Cougar. This isn't surprising, as the proposals themselves are open to change—W3C describes them as 'work in progress'. In particular, the current release of Netscape Communicator (4.0) suffers from being first to market. The range of tags it supports is quite different from those described in the working drafts of HTML 4.0. However, Netscape have assured the industry that they will be adopting the recommendations as soon as they are ratified.

Microsoft's Internet Explorer 4 is, in many ways, a much more wide-ranging project than Netscape has taken on with Communicator. It aims to link directly into the core of the Windows operating system to provide a seamless Web/Internet/Desktop environment. This will of course mean that the Active Desktop features of Internet Explorer will be locked into the Windows operating system. Communicator, on the other hand, has always been available for a wide range of platforms—including Unix and its derivatives. Unix is still at the heart of the Internet as a whole, so cross-platform compatibility remains very high on their agenda.

So, it's possible that everything could change in the months to come, as the standard gets closer to ratification. In the meantime, it means that you, the web page author, need to be aware of which way the HTML ship is sailing, and how close each browser is likely to be to its destination port.

Internet Explorer 4

In this book, we've based our exploration of Dynamic HTML on Microsoft's browser, Internet Explorer 4 (IE4). It provides support for almost the entire set of current Project Cougar Document Object Model proposals. This isn't to say that the final specification of Project Cougar will use the same object model, properties, methods and events as Internet Explorer—but there is a strong case to be made that IE4 is the more compatible of the two contenders at the moment. However, we'll compare the two browsers by feature, where possible.

First, we'll look at the new features of IE4 in relation to Project Cougar and HTML 4.0 as it stands today. As you've seen, IE4 provides the conditions necessary for the three main requirements—a defined object structure accessible from VBScript and JavaScript (and other scripting languages that may become available), access to all the elements in the page and event bubbling throughout the object hierarchy.

Structure Navigation, Document and Content Manipulation

IE4 contains methods and properties that meet the requirements that have been laid down for structure navigation and document and content manipulation. Each element has a **parentElement** property, and the object model provides a collection (or array) named **all**—as well as the usual **images**, **links**, **anchors**, **forms**, **elements** and so on. It also provides a **contains** method for each element, enabling script to track which elements are contained within others.

New methods such as **innerText** and **outerText** allow script to access, determine and change any of the contents of the document—including the HTML source—without it having to be within a separate container such as a **<DIV>**. Properties of any element can be accessed and changed using the **getAttribute**, **setAttribute** and **removeAttribute** methods. In certain cases, new elements can be created and existing ones removed.

IE4 can retrieve the contents of the current user's selection in the document using the new **Selection** object, and provide a range of properties—including the selection type and content—and can also search for text within the page.

The Event Model

IE4 provides a rich selection of events for all objects, with a raft of new events. All visible elements provide at least a subset of these. For example, even simple text tags like **<H1>** and **<B>** support the **onclick** and **ondblclick** events, plus a full range of mouse events.

On top of this, the event model allows events to bubble up through the object hierarchy by default, and a new **Event** object provides global access to extra parameters of each event—allowing control of this event bubbling.

Styles and Style Sheet Object Model Support

IE4 supports the CSS1 cascading style sheet standards in general. It also implements an internal **style** object for each element—as required by Project Cougar. This provides script code with access to the style properties for all the elements in the page, and the ability to change them as required. However, IE4 doesn't support the full range of style properties that CSS1 currently includes, such as **white-space**. A full list of IE4 CSS1 omissions can be found at the end of section C.

The major advantages of Dynamic HTML, which we've been learning about and developing with in this book, are based on the support for a style sheet object model. This includes absolute and relative positioning, control of the z-order, and the ability to move objects around on the page. IE4 appears to fully support the Project Cougar recommendations in this area. However, there are also proposed additions to the existing style sheet standards, which will allow frames to be created in a document and content to be piped to different frames. Currently this is done using a **<FRAMESET>** and by loading different pages into each frame. Using the new method, a single page will be able to create the frames and divide its content between them. This is not supported in IE4 or Communicator at present.

232

Finally, IE4 also provides support for the two tags, `<SPAN>` and `<DIV>`, in a way that is compatible with the current proposals.

Document and Error Information

The requirement to expose information about the document, its embedded objects, the user agent (browser) itself and any cookies is met in the same way in both IE4 and Netscape Communicator 4. The existing parts of the **window** and **document** object model, plus the subsidiary objects and collections (or arrays), have been generally compatible over previous versions of the two browsers (especially in version 3) and can provide this information.

The document-wide error reporting and logging system required by Project Cougar is not fully implemented in IE4, though new objects within the object model now provide properties to indicate the status of various objects, and the scripting languages can provide an object that records and reports scripting errors.

Scripting Languages

One very important development in scripting languages, which occurred while this book was being written, was the adoption of JavaScript by ECMA (a European standards organization) as the standard ECMA scripting language. There is no standard for VBScript currently. It's noticeable that Microsoft has moved the emphasis in their own documentation and examples away from VBScript and much more towards JavaScript between platform preview releases 1 and 2. This isn't to say that Microsoft is planning to kill off VBScript, since it will undoubtedly still feature very heavily in server side applications. However, Microsoft has announced its strong commitment to supporting standards, and if there is to be one standard scripting language that, for compatibility, all vendors will have to support, it will be JavaScript. Consequently, Microsoft will have to give preference to JavaScript (or their own implementation of it, JScript).

> For more details on the ECMA standards please go to
> `http://www.ecma.ch.`

Also at present, IE4 doesn't support the new proposals for the `<SCRIPT>` tag, including the **SRC** and **TYPE** attributes. However, it does contain updated versions of the JScript (which is compatible with JavaScript 1.1) and VBScript languages.

Enhanced HTML Forms

One area we explored in detail in the previous chapter was the construction of forms in Dynamic HTML. The description and techniques we used there are based on the Project Cougar proposals for enhanced forms, and are either already either supported by, or under development in, IE4. There are also more intrinsic controls such as scroll bars, tabular entry fields and multiple page layouts.

The Future of the <OBJECT> Tag

In the previous chapter, we also previewed the proposed changes in HTML 4.0 that will make the <OBJECT> tag a generic tag for inserting all kinds of content into a web page. Internet Explorer introduced this tag with support for ActiveX controls, and Microsoft has continued to develop around it. Microsoft originally introduced <OBJECT> to provide a way to insert ActiveX controls into a web page, but it is also proposed as a generic tag to be used to insert any kind of object—including Java applets. For that reason, it supports the CODE attribute, so that the Java class file can be specified. In Netscape Communicator, this is still done using the <APPLET> tag because the <OBJECT> tag is not supported.

However, the W3C working discussion documents propose to go even further than that. They envisage the <OBJECT> tag being used to insert any kind of object, be it Java applets, ActiveX controls or other components, plug-ins, images, audio, video and rich-text formatted files, and embedded documents. In other words, the <OBJECT> tag is cited to supercede the <APPLET>, <EMBED> and <IMG> tags, and Microsoft's existing DYNASRC attribute. This will provide a single means of embedding a whole range of objects into web documents, and is designed to offer more universal, cross-platform support for our pages.

New Ways to Use the <OBJECT> Tag Attributes

In order to cope with all the different types of content, the CODETYPE and TYPE attributes of the <OBJECT> tag are used to indicate the type of data that the object comprises. TYPE is a string description of the content, such as application/java-vm for a Java applet requiring a virtual machine to run, or application/avi for an AVI file. In general terms, the application that is required is defined by application/<document_type>. The CODETYPE argument can be a standard mime type, in much the same way as the TYPE attribute.

The DATA attribute provides the data for the object, either as a URL from where it can be downloaded, or in-line as a string of values. This is much the same way as ActiveX controls work at present. As an example, this code will display an AVI file named MyVideo.avi. If the browser can't support the object, it will display the text My Video:

```
<OBJECT DATA="http://mysite.com/video/MyVideo.avi" TYPE="application/avi"
ALT="My Video">
</OBJECT>
```

Here's an example that embeds a local Microsoft Word document into the page. When activated, Word will be used to allow it to be edited:

```
<OBJECT DATA="BankLetter.doc" TYPE="application/msword" ALT="Letter to the
bank">
</OBJECT>
```

A list of the mime types supported by your machine can be found in the Windows registry under
HKEY_CLASSES_ROOT\MIME\Database\ContentType\.

If the data content is reasonably small, the object can be defined by including the data itself in the <OBJECT> tag. This is called an in-line definition:

```
<OBJECT CLASSID="clsid:663CA835-1E82-3BB2-4112-66FF428C18E3"
   DATA="data:application/x-oleobject;3300,FF00,2756,E5A0,E3A0,22F6, ... etc">
</OBJECT>
```

As you can see from the last example, the **TYPE** and **CODETYPE** attributes are optional. However, in this case, the only way that the browser can be sure of knowing if it can handle the file is by downloading it first—not all files can be uniquely identified from, say, a file extension, and not all systems use file extensions anyway. By including the **TYPE** or **CODETYPE** attribute, we can tell the browser exactly what type of file it is. Then, if the browser can't handle it, it won't waste time and bandwidth downloading it.

Fall Back in Browsers That Don't Support an Object

If the browser can't display the object, it will usually provide some text alternative—as defined either by the **ALT** or **STANDBY** attributes of the <OBJECT> tag. However, we can do better than this. We can include text and other elements that are only visible on browsers that either don't recognize the <OBJECT> tag, or that can't handle the content type of the data it specifies. This is done by placing it between the opening and closing <OBJECT> tags, and outside any parameter tags:

```
<OBJECT DATA="http://mysite.com/video/MyVideo.avi" TYPE="application/avi"
ALT="My Video">
   Sorry, your browser can't support video files, you should upgrade.
</OBJECT>
```

We can also use other elements here, perhaps a still image as a `gif` file:

```
<OBJECT DATA="http://mysite.com/video/MyVideo.avi" TYPE="application/avi"
ALT="My Video">
   <IMG SRC="http://mysite.com/stills/MyPicture.gif">
</OBJECT>
```

Inserting Images with an <OBJECT> Tag

One of the most intriguing proposals is for the use of the <OBJECT> tag as a means to embed ordinary graphics files, such as `gif` and `jpg` files. This is also likely to extend the kinds of graphic files that are supported, possibly to include Windows `bmp` files and `wmf` or other graphics meta files. In its most basic form the use is simple:

```
<OBJECT DATA="MyPicture.gif">
</OBJECT>
```

The **DATA** attribute works just like the **SRC** attribute, but can also accept in-line data where the image is small. This can reduce the time needed to view a page, by reducing the number of server connections required.

```
<OBJECT TYPE="image/jpeg"
   DATA="data:image/jpeg;3300,FF00,2756,E5A0,E3A0,22F6, ... etc">
</OBJECT>
```

235

And finally, by adding the usual **WIDTH, HEIGHT, ALT** and **ALIGN** attributes, we have a system that can emulate all the usual **<IMG>** attributes:

```
<OBJECT DATA="MyDog.gif" WIDTH=120 HEIGHT=100 ALIGN=LEFT ALT="A picture of my
dog">
</OBJECT>
```

There are occasions, however, when we use an image to provide a set of clickable hot spots, such as in a graphical menu. These are called image maps, and the **<OBJECT>** tag will provide these as well.

Server-side Image Maps

If we include the **SHAPES** attribute in the opening **<OBJECT>** tag any **<A>** tags between this and the closing **<OBJECT>** tag which themselves contain the **SHAPE** attribute, are considered to be definitions of hot-spots in the image. In Dynamic HTML-terminology, these are called areas—all image maps expose this set of areas through their **areas** collections.

If the **<A>** tag contains the attribute **ISMAP**, with the **SHAPE** definition of **DEFAULT**, the browser will access the URL in the **<A>** tag and send it the x and y offsets of the mouse pointer within the image as parameters. These can be decoded at the server end in the usual way, and the appropriate page sent back to the browser:

```
<OBJECT TYPE="image/gif" DATA=MyMenu.gif SHAPES>
  <A HREF="/scripts/imagemap.pl" ISMAP SHAPE=DEFAULT> Click here </A>
</OBJECT>
```

Client-side Image Maps

Instead of a round trip to the server to find out which page to load, recent browsers have implemented client-side image maps. The **<OBJECT>** tag can create these as well, by simply adding the list of **<A>** tags inside the **<OBJECT>** tag:

```
<OBJECT TYPE="image/gif" DATA=MyMenu.gif SHAPES>
  <A HREF="page1.htm" SHAPE=RECT    COORDS=5,5,50,35> Page 1</A>
  <A HREF="page2.htm" SHAPE=CIRCLE COORDS=25,50,50>  Page 2</A>
  <A HREF="page3.htm" SHAPE=POLY    COORDS=50,60,125,200,20,200>
     Page 3 </A>
</OBJECT>
```

However, if you are converting existing pages that contain client-side image maps, you may prefer to leave the existing **<MAP>** section intact and reference it separately. This too is possible with the **<OBJECT>** tag and a **USEMAP** attribute:

```
<OBJECT TYPE="image/gif" DATA=MyMenu.gif USEMAP="#MyMap">
</OBJECT>
  ...
  ...
<MAP NAME="MyMap">
  <AREA HREF="page1.htm" SHAPE=RECT
        COORDS=10,10,50,35 ALT="Page 1">
  <AREA HREF="page2.htm" SHAPE=CIRCLE
        COORDS=150,150,50  ALT="Page 2">
  <AREA HREF="page3.htm" SHAPE=POLY
        COORDS=40,60,125,200,20,200 ALT="Page 3">
</MAP>
```

*To learn more about client-side image maps, and other HTML 3.2 tags, look
out for* Instant HTML Programmers Reference, *ISBN 1-861000-76-6,
from Wrox Press.*

The Declare Attribute

The new proposals under discussion at the time of writing also suggest a new
attribute named **DECLARE**. This will allow the browser to download the object,
and embed a container for it in the page, but not actually instantiate it. In other
words, its own internal code will not start to run when downloading completes,
as is the case with objects at present. This means that you can download and
install objects on the users' systems, and set references to them in the page,
without allowing them to execute immediately.

Netscape Communicator 4

Having seen in outline how Internet Explorer 4 meets the current W3C
proposals for Project Cougar, let's compare the same feature list with Netscape's
new browser, Communicator 4 (NC4). We won't be attempting to explain the
features in full, because our aim is simply to indicate how close they come to
Project Cougar. However, at the end of this section, we'll look briefly at some
of the other new features of NC4.

Structure Navigation, Document and Content Manipulation

Netscape Communicator 4's current incarnation does not follow the working
drafts for HTML 4.0 as closely as Netscape would probably have preferred.
However, in most areas, it does provide much of the functionality that Project
Cougar is attempting to bring to the language.

The first thing to note is that NC4 doesn't attempt to provide access to *all* the
elements in the page. The element object arrays that were part of the previous
browser object model— such as **plugins**, **embeds**, **applets**, **forms**,
elements, etc—are still available through JavaScript, but there is no universal
array of all the element tags. The **tags** and **ids** arrays only provide access to
the styles that have been applied to individual elements. These arrays are not
'true' document object arrays either, in that they have no **length** property and
cannot be iterated through like the other element arrays.

The major new system for providing dynamic content is based on two new
tags, **<LAYER>** and **<ILAYER>**. These can be positioned (absolutely in the case
of the **<LAYER>** tag), moved, hidden, and their content and z-order changed,
while the main document is displayed in the browser. They also provide a
parent/child navigation system through special properties. However, few of the
other existing elements have these kinds of abilities. For example, it isn't
possible to absolutely position headings, images, or other block elements,
without placing them within a **<LAYER>** element.

NC4 can retrieve the contents of the current user's selection in the document, as
a simple string, using the **getSelection** method. It can search for text in the
page using the new **find** method. There is no system for changing the
displayed content outside a layer, although this is not generally a problem.

Layers are flexible enough to allow a page to be created where the contents can be changed dynamically by code running in the browser.

The Event Model

The Project Cougar proposals include the requirement for the browser to provide a rich selection of events for all objects, which can be bound to script code in order to allow the construction of completely interactive documents.

NC4 implements a new **Event** object that provides information about all the scriptable events that are occurring in the browser. Instead of providing event bubbling as the default, as discussed by W3C, Communicator implements a system called event capturing. The **document** or **window** can be instructed, with the **captureEvents** method, to capture events originally destined for a contained element. The event can then be handled or routed to the original element with a **routeEvent** method call. This system also allows events to be captured in other documents loaded into a **<FRAMESET>**, depending on the security settings in those documents.

Project Cougar specifies a 'rich set of events for all elements', and NC4 doesn't fully deliver at present. New events are available, but the range of elements to which they apply is very limited. For example, the new **mouse** and **key-press** events provide a lot of opportunity to make pages more reactive to the viewer. However, they are generally restricted to elements like the document, links, and in some cases images.

Styles and Style Sheet Object Model Support

Netscape were early adopters of styles and style sheets, and NC4 is documented as offering 'full support for the CSS1 standards'. This includes the recommendations for the new positioning properties and—once defined—the styles can be accessed using JavaScript to provide dynamic pages.

Netscape have also developed a separate style language called **JavaScript Style Sheets** (JSS), which uses the hyphen-less syntax for the style property names. This works in a similar way to the CSS methods we've seen in this book, but uses JavaScript methods to assign the styles to elements. It provides absolute positioning and access to the style properties of elements.

NC4 now contains a JavaScript **delete** method that can remove objects, properties or elements from the page. Finally, NC4 provides support for the two tags **<SPAN>** and **<DIV>**, in a way that is documented to be compatible with the current proposals. Remember, however, that the **<DIV>** tag in NC4 does not provide any events, and so is not compatible with IE4 dynamic pages that uses events generated from a **<DIV>** tag.

Document and Error Information

The Project Cougar proposals require the browser to expose information about the document, its embedded objects, the user agent (browser) itself and any cookies available for the current document. This is done using the window and document objects, plus their subsidiary objects (such as **navigator**), and the various arrays of contained objects (such as **images**, **links**, **forms**, etc.).

Project Cougar also requires a document-wide error reporting and logging system to be in place. Through JavaScript, NC4 provides an **onerror** event for images and the script in the page. There is no indication of how it will support other document-based errors at present.

Scripting Languages

The Project Cougar Scripting proposals include the requirement for support of the **SRC** and **TYPE** attributes in a **<SCRIPT>** tag, allowing a script to be downloaded separately from the initial document.

NC4 implements an interpreter for JavaScript, and the **<SCRIPT>** tag supports the **SRC** attribute in order to allow signed (secure) scripts to be imported into a page. Although, this is not completely in line with current Project Cougar proposals, although it is closer than Internet Explorer 4 at present.

Changes are also proposed in the HTML 4.0 working drafts to replace the **LANGUAGE** attribute with **TYPE**, i.e. **TYPE="script/javascript"**. This is not supported at present.

Enhanced HTML Forms

Project Cougar, and the HTML 4.0 working draft, talk about providing better access to elements on a form. This is with new attributes such as **DISABLED**, **READONLY**, **ACCESSKEY** and **TABINDEX**. There are also new tags proposed— **<BUTTON>**, **<FIELDSET>**, **<LEGEND>** and **<LABEL>**. There are even indications of future direction in the provision of more intrinsic controls such as scroll bars, tabular entry fields and multiple page layouts.

In Communicator version 4.0, there is no support for these enhanced HTML forms. As enhanced forms were originally a Microsoft proposal, it's perhaps not surprising that this feature is yet to be implemented in NC4. It's likely that there will be some considerable changes to the working drafts in this area before final ratification.

Communicator and the <OBJECT> Tag

Communicator does not support the **<OBJECT>** tag at present, despite rumors circulating during its development. In general, executable objects are inserted using an **<APPLET>** tag, and embedded documents and other files with an **<EMBED>** tag. The proposals for HTML 4.0 suggest that both these tags will disappear, to be replaced with **<OBJECT>**. In fact, even the **<IMG>** tag is destined to be replaced by extensions to the **<OBJECT>** tag, as mentioned earlier.

New Features in Netscape Communicator

The new document-oriented features in NC4 do provide the web page author with some interesting new possibilities, although not fully in line with the current scope of Project Cougar. One of the biggest changes is a new system of creating layers in a page, and placing elements and scripts into each layer. The layers can even be separate pages, loaded from the server. They are created with the new `<LAYER>` and `<ILAYER>` tags, which also provide positioning and z-order control and respond to a limited range of events.

The `<LAYER>` tag behaves like an element with a **position** style of **absolute**, while `<ILAYER>` (short for in-line layer) behaves like an element with a **position** style setting of **relative**. By moving and resizing the layers, in a way similar to the method we demonstrated with a `<DIV>` document division in earlier chapters, a dynamic page can be created.

In NC4, you can now take advantage of a 'proper' in-built timer, that doesn't need to be reset after each **timeOut** event. The new **setInterval** and **clearInterval** methods of the **window** object start and stop a repeating internal timer.

NC4 also adds methods to print the contents of the page, and—like IE4—now includes an object that provides information about the user's display capabilities, the **screen** object. Finally, NC4 offers a feature known as Dynamic Fonts, which allows the web page author to take advantage of different fonts in any document, by explicitly providing a link to the 'new' fonts it uses. This allows the author to get away from the Courier, Arial and Times Roman fonts that give all current HTML pages a 'samey' feel.

> *For a full list of the new features in Netscape Communicator 4, visit their web site at:* `http://developer.netscape.com/library`. *If you want to know more about Netscape Communicator 4's version of Dynamic HTML then look out for the companion book to this one:*
>
> Instant Netscape Dynamic HTML Programmer's Reference, NC4 edition *ISBN 1-861001-193*

Backward Compatibility Issues

Just because a new version of HTML is starting to appear, and new browsers are available to support it, doesn't mean that everyone will be rewriting their site just to take advantage of this. All software (and hardware for that matter) has to cope with issues of backward compatibility.

This is an issue that is perhaps more important on the Web than in most other situations. The geographical and technical spread of the source documents, and the already confusing mixture of HTML versions and browser-specific language extensions in use, means that any new browser must make every effort to support a huge range of tags and attributes.

It also needs to be forgiving, and to be able to cope with pages that may not follow the exact syntactical rules of HTML wherever possible (such as missing `</BODY>` tags, for example), as well as those containing tags it can't handle or simply doesn't recognize.

Microsoft Internet Explorer 4

Microsoft have made sure that Internet Explorer 4 will support all existing pages designed for earlier versions of Internet Explorer. However, they have also 'extended the olive branch' to some extent, by adding features which provide more support for old Navigator-specific pages.

Internet Explorer with Old IE Pages

Internet Explorer 4 supports all the existing tags and attributes from earlier versions of this browser, such as the `<MARQUEE>` tag, and the `DYNASRC` image attribute. This is despite the fact that these will be superceded by the ability of Dynamic HTML to create the same kinds of effects with the core language and the extensions proposed to the `<OBJECT>` tag.

Internet Explorer 4 also brings with it new versions of JScript and VBScript. These are fully compatible with earlier versions of the interpreter, and existing scripts will still work without being changed. However, if pages take advantage of the new features of these languages, while running on the older version, errors will occur. Unlike NC4, IE4 doesn't support the scripting version number as part of the `LANGUAGE` attribute. However, it does provide the new `ScriptEngine`, `ScriptEngineMajorVersion`, `ScriptEngineMinorVersion` and `ScriptEngineBuildVersion` properties.

Internet Explorer with Old Navigator Pages

Microsoft have also added new tags, attributes and integral browser objects to make Internet Explorer 4 more able to handle pages that were aimed at Netscape Navigator 3 and earlier. These are not part of the proposals for Dynamic HTML, but are included simply to widen the browser's appeal, and allow it to do a better job with sites that pronounce themselves Designed for Netscape Navigator.

These additions include new collections of **applets**, **embeds** and **plugins**, and support for a wider range of **ALIGN** attribute values and named colors. In general, pages aimed at Navigator should display more intelligently in Internet Explorer 4 than in previous versions of Internet Explorer.

VBScript vs VBScript3

Internet Explorer 4 uses the latest version of VBScript, called rather uninspiringly VBScript3, and which was originally part of Microsoft's Active Server Pages technology. Pages that use 'ordinary' VBScript will still run with the new VBScript3 interpreter, but the opposite is not true. However, unlike Netscape Communicator, it isn't possible to specify the language version in the `<SCRIPT>` tag. If you want to be sure that pages are compatible with older browsers, you need to avoid these new features of VBScript3:

 The formatting functions `FormatNumber`, `FormatCurrency`, `FormatPercent` and `FormatDateTime`

 The time and date functions `DateAdd`, `DateDiff`, `DatePart`, `MonthName`, `WeekdayName`

241

The string handling functions **Filter**, **Join**, **Replace**, **Split**, **StrComp** and **StrReverse**

 The named constants, such as **vbYes** and **vbExclamation**

 The mathematical function **Round**

Netscape Communicator 4

Just as Microsoft have made it a priority to support all existing Internet Explorer pages, Netscape's new browser, Communicator 4, is designed to be fully compatible with pages designed for all earlier versions of the Navigator browser. As you'd expect, all the tags and attributes from Navigator 3 and earlier are fully supported and handled in a way that produces the same effect.

Communicator with Old Navigator Pages

Although Communicator 4 contains some changes to the core JavaScript scripting language, these have cleverly been hidden from existing pages. When **LANGUAGE="JavaScript1.2"** is included in the **<SCRIPT>** tag, the browser 'turns on' the new features in the JavaScript interpreter. With any other **LANGUAGE** attribute they are not activated, so existing scripts will work without being changed. Likewise, you can specify **"JavaScript1.1"** or **"JavaScript1.0"** if scripts are written to a particular version of JavaScript.

Communicator with Old Internet Explorer Pages

However, Netscape have made no move towards supporting the features that Microsoft added to version 3 of their browser. Up until then, Microsoft were playing a catch-up game with Navigator, as well as adding their own proprietary tags and attributes. This diversity has been only too clear in the number of sites that display messages such as Designed for Netscape Navigator or Best viewed with Internet Explorer.

In particular, Netscape have not added support for things like the **<MARQUEE>** tag, the **DYNASRC** image attribute, or ActiveX controls. Even VBScript still requires a separate plug-in to work in Communicator. And Communicator still handles Java Applets using the LiveConnect mechanism, while Internet Explorer wraps them up in an ActiveX/COM interface.

Pages that Work in All Older Browsers

Of course, compatibility issues become even more of a headache if we have to support a range of older browsers. In this case, we can create pages that only use the new features of Dynamic HTML for non-core tasks and effects.

For example, we can create a form that uses the integral HTML controls and works in older browsers; then add extra effects using Dynamic HTML-specific **STYLE** attributes and event code to react to the events that are supported in newer browsers. In an old browser, these new style properties will not be recognized or applied, and the new events will not be fired. However, the page will behave well on most systems.

In general, we can always add **STYLE** and other new attributes to existing tags, and handlers for events that might not be available, without upsetting the older browser. The problem is that there is only so much 'decorative' work you can do in a page without affecting the usability. By trying to maintain backward compatibility, even to the version 3 browsers, all the real advantages of Dynamic HTML must be abandoned.

Creating Compatible Sites and Pages

As you'll have gathered from the previous discussions, we have some difficulties to face if we need to build a web page, or a complete web site, which performs properly for all our visitors. It's pretty obvious that anything designed specifically for a browser that supports Dynamic HTML is not going to look good on an earlier browser unless we go to some lengths to make this happen—it's never going to be an automatic process.

So, let's consider the issues we have to face. At the moment, we could aim to produce pages that:

 Are specific to one Dynamic HTML browser, either Internet Explorer 4 or Netscape Communicator 4.

 Are designed to produce a similar output on both Dynamic HTML browsers.

 Work on Dynamic HTML browsers, but still work on version 3 browsers as well.

Look OK on all kinds of browsers, on any platform.

Of these options, of course, only the first two make sense when using the new features of Dynamic HTML. At the end of the day, the only real answer is to maintain at least two different versions of your complete web site. An alternative is have one site with different sections for the areas where you want to exploit the features offered by Dynamic HTML.

Maintaining Separate Sets of Pages

Maintaining two separate sets of pages for a site seems a crazy idea, though it is done already where sites still need to support very old browser, or specialist, text-only browsers, or those designed for people with disabilities. How much extra effort this involves is hard to say, and depends on the size and complexity of the site. Perhaps only a section of it needs to be duplicated, anyway.

Of course, it's safe to assume that in time the majority of visitors will be using the new browsers. You may even make a decision to build a new copy of your site using Dynamic HTML to full effect and abandon development of the existing site, or a section of its pages.

Navigating by Browser Type

To be able to offer separate sites, depending on the browser version, means that we must be able to differentiate between the browsers when they hit our index or 'welcome' page. We could offer the two separate sets of pages as different choices on the main menu, but this can produce a negative effect. People with old browsers may feel like second-class citizens and may still select the new pages anyway. Instead, we need to make the choice for them in the background. There are different ways of doing this; we'll show you some examples.

Redirecting Visitors Automatically

The easiest way to automatically load a different page, depending on the browser that is accessing our site, is to create a **redirector page**. It is loaded as the default page for the whole site, and uses the different properties or capabilities of each browser to load another page. This second page will be the home page, or index, of the set of pages appropriate for that browser.

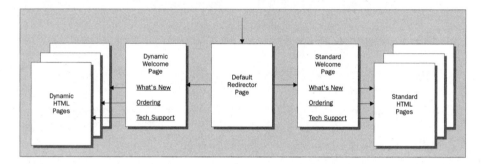

The default redirector page appears as a blank document, and the code in it loads the appropriate home page, a menu for a set of other pages or a single page that is browser specific. All the viewer sees is the browser window clearing, followed by the new page loading.

We could include a welcome message, and even a logo or graphic. However, this slows down loading of the page, and—depending on how we load the next page—may disappear again as soon as it's finished loading. Visitors might not get time to read it. Instead, we can give the redirector page a `<TITLE>` of Loading, please wait, which is displayed in the title bar while the next page loads.

Redirection with a META HTTP-EQUIV Tag

One of the most reliable ways to redirect the user is to include a **meta-refresh instruction** in the `<HEAD>` section of the page. This tells the browser to fetch a different page, and we can specify a delay before it does so:

```
<HTML>
<HEAD>
   <TITLE> Loading, please wait </TITLE>
   <META HTTP-EQUIV=REFRESH CONTENT="2;URL=http://mysite.com/std_menu.htm">
</HEAD>
```

```
<BODY>
</BODY>
</HTML>
```

This waits 2 seconds (the first part of the **CONTENT** attribute), then loads the URL specified. However, this will always load the *same* new page. We want to be able to load a different page if the browser can support it. This is done by adding some script that redirects the browser before the 2 second delay has expired:

```
...
<BODY>
<SCRIPT LANGUAGE=VBSCRIPT>
  location.href="http://www.mysite.com/vbs_menu.htm"
</SCRIPT>
</BODY>
...
```

Now, the browser will load the page **vbs_menu.htm** if the browser supports VBScript, or wait 2 seconds and load **std_menu.htm** if it doesn't. This doesn't really help, though, because lots of browsers support JavaScript—including the older ones. If we have a special menu page for Netscape Communicator, we can take advantage of the way the **<SCRIPT>** tag in Communicator can identify the language version:

```
...
<BODY>
  <SCRIPT LANGUAGE="JavaScript1.2">
    location.href = "http://www.mysite.com/nc4_menu.htm";
  </SCRIPT>
  <SCRIPT LANGUAGE=VBSCRIPT>
    location.href = "http://www.mysite.com/vbs_menu.htm"
  </SCRIPT>
  <SCRIPT LANGUAGE=JAVASCRIPT>
    location.href = "http://www.mysite.com/js_menu.htm";
  </SCRIPT>
</BODY>
...
```

This loads the page **nc4_menu.htm** only if the browser can execute JavaScipt version 1.2. Other browsers will then get **vbs_menu.htm** if they support VBScript or just get **js_menu.htm** if they support JavaScript in any form. Finally, if they support none of these, they will get **std_menu.htm** (via the **HTTP-EQUIV** tag). Notice that we place the JavaScript 1.2 section before the 'vanilla' JavaScript section, so that it will execute first if the browser supports it. Note that, as IE is designed to be script compatible with Javascript 1.2, this may change in future.

There is one problem that arises and that is when redirecting using VBScript, we can't detect which version of the browser it is just from this. Both IE3 and IE4 support the 'vanilla' VBScript. To get round this, we need to use some other properties of the browser.

Redirection Using the Browser's Properties

All browsers that support scripting should make available one or more properties that contain the name and version of the browser. These will generally be properties of the **navigator** object:

245

Property	Description
appCodeName	The code name of the browser.
appName	The product name of the browser.
appVersion	The version of the browser.
userAgent	The user-agent (browser name) header sent as part of the HTTP protocol.

If we use the **appName** and **appVersion** properties, we can easily identify the manufacturer and the actual version number string. This code will display both in an **alert** dialog:

```
...
<SCRIPT LANGUAGE="JavaScript">
  alert(navigator.appName + ' : ' + navigator.appVersion)
</SCRIPT>
...
```

The results with Internet Explorer 3.01, Internet Explorer 4 and Communicator 4 are shown here:

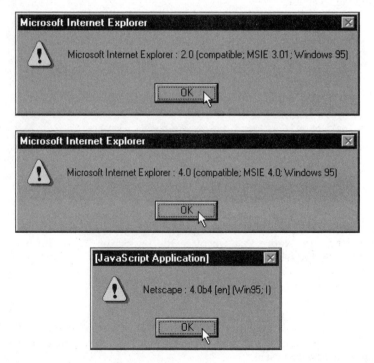

So, our code can read these properties, and decide what to do next. Here's an example—it's written in 'generic' JavaScript, so that it will work on any script-enabled browser. We've also used a **<NOSCRIPT>** tag to provide a message for users whose browser doesn't support scripting at all. They can click on the link we place in the page in this case, and it means that the page can still be used in browsers that don't support the **META HTTP-EQUIV** method either:

```
<HTML>
<HEAD>
<TITLE> Loading, please wait </TITLE>
<META HTTP-EQUIV=REFRESH CONTENT="2;URL=http://mysite.com/std_menu.htm">
</HEAD>
<BODY>
<SCRIPT LANGUAGE="JavaScript">

   // Get the manufacturer and version information
   manufacturer=navigator.appName
   version=navigator.appVersion;

   // Look for Communicator 4
   if (manufacturer.indexOf('Netscape')>=0 && version.indexOf('4.0')>=0)
     location.href='http://mysite.com/nc4_menu.htm';

   // Look for Internet Explorer 4
   if (manufacturer.indexOf('Microsoft')>=0 && version.indexOf('4.0')>=0)
     location.href='http://mysite.com/ie4_menu.htm';

   // Look for some version 3.0x browser
   if (version.indexOf('3.0')>=0)
     location.href='http://mysite.com/v3_menu.htm';

</SCRIPT>

<NOSCRIPT>
   Your browser doesn't support scripting. However, we do
   have a special area of our site for you to visit.
   <A HREF="http://mysite.com/std_menu.htm"> Click here to continue </A>
</NOSCRIPT>

</BODY>
</HTML>
```

You can see an example of automatic redirection, based on the browser version, by visiting the site `http://www.stonebroom.com`.

Cross-Browser Compatible Pages

Having seen how we can offer different pages for different browsers, let's move on to look at what is probably the major topic of concern as the two newest browsers are being developed. We've already seen that each browser is not fully compatible with pages written for the other, but we would like to be able to create Dynamic HTML pages that will work in both of them.

How easy this is depends on the complexity of the page, and the actual effects we are trying to achieve. We'll look at three general situations, static 2.5-D pages using style and font properties, pages that simply access the browser object model in script, and pages that use more complex mixtures of scripting and event handling techniques.

Compatible Style and Font Properties

One of the simplest pages we looked at back in Chapter 3 used the new absolute positioning properties of Dynamic HTML Cascading Style Sheets, in conjunction with some font style properties, to create a simple 3-D title. Loading it into Netscape Communicator as it stands doesn't look very encouraging at first:

247

Obviously, we have lost the font family and font size properties somewhere. Here's the original code for the page:

```
<HTML>
<HEAD><TITLE> Cheating with 3D Title </TITLE></HEAD>

<STYLE>
  P { font-family:"Impact, sans-serif"; font-size:96; color:red }
  P.highlight { color:silver }
  P.shadow { color:darkred }
</STYLE>

<BODY BGCOLOR=408080>

<DIV STYLE="position:absolute; top:5; left:5; width:600; height:100;
margin:10">
<P CLASS=shadow>Wrox Press</P>
</DIV>

<DIV STYLE="position:absolute; top:0; left:0; width:600; height:100;
margin:10">
<P CLASS=highlight>Wrox Press</P>
</DIV>

<DIV STYLE="position:absolute; top:2; left:2; width:600; height:100;
margin:10">
<P>Wrox Press</P>
</DIV>

</BODY>
</HTML>
```

Managing Incompatible Style Property Names

We know that Communicator supports the `<DIV>` tag, and absolute positioning of the divisions. This much is obvious from the screen shot. It also recognizes the color property for the font. The problem is those two hyphenated style properties, `font-family` and `font-size`.

The other thing we need to change is the way the multiple fonts are defined. Netscape requires each one to be in quotation marks separately. So we need the `<STYLE>` tag to be:

```
P { fontfamily:"Impact", "sans-serif"; fontsize:96; color:red }
```

248

The problem now is that Internet Explorer won't recognize the font family and size properties. However, browsers will ignore style properties that they don't support, so we can make our page work on both browsers by including both sets of styles. Here, we've separated the original P definition into three separate ones. The first works for both browsers, and sets the font color. The next one applies the properties appropriate to Communicator, and the one after that the properties appropriate for Internet Explorer:

```
<STYLE>
    P { color:red }
    P { fontfamily:"Impact", "sans-serif"; fontsize:96 }
    P { font-family:"Impact, sans-serif"; font-size:96 }
    P.highlight { color:silver }
    P.shadow { color:darkred }
</STYLE>
```

Now the page works fine on both browsers:

*Notice that placing the different browser-specific properties all in the **same** definition does not work. You need to split them into separate definitions, even though they are applied to the same element type.*

Accessing the Browser Object Model

In Chapter 3, we used a simple page to demonstrate some of the properties that are available from the browser's **location**, **history**, **navigator** and **visual** objects. It worked by creating the complete HTML for the table and the contents in a string variable, then using the **write** method of the **document** object to display it. The page also contained two buttons which, when clicked, used methods of the **history** object to load a different page.

Both of these tasks rely on a common object model, and in these areas the two browsers are reasonably compatible. They both provide the **document.write** and **history.go** methods, and (in the main) the same object properties to include in our table. So we can quite easily achieve a similar effect in Communicator, using JavaScript—in this example we have removed some of the properties originally included in the example in Chapter 3:

```
<SCRIPT LANGUAGE="JAVASCRIPT">

var strInfo = "<CENTER><TABLE WIDTH=100%>" +
             "<TR><TD>[window.] location.href</TD>\n" +
             "<TD><B>" + window.location.href + "</TD></TR>\n" +
             "<TR><TD>[window.] history.length</TD>\n" +
             "<TD><B>" + window.history.length + "</TD></TR>\n" +
             "<TR><TD>navigator.appCodeName</TD>\n" +
             "<TD><B>" + navigator.appCodeName + "</TD></TR>\n" +
             "<TR><TD>navigator.appName</TD>\n" +
             "<TD><B>" + navigator.appName + "</TD></TR>\n" +
             "<TR><TD>navigator.appVersion</TD>\n" +
             "<TD><B>" + navigator.appVersion + "</TD></TR>\n" +
             "<TR><TD>navigator.javaEnabled</TD>\n" +
             "<TD><B>" + navigator.javaEnabled() + "</TD></TR>\n" +
             "<TR><TD>navigator.userAgent</TD>\n" +
             "<TD><B>" + navigator.userAgent + "</TD></TR>\n" +
           "<TR><TD>screen.colorDepth</TD>\n" +
             "<TD><B>" + screen.colorDepth + "</TD></TR>\n" +
             "</TABLE></CENTER><P>\n";
document.write(strInfo);

function history_OnClick(dir, dirs) {
  var intPlaces;
  intPlaces = Math.floor((Math.random() * 3) + 1);
  alert("Trying to go " + dirs + " " + intPlaces + " places.");
  window.history.go(dir * intPlaces);
}

</SCRIPT>

<FORM>
  <INPUT TYPE=button VALUE="Go Back" NAME="cmdBack"
         onClick="history_OnClick(-1, 'back')">
  <INPUT TYPE=button VALUE="Go Forward" NAME="cmdForward"
         onClick="history_OnClick(1, 'forward')">
</FORM>
```

Managing Incompatible Browser Objects

When we open this page in Communicator, things at first appear to be fine—the next screenshot shows the results:

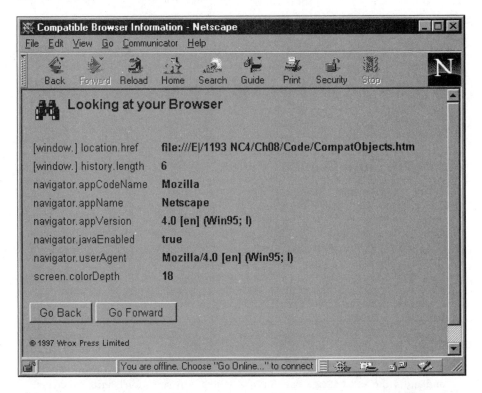

Of course, we've lost the style formatting of the text, because the STYLE properties we defined are Communicator-specific. However, the more worrying problem is in the last line in the table. It uses the **screen** object to retrieve the color depth setting. In Communicator, this is the number of colors used, but in Internet Explorer 4 this property returns the number of bits per pixel. Both the screenshots were taken with the system set to 256 colors, but Communicator returns **18** while Internet Explorer returns **8**. To return the 'bits per pixel' in Communicator, we need to refer to the **pixelDepth** property and not the **colorDepth** property.

To get round this, we can use the technique we saw earlier of examining the **navigator.appName** and **navigator.appVersion** to see which browser we're running under, then create the appropriate code in the string that defines the table. Here are the modifications to the code:

```
    . . .
    manufacturer = navigator.appName
    version = navigator.appVersion;
    if (manufacturer.indexOf('Netscape')>=0 && version.indexOf('4.0')>=0)
        tablerow = "<TR><TD>screen.pixelDepth</TD>\n" +
                   "<TD><B>" + screen.pixelDepth + "</TD></TR>\n";
```

```
    if (manufacturer.indexOf('Microsoft')>=0 && version.indexOf('4.0')>=0)
    tablerow = "<TR><TD>screen.colorDepth</TD>\n" +
               "<TD><B>" + screen.colorDepth + "</TD></TR>\n";
var strInfo = "<CENTER><TABLE WIDTH=100%>" +
               ...
               ...
               "<TD><B>" + navigator.userAgent + "</TD></TR>\n" +
               tablerow +
               "</TABLE></CENTER><P>\n";
document.write(strInfo);
    ...
```

Now, we get the correct answer, 8, under both browsers. You can load the finished page, **CompatObjects.htm**, from our web site at **http://rapid.wrox.co.uk/books/0685**, and view it in either Internet Explorer 4 or Netscape Communicator 4.

Managing More Complex Pages

When we have pages that are more complex than those you've seen so far in this chapter, we have to do a great deal more work to make them compatible with both Internet Explorer 4 and Netscape Communicator 4. We'll demonstrate some of the techniques available and offer you some tips on how you can adapt these to suit your own pages

In general, we can use a mixture of the techniques we've seen so far to create a page where parts of the content are either ignored by one of the browsers or an appropriate section of HTML code is generated dynamically as the page loads.

Coping with <LAYER> and <DIV> Compatibility

Communicator supports the **<LAYER>** tag to create dynamic document divisions and adds the **<NOLAYER>** tag for use when browsers don't support layers. Internet Explorer uses the **<DIV>** tag to create dynamic document divisions and doesn't recognize the **<LAYER>** or **<NOLAYER>** tags. However, Communicator also recognizes the **<DIV>** tag, though it doesn't behave quite the same way when we use events in our page.

So, if we need to create an area in the page that responds to mouse events, we have to use a **<LAYER>** tag in Communicator, and a **<DIV>** tag in Internet Explorer. The trick is to get the browser to react correctly in both cases.

By enclosing the **<DIV>** tags inside **<NOLAYER>** and **</NOLAYER>** tags, we prevent Communicator from seeing them, while Internet Explorer will—but it won't recognize the **<LAYER>** tags. We have to do this with the opening and closing **<DIV>** tags separately, however, so that the content of the layer/division is only included once.

```
<LAYER ... >        <- start of layer in NC4

   <NOLAYER>
     <DIV ... >      <- start of division in IE4
   </NOLAYER>

   Content          <- the contents of the layer or division
```

```
    <NOLAYER>
      </DIV>              <- end of division in IE4
    </NOLAYER>

  </LAYER>                <- end of layer in NC4
```

Here's the body section of our page, **CompatLayers.htm**. You can load this from our web site at **http://rapid.wrox.co.uk/books/0685**:

```
<LAYER NAME=MyLayer BGCOLOR="white" TOP=50 LEFT=50
ONMOUSEOVER="colorlayer('red')" ONMOUSEOUT="colorlayer('white')" >

  <NOLAYER>
    <DIV ID=MyDiv STYLE="position:absolute; top:50; left:50">
  </NOLAYER>

    <P>Wrox Press</P>

  <NOLAYER>
    </DIV>
  </NOLAYER>

  <SCRIPT LANGUAGE=JavaScript1.2>
    function colorlayer(changeto)
    { bgColor=changeto }
  </SCRIPT>
</LAYER>

<SCRIPT LANGUAGE=VBSCRIPT>
  Sub MyDiv_onmouseover()
    document.all.MyDiv.style.backgroundColor = "red"
  End Sub
  Sub MyDiv_onmouseout()
    document.all.MyDiv.style.backgroundColor = "white"
  End Sub
</SCRIPT>
```

In Communicator, we can include a script section inside a layer, and it then applies to that layer only. This is what we've done in the code above, using **LANGUAGE=JavaScript1.2** so that Internet Explorer won't see it. Outside the layer, we've placed a section of code that uses VBScript. The subroutines here are directly linked to the **<DIV>** element **MyDiv** through the event names and the **ID** of the element. Even if Communicator has a VBScript interpreter installed, it can't execute these routines because it can't see the division tag with the **ID** of **MyDiv**.

The result in both cases is that the area around the text changes color when the mouse pointer is moved over it. OK, so there are other ways of doing the same thing, but this serves to demonstrate the way we can use layers and document divisions to provide compatible pages.

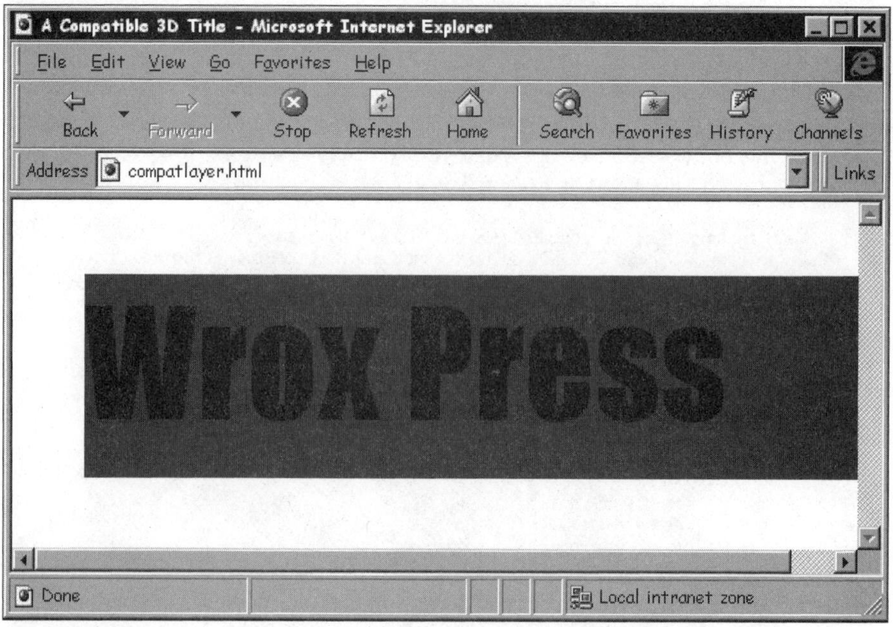
A Compatible 3D Title - Microsoft Internet Explorer
File Edit View Go Favorites Help
Back Forward Stop Refresh Home Search Favorites History Channels
Address compatlayer.html
Links
Wrox Press
Done
Local intranet zone

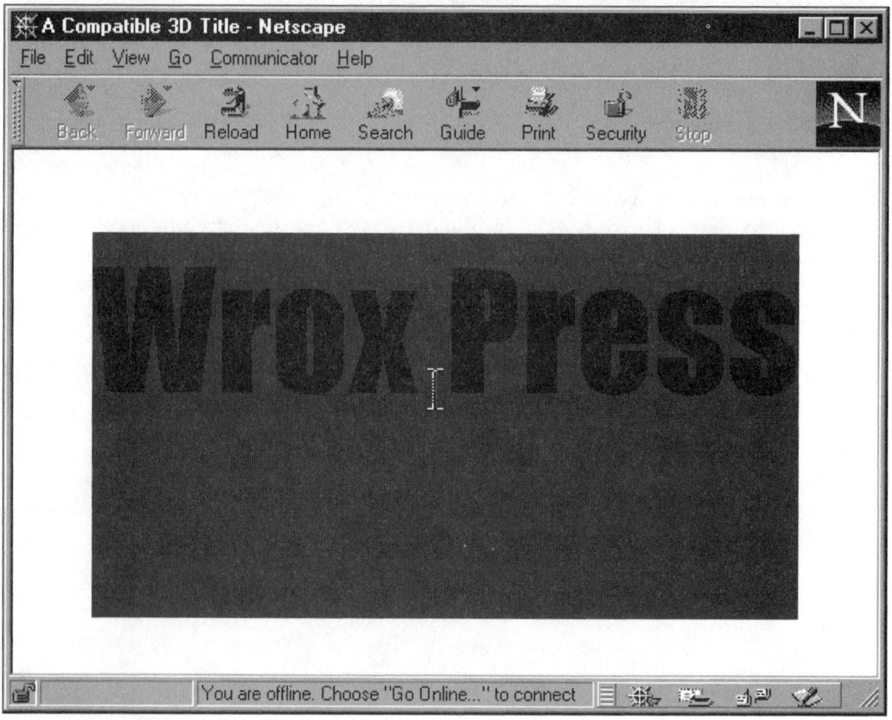
A Compatible 3D Title - Netscape
File Edit View Go Communicator Help
Back Forward Reload Home Search Guide Print Security Stop
Wrox Press
You are offline. Choose "Go Online..." to connect

Including Two Script Sections

As you've just seen again in the previous example, we can use the trick we saw earlier of creating two script sections in the page, only one of which is executed in either browser. This provides us with a way of writing content dynamically to the page. Here's a compatible version of the code for the keypress example we first used in Chapter 5. You can load it from our web site as `CompatKeys.htm`:

```
<HTML>
<HEAD>
<TITLE> A Compatible Keypress Page </TITLE>

<SCRIPT LANGUAGE="JavaScript1.2">
function stringify_event(e) {
    strMesg = "You pressed the " + String.fromCharCode(e.which) + " key, "
        + "which has an ASCII value of " + String(e.which);
    strMesg = strMesg + String.fromCharCode(10) + "while holding down the ";
    if (e.modifiers & Event.SHIFT_MASK)    strMesg = strMesg + "Shift key ";
    if (e.modifiers & Event.CONTROL_MASK)    strMesg = strMesg + "Ctrl key ";
    if (e.modifiers & Event.ALT_MASK)    strMesg = strMesg + "Alt key ";
    strMesg = strMesg + String.fromCharCode(10)
        + "The mouse pointer is at position " + "x = " + e.x + ", y = " + e.y;
    return strMesg;
}
function report_key1(e) {
    var strMesg = stringify_event(e);
    alert(strMesg);
}
document.onkeyup=report_key1;
</SCRIPT>

<SCRIPT LANGUAGE=VBSCRIPT>
Sub document_onkeypress()
    If InStr(navigator.appName, "Microsoft") Then
        strMesg = "You pressed the " & Chr(window.event.keyCode) & " key, " _
            & "which has an ASCII value of " & window.event.keyCode
        strMesg = strMesg & Chr(10) & "while holding down the "
        If window.event.shiftKey Then strMesg = strMesg & "Shift key "
        If window.event.ctrlKey Then strMesg = strMesg & "Ctrl key "
        If window.event.altKey Then strMesg = strMesg & "Alt key "
        strMesg = strMesg & Chr(10) & "The mouse pointer is at position " _
            & "x = " & window.event.x & ", y = " & window.event.y
        MsgBox strMesg, vbInformation, "The Event object parameters"
    End If
End Sub
</SCRIPT>

</HEAD>
<BODY >
    <H2>Press a key, holding down Shift, Ctrl, Alt if you like... </H2>
</BODY>
</HTML>
```

Notice that we have a script section that will only be executed when the browser supports JavaScript version 1.2 (i.e. Communicator), and a VBScript section that will be executed in Internet Explorer. The only catch is if Communicator has a VBScript interpreter plug-in installed. To prevent any problems in this case, we check that the browser is in fact a Microsoft product before we carry out the action in the **onkeypress** event handler.

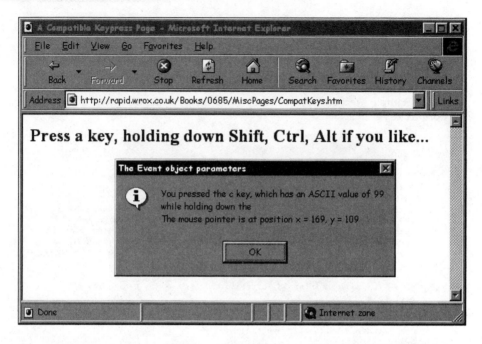

Of course, we can always just use a single script section written in 'vanilla' JavaScript. Within it we can then determine what actions to take depending on the values of the **appName** and **appVersion** properties of the **navigator** object—much as we did with the properties of the browser earlier in this chapter.

Doing It on the Server

Finally, we might decide to do all the work on the server instead. Technologies like Active Server Pages, or other CGI programming methods, can create pages dynamically. We simply need to read the user agent details from the HTTP header that the browser sends to the server when it requests a page, and dynamically create a fully compatible page to send back.

> *This topic is outside the scope of the book, but you can learn more about server-side programming techniques from other books in our range:*
>
> Professional Active Server Pages Programming, ISBN 1-861000-766
>
> Professional NT C++ ISAPI Programming, ISBN 1-8614416-66-4

Going Your Own Way

Of course, when it comes down to your own site, you don't *have* to do any of this. If you want to get the best out of your chosen browser, you might decide to program it all in one scripting language, and not worry about backwards compatibility. After all, getting your page to display correctly in one browser is often enough of a task. In this case, you just stick the 'Best viewed in Internet Explorer / Netscape Communicator' logo at the foot of your page. But while your pages will look much better if you just exploit all the latest features of your preferred browser, you'll be well on the way to admitting that the intense rivalry of the two market-leader browser vendors is destroying the heart of the Web as an inherently cross-platform medium.

Summary

This completes our tour of browser compatibility. We looked at the main Project Cougar proposals, and tried to see to what extent they have been adopted by Microsoft and Netscape. We looked at how you can make your pages backward compatible over previous releases of the same browser. Finally we looked at how you could make your pages function on both Communicator and IE4.

Having read this book, and this chapter, you may feel that it is slanted unduly towards one or other of the two main *Windows*-based browsers. Previously, HTML had been a truly cross-platform language, and Microsoft's non-compliance with proposals and standards (interpreted as setting future guidelines) was as confounding as Netscape's current stance. This is a book about Dynamic HTML, and isn't intended to favor either browser. However, you want to know about more it than just concepts, as documented in the W3C proposals and discussed in this chapter. To do that we had to choose a browser to work with—trying to cover both together is not an option, due to the totally different way most of the new features are implemented.

Despite the recent release of the HTML 4.0 working draft, Dynamic HTML isn't a finished language, and will undoubtedly evolve over future browser releases and future standards upgrades. We've tried to capture the main concepts at the heart of the proposals. We would like to have seen a language that was supported by both browsers, but instead we've ended up with two editions of what should have been one book. If you wish to know more about Netscape's implementation of Dynamic HTML, look out for the 'NC4' edition of this book Instant Netscape Dynamic HTML Programmer's Reference, NC4 edition *ISBN 1-861001-193*. And if this book has made you want to learn more about the whole concept of Internet Explorer 4 and the Active Desktop, look out for Professional Dynamic HTML and IE4 Programming – *ISBN 1-861000-70-7*.

INSTANT

Dynamic HTML

Reference Section

This section of the book is designed to help you to quickly and efficiently find the information you need while working with Dynamic HTML. To achieve this, we've split it up into separate, but inter-related, sections.

For example, when working with a `<DIV>` tag, you can look in Section **B** to find a full list of the Properties, Methods and Events it supports, plus the Attributes you can include in the tag itself and a list of the equivalent Style properties.

Then, to get a description of what each of these actually do, you can use the lists of Properties, Methods and Events in Section **A**. If you then need to know how to reference the division, using the browser's Object Model, you can see the overall structure, and you can look up individual objects within the hierarchy, in Section **E**.

Section A - Lists of Properties, Methods and Events

The list of **Properties** includes the equivalent HTML **Attributes** and **CSS Styles**, plus the type of data or individual values you can use with each one.

Section B - List of Dynamic HTML Tags

An alphabetical list of all the **HTML Tags** that can be used in Dynamic HTML files. The entry for each tag provides the following information:

 A short description of the tag.

 Tables of the Properties, Methods and Events it provides.

 The Attributes it accepts and the data types or values that can be used with them.

 The equivalent Style values.

 Some sample code, where appropriate, to show you how it is used.

Reference Section

Section C - Style Sheet Properties Reference

This listing contains all the attributes and values that can be used in **Cascading Style Sheets**, `<STYLE>` sections of a page, and in-line HTML `STYLE` attributes.

Section D - List of HTML Tags by Category

This section will help you to find which tag you need. It lists all the HTML tags by name, divided into **categories** like **Tables**, **Graphics**, **Forms**, etc.

Section E - The Browser Object Model Reference

This section covers the **object model** that is available in the browser through Dynamic HTML.
It contains a view of the overall structure, and a list of all the **objects** and **collections** that are provided. It goes on to show the Properties, Methods and Events which each object and collection supports.

Section F - HTML Color Names and Values

Many Dynamic HTML properties and methods expect you to provide a **color value**. This can be one of the accepted color names, or a numeric value that indicates the red green and blue (RGB) components of the color (also known as the hexadecimal value). This section lists all the color names, and shows the equivalent RGB values.

Section G - Special HTML Characters

Many of the **common symbols** we use in web pages cannot be transmitted as ASCII code because HTTP only supports 7-bit characters. Instead we use special codes in the page to indicate which of the **special characters** we want the browser to display. This section lists all the available characters and their equivalent codes.

Section H - VBScript2 Language Reference and Tutorial

Dynamic HTML is available in any **scripting language** that is supported by the browser. This section contains a reference to the VBScript language, listing all the keywords, functions, statements, built-in constants, etc. It also contains a tutorial to help those not so familiar with the language.

Section I - JavaScript Language Reference

The other language that most browsers, including Microsoft's Internet Explorer and Netscape's Navigator and Communicator, support is **JavaScript**. This section contains a reference to the **JavaScript language**, including the built-in objects, functions, keywords, and constants.

Section J - Support and Errata

Explains in detail how to contact us for support on this book, and how to log any errata that you may find in it.

Lists of Properties, Methods and Events

This section consists of three tables; the listing of Properties, Attributes and CSS Equivalents below, a listing of Dynamic HTML Methods and a listing of Dynamic HTML Events. Where there is more than one possible use/description for an item there will sometimes be more than one entry for it in the table. To find out more about any of the items listed here, check out the Microsoft Dynamic HTML Authoring reference section at **http://www.microsoft.com/workshop/author/dynhtml**.

The notation for the CSS Values is as follows:

 One vertical bar means either/or; that is, only one of the items is allowed.

 Two vertical bars mean either/both/any; that is, any number of the items are allowed.

<> mean the actual value of the items needs to be substituted, for example **#FFCC00** for **<color>**.

[] indicate grouping.

{} denote each style sheet within the **STYLE** tag, which have to be enclosed between braces.

 {A,B} within the CSS Values indicate that the preceding group must be repeated between **A** and **B** times, for example within **padding**, **{1,4}** indicates that the individual values may be specified up to four times, for top, right, bottom and left respectively.

 An asterisk means that the preceding group is repeated zero or more times

A question mark indicates that the preceding group is optional

List of Properties, Attributes and CSS Equivalents

This table lists Properties, with their associated Attributes and CSS Equivalents where appropriate. Not all properties have attributes, and occasionally you will find an entry for a CSS Equivalent which has neither a Property nor an Attribute associated with it.

Property Name	Attribute Name	CSS Values	Description
		@fontface{ <font-family> ; url (<url>);}	Specifies a font to embed in your HTML document. Allows you to use fonts not found locally.
		@import{ url (<url>) }	Specifies a style sheet to import.
accessKey	ACCESSKEY		Specifies an accelerator or 'hot key' for the element.
action	ACTION		The URL for the ACTION of the form. If not specified document's base URL is used.
activeElement			Identifies the element that has the focus.
align	ALIGN		Specifies how the element is aligned with respect to the rest of the page.
alinkColor	ALINK		The color for active links in the page - i.e. while the mouse button is held down.
alt	ALT		Text to be used as an alternative to the object in non-graphical environments.
altKey			Returns the state of the ALT key when an event occurs.
appCodeName			The code name of the browser.
appName			The product name of the browser.
appVersion			The version of the browser.

background	BACKGROUND	{ background: transparent | <color> || <url> || <repeat> || <scroll> || <position>)	Specifies a background picture that is tiled behind text and graphics.
backgroundattachment		{ background-attachment: scroll| fixed}	Defines if a background image should be fixed on the page or scroll with the content.
backgroundColor		{ background-color: <color> | transparent}	Specifies the background color of the page or element.
backgroundImage		{ background-image: <url> | none}	Specifies a URL for the background image for the page or element.
backgroundPosition		{ background-position: [<position> | <length>] {1,2} | [top | center | bottom] || [left | center | right])	The initial position of a background image on the page.
backgroundPositionX			The x-coordinate of the background image in relation to the containing window.
backgroundPositionY			The y-coordinate of the background image in relation to the containing window.
backgroundRepeat		{ background-repeat: repeat | repeat-x | repeat-y | no-repeat}	Defines if and how a background image is repeated on the page.
balance	BALANCE		Returns the left-to-right balance value for a background sound.
behavior	BEHAVIOR		Specifies how the text scrolls in a marquee element.
bgColor	BGCOLOR	{ background-color: <color> | transparent}	Specifies the background color to be used for an element.
bgProperties	BGPROPERTIES	{ background-attachment: scroll | fixed}	Sets or retrieves properties for the background picture.

Property Name	Attribute Name	CSS Values	Description
body			Read-only reference to the document's implicit body object, as defined by the `<BODY>` tag.
border	BORDER	`{ border: <border-width> || <border-style> || <color>}`	Specifies the border to be drawn around the element or between frames.
borderBottom		`{ border-bottom: <border-bottom-width> || <border-style> || <color>}`	Used to specify several attributes of the bottom border of an element.
borderBottomColor		`{ border-bottom-color: <color>}`	The color of the bottom border for an element.
borderBottomStyle		`{ border-bottom-style: none | solid | double | groove | ridge | inset | outset}`	The style of the bottom border for an element.
borderBottomWidth		`{ border-bottom-width: thin | medium| thick | <length>}`	The width of the bottom border for an element.
borderColor	BORDERCOLOR	`{ border-color: <color>{1,4}}`	The color of all or some of the borders for an element.
borderColorDark	BORDERCOLORDARK		The color used to draw the bottom and right borders for a 3-D element border.
borderColorLight	BORDERCOLORLIGHT		The color used to draw the top and left borders for a 3-D element border.
borderLeft		`{ border-left: <border-left-width> || <border-style> || <color>}`	Used to specify several attributes of the left border of an element.
borderLeftColor		`{ border-left-color: <color>}`	The color of the left border for an element.

`borderLeftStyle`	`{ border-left-style: none	solid	double	groove	ridge	inset	outset}`	The style of the left border for an element.
`borderLeftWidth`	`{ border-left-width: thin	medium	thick	<length>}`	The width of the left border for an element.
`borderRight`	`{ border-right: <border-right-width> || <border-style> || <color>}`	Used to specify several attributes of the right border of an element.
`borderRightColor`	`{ border-right-color: <color>}`	The color of the right border for an element.
`borderRightStyle`	`{ border-right-style: none	solid	double	groove	ridge	inset	outset}`	The style of the right border for an element.
`borderRightWidth`	`{ border-right-width: thin	medium	thick	<length>}`	The width of the right border for an element.
`borderStyle`	`{ border-style: none	solid	double	groove	ridge	inset	outset}`	Used to specify the style of one or more borders of an element.
`borderTop`	`{ border-top: <border-top-width> || <border-style> || <color>}`	Used to specify several attributes of the top border of an element.
`borderTopColor`	`{ border-top-color: <color>}`	The color of the top border for an element.
`borderTopStyle`	`{ border-top-style: none	solid	double	groove	ridge	inset	outset}`	The style of the top border for an element.
`borderTopWidth`	`{ border-top-width: thin	medium	thick	<length>}`	The width of the top border for an element.

Property Name	Attribute Name	CSS Values	Description
borderWidth		{ border-width: [thin | medium | thick | <length>] {1,4} }	Used to specify the width of one or more borders of an element.
bottomMargin	BOTTOMMARGIN		Sets or returns the bottom margin for the entire page. Overrides default margin.
bufferDepth			Specifies if and how an off-screen bitmap buffer should be used.
button			The mouse button, if any, that was pressed to fire the event.
cancelBubble			Set to prevent the current event from bubbling up the hierarchy.
cellPadding	CELLPADDING		Specifies the amount of space between the border of the cell and its contents.
cellSpacing	CELLSPACING		Specifies the amount of space between cells in a table.
charset			Sets or returns the character set of the document.
checked	CHECKED		For check boxes and radio buttons, indicates that they are selected.
classid	CLASSID		Used to specify the class identifier for the object.
className	CLASS		Specifies the class of the tag, used to associate a sub-classed style sheet with the tag.
clear	CLEAR	{ clear: none | left | right | both }	Causes the next element or text to be displayed below left-aligned or right-aligned images.
client			A reference that returns the navigator object for the browser, used to retrieve information on the browser name and version.

clientHeight		Returns the height of the element, excluding borders, margins, padding, scrollbars, etc.
clientWidth		Returns the width of the element, excluding borders, margins, padding, scrollbars, etc.
clientX		Returns the x-coordinate of the element, excluding borders, margins, padding, scrollbars, etc.
clientY		Returns the y-coordinate of the element, excluding borders, margins, padding, scrollbars, etc.
clip	{ clip: <shape> | auto }	Specifies how an element's contents should be displayed if larger than the available client area.
closed		Indicates if a window is closed.
code	CODE	The name of the file containing the compiled Java class.
codeBase	CODEBASE	The URL where the code implementation of the object can be found if required.
codeType	CODETYPE	The media type of the code for an externally implemented object.
color	{ color: <color> }	The text or foreground color of an element.
colorDepth		Returns the number of bits per pixel of the user's display device or screen buffer.
cols	COLS	The number of columns in the table or a frameset, or the number of characters in an input element.
colSpan	COLSPAN	Specifies the number of columns in the table that this cell should span.
compact	COMPACT	Specifies that the list should be compacted to remove extra space between its elements.
complete		Indicates whether the contents of the image have finished loading.

Property Name	Attribute Name	CSS Values	Description
content	CONTENT		Information in a <META> tag to be associated with the given name or HTTP response header.
cookie			The string value of a cookie stored by the browser.
cookieEnabled			Indicates if client-side cookies are enabled in the browser.
coords	COORDS		The coordinates that define the hot spot's shape in a client-side image map.
cssText			The text value of the element's entire STYLE attribute.
ctrlKey			Returns the state of the *CTRL* key when an event occurs.
cursor		{ cursor: auto | crosshair | default | hand | move | e-resize | ne-resize | nw-resize | n-resize | se-resize | sw-resize | s-resize | w-resize | text | wait | help}	Specifies the type of cursor to display when the mouse pointer is over the element.
data	DATA		Specifies a URL that references the source of the object's data.
dataFld	DATAFLD		Specifies the column or field name in the object's data source bound to this element.
dataFormatAs	DATAFORMATAS		Specifies the format of the data, can be 'text', 'html' or 'none'.
dataPageSize	DATAPAGESIZE		Defines the maximum number of records to be displayed at one time, as pages.
dataSrc	DATASRC		Specifies the source of the object's data for data binding.

`defaultChecked`		Denotes if this control element is checked (on) by default.
`defaultSelected`		Denotes if this list option is selected by default.
`defaultStatus`		The default message displayed in the status bar at the bottom of the window.
`defaultValue`		The text that is displayed as the initial contents of a control.
`dialogArguments`		Returns the arguments that were passed into a dialog window, as an array.
`dialogHeight`		Sets or returns the height of a dialog window.
`dialogLeft`		Sets or returns the x coordinate of a dialog window.
`dialogTop`		Sets or returns the y coordinate of a dialog window.
`dialogWidth`		Sets or returns the width of a dialog window.
`direction`	`DIRECTION`	Specifies which direction the text should scroll in a `<MARQUEE>`.
`disabled`	`DISABLED`	Sets or returns whether an element is disabled.
`display`	`{ display: none	<empty string>}`	Specifies if the element will be visible (displayed) in the page.
`document`		Read-only reference to the window's document object.
`domain`		Sets or returns the domain of the document for use in cookies and security.
`duration`		Sets the default length of time a filter transition will take to complete.
`dynsrc`	`DYNSRC`	Specifies the address of a dynamic source (video clip or `VRML`) be displayed in the element.
`encoding`	`ENCTYPE`	The type of encoding to apply to the contents of a form when submitted.

Property Name	Attribute Name	CSS Values	Description
event	`<event_name>`		Name of the event handler to be called when the specified event occurs.
event	EVENT		Read-only reference to the global event object.
face	FACE	`{ font-family: [[` `<family-name>` | `<generic-family> ] , ]*` `[ <family-name> ]` `<generic-family> ]}`	Sets the typeface of the current font.
fgColor	TEXT		Sets the color of the document foreground text.
filter		`{ filter: blendtrans ]` `revealtrans ] alpha ] blur` `] chroma ] dropshadow ]` `fliph ] flipv ] glow ]` `gray ] invert ] light ]` `mask ] shadow ] wave ]` `xray }`	Sets or returns an array of all the filters specified in the element's style property.
font		`{ font: [ <font-style>` `]] <font-variant> ]]` `<font-weight> ]? <font-` `size> [ / <line-height> ]?` `<font-family>}`	Defines various attributes of the font for an element, or imports a font.
fontFamily		`{ font-family: [[ <family-` `name> ] <generic-family> ]` `, ]* [ <family-name> ]` `<generic-family> ]}`	Specifies the name of the typeface, or 'font family'.
fontSize		`{ font-size: [xx-large ]` `x-large ] large ] medium` `] small ] x-small ]` `xx-small] ] [larger ]`	Specifies the font size.

Property	Syntax	Description
	`smaller]	<percentage>	<length>}`	
fontStyle	`{ font-style: normal	italic	oblique}`	Specifies the style of the font, i.e. normal or italic.
fontVariant	`{ font-variant: normal	small-caps}`	Specifies the use of small capitals for the text.
fontWeight	`{ font-weight: normal	bold	bolder	lighter	100	200	300	400	500	600	700	800	900}`	Specifies the weight (boldness) of the text.
form		Returns a reference to the form that contains the element.
frame	FRAME	Controls the appearance of the border frame around a table.
frameBorder	FRAMEBORDER	Controls the appearance of the border frame around a frame.
frameSpacing	FRAMESPACING	Specifies the spacing between frames in a frameset.
fromElement		Returns the element being moved from for an `onmouseover` or `onmouseout` event.
hash		The string following the # symbol in the URL.
height	HEIGHT	`{ height: <length>	auto}`	Specifies the height at which the element is to be drawn, and sets the `posHeight` property.
height		Returns the height of the user's display screen in pixels.
hidden	HIDDEN	Forces the embedded object to be invisible in an `<EMBED>` tag.
history		Read-only reference to the window's history object.

Property Name	Attribute Name	CSS Values	Description
host			The hostname:port part of the location or URL.
hostname			The hostname part of the location or URL.
href	HREF		The entire URL as a string.
hspace	HSPACE		Specifies the horizontal spacing or margin between an element and its neighbors.
htmlFor	FOR		Specifies the element to which the event script or label is linked.
htmlText			Returns the contents of a TextRange as text and HTML source.
httpEquiv	HTTP-EQUIV		Used to bind the content of the element to an HTTP response header.
id	ID		Identifier or name for an element in a page or style sheet, or as the target for hypertext links.
indeterminate			Sets the value of a checkbox to a gray background, representing an indeterminate state.
index			Returns the ordinal position of the option in a list box.
innerHTML			Sets or returns the text and HTML between an element's opening and closing tags in the HTML source.
innerText			Sets or returns only the text between an element's opening and closing tags in the HTML source.
isMap	ISMAP		Identifies the picture as being a server-side image map.
isTextEdit			Indicates if the element can be used as the source to create a TextRange object.

Property	Attribute	Syntax	Description
keyCode			ASCII code of the key being pressed. Changing it sends a different character to the object.
lang	LANG		The ISO description of the language for the element, as in `"text/javascript"`.
language	LANGUAGE		The browser-specific description of the scripting language in use, such as `"javascript"`.
lastModified			The date that the source file for the page was last modified, as a string, where available.
left		`{ left: <length>	<percentage>	auto}`	Specifies the position of the left of the element, and sets the `posLeft` property.
leftMargin	LEFTMARGIN	`{ margin-left: [<length>	<percentage>	auto] }`	Specifies the left margin for the entire body of the page, overriding the default margin.
length			Returns the number of elements in a collection.
letterSpacing		`{ letter-spacing: normal	<length>}`	Indicates the additional space to be placed between characters in the text.
lineHeight		`{ line-height: normal	<number>	<length>	<percentage>}`	The distance between the baselines of two adjacent lines of text.
linkColor	LINK		The color for unvisited links in the page.
listStyle		`{ list-style: <type> || <position> || <url>}`	Allows several style properties of a list element to be set in one operation.
listStyleImage		`{ list-style-image: <url>	none}`	Defines the image used as a background for a list element.
listStylePosition		`{ list-style-position: inside	outside}`	Defines the position of the bullets used in a list element.
listStyleType		`{ list-style-type: disk	circle	square	decimal	lower-roman	upper-roman	lower-alpha	upper-alpha	none}`	Defines the design of the bullets used in a list element.

Property Name	Attribute Name	CSS Values	Description
location			The full URL of the document.
loop	LOOP		Number of times sound or video clips should play when activated, or text in a MARQUEE should loop.
lowsrc	LOWSRC		Specifies the URL of a lower resolution image to display.
map			Identifies the element as representing an image map.
margin		{ margin: [<length> | <percentage> | auto] {1,4} }	Allows all four margins to be specified with a single attribute.
marginBottom		{ margin-bottom: [<length> | <percentage> | auto] }	Specifies the bottom margin for the page or text block.
marginHeight	MARGINHEIGHT		Specifies the top and bottom margins for displaying text in a frame.
marginLeft		{ margin-left: [<length> | <percentage> | auto] }	Specifies the left margin for the page or text block.
marginRight		{ margin-right: [<length> | <percentage> | auto] }	Specifies the right margin for the page or text block.
marginTop		{ margin-top: [<length> | <percentage> | auto] }	Specifies the top margin for the page or text block.
marginWidth	MARGINWIDTH		Specifies the left and right margins for displaying text in a frame.
maxLength	MAXLENGTH		Indicates the maximum number of characters that can be entered into a text control.
method	METHOD		Indicates how the form data should be sent to the server, either GET or POST.

methods	METHODS	Provides information about the functions that the user may perform on an object.
mimeTypes		An array of `MimeTypes` supported by the browser. Returns an empty collection in IE4.
multiple	MULTIPLE	Indicates that multiple items in the select list can be selected.
name	NAME	Specifies the name of the window, frame, element, control, bookmark or applet.
navigator		Read-only reference to the window's `navigator` object.
noHref	NOHREF	Indicates that clicks in this region of an image map should cause no action.
noResize	NORESIZE	Indicates that a frame is not resizable by the user.
noShade	NOSHADE	Draws the horizontal rule without 3-D shading.
noWrap	NOWRAP	Indicates that the browser should not perform automatic word wrapping of the text.
object	OBJECT	Reference to the object contained in an `<OBJECT>` tag, for use with duplicated property names.
offScreenBuffering		Specifies whether to use off-screen buffering for the document.
offsetHeight		Returns the total height of the content of an element in pixels, including that not currently visible without scrolling.
offsetLeft		Returns the x coordinate of the left of the content of an element in pixels, relative to the containing element.
offsetParent		Returns a reference to the element that contains this element, and that defines the top and left positions.

Property Name	Attribute Name	CSS Values	Description
offsetTop			Returns the y coordinate of the top of the content of an element in pixels, relative to the containing element.
offsetWidth			Returns the total width of the content of an element in pixels, including that not currently visible without scrolling.
offsetX			Returns the x coordinate of the mouse pointer when an event occurs, relative to the containing element.
offsetY			Returns the y coordinate position of the mouse pointer when an event occurs, relative to the containing element.
opener			Returns a reference to the window that created the current window.
outerHTML			Sets or returns the text and HTML for an element, including the opening and closing tags in the HTML source.
outerText			Sets or returns only the text for an element, including the opening and closing tags in the HTML source.
overflow		{ overflow: none | clip | scroll}	Defines how text that overflows the element is handled.
owningElement			Returns the style sheet that imported or referenced the current style sheet, usually through a <LINK> tag.
padding		{ padding: [<length> | <percentage>] {1,4} }	Sets the amount of space between the border and content for up to four sides of an element in operation.

paddingBottom	{ padding-bottom: [<length> | <percentage>] }	Sets the amount of space between the bottom border and content of an element.
paddingLeft	{ padding-left: [<length> | <percentage>] }	Sets the amount of space between the left border and content of an element.
paddingRight	{ padding-right: [<length> | <percentage>] }	Sets the amount of space between the right border and content of an element.
paddingTop	{ padding-top: [<length> | <percentage>] }	Sets the amount of space between the top border and content of an element.
pageBreakAfter	{ page-break-after: auto | always | left | right }	Specifies if a page break should occur after the element.
pageBreakBefore	{ page-break-before: auto | always | left | right }	Specifies if a page break should occur before the element.
palette PALETTE		Defines a palette to be used with an embedded document.
parent		Returns the parent window or frame in the window/frame hierarchy.
parentElement		Returns the parent element. The topmost element returns null for its parent.
parentStyleSheet		Returns the style sheet that imported the current style sheet, or null for a non-imported stylesheet.
parentTextEdit		Returns the closest parent of the element that can be used as the source to create a TextRange object.
parentWindow		Returns the parent window that contains the document.
pathname		The file or object path name following the third slash in a URL.
pixelHeight	{ height: <length> | auto }	Sets or returns the height style property of the element in pixels, as a number rather than a string.

Property Name	Attribute Name	CSS Values	Description
pixelLeft		{left: <length> | <percentage> | auto}	Sets or returns the left style property of the element in pixels, as a number, rather than a string.
pixelTop		{top: <length> | <percentage> | auto}	Sets or returns the top style property of the element in pixels, as a number, rather than a string.
pixelWidth		{width: <length> | <percentage> | auto}	Sets or returns the width style property of the element in pixels, as a number, rather than a string.
plugins			An array of plugins available in the browser. Returns an empty collection in IE4.
pluginspage	PLUGINSPAGE		Defines the plug-in to be used with an embedded document.
port			The port number in a URL.
posHeight		{ height: <length> | auto}	Returns the value of the height style property in its last specified units, as a number rather than a string.
position		{ position: absolute | relative | static}	Returns the value of the position style property, defining whether the element can be positioned.
posLeft		{left: <length> | <percentage> | auto}	Returns the value of the left style property in its last specified units, as a number rather than a string.
posTop		{top: <length> | <percentage> | auto}	Returns the value of the top style property in its last specified units, as a number rather than a string.
posWidth		{width: <length> | <percentage> | auto}	Returns the value of the width style property in its last specified units, as a number rather than a string.

protocol		The initial substring up to and including the first colon, indicating the URL's access method.
readonly	READONLY	Indicates that an element's contents are read-only, or that a rule in a style sheet cannot be changed.
readyState		Specifies the current state of an object being downloaded.
reason		Indicates whether data transfer to an element was successful, or why it failed.
recordNumber		Returns the ordinal number of the current record for a data-bound table element.
recordset		Returns the recordset for the object, if the object is a data provider.
	REF	Indicates that the value is a URL.
referrer		The URL of the page that referenced (loaded) the current page.
rel	REL	Relationship described by a hypertext link from an anchor to the target. Opposite to **rev**.
returnValue		Allows a return value to be specified for the event or a dialog window.
rev	REV	Relationship described by a hypertext link from the target to its anchor. Opposite of **rel**.
rightMargin	RIGHTMARGIN	Specifies the right margin for the entire body of the page, over-riding the default margin.
rows	ROWS	Number of rows in a **TEXTAREA** control, or the height of the frames in a frameset.
rowSpan	ROWSPAN	Specifies the number of rows in the table that this cell should span.
rules	RULES	Specifies which dividing lines (inner borders) are displayed in a table.

Property Name	Attribute Name	CSS Values	Description
screen			Read-only reference to the global screen object.
screenX			Returns the x coordinate of the mouse pointer when an event occurs, in relation to the screen.
screenY			Returns the y coordinate of the mouse pointer when an event occurs, in relation to the screen.
scroll	SCROLL		Turns the scrollbars in a frame on or off.
scrollAmount	SCROLLAMOUNT		Number of pixels that the text scrolls between each subsequent drawing of the MARQUEE.
scrollDelay	SCROLLDELAY		Specifies the time between redraws of the MARQUEE in milliseconds.
scrollHeight			Total height in pixels of the content of an element that can be viewed without moving any scroll bars.
scrolling	SCROLLING		Specifies whether a frame can be scrolled.
scrollLeft			The scrolled distance in pixels between the left edge of the content of an element and the left edge of its container.
scrollTop			The scrolled distance in pixels between the top edge of the content of an element and the top edge of its container.
scrollWidth			Total width in pixels of the content of an element that can be viewed without moving any scroll bars.
search			The contents of the query string or form data following the ? in the complete URL.
selected	SELECTED		Indicates that this item is the default and will be selected in a select list.
selectedIndex			An integer specifying the index of the currently selected option in a select list.

selection		Read-only reference to the document's **selection** object.
self		Provides a reference to the current window.
shape	**SHAPE**	Specifies the type of shape used in a client-side image map.
shiftKey		Returns the state of the *SHIFT* key when an event occurs.
size	**SIZE**	Specifies the size of the control, horizontal rule or font.
sourceIndex		Returns the ordinal position of the element in the source order, and in the **all** collection.
span	**SPAN**	Specifies how many columns are in a **COLGROUP**.
src	**SRC**	Specifies an external file that contains the source data for the element.
srcElement		Returns the element deepest in the object hierarchy over which a specified event occurred.
srcFilter		Returns the filter that caused the element to produce an **onfilterchange** event.
start	**START**	Sets or returns the start number of a list, or when a video clip should begin playing.
status		Text displayed in the window's status bar, or an alias for the value of an option button.
status		Returns the current status of the filter transition.
style	**STYLE**	Specifies an in-line style sheet (or set of style properties) for the element.
styleFloat	`{ float: left | right | none}`	Specifies if the element will float above the other elements in the page, or cause them to flow round it.

Property Name	Attribute Name	CSS Values	Description
tabIndex	TABINDEX		Sets the Tab index for the element within the tabbing order of the page.
tagName			Returns the HTML tag as a lower-case string, without the < and > delimiters.
target	TARGET		Specifies the window or frame where the new page will be loaded.
text	TEXT		Sets or retrieves the color of the foreground text in the page.
text			The plain text contained within a block element, a TextRange or an <OPTION> tag.
textAlign		{ text-align: left | right | center | justify}	Indicates how text should be aligned within the element.
textDecoration		{ text-decoration: none | [underline || overline || line-through]}	Specifies several font decorations (underline, overline, strikethrough) added to the text of an element.
textDecorationBlink		{ text-decoration: none | [underline || overline || line-through]}	Specifies if the font should blink or flash. Has no effect in IE4.
textDecorationLineThrough		{ text-decoration: none | [underline || overline || line-through]}	Specifies if the text is displayed as strikethrough, i.e. with a horizontal line through it.
textDecorationNone		{ text-decoration: none | [underline || overline || line-through]}	Specifies if the text is displayed with no additional decoration.
textDecorationOverline		{ text-decoration: none | [underline || overline || line-through]}	Denotes if the text is displayed as overline, i.e. with a horizontal line above it.

Property	Attribute	Syntax	Description
textDecorationUnderline		{ text-decoration: none | [underline || overline || line-through] }	Denotes if the text is displayed as underline, i.e. with a horizontal line below it.
textIndent		{ text-indent: <length> | <percentage>}	Specifies the indent for the first line of text in an element; may be negative.
textTransform		{ text-transform: capitalize | uppercase | lowercase | none}	Specifies how the text for the element should be capitalized.
title	TITLE		Provides advisory information about the element, such as when loading or as a tooltip.
toElement			Returns the element being moved to for an onmouseover or onmouseout event.
top		{ top: <length> | <percentage> | auto}	Position of the top of the element, sets the posTop property. Also returns topmost window object.
topMargin	TOPMARGIN	{ margin-top: [<length> | <percentage> | auto] }	Specifies the margin for the top of the page, overriding the default top margin.
trueSpeed	TRUESPEED		Specifies how a MARQUEE element calculates the scrolling speed, compared to IE3.
type	TYPE		Specifies type of liststyle, link, selection, control, button, Mime-type, rel, or CSS language.
type			Returns the name of the event as a string, without the 'on' prefix, such as 'click' instead of 'onclick'.
updateInterval			Sets or returns the interval between screen updates on the client.
url	URL		Uniform Resource Locator (address) for the current document or in a <META> tag.
urn	URN		Uniform Resource Name for a target document.
useMap	USEMAP		Identifies the picture as a client-side image map, and indicates the map to be used with it.

Property Name	Attribute Name	CSS Values	Description
userAgent			The user-agent (browser name) header sent in the HTTP protocol from the client to the server.
vAlign	VALIGN		Specifies how the contents should aligned at the top or bottom of an element.
value	VALUE		The default value of text/numeric controls, or the value when control is 'on' for boolean controls.
verticalAlign		{ vertical-align: baseline | sub | super | top | text-top | middle | bottom | text-bottom | <percentage>}	Sets or returns the vertical alignment style property for an element.
visibility		{ visibility: visible | hidden | inherit}	Indicates if the element or contents are visible on the page.
vlinkColor	VLINK		The color for visited links in the page.
volume	VOLUME		Returns the volume setting for a background sound.
vspace	VSPACE		Specifies the vertical spacing or margin between an element and its neighbors.
width	WIDTH	{ width: <length> | <percentage> | auto}	Specifies the width at which the element is to be drawn, and sets the posWidth property.
width			Returns the width of the user's display screen in pixels.
window			Read-only reference to the current window object, same as self.
wrap	WRAP		Specifies how wrapping is handled in a Textarea control element.
x			Returns the x coordinate of the mouse pointer relative to a positioned parent, or otherwise to the window.

y	Returns the y coordinate of the mouse pointer relative to a positioned parent, or otherwise to the window.
zIndex	Sets or returns the z-index for the element, indicating whether it appears above or below other elements.
`{ z-index: <number> }`	

Listing of Dynamic HTML Methods

Method Name	Syntax	Description
add	*object*.add(*element* [, *index*])	Adds an area or option element to the appropriate collection.
addAmbient	*object*.style.filters.Light(*n*).addAmbient(*R*, *G*, *B*, *strength*)	Adds an ambient light to the **Light Filter Effect** object.
addCone	*object*.style.filters.Light(*n*).addCone(*x1*, *y1*, *z1*, *x2*, *y2*, *R*, *G*, *B*, *strenth*, *spread*)	Adds a cone light to the **Light Filter Effect** object to cast a directional light on the page.
addImport	*Integer* = *object*.addImport(*url* [, *index*])	Adds a style sheet from *url* to the current document, optionally at index in the **styleSheets** collection.
addPoint	*object*.style.filters.Light(*n*).addPoint(*x*, *y*, *z*, *R*, *G*, *B*, *strength*)	Adds a point light source to the **Light Filter Effect** object.
addRule	*Integer* = *object*.addRule(*selector*, *style*)	Adds a new property rule to a style sheet.
alert	*object*.alert([*message*])	Displays an **Alert** dialog box with a message and an OK button.
apply	*object*.style.filters.transition(*index*).apply	Applies a transition to the designated object.
assign	*object*.assign(*url*)	Loads another page. Equivalent to changing the **window.location.href** property.
back	*object*.back()	Loads the previous URL in the browser's history list.
blur	*object*.blur()	Causes a control to lose focus and fire its **onblur** event.
changeColor	*object*.style.filters.Light(*n*).changeColor(*lightnumber*, *r*, *g*, *b*, *fAbsolute*)	Changes the light color for any light on the page.
changeStrength	*object*.style.filters.Light(*n*).changeStrength(*lightnumber*, *strength*, *fAbsolute*)	Changes the intensity of the light.
clear	*object*.style.filters.Light(*n*).clear	Deletes all lights associated with the specified **Lightfilter**.

clear	`object.clear()`	Clears the contents of a selection or document object.
clearInterval	`object.clearInterval(intervalID)`	Cancels an interval timer that was set with the `setInterval` method.
clearTimeout	`object.clearTimeout(timeoutID)`	Cancels a timeout that was set with the `setTimeout` method.
click	`object.click()`	Simulates a click on an element, and fires its **onclick** event.
close	`object.close()`	Closes a document forcing written data to be displayed, or closes the browser window.
collapse	`object.collapse([start])`	Shrinks a **TextRange** to either the start or end of the current range.
compareEndPoints	`object.compareEndPoints(comparetype, range)`	Compares two text ranges and returns a value indicating the result.
confirm	`object.confirm([message])`	Displays a **Confirm** dialog box with a message and OK and Cancel buttons.
contains	`Boolean = object.contains(element)`	Denotes if another element is contained within the current element.
createElement	`element = object.createElement(tag)`	Creates an instance of an image or option element object.
createRange	`object.createRange()`	Returns a copy of the current selection in the document.
createTextRange	`TextRange = object.createTextRange()`	Returns a new **TextRange** from the document or a text-based control.
duplicate	`TextRange = object.duplicate()`	Returns a duplicate of a **TextRange** object.
elementFromPoint	`element = object.elementFromPoint(x, y)`	Returns the element at the specified x and y coordinates with respect to the window.
empty	`object.empty()`	Deselects the current selection. Sets selection type to none and the item property to null.
execCommand	`Boolean = object.execCommand(command [, bool [, value]])`	Executes a command over the document selection or range.

289

Method Name	Syntax	Description
execScript	object.execScript(expression [, language])	Executes a script in the language defined. The default language is JScript.
expand	Boolean = object.expand(unit)	Expands the range by a character, word, sentence or story so that partial units are completely contained.
findText	Boolean = object.findText(text)	Sets the range start and end points to cover the text if found within the current document.
focus	object.focus()	Causes a control to receive the focus and fire its onfocus event.
forward	object.forward()	Loads the next URL in the browser's history list.
getAttribute	Variant = object.getAttribute(attrName [, caseSensitive])	Returns the value of an attribute defined in an HTML tag.
getBookmark	String = object.getBookmark()	Sets String to a unique bookmark value to identify that position in the document.
go	object.go(delta | location)	Loads the specified URL from the browser's history list.
inRange	Boolean = object.inRange(compareRange)	Denotes if the specified range is within or equal to the current range.
insertAdjacentHtml	object.insertAdjacentHtml(where, html)	Inserts text and HTML into the element at a given point, parsing the HTML.
insertAdjacentText	object.insertAdjacentText(where, text)	Inserts text into the element at a given point. Any HTML tags are displayed as text.
isEqual	Boolean = object.isEqual(compareRange)	Denotes if the specified range is equal to the current range.
item	element = object.item(index [, subindex])	Returns an object from a collection using its index. If the element returned is a collection, a subindex can be used.
javaEnabled	Boolean = object.javaEnabled()	Returns True or False, depending on whether a Java VM is installed and enabled.

move	`Long = object.move(unit [, count])`	Changes the start and end points of a **TextRange** to cover different text.
moveEnd	`Long = object.moveEnd(unit [, count])`	Causes the range to grow or shrink from the end of the range.
moveLight	`object.style.filters.Light(n).moveLight(x,y,z,fAbsolute)`	Moves the light effect on the page.
moveStart	`Long = object.moveStart(unit [, count])`	Causes the range to grow or shrink from the beginning of the range.
moveToBookmark	`Boolean = object.moveToBookmark(bookmark)`	Moves range to encompass the range with a bookmark value previously defined in **String**.
moveToElementText	`object.moveToElement(Element)`	Moves range to encompass the text in the element specified.
moveToPoint	`object.moveToPoint(x, y)`	Moves and collapses range to the point specified in x and y relative to the document.
navigate	`object.navigate(url)`	Loads another page (VBScript only). Equivalent to changing the **window.location.href** property.
nextPage	`object.nextPage()`	Displays the next page of records in a repeated databound table element.
open	`object.open()`	Opens the document as a a stream to collect output of **write** or **writeln** methods.
open	`window = object.open(url [, name [, features [,replace]]])`	Opens a new browser window and loads the document defined in the *url* parameter.
parentElement	`element = object.parentElement()`	Returns the parent element that completely encloses the current range.
pasteHTML	`object.pasteHTML(htmlText)`	Pastes HTML and/or plain text into the current range.
play	`object.style.filters.transition.play(duration)`	Plays the transition.
prevPage	`object.prevPage()`	Displays the previous page of records in a repeated databound table element.

291

Method Name	Syntax	Description
prompt	*object*.**prompt** ([*message* [, *inputDefault*]])	Displays a **Prompt** dialog box with a message and an input field.
queryCommandEnabled	*Boolean* = *object*.**queryCommandEnabled** (*command*)	Denotes whether the specified command is available for a document or **TextRange**.
queryCommandIndeterm	*Boolean* = *object*.**queryCommandIndeterm** (*command*)	Denotes whether the specified command is in the indeterminate state.
queryCommandState	*Boolean* = *object*.**queryCommandState** (*command*)	Returns the current state of the command for a document or **TextRange** object.
queryCommandSupported	*Boolean* = *object*.**queryCommandSupported** (*command*)	Denotes whether the specified command is supported for a document or **TextRange** object.
queryCommandText	*String* = *object*.**queryCommandText** (*command*)	Returns the string associated with a command for a document or **TextRange** object.
queryCommandValue	*String* = *object*.**queryCommandValue** (*command*)	Returns the value of the command specified for a document or **TextRange** object.
refresh	*object*.**refresh** ( )	Refreshes the contents of the table.
reload	*object*.**reload** ( )	Reloads the current page.
remove	*object*.**remove** (*index*)	Removes an element from an areas or options collection.
removeAttribute	*Boolean* = *object*.**removeAttribute** (*attrName* [, *caseSensitive*])	Causes the specified attribute to be removed from the HTML element and the current page.
replace	*object*.**replace** (*url*)	Loads a document, replacing the current document's session history entry with its URL.
reset	*object*.**reset** ( )	Simulates a mouse click on a **RESET** button in a form.
scroll	*object*.**scroll** (*x*, *y*)	Scrolls the window to the specified x and y offset relative to the entire document.
scrollIntoView	*object*.**scrollIntoView** ([*start*])	Scrolls the element or **TextRange** into view in the browser, optionally at the top of the window.

Method	Syntax	Description
`select`	`object.select()`	Makes the active selection equal to the current object, or highlights the input area of a form element.
`setAttribute`	`object.setAttribute(attrName, value [, caseSensitive])`	Adds and/or sets the value of an attribute in a HTML tag.
`setEndPoint`	`object.setEndPoint(type, range)`	Sets the end point of the range based on the end point of another range.
`setInterval`	`intervalID = object.setInterval(expression, msec [, language])`	Denotes a code routine to execute repeatedly every specified number of milliseconds.
`setTimeout`	`timeoutID = object.setTimeout(expression, msec [, language])`	Denotes a code routine to execute a specified number of milliseconds after loading the page.
`showHelp`	`object.showHelp(url [, arguments])`	Opens a window to display a Help file.
`showModalDialog`	`Variant = object.showModalDialog(url [, arguments [, features]])`	Displays an HTML dialog window, and returns the returnValue property of its document when closed.
`start`	`object.start()`	Begins scrolling the text in a MARQUEE.
`stop`	`object.stop()`	Stops scrolling the text in a MARQUEE.
`stop`	`object.style.filters.transition.(index).stop`	Stops the transition playback.
`submit`	`object.submit()`	Submits a form, as when the SUBMIT button is clicked.
`tags`	`element = object.tags(tag)`	Returns a collection of all the elements for the specified tagname.
`taintEnabled`	`Boolean = object.taintEnabled()`	Returns False, included for compatibility with Netscape Navigator
`write`	`object.write(string)`	Writes text and HTML to a document in the specified window.
`writeln`	`object.writeln(string)`	Writes text and HTML to a document in the specified window, followed by a carriage return.
`zOrder`	`object.zOrder([position])`	Sets the z-index or layering in fixed layout regions.

293

Listing of Dynamic HTML Events

Event Name	Description
onabort	Occurs if the user aborts the downloading of the image.
onafterupdate	Occurs when transfer of data from the element to the data provider is complete.
onbeforeunload	Occurs just before the page is unloaded, allowing the databound controls to store their data.
onbeforeupdate	Occurs before transfer of changed data to the data provider when an element loses focus or the page is unloaded.
onblur	Occurs when the control loses the input focus.
onbounce	Occurs in a <MARQUEE> when BEHAVIOR is ALTERNATE, and the contents reach the edge.
onchange	Occurs when the contents of the element have changed.
onclick	Occurs when the user clicks the mouse button on an element, or when the value of a control is changed.
ondataavailable	Occurs periodically while data is arriving from an asynchronous data source.
ondatasetchanged	Occurs when the dataset changes, such as when a different data filter is applied.
ondatasetcomplete	Occurs once all the data is available from the data source object.
ondblclick	Occurs when the user double-clicks on an element.
ondragstart	Occurs when the user first starts to drag an element or selection.
onerror	Occurs when an error loading a document or image arises.
onerrorupdate	Occurs when an onbeforeupdate event cancels update of the data, replacing the onafterupdate event.
onfilterchange	Occurs when a filter changes state, or when a filter transition is complete.
onfilterevent	Occurs when a specified transition is complete.
onfinish	Occurs when looping is complete in a <MARQUEE> element.

onfocus	Occurs when a control receives the input focus.
onhelp	Occurs when the user presses the *F1* or *Help* key.
onkeydown	Occurs when the user presses a key.
onkeypress	Occurs when the user presses a key and a character is available.
onkeyup	Occurs when the user releases a key.
onload	Occurs when the element has completed loading.
onmousedown	Occurs when the user presses a mouse button.
onmousemove	Occurs when the user moves the mouse.
onmouseout	Occurs when the mouse pointer leaves the element.
onmouseover	Occurs when the mouse pointer first enters the element.
onmouseup	Occurs when the user releases a mouse button.
onreadystatechange	Occurs when the `readyState` for an object has changed.
onreset	Occurs when the `RESET` button on a form is clicked or a form is reset.
onresize	Occurs when the element or object is resized by the user.
onrowenter	Occurs when data in the current row has changed and new values are available.
onrowexit	Occurs before the data source changes data in the current row.
onscroll	Occurs when the user scrolls a page or element.
onselect	Occurs when the current selection in an element is changed.
onselectstart	Occurs when the user first starts to select contents of an element.
onstart	Occurs in a `<MARQUEE>` when looping begins, or a bounce occurs when `BEHAVIOR` is `ALTERNATE`.
onsubmit	Occurs when the `SUBMIT` button on a form is clicked or a form is submitted.
onunload	Occurs immediately before the page is unloaded.

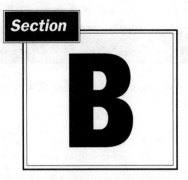

List of Dynamic HTML Tags

This section provides an alphabetical list of all the **HTML Tags** which can be used in Dynamic HTML files. The entry for each tag provides the following information; a short description of the tag, tables of the Properties, Methods and Events it provides, the Attributes it accepts and the data types or values that can be used with them, the equivalent CSS values and some sample code, where appropriate, to show you how it is used.

!–

Denotes a comment that is ignored by the HTML parser.

No Properties, Methods or Events.

Can be a single tag containing a comment, or span several lines. Often used to hide features that may not be supported in older browsers.

```
<! this is a comment that will be ignored>

    <SCRIPT LANGUAGE=VBSCRIPT>
<!-- hide the script from older browsers
    Sub DoSomething()
       ...
    End Sub
-->
    </SCRIPT>
```

!DOCTYPE

Declares the type and content format of the document.

No Properties, Methods or Events.

A rigorous HTML-checking program will reject any documents that do not contain this tag. However, most browsers are not so fussy, and most documents on the Web do not include this tag, even though it is required by the HTML 3.2 standard.

It must be the first item in the document. For documents written to HTML 3.2 standard use:

```
<!DOCTYPE HTML PUBLIC "-//W3C//DTD HTML 3.2// EN">
```

As Dynamic HTML is not yet a W3C standard, there is no agreed format of the **DOCTYPE** tag for this.

Defines a hypertext link. The **HREF** or the **NAME** attribute must be specified.

Properties	Attributes	Properties	Attributes
accessKey	ACCESSKEY=*string*	offsetLeft	
className	CLASS=*string*	offsetParent	
dataFld	DATAFLD=*column-name*	offsetTop	
dataSrc	DATASRC=*id*	offsetWidth	
document		outerText	
event	<event_name>=*name of script*	parentElement	
		parentTextEdit	
hash		pathname	
host		port	
hostname		protocol	
href	HREF=*string*	rel	REL=*string*
id	ID=*string*	rev	REV=*string*
innerText		search	
isTextEdit		sourceIndex	
lang	LANG=*string*	style	STYLE=*string*
language	LANGUAGE= JAVASCRIPT | JSCRIPT | VBSCRIPT | VBS	tagName	
		target	TARGET= <window_name> | _parent | _blank | _top | _self
Methods	METHODS=*string*		
name	NAME=*string*	title	TITLE=*string*
offsetHeight		urn	URN=*string*

Methods
blur click contains focus getAttribute insertAdjacentHTML
insertAdjacentText removeAttribute scrollIntoView
setAttribute

Events
onblur onclick ondblclick ondragstart onerrorupdate
onfilterchange onfocus onhelp onkeydown onkeypress
onkeyup onmousedown onmousemove onmouseout
onmouseover onmouseup onselectstart

```
<A HREF="http://www.wrox.com" onclick="MsgBox 'Switching to the Wrox web site'">Click
here to go to Wrox!</A>
```

ADDRESS

Specifies information such as address, signature and authorship.

Properties	Attributes	Properties	Attributes
className	CLASS=*string*	sourceIndex	
event	<event_name>=*name of script*	tagName	
		document	
innerHTML		id	ID=*string*
isTextEdit		innerText	
language	LANGUAGE= JAVASCRIPT | JSCRIPT | VBSCRIPT | VBS	lang	LANG=*string*
		offsetHeight	
		offsetParent	
offsetLeft		offsetWidth	
offsetTop		outerText	
outerHTML		parentTextEdit	
parentElement		style	STYLE=*string*
		title	TITLE=*string*

Methods
click contains getAttribute insertAdjacentHTML
insertAdjacentText removeAttribute scrollIntoView
setAttribute

Events
onclick ondblclick ondragstart onhelp onkeydown onkeypress
onkeyup onmousedown onmousemove onmouseout onmouseover
onmouseup onselectstart

Collection	Description
filters	Collection of all the filter objects for an element.

Normally displays text in italics:

```
Produced by:
<ADDRESS>
  Wrox Press Limited, US
  1512 North Fremont
  Suite 103
  Chicago
  IL 60622
</ADDRESS>
```

Places a Java Applet or other executable content in the page.

Properties	Attributes	Properties	Attributes
accessKey		name	NAME=*string*
align	ALIGN=CENTER | LEFT | RIGHT	offsetHeight	
	ALT=*string*	offsetLeft	
		offsetParent	
className	CLASS=*string*	offsetTop	
code	CODE=*string*	offsetWidth	
codeBase	CODEBASE=*string*	outerHTML	
dataFld	DATAFLD=*columnname*	outerText	
dataSrc	DATASRC=*id*	parentElement	
disabled		parentTextEdit	
document		sourceIndex	
hspace	HSPACE=*number*	src	SRC=*url*
id	ID=*string*	style	STYLE=*string*
isTextEdit		tagName	
lang	LANG=*string*	title	TITLE=*string*
language	LANGUAGE= JAVASCRIPT | JSCRIPT | VBSCRIPT | VBS	vspace	VSPACE=*number*
			WIDTH=*number*

Methods
blur click contains focus getAttribute insertAdjacentHTML
insertAdjacentText removeAttribute scrollIntoView
setAttribute

Events
onafterupdate onbeforeupdate onblur onclick
ondataavailable ondatasetchanged ondatasetcomplete
ondblclick ondragstart onerrorupdate onfocus onhelp
onkeydown onkeypress onkeyup onload onmousedown
onmousemove onmouseout onmouseover onmouseup
onreadystatechange onresize onrowenter onrowexit
onselectstart

AREA

Specifies the shape of a "hot spot" in a client-side image map.

Properties	Attributes	Properties	Attributes
alt	ALT=*string*	offsetTop	
className	CLASS=*string*	offsetWidth	
coords	COORDS=*string*	outerHTML	
document		outerText	
event	<event_name>=*name of script*	parentElement	
		parentTextEdit	
hash		pathname	
host		port	
hostname		protocol	
href	HREF=*string*	search	
id	ID=*string*	shape	SHAPE=CIRC | CIRCLE | POLY | POLYGON | RECT | RECTANGLE
isTextEdit			
lang	LANG=*string*		
language	LANGUAGE= JAVASCRIPT | JSCRIPT | VBSCRIPT | VBS	sourceIndex	
		style	STYLE=*string*
		tagName	
noHref	NOHREF	target	TARGET= <window_name> | _parent | _blank | _top | _self
offsetHeight			
offsetLeft			
offsetParent		title	TITLE=*string*

Methods
blur click contains focus getAttribute insertAdjacentHTML
insertAdjacentText removeAttribute scrollIntoView
setAttribute

Events
onblur onclick ondblclick ondragstart onfilterchange
onfocus onhelp onkeydown onkeypress onkeyup onmousedown
onmousemove onmouseout onmouseover onmouseup

Collection	Description
`filters`	Collection of all the filter objects for an element.

See also **Map**

```
<MAP NAME="toolbar">
<AREA SHAPE="RECT" COORDS="12,216,68,267" HREF="wrox.html">
</MAP>
```

B

Renders text in boldface where available.

Properties	Attributes	Properties	Attributes
`className`	`CLASS=`*string*	`offsetHeight`	
`document`		`offsetLeft`	
`event`	`<event_name>=`*name of script*	`offsetParent`	
		`offsetTop`	
`id`	`ID=`*string*	`offsetWidth`	
`innerHTML`		`outerHTML`	
`innerText`		`outerText`	
`isTextEdit`		`parentElement`	
`lang`	`LANG=`*string*	`parentTextEdit`	
`language`	`LANGUAGE= JAVASCRIPT	JSCRIPT	VBSCRIPT	VBS`	`sourceIndex`	
		`style`	`STYLE=`*string*
		`tagName`	
		`title`	`TITLE=`*string*

Methods
`click contains getAttribute insertAdjacentHTML insertAdjacentText removeAttribute scrollIntoView setAttribute`

Events
`onclick ondblclick ondragstart onfilterchange onhelp onkeydown onkeypress onkeyup onmousedown onmousemove onmouseout onmouseover onmouseup onselectstart`

...B

Collection	Description
`filters`	Collection of all the filter objects for an element.

```
<B>BOLD</B>
```

This example would produce the word **BOLD** in bold font.

BASE

Specifies the document's base URL.

Properties	Attributes	Properties	Attributes
`className`	`CLASS=`*string*	`parentElement`	
`document`		`parentTextEdit`	
`href`	`HREF=`*string*	`sourceIndex`	
`id`	`ID=`*string*	`tagName`	
`isTextEdit`		`target`	`TARGET=` `<window_name>` | `_parent` | `_blank` | `_top` | `_self`
`lang`	`LANG=`*string*		
`outerHTML`			
`outerText`		`title`	`TITLE=`*string*

Methods
`contains getAttribute removeAttribute setAttribute`

This is the address used to reference other resources, such as documents, graphics, etc., which do not specify a full URL. For example:

```
<IMG SRC="MyGraphic.gif">
```

If you have set up a `<BASE>` tag defining the base directory, MyGraphic.gif will be loaded from the directory defined by the `<BASE>` tag.

There are no events for this tag.

304

Sets a base font value to be used as the default font when rendering text.

Properties	Attributes	Properties	Attributes
className	CLASS=*string*	outerText	
color	COLOR=*color*	parentElement	
document		parentTextEdit	
face	FACE=*string*	size	SIZE=*number*
id	ID=*string*	sourceIndex	
isTextEdit		tagName	
outerHTML			TITLE=*string*

Methods
contains getAttribute removeAttribute setAttribute

Once the **BASEFONT** for a document has been set, you can use relative sizes for the font in different places, or specify individual sizes as required:

```
<BASEFONT SIZE=4 FACE="Arial,Tahoma,sans-serif">
...
<FONT SIZE=-1> A bit smaller font than the base </FONT>
...
<FONT SIZE=+3> A larger font than the base will be used here </FONT>
...
<FONT SIZE=2> This is small and not related to BASEFONT </FONT>
```

There are no events for this tag.
See also **FONT**.

BGSOUND

Specifies a background sound to be played while the page is loaded.

Properties	Attributes	Properties	Attributes
balance	BALANCE=*number*	offsetWidth	
className	CLASS=*string*	outerHTML	
document		outerText	
id	ID=*string*	parentElement	
isTextEdit		parentTextEdit	
	LANG=*string*	sourceIndex	
loop	LOOP=*number*	src	SRC=*url*
offsetHeight		style	
offsetLeft		tagName	
offsetParent		title	TITLE=*string*
offsetTop		volume	VOLUME=*number*

Methods
contains getAttribute removeAttribute setAttribute

The **SRC** attribute identifies the file through a URL, and the **LOOP** attribute defines how often it will be played. Setting **LOOP** to **-1** or the special value **INFINITE** causes the sound to be repeated all the time the page is displayed:

```
<BGSOUND SRC="http://www.wrox.com/sounds/crash.wav" LOOP=INFINITE>
<BGSOUND SRC="http://www.wrox.com/sounds/crash.wav" LOOP=-1>
```

Otherwise, **LOOP** can be set to a value starting at **1** to play the file that many times:

```
<BGSOUND SRC="http://www.wrox.com/sounds/crash.wav" LOOP=3>
```

There are no events for this tag.

Renders text in a relatively larger font than the current font.

Properties	Attributes	Properties	Attributes
className	CLASS=*string*	offsetHeight	
document		offsetLeft	
event	<event_name>=*name of script*	offsetParent	
		offsetTop	
id	ID=*string*	offsetWidth	
innerHTML		outerHTML	
innerText		outerText	
isTextEdit		parentElement	
lang	LANG=*string*	parentTextEdit	
language	LANGUAGE= JAVASCRIPT | JSCRIPT | VBSCRIPT | VBS	sourceIndex	
		style	STYLE=*string*
		tagName	
		title	TITLE=*string*

Methods
click contains getAttribute insertAdjacentHTML
insertAdjacentText removeAttribute scrollIntoView
setAttribute

Events
onclick ondblclick ondragstart onfilterchange onhelp
onkeydown onkeypress onkeyup onmousedown onmousemove
onmouseout onmouseover

Collection	Description
filters	Collection of all the filter objects for an element.

```
<BIG> This text will be one size larger than the rest. </BIG>
```

BLOCKQUOTE

Denotes a quotation in text.

Properties	Attributes	Properties	Attributes
className	CLASS=*string*	offsetHeight	
document		offsetLeft	
event	<event_name>=*name of script*	offsetParent	
		offsetTop	
id	ID=*string*	offsetWidth	
innerHTML		outerHTML	
innerText		outerText	
isTextEdit		parentElement	
lang	LANG=*string*	parentTextEdit	
language	LANGUAGE= JAVASCRIPT | JSCRIPT | VBSCRIPT | VBS	sourceIndex	
		style	STYLE=*string*
		tagName	
		title	TITLE=*string*

Methods
click contains getAttribute insertAdjacentHTML
insertAdjacentText removeAttribute scrollIntoView
setAttribute

Events
onclick ondblclick ondragstart onfilterchange onhelp
onkeydown onkeypress onkeyup onmousedown onmousemove
onmouseout onmouseover onmouseup onselectstart

Collection	Description
filters	Collection of all the filter objects for an element.

Normally displays text indented:

```
<HTML>
<HEAD>
</HEAD>
<BODY>
This is normal text
<BR>
<BLOCKQUOTE>This is a blockquote which will produce indented text</BLOCKQUOTE>
</BODY>
</HTML>
```

308

Defines the beginning and end of the body section of the page.

Properties	Attributes	Properties	Attributes
accessKey	ACCESSKEY=*string*	leftMargin	LEFTMARGIN=*number*
	ALINK=*color*	linkColor	LINK=*color*
background	BACKGROUND=*string*	offsetHeight	
bgColor	BGCOLOR=*color*	offsetLeft	
bgProperties	BGPROPERTIES= FIXED	offsetParent	
		offsetTop	
bottomMargin	BOTTOMMARGIN= *number*	offsetWidth	
		parentElement	
className	CLASS=*string*	parentTextEdit	
clientHeight		rightMargin	RIGHTMARGIN= *number*
clientWidth			
document		scroll	SCROLL=YES | NO
event	<event_name>=*name of script*	scrollHeight	
		scrollLeft	
	TEXT=*color*	scrollTop	
id	ID=*string*	scrollWidth	
innerHTML		sourceIndex	
innerText		style	STYLE=*string*
isTextEdit		tagName	
lang	LANG=*string*	text	
language	LANGUAGE= JAVASCRIPT | JSCRIPT | VBSCRIPT | VBS	title	TITLE=*string*
		topMargin	TOPMARGIN=*number*
		vlinkColor	VLINK=*color*

Methods
blur click contains createTextRange focus getAttribute
insertAdjacentHTML insertAdjacentText removeAttribute
scrollIntoView setAttribute

Events
onafterupdate onbeforeupdate onblur onclick ondblclick
ondragstart onfocus onhelp onkeydown onkeypress onkeyup
onmousedown onmousemove onmouseout onmouseover onmouseup
onresize onrowenter onrowexit onscroll onselectstart

...BODY

To set the colors of the links in the page, we include the **LINK** and **VLINK** attributes in the **BODY** tag. To set the color of the page itself, and the color of the text, we use the **BGCOLOR** and **TEXT** attributes:

```
<BODY BGCOLOR="red" TEXT="white" LINK="blue" ALINK="maroon">
```

Alternatively, we can specify the colors using their RGB values:

```
<BODY BGCOLOR="#ff0000" TEXT="#ffffff" LINK="#ff" ALINK="#ff00ff">
```

To display a picture on the page as a background, we use the **BACKGROUND** attribute:

```
<BODY BACKGROUND="bgpattern.gif">
```

We can also align the text in the page, and set the margins:

```
<BODY ALIGN=LEFT LEFTMARGIN=100>
```

Finally, we can also prevent the image used as the page background from scrolling with the page by setting the **BGPROPERTIES** attribute, and remove the default scroll bars with the **SCROLL** attribute:

```
<BODY BACKGROUND="bgpattern.gif" BGPROPERTIES=FIXED SCROLL=NO>
```

Inserts a line break.

Properties	Attributes	Properties	Attributes
className	CLASS=*string*	offsetParent	
clear	CLEAR=ALL | LEFT | RIGHT	offsetTop	
		offsetWidth	
document		outerHTML	
id	ID=*string*	outerText	
isTextEdit		parentElement	
language	LANGUAGE= JAVASCRIPT | JSCRIPT | VBSCRIPT | VBS	parentTextEdit	
		sourceIndex	
		style	STYLE=*string*
offsetHeight		tagName	
offsetLeft		title	TITLE=*string*

Methods
contains getAttribute insertAdjacentHTML insertAdjacentText
removeAttribute setAttribute

If we want the line break to move following text or elements down past another element, such as an image, which is left or right aligned, we use the **CLEAR** attribute. Without it, the following text or elements would continue to wrap around the other element.

To move the following elements below a left-aligned image, for example, we can use:

```
<BR CLEAR=LEFT>
```

To move the following elements below both left and right-aligned images we use:

```
<BR CLEAR=ALL>
```

There are no Events for this tag.

BUTTON

Renders an HTML button with the text or other elements between the opening and closing tags being rendered as the button face.

Properties	Attributes	Properties	Attributes
accessKey	ACCESSKEY=*string*	name	
className	CLASS=*string*	offsetHeight	
dataFld	DATAFLD=*columnname*	offsetLeft	
dataFormatAs	DATAFORMATAS=*string*	offsetParent	
dataSrc	DATASRC=*id*	offsetTop	
disabled	DISABLED	offsetWidth	
document		outerHTML	
event	<event_name>= *name of script*	outerText	
form		parentElement	
id	ID=*string*	parentTextEdit	
innerHTML		sourceIndex	
innerText		status	
isTextEdit		style	STYLE=*string*
lang	LANG=*string*	tagName	
language	LANGUAGE= JAVASCRIPT | JSCRIPT | VBSCRIPT | VBS	title	TITLE=*string*
		type	TYPE=*string*
		value	

Methods
blur click contains createTextRange focus getAttribute
insertAdjacentHTML insertAdjacentText removeAttribute
scrollIntoView setAttribute

Events
onafterupdate onbeforeupdate onblur onclick ondblclick
ondragstart onfilterchange onfocuson mousedown onmousemove
onmouseout onmouseover onmouseup onresize onrowenter
onrowexit onscroll onselectstart

Collection	Description
filters	Collection of all the filter objects for an element.

```
<BUTTON>Button Caption</BUTTON>
```

```
<BUTTON ID=MyBTN>
    <IMG SRC="ButtonPic.gif" WIDTH=100 HEIGHT=100> <BR> My Button
</BUTTON>
```

We can even specify what the button should do when it is clicked

```
<BUTTON onclick="alert('You just clicked the button')">Button Caption</BUTTON>
```

CAPTION

Specifies a caption for a table.

Properties	Attributes
align	ALIGN=BOTTOM | CENTER | LEFT | RIGHT | TOP
className	CLASS=*string*
clientHeight	
clientWidth	
document	
event	<event_name>=*name of script*
id	ID=*string*
innerText	
isTextEdit	
lang	LANG=*string*
language	LANGUAGE= JAVASCRIPT | JSCRIPT | VBSCRIPT | VBS

Properties	Attributes
offsetHeight	
offsetLeft	
offsetParent	
offsetTop	
offsetWidth	
outerText	
parentElement	
parentTextEdit	
sourceIndex	
style	STYLE=*string*
tagName	
title	TITLE=*string*
vAlign	VALIGN=BOTTOM | TOP

Methods
blur click contains focus getAttribute insertAdjacentHTML
insertAdjacentText removeAttribute scrollIntoView
setAttribute

...CAPTION

Events

onafterupdate onbeforeupdate onblur onclick ondblclick ondragstart onfilterchange onfocus onhelp onkeydown onkeypress onkeyup onmousedown onmousemove onmouseout onmouseover onmouseup onresize onrowenter onrowexit onscroll onselectstart

Collection	Description
filters	Collection of all the filter objects for an element.

See also **TABLE**

```
<TABLE>
   <CAPTION ALIGN=LEFT> This is the table caption </CAPTION>
   <TR> <TD> table content </TD> </TR>
</TABLE>
```

CENTER

Causes subsequent text and other elements to be centered on the page.

Properties	Attributes	Properties	Attributes
className	CLASS=*string*	offsetHeight	
document		offsetLeft	
event	<event_name>=*name of script*	offsetParent	
		offsetTop	
id	ID=*string*	offsetWidth	
innerHTML		outerHTML	
innerText		outerText	
isTextEdit		parentElement	
lang	LANG=*string*	parentTextEdit	
language	LANGUAGE= JAVASCRIPT | JSCRIPT | VBSCRIPT | VBS	sourceIndex	
		style	STYLE=*string*
		tagName	
		title	TITLE=*string*

Methods
click contains getAttribute insertAdjacentHTML
InsertAdjacentText removeAttribute scrollIntoView
setAttribute

Events
onclick ondblclick ondragstart onfilterchange onhelp
onkeydown onkeypress onkeyup onmousedown onmousemove
onmouseout onmouseover onmouseup onselectstart

Collection	Description
filters	Collection of all the filter objects for an element.

```
<CENTER>
    This text will be centered on the page.
    <H1> So will this heading </H1>
    <IMG SRC="MyImage.gif"> <P>
    And so will the image above.
</CENTER>
```

The center tag is still available for backward compatibility purposes, but the
W3C recommendation is that you use **ALIGN** instead.

CITE

Renders text in italics, as a citation. Often used for copyright statements.

Properties	Attributes	Properties	Attributes
className	CLASS=*string*	offsetLeft	
document		offsetParent	
event	<event_name>=*name of script*	offsetTop	
		offsetWidth	
id	ID=*string*	outerHTML	
innerHTML		outerText	
innerText		parentElement	
isTextEdit		parentTextEdit	
lang	LANG=*string*	sourceIndex	
language	LANGUAGE= JAVASCRIPT | JSCRIPT | VBSCRIPT | VBS	style	STYLE=*string*
		tagName	
		title	TITLE=*string*
offsetHeight			

Methods
click contains getAttribute insertAdjacentHTML
insertAdjacentText removeAttribute scrollIntoView
setAttribute

Events
onclick ondblclick ondragstart onfilterchange onhelp
onkeydown onkeypress onkeyup onmousedown onmousemove
onmouseout onmouseover onmouseup onselectstart

Collection	Description
filters	Collection of all the filter objects for an element.

<CITE> © 1997 Wrox Press Limited, UK </CITE>

Renders text as a code sample in a fixed width font.

Properties	Attributes	Properties	Attributes
className	CLASS=*string*	offsetLeft	
document		offsetParent	
event	<event_name>=*name of script*	offsetTop	
		offsetWidth	
id	ID=*string*	outerHTML	
innerHTML		outerText	
innerText		parentElement	
isTextEdit		parentTextEdit	
lang	LANG=*string*	sourceIndex	
language	LANGUAGE= JAVASCRIPT | JSCRIPT | VBSCRIPT | VBS	style	STYLE=*string*
		tagName	
offsetHeight		title	TITLE=*string*

Methods
```
click contains getAttribute insertAdjacentHTML
insertAdjacentText removeAttribute scrollIntoView
setAttribute
```

Events
```
onclick ondblclick ondragstart onfilterchange onhelp
onkeydown onkeypress onkeyup onmousedown onmousemove
onmouseout onmouseover onmouseup onselectstart
```

Collection	Description
filters	Collection of all the filter objects for an element.

```
<CODE> <! following is rendered as a code listing on the screen>
 Sub MyRoutine(datToday)
    If datToday = "Saturday" Then
      strDestination = "The beach."
    Else
      strDestination = "The office again."
    End If
  End Sub
</CODE>
```

COL

Used to specify column based defaults for a table.

Properties	Attributes	Properties	Attributes
align	ALIGN=CENTER | LEFT | RIGHT	span	SPAN=*number*
className	CLASS=*string*	style	STYLE=*string*
document		tagName	
id	ID=*string*	title	TITLE=*string*
isTextEdit		vAlign	VALIGN=BASELINE | BOTTOM | MIDDLE | TOP
parentElement			
parentTextEdit			WIDTH=*number*

Methods
contains getAttribute removeAttribute setAttribute

```
<TABLE>
   <COLGROUP>
   <COL ALIGN=LEFT WIDTH=100 SPAN=2>
   <COLGROUP ALIGN=LEFT WIDTH=100 SPAN=4>
   <TR><TD> table content </TD ></TR>
   ...
</TABLE>
```

There are no events for this tag.

Used as a container for a group of columns.

Properties	Attributes	Properties	Attributes
align	ALIGN=CENTER | LEFT | RIGHT	span	SPAN=*number*
		style	STYLE=*string*
className	CLASS=*string*	tagName	
document		title	TITLE=*string*
id	ID=*string*	vAlign	VALIGN=BASELINE | BOTTOM | MIDDLE | TOP
isTextEdit			
parentElement			
parentTextEdit			WIDTH=*number*

Methods
contains getAttribute removeAttribute setAttribute

There are no Events for this tag.

Denotes a comment that will not be displayed.

Properties	Attributes	Properties	Attributes
className	CLASS=*string*	parentElement	
document		parentTextEdit	
id	ID=*string*	sourceIndex	
isTextEdit		tagName	
lang	LANG=*string*	title	TITLE=*string*

Methods
contains getAttribute removeAttribute setAttribute

```
<COMMENT>
   Anything here will be ignored by the browser while rendering the page.
   The COMMENT tag is good for commenting out several lines at a time.
</COMMENT>
```

There are no Events for this tag.

DD

The DD tag is used inside a definition list to provide the definition of the text in the DT tag. It may contain block elements, as well as plain text and markup. The end tag is optional, as it's always clear from the context where the tag's contents end.

Properties	Attributes	Properties	Attributes
className	CLASS=*string*	offsetLeft	
document		offsetParent	
event	<event_name>=*name of script*	offsetTop	
id	ID=*string*	offsetWidth	
innerHTML		outerHTML	
innerText		outerText	
isTextEdit		parentElement	
lang	LANG=*string*	parentTextEdit	
language	LANGUAGE= JAVASCRIPT | JSCRIPT | VBSCRIPT | VBS	sourceIndex	STYLE=*string*
		tagName	
offsetHeight		title	TITLE=*string*

Methods
click contains getAttribute insertAdjacentHTML insertAdjacentText removeAttribute scrollIntoView setAttribute

Events
onclick ondblclick ondragstart onfilterchange onhelp onkeydown onkeypress onkeyup onmousedown onmousemove onmouseout onmouseover onmouseup onselectstart

See also **DL** and **DT**

```
<DL>
<DT>Wrox</DT>
<DD>The publisher of Professional IE4 and Dynamic HTML Programming</DD>
</DL>
```

DFN is used to mark out terms which are being used for the first time. These are often rendered in italics.

Properties	Attributes	Properties	Attributes
className	CLASS=*string*	offsetLeft	
document		offsetParent	
event	<event_name>=*name of script*	offsetTop	
		offsetWidth	
id	ID=*string*	outerHTML	
innerHTML		outerText	
innerText		parentElement	
isTextEdit		parentTextEdit	
lang	LANG=*string*	sourceIndex	
language	LANGUAGE= JAVASCRIPT | JSCRIPT | VBSCRIPT | VBS	style	STYLE=*string*
		tagName	
		title	TITLE=*string*
offsetHeight			

Methods
click contains getAttribute insertAdjacentHTML
insertAdjacentText removeAttribute scrollIntoView
setAttribute

Events
onclick ondblclick ondragstart onfilterchange onhelp
onkeydown onkeypress onkeyup onmousedown onmousemove
onmouseout onmouseover onmouseup onselectstart

Collection	Description
filters	Collection of all the filter objects for an element.

DHTML –
<DFN>Dynamic HTML</DFN>

DIR

Renders text as a directory listing.

Properties	Attributes	Properties	Attributes
className	CLASS=*string*	offsetLeft	
document		offsetParent	
event	<event_name>=*name of script*	offsetTop	
		offsetWidth	
id	ID=*string*	outerHTML	
innerHTML		outerText	
innerText		parentElement	
isTextEdit		parentTextEdit	
lang	LANG=*string*	sourceIndex	
language	LANGUAGE= JAVASCRIPT | JSCRIPT | VBSCRIPT | VBS	style	STYLE=*string*
		tagName	
offsetHeight		title	TITLE=*string*

Methods
click contains getAttribute insertAdjacentHTML
insertAdjacentText removeAttribute scrollIntoView
setAttribute

Events
onclick ondblclick ondragstart onfilterchange onhelp
onkeydown onkeypress onkeyup onmousedown onmousemove
onmouseout onmouseover onmouseup onselectstart

Collection	Description
filters	Collection of all the filter objects for an element.

```
<DIR>
  properties.doc    421,564
  methods.doc        23,518
  events.doc          6,386
</DIR>
```

Defines a logical division within a document.

Properties	Attributes	Properties	Attributes
		offsetHeight	
align	ALIGN=CENTER | LEFT | RIGHT	offsetLeft	
		offsetParent	
className	CLASS=*string*	offsetTop	
clientHeight		offsetWidth	
clientWidth		outerText	
dataFld	DATAFLD=*column-name*	parentElement	
dataFormatAs	DATAFORMATAS=*string*	parentTextEdit	
dataSrc	DATASRC=*id*	scrollHeight	
document		scrollLeft	
event	<event_name>=*name of script*	scrollTop	
id	ID=*string*	scrollWidth	
innerText		sourceIndex	
isTextEdit		style	STYLE=*string*
lang	LANG=*string*	tagName	
language	LANGUAGE= JAVASCRIPT | JSCRIPT | VBSCRIPT | VBS	title	TITLE=*string*

Methods
blur click contains focus getAttribute insertAdjacentHTML
insertAdjacentText removeAttribute scrollIntoView
setAttribute

Events
onafterupdate onbeforeupdate onblur onclick ondblclick
ondragstart onfocus onhelp onkeydown onkeypress onkeyup
onmousedown onmousemove onmouseout onmouseover onmouseup
onresize onrowenter onrowexit onscroll onselectstart

Collection	Description
filters	Collection of all the filter objects for an element.

```
<DIV ID=MyDiv STYLE="position:absolute;top:20;left:50;width:500;height:100>
This text is inside an absolutely positioned document division.
</DIV>
```

DL

DL is used to provide a list of items with associated definitions. Every item should be put in a DT, with its definition in the DD immediately following it. This list is typically rendered without bullets of any kind. While it is legal to have a DL with only DD or DT tags, it doesn't make much sense - what good is a definition without a term? - and you should not expect it to get rendered as a normal list.

Properties	Attributes	Properties	Attributes
className	CLASS=*string*	offsetHeight	
compact	COMPACT	offsetLeft	
document		offsetParent	
event	<event_name>=*name of script*	offsetTop	
		offsetWidth	
id	ID=*string*	outerHTML	
innerHTML		outerText	
innerText		parentElement	
isTextEdit		parentTextEdit	
lang	LANG=*string*	sourceIndex	
language	LANGUAGE= JAVASCRIPT | JSCRIPT | VBSCRIPT | VBS	style	STYLE=*string*
		tagName	
		title	TITLE=*string*

Methods
click contains getAttribute insertAdjacentHTML
insertAdjacentText removeAttribute scrollIntoView
setAttribute

Events
onclick ondblclick ondragstart onfilterchange onhelp
onkeydown onkeypress onkeyup onmousedown onmousemove
onmouseout onmouseover onmouseup onselectstart

Collection	Description
filters	Collection of all the filter objects for an element.

```
<DL>
<DT>Wrox</DT>
<DD>The publisher of Professional Dynamic HTML and IE4 Programming</DD>
</DL>
```

See also **DT**, **DD**.

The DT tag is used inside a DL tag. It marks a term whose definition is provided by the next DD. The DT tag may only contain text-level markup.

Properties	Attributes	Properties	Attributes
className	CLASS=*string*	offsetLeft	
document		offsetParent	
event	<event_name>=*name of script*	offsetTop	
		offsetWidth	
id	ID=*string*	outerHTML	
innerHTML		outerText	
innerText		parentElement	
isTextEdit		parentTextEdit	
lang	LANG=*string*	sourceIndex	
language	LANGUAGE= JAVASCRIPT | JSCRIPT | VBSCRIPT | VBS	style	STYLE=*string*
		tagName	
		title	TITLE=*string*
offsetHeight			

Methods
click contains getAttribute insertAdjacentHTML
insertAdjacentText removeAttribute scrollIntoView
setAttribute

Events
onclick ondblclick ondragstart onfilterchange onhelp
onkeydown onkeypress onkeyup onmousedown onmousemove
onmouseout onmouseover onmouseup onselectstart

Collection	Description
filters	Collection of all the filter objects for an element.

```
<DL>
<DT>Wrox</DT>
<DD>The publisher of Professional Dynamic HTML and IE4 Programming</DD>
</DL>
```

See also DD, DL.

EM

Renders text as emphasized, usually in italics.

Properties	Attributes	Properties	Attributes
className	CLASS=*string*	offsetLeft	
document		offsetParent	
event	\<event_name\>= *name of script*	offsetTop	
		offsetWidth	
id	ID=*string*	outerHTML	
innerHTML		outerText	
innerText		parentElement	
isTextEdit		parentTextEdit	
lang	LANG=*string*	sourceIndex	
language	LANGUAGE= JAVASCRIPT | JSCRIPT | VBSCRIPT | VBS	style	STYLE=*string*
		tagName	
		title	TITLE=*string*
offsetHeight			

Methods
click contains getAttribute insertAdjacentHTML
insertAdjacentText removeAttribute scrollIntoView
setAttribute

Events
onclick ondblclick ondragstart onfilterchange onhelp
onkeydown onkeypress onkeyup onmousedown onmousemove
onmouseout onmouseover onmouseup onselectstart

Collection	Description
filters	Collection of all the filter objects for an element.

The word \<EM\>emphasis\</EM\> will be emphasized by being rendered in italics

Embeds documents of any type in the page, to be viewed in another suitable application.

Properties	Attributes	Properties	Attributes
accessKey		offsetHeight	
align	ALIGN=ABSBOTTOM | ABSMIDDLE | BASELINE | BOTTOM | LEFT | MIDDLE | RIGHT | TEXTTOP | TOP	offsetLeft	
		offsetParent	
		offsetTop	
		offsetWidth	
	ALT=*string*	outerHTML	
className	CLASS=*string*	outerText	
	CODE=*string*	palette	
	CODEBASE=*string*	parentElement	
document		parentTextEdit	
height	HEIGHT=*string*	pluginspage	
Hidden		sourceIndex	
	HSPACE=*number*	src	SRC=*url*
id	ID=*string*	style	STYLE=*string*
isTextEdit		tagName	
lang		title	TITLE=*string*
language			VSPACE=*number*
	NAME=*string*	width	WIDTH=*number*

Methods
blur contains focus getAttribute insertAdjacentHTML insertAdjacentText removeAttribute scrollIntoView setAttribute

Events
onblur onfocus

```
<EMBED SRC="MyMovie.mov" WIDTH=300 HEIGHT=200>
<EMBED SRC="Letter.doc" WIDTH=600 HEIGHT=400 ALIGN=CENTER>
```

327

FIELDSET

Draws a box around the contained elements to indicate related items.

Properties	Attributes	Properties	Attributes
accessKey		offsetParent	
align		offsetTop	
className	CLASS=*string*	offsetWidth	
clientHeight		outerHTML	
clientWidth		outerText	
document		parentElement	
event	<event_name>=*name of script*	parentTextEdit	
		recordNumber	
id	ID=*string*	scrollHeight	
innerHTML		scrollLeft	
innerText		scrollTop	
isTextEdit		scrollWidth	
lang	LANG=*string*	sourceIndex	
language	LANGUAGE= JAVASCRIPT | JSCRIPT | VBSCRIPT | VBS	style	STYLE=*string*
		tabIndex	
		tagName	
offsetHeight		title	TITLE=*string*
offsetLeft			

Methods
blur click contains focus getAttribute insertAdjacentHTML
insertAdjacentText removeAttribute scrollIntoView
setAttribute

Events
onafterupdate onbeforeupdate onblur onclick ondblclick
ondragstart onerrorupdate onfocus onhelp onkeydown
onkeypress onkeyup onmousedown onmousemove onmouseout
onmouseover onmouseup onresize onrowenter onrowexit
onscroll onselectstart

Collection	Description
filters	Collection of all the filter objects for an element.

Specifies the font face, size and color for rendering the text.

Properties	Attributes	Properties	Attributes
className	CLASS=*string*	offsetHeight	
color	COLOR=*color*	offsetLeft	
document		offsetParent	
event	\<event_name\>=*name of script*	offsetTop	
		offsetWidth	
face	FACE=*string*	outerHTML	
id	ID=*string*	outerText	
innerHTML		parentElement	
innerText		parentTextEdit	
isTextEdit		size	SIZE=*number*
lang	LANG=*string*	sourceIndex	
language	LANGUAGE= JAVASCRIPT | JSCRIPT | VBSCRIPT | VBS	style	STYLE=*string*
		tagName	
		title	TITLE=*string*

Methods
click contains getAttribute insertAdjacentHTML
insertAdjacentText removeAttribute scrollIntoView
setAttribute

Events
onclick ondblclick ondragstart onfilterchange onhelp
onkeydown onkeypress onkeyup onmousedown onmousemove
onmouseout onmouseover onmouseup onselectstart

Collection	Description
filters	Collection of all the filter objects for an element.

We can change the size in relation to the current **BASEFONT** setting -

```
<FONT SIZE="+1">font</FONT>
```

will render the word font as slightly bigger than the other text.

We can also specify the font face (fontname) and color

```
<FONT FACE="ARIAL" SIZE="+1" COLOR="#FFFFFF">font</FONT>
```

will render the word font in slightly larger, white Arial font.

FORM

Denotes a form on the page that can contain other controls and elements.

Properties	Attributes	Properties	Attributes
action	ACTION=*string*	offsetHeight	
className	CLASS=*string*	offsetLeft	
document		offsetParent	
encoding	ENCTYPE=*string*	offsetTop	
event	<event_name>=*name of script*	offsetWidth	
		outerHTML	
id	ID=*string*	outerText	
innerHTML		parentElement	
innerText		parentTextEdit	
isTextEdit		sourceIndex	
lang	LANG=*string*	style	STYLE=*string*
language	LANGUAGE= JAVASCRIPT | JSCRIPT | VBSCRIPT | VBS	tagName	
		target	TARGET= <window_name> | _parent | _blank | _top | _self
method	METHOD=GET | POST		
name	NAME=*string*	title	TITLE=*string*

Methods
```
click contains getAttribute insertAdjacentHTML
insertAdjacentText removeAttribute reset scrollIntoView
setAttribute submit
```

Events
```
onclick ondblclick ondragstart onfilterchange onhelp
onkeydown onkeypress onkeyup onmousedown onmousemove
onmouseout onmouseover onmouseup onreset onselectstart
onsubmit
```

Collection	Description
elements	Collection of all controls and elements in the form.
filters	Collection of all the filter objects for an element.

```
<FORM NAME="MyForm" ACTION="http://mysite.com/scripts/handler.pl">
   This is a form which can be submitted to the server.
   Enter Your Opinion: <INPUT TYPE="TEXT" NAME="txtOpinion">
   <INPUT TYPE="SUBMIT" VALUE="Send Opinion">
   <INPUT TYPE="RESET" VALUE="Clear Form">
</FORM>
```

Specifies an individual frame within a frameset.

Properties	Attributes	Properties	Attributes
borderColor	BORDERCOLOR=*color*	marginWidth	MARGINWIDTH= *number*
className	CLASS=*string*	name	NAME=*window_name* |
dataFld	DATAFLD=*column-name*		_blank | _parent |
dataSrc	DATASRC=*id*		self | top
document		noResize	NORESIZE=NORESIZE
event	<event_name>=*name* of script		| RESIZE
		parentElement	
frameBorder	FRAMEBORDER=*string*	parentTextEdit	
height	HEIGHT=*string*	scrolling	SCROLLING=AUTO |
id	ID=*string*		YES | NO
isTextEdit		sourceIndex	
lang	LANG=*string*	src	SRC=*url*
language	LANGUAGE= JAVASCRIPT | JSCRIPT | VBSCRIPT | VBS	style	
		tagName	
		title	TITLE=*string*
marginHeight	MARGINHEIGHT= *number*		WIDTH=*number*

Methods
contains getAttribute removeAttribute setAttribute

The frame tag has no associated Events or Collections.

See also **Frameset**

```
<FRAMESET FRAMESPACING=0 COLS="140,*" BORDER=1>
    <FRAME  SRC="menu.htm" NAME="menuframe" MARGINWIDTH=0 SCROLLING=NO NORESIZE>
    <FRAME  SRC="menu.htm" NAME="menuframe" MARGINWIDTH=10 MARGINHEIGHT=10>
</FRAMESET>
```

FRAMESET

Specifies a frameset containing multiple frames and other nested framesets.

Properties	Attributes	Properties	Attributes
border	BORDER=*number*	language	LANGUAGE=
borderColor	BORDERCOLOR=*color*		JAVASCRIPT |
className	CLASS=*string*		JSCRIPT | VBSCRIPT
cols	COLS=*number*		| VBS
document		parentElement	
frameBorder	FRAMEBORDER=NO |	parentTextEdit	
	YES | 0 | 1	rows	ROWS=*number*
frameSpacing	FRAMESPACING=*string*	sourceIndex	
id	ID=*string*	style	
isTextEdit		tagName	
lang	LANG=*string*	title	TITLE=*string*

Methods
contains getAttribute emoveAttribute setAttribute

```
<FRAMESET FRAMESPACING=0 COLS="140,*" BORDER=1>
    <FRAME   SRC="menu.htm" NAME="menuframe" MARGINWIDTH=0 SCROLLING=NO NORESIZE>
    <FRAME   SRC="menu.htm" NAME="menuframe" MARGINWIDTH=10 MARGINHEIGHT=10>
</FRAMESET>
```

There are no Events for this tag.

Contains tags holding unviewed information about the document.

Properties	Attributes	Properties	Attributes
className	CLASS=*string*	parentElement	
document		sourceIndex	
id	ID=*string*	tagName	
isTextEdit		title	TITLE=*string*

Methods
contains getAttribute removeAttribute setAttribute

Usually only contains **TITLE, META, BASE, ISINDEX, LINK, SCRIPT** and **STYLE** tags.

```
<HEAD>
    <TITLE> My Web Page </TITLE>
    <META NAME="Updated" CONTENT="15-Aug-97">
    <BASE HREF="http://mysite.com/pages/thispage.htm">
</HEAD>
```

There are no Events for this tag.

H*n*

Renders text as a heading style (**H1** to **H6**).

Properties	Attributes	Properties	Attributes
align	ALIGN=CENTER | LEFT | RIGHT	offsetHeight	
		offsetLeft	
className	CLASS=*string*	offsetParent	
document		offsetTop	
event	<event_name>=*name of script*	offsetWidth	
		outerHTML	
id	ID=*string*	outerText	
innerHTML		parentElement	
innerText		parentTextEdit	
isTextEdit		sourceIndex	
lang	LANG=*string*	style	STYLE=*string*
language	LANGUAGE= JAVASCRIPT | JSCRIPT | VBSCRIPT | VBS	tagName	
		title	TITLE=*string*

Methods
click contains getAttribute insertAdjacentHTML
insertAdjacentText removeAttribute scrollIntoView
setAttribute

Events
onclick ondblclick ondragstart onfilterchange onhelp
onkeydown onkeypress onkeyup onmousedown onmousemove
onmouseout onmouseover onmouseup onselectstart

Collection	Description
filters	Collection of all the filter objects for an element.

```
<H1> This is the largest size of heading </H1>
<H6> This is the smallest size of heading </H6>
<H4> And this is somewhere in between </H4>
```

Places a horizontal rule in the page.

Properties	Attributes	Properties	Attributes
align	ALIGN=CENTER | LEFT | RIGHT	offsetLeft	
		offsetParent	
className	CLASS=*string*	offsetTop	
color	COLOR=*color*	offsetWidth	
document		outerHTML	
event	<event_name>=*name of script*	outerText	
		parentElement	
id	ID=*string*	parentTextEdit	
isTextEdit		size	SIZE=*number*
lang	LANG=*string*	sourceIndex	
language	LANGUAGE= JAVASCRIPT | JSCRIPT | VBSCRIPT | VBS		SRC=*url*
		style	STYLE=*string*
		tagName	
noShade	NOSHADE	title	TITLE=*string*
offsetHeight		width	WIDTH=*number*

Methods
blur click contains focus getAttribute insertAdjacentHTML
insertAdjacentText removeAttribute scrollIntoView
setAttribute

Events
onbeforeupdate onblur onclick ondblclick ondragstart
onfilterchange onfocus onhelp onkeydown onkeypress onkeyup
onmousedown onmousemove onmouseout onmouseover onmouseup
onresize onrowenter onrowexit onselectstart

Collection	Description
filters	Collection of all the filter objects for an element.

For a red horizontal rule half the page width, 5 pixels deep, and with no 3D effect, we can use:

```
<HR SIZE=5 WIDTH=50% COLOR="#ff0000" NOSHADE>
```

HTML

Identifies the document as containing HTML elements.

Properties	Attributes	Properties	Attributes
className		parentElement	
document		sourceIndex	
id		style	
isTextEdit		tagName	
language	LANG=*language*	title	TITLE=*string*

Methods
`contains  getAttribute  removeAttribute  setAttribute`

A standard HTML document MUST BE enclosed by the **HTML** tags. Inside these, the **HEAD** and **BODY** tags are used to divide the document up into sections

The **HEAD** section contains information about the document, specifies how it should be displayed, and issues other instructions to the browser.

The **BODY** section contains the elements of the document designed to be displayed by the browser.

```
<!DOCTYPE ...>
<HTML>
  <HEAD>
    <META ... >
    <TITLE> Page title goes here </TITLE>
  </HEAD>
  <BODY>
    ...
      This is the main visible part of the page
    ...
  </BODY
</HTML>
```

There are no Events for this tag.

336

Renders text in an italic font where available.

Properties	Attributes	Properties	Attributes
className	CLASS=*string*	offsetLeft	
document		offsetParent	
event	<event_name>=*name of script*	offsetTop	
		offsetWidth	
id	ID=*string*	outerHTML	
innerHTML		outerText	
innerText		parentElement	
isTextEdit		parentTextEdit	
lang	LANG=*string*	sourceIndex	
language	LANGUAGE= JAVASCRIPT | JSCRIPT | VBSCRIPT | VBS	style	STYLE=*string*
		tagName	
		title	TITLE=*string*
offsetHeight			

Methods
`click contains getAttribute insertAdjacentHTML insertAdjacentText removeAttribute scrollIntoView setAttribute`

Events
`onclick ondblclick ondragstart onfilterchange onhelp onkeydown onkeypress onkeyup onmousedown onmousemove onmouseout onmouseover onmouseup onselectstart`

Collection	Description
filters	Collection of all the filter objects for an element.

`<I> This text will be displayed in italic font style. </I>`

IFRAME

Used to create in-line floating frames within the page.

Properties	Attributes	Properties	Attributes
align	ALIGN=ABSBOTTOM | ABSMIDDLE | BASELINE | BOTTOM | LEFT | MIDDLE | RIGHT | TEXTTOP | TOP	marginHeight	MARGINHEIGHT= *number*
		marginWidth	MARGINWIDTH=*number*
		name	NAME=*string*
		noResize	NORESIZE=NORESIZE | RESIZE
border	BORDER=*number*	offsetHeight	
borderColor	BORDERCOLOR=*color*	offsetLeft	
className	CLASS=*string*	offsetParent	
dataFld	DATAFLD=*columnname*	offsetTop	
dataSrc	DATASRC=*id*	offsetWidth	
document		outerHTML	
event	<event_name>=*name of script*	outerText	
frameBorder	FRAMEBORDER=NO | YES | 0 | 1	parentElement	
		parentTextEdit	
frameSpacing	FRAMESPACING=*string*	scrolling	SCROLLING=AUTO | YES | NO
height	HEIGHT=*string*		
hspace	HSPACE=*number*	sourceIndex	
id	ID=*string*	src	SRC=*url*
innerHTML		style	STYLE=*string*
innerText		tagName	
isTextEdit		title	TITLE=*string*
lang	LANG=*string*	vspace	VSPACE=*number*
language	LANGUAGE= JAVASCRIPT | JSCRIPT | VBSCRIPT | VBS	width	WIDTH=*number*

Methods
contains getAttribute insertAdjacentHTML insertAdjacentText
removeAttribute scrollIntoView setAttribute

There are no Events for this tag.

338

Embeds an image or a video clip in the document. Most browsers only support **GIF** and **JPEG** file types for inline images. Video clips are more usually handled by the **EMBED** tag.

Properties	Attributes	Properties	Attributes
align	ALIGN=ABSBOTTOM | ABSMIDDLE | BASELINE | BOTTOM | LEFT | MIDDLE | RIGHT | TEXTTOP | TOP	name	NAME=*string*
		offsetHeight	
		offsetLeft	
		offsetParent	
		offsetTop	
alt	ALT=*string*	offsetWidth	
border	BORDER=*number*	outerHTML	
className	CLASS=*string*	outerText	
dataFld	DATAFLD=*columnname*	parentElement	
dataSrc	DATASRC=*id*	parentTextEdit	
document		readyState	
dynsrc	DYNSRC=*string*	scrollHeight	
event	<event_name>= *name of script*	scrollLeft	
		scrollTop	
height	HEIGHT=*string*	scrollWidth	
hspace	HSPACE=*number*	sourceIndex	
id	ID=*string*	src	SRC=*url*
isMap	ISMAP	start	
isTextEdit		style	STYLE=*string*
lang	LANG=*string*	tagName	
language	LANGUAGE= JAVASCRIPT | JSCRIPT | VBSCRIPT | VBS	title	TITLE=*string*
		useMap	USEMAP=*string*
		vspace	VSPACE=*number*
loop	LOOP=*number*	width	WIDTH=*number*
lowsrc	LOWSRC=*url*		

Methods
blur click contains focus getAttribute insertAdjacentHTML
insertAdjacentText removeAttribute scrollIntoView
setAttribute

...IMG

Events

```
onabort onafterupdate onbeforeupdate onblur onclick
ondblclick ondragstart onerror onfilterchange onfocus
onhelp onkeydown onkeypress onkeyup onload onmousedown
onmousemove onmouseout onmouseover onmouseup onresize
onrowenter onrowexit onscroll onselectstart
```

Collection	Description
`filters`	Collection of all the filter objects for an element.

This example inserts an image named "MyDog.gif" into the page:

```
<IMG SRC="MyDog.gif">
```

We can speed up the loading of the image by setting the size for it in the page:

```
<IMG SRC="MyDog.gif" WIDTH=200 HEIGHT=100>
```

We can also supply text that is displayed if the image is not loaded:

```
<IMG SRC="MyDog.gif" WIDTH=200 HEIGHT=100 ALT="Picture of my dog">
```

The **IMG** tage can also display .avi files in Internet Explorer. This example will play the AVI file MyDog.avi if possible, or include the picture MyDog.gif if not. If the video can be shown it will start when the page opens and repeat indefinitely:

```
<IMG DYNASRC="MyDog.avi" SRC="MyDog.gif" START=FILEOPEN LOOP=INFINITE>
```

Specifies a form input control.

Properties	Attributes	Properties	Attributes
accessKey	ACCESSKEY=*string*	offsetHeight	
checked		offsetLeft	
className	CLASS=*string*	offsetParent	
dataFld		offsetTop	
dataFormatAs		offsetWidth	
dataSrc		outerHTML	
defaultChecked		outerText	
defaultValue		parentElement	
disabled	DISABLED	parentTextEdit	
document		readOnly	
event	<event_name>= *name of script*	recordNumber	
		size	SIZE=*number*
form		sourceIndex	
id	ID=*string*	src	SRC=*url*
indeterminate		status	
innerHTML		style	STYLE=*string*
innerText		tabIndex	TABINDEX=*number*
isTextEdit		tagName	
lang	LANG=*string*	title	TITLE= *string*
language	LANGUAGE= JAVASCRIPT | JSCRIPT | VBSCRIPT | VBS	type	TYPE= BUTTON | CHECKBOX | FILE | HIDDEN | IMAGE | PASSWORD | RADIO | RESET | SUBMIT | TEXT
maxLength	MAXLENGTH=*number*		
name	NAME=*string*	value	VALUE=*string*

Methods
blur click contains createTextRange focus getAttribute
insertAdjacentHTML insertAdjacentText removeAttribute
scrollIntoView select setAttribute

...INPUT

Events

```
onafterupdate onbeforeupdate onblur onchange onclick
ondblclick ondragstart onerrorupdate onfilterchange
onfocus onhelp onkeydown onkeypress onkeyup onmousedown
onmousemove onmouseout onmouseover onmouseup onresize
onselect onselectstart
```

Collection	Description
`filters`	Collection of all the filter objects for an element.

The **INPUT** tag is used to create a range of HTML controls, depending on the setting of the **TYPE** attribute.

The **VALUE** attribute provides the default value for a text-type control, or the caption for a button-type control:

```
<INPUT TYPE="TEXT" NAME="txtFavorite" VALUE="Enter your Favorite" SIZE=30>
<INPUT TYPE="BUTTON" NAME="btnOK" VALUE="OK" ONCLICK="MyClickCode()">
<INPUT TYPE="CHECKBOX" NAME="chkYes" CHECKED>
<INPUT TYPE="SUBMIT" NAME="btnSubmit" VALUE="Send Details">
<INPUT TYPE="RESET" NAME="btnReset" VALUE="Clear Form">
<INPUT TYPE="HIDDEN" NAME="hidMyValue" VALUE="Hidden from view">
<INPUT TYPE="PASSWORD" NAME="txtPassword">
```

When creating sets of **RADIO** type controls, or option buttons, use the same **NAME** attribute if you want only one of the controls to be set at any time:

```
<INPUT TYPE="RADIO" NAME="optColor" VALUE="RED" CHECKED>
<INPUT TYPE="RADIO" NAME="optColor" VALUE="YELLOW">
<INPUT TYPE="RADIO" NAME="optColor" VALUE="GREEN">
```

When controls are placed on a form, their values are sent to the server when a **SUBMIT**-type button is clicked:

```
<FORM NAME="MyForm"  ACTION="http://mysite.com/scripts/handler.pl">
    This is a form which can be submitted to the server.
    Enter Your Opinion: <INPUT TYPE="TEXT" NAME="txtOpinion">
    <INPUT TYPE="SUBMIT" VALUE="Send Opinion">
</FORM>
```

See Reference Section E for more information about the different types of control that an `<INPUT>` tag can create.

KBD is used to indicate text which should be entered by the user. It is often drawn in a monospaced font, although this is not required. It differs from **CODE** in that **CODE** indicates code fragments and **KBD** indicates input.

Properties	Attributes	Properties	Attributes
className	CLASS=*string*	offsetLeft	
document		offsetParent	
event	\<event_name\>= *name of script*	offsetTop	
		offsetWidth	
id	ID=*string*	outerHTML	
innerHTML		outerText	
innerText		parentElement	
isTextEdit		parentTextEdit	
lang	LANG=*string*	sourceIndex	
language	LANGUAGE= JAVASCRIPT | JSCRIPT | VBSCRIPT | VBS	style	STYLE=*string*
		tagName	
		title	TITLE=*string*
offsetHeight			

Methods
click contains getAttribute insertAdjacentHTML
insertAdjacentText removeAttribute scrollIntoView
setAttribute

Events
onclick ondblclick ondragstart onfilterchange onhelp
onkeydown onkeypress onkeyup onmousedown onmousemove
onmouseout onmouseover onmouseup onselectstart

Collection	Description
filters	Collection of all the filter objects for an element.

This tag is useful to indicate that \<KBD\> something \</KBD\> is to be typed.

LABEL

Defines the text of a label for a control-like element.

Properties	Attributes	Properties	Attributes
accessKey	ACCESSKEY=*string*	offsetHeight	
className	CLASS=*string*	offsetLeft	
document		offsetParent	
	DATAFLD=*colname*	offsetTop	
	DATAFORMATAS=HTML | TEXT	offsetWidth	
		outerHTML	
	DATASRC=*id*	outerText	
event	<event_name>= *name of script*	parentElement	
		parentTextEdit	
htmlFor	FOR=*string*	sourceIndex	
id	ID=*string*	style	STYLE=*string*
innerHTML		tagName	
innerText		title	TITLE=*string*
isTextEdit			
lang	LANG=*string*		
language	LANGUAGE= JAVASCRIPT | JSCRIPT | VBSCRIPT | VBS		

Methods
click contains getAttribute insertAdjacentHTML insertAdjacentText removeAttribute scrollIntoView setAttribute

Events
onclick ondblclick ondragstart onfilterchange onhelp onkeydown onkeypress onkeyup onmousedown onmousemove onmouseout onmouseover onmouseup onselectstart

Collection	Description
filters	Collection of all the filter objects for an element.

```
<LABEL ACCESSKEY=F FOR="txtFavorite" ID="MyLabel">
   Favorite Color:
   <INPUT TYPE="TEXT" NAME=txtFavorite>
</LABEL>
```

Defines the text to place in the box created by the **FIELDSET** tag.

Properties	Attributes	Properties	Attributes
accessKey		offsetParent	
align	ALIGN=BOTTOM | CENTER | LEFT | RIGHT | TOP	offsetTop	
		offsetWidth	
className	CLASS=*string*	outerHTML	
clientHeight		outerText	
clientWidth		parentElement	
document		parentTextEdit	
event	<event_name>= *name of script*	recordNumber	
		scrollHeight	
id	ID=*string*	scrollLeft	
innerHTML		scrollTop	
innerText		scrollWidth	
isTextEdit		sourceIndex	
lang	LANG=*string*	style	STYLE=*string*
language	LANGUAGE= JAVASCRIPT | JSCRIPT | VBSCRIPT | VBS	tabIndex	
		tagName	
		title	TITLE=*string*
offsetHeight			VALIGN= BOTTOM | TOP
offsetLeft			

Methods
blur click contains focus getAttribute insertAdjacentHTML
insertAdjacentText removeAttribute scrollIntoView
setAttribute

Events
onafterupdate onbeforeupdate onblur onclick ondblclick
ondragstart onerrorupdate onfocus onhelp onkeydown
onkeypress onkeyup onmousedown onmousemove onmouseout
onmouseover onmouseup onresize onrowenter onrowexit
onscroll onselectstart

Collection	Description
filters	Collection of all the filter objects for an element.

LI

Denotes one item within an ordered or unordered list.

Properties	Attributes	Properties	Attributes
className	CLASS=*string*	offsetParent	
document		offsetTop	
event	<event_name>= *name of script*	offsetWidth	
		outerHTML	
id	ID=*string*	outerText	
innerHTML		parentElement	
innerText		parentTextEdit	
isTextEdit		sourceIndex	
lang	LANG=*string*	style	STYLE=*string*
language	LANGUAGE= JAVASCRIPT | JSCRIPT | VBSCRIPT | VBS	tagName	
		title	TITLE=*string*
		type	TYPE=1 | a | A | i | I
offsetHeight			
offsetLeft		value	VALUE=*string*

Methods
click contains getAttribute insertAdjacentHTML
insertAdjacentText removeAttribute scrollIntoView
setAttribute

Events
onclick ondblclick ondragstart onfilterchange onhelp
onkeydown onkeypress onkeyup onmousedown onmousemove
onmouseout onmouseover onmouseup onselectstart

Collection	Description
filters	Collection of all the filter objects for an element.

Used to create indented lists of items, either in an ordered or unordered list. Tags can be nested to provide sub-lists:

See also UL, OL.

```
<OL>
   <LI> This is item one in an ordered list
   <LI> This is item two in an ordered list
</OL>
```

LINK is used to indicate relationships between documents. **REL** indicates a normal relationship to the document specified in the **URL**. The **TITLE** attribute can be used to suggest a title for the referenced **URL** or relation.

Properties	Attributes	Properties	Attributes
className		readyState	
disabled	DISABLED	rel	REL=*string*
document		sourceIndex	
href	HREF=*string*	tagName	
id	ID=*string*	title	TITLE=*string*
parentElement		type	TYPE=*string*

Methods
contains getAttribute removeAttribute setAttribute

Events
onerror onload onreadystatechange

The following **LINK** tags allow advanced browsers to automatically generate a navigational buttonbar for the site. For each possible value, the **URL** can be either absolute or relative.

REL="copyright"	Indicates the location of a page with copyright information for information and such on this site.
REL="glossary"	Indicates the location of a glossary of terms for this site.
REL="help"	Indicates the location of a help file for this site. This can be useful if the site is complex, or if the current document may require explanation to be used correctly (for example, a large fill-in form)
REL="home"	Indicates the location of the homepage, or starting page in this site.
REL="index"	Indicates the location of the index for this site. This doesn't have to be the same as the table of contents. The index could be alphabetical, for example.
REL="next"	Indicates the location of the next document in a series, relative to the current document.
REL="previous"	Indicates the location of the previous document in a series, relative to the current document.
REL="toc"	Indicates the location of the table of contents, or overview of this site.
REL="up"	Indicates the location of the document which is logically directly above the current document.

```
<LINK REL="stylesheet" HREF="http://mysite.com/styles/mystyle.css">
```

```
<LINK REL="subdocument" HREF="http://mysite.com/docs/subdoc.htm">
```

347

LISTING

Renders text in fixed-width type.

Properties	Attributes	Properties	Attributes
className	CLASS=*string*	offsetLeft	
document		offsetParent	
event	<event_name>= *name of script*	offsetTop	
		offsetWidth	
id	ID=*string*	outerHTML	
innerHTML		outerText	
innerText		parentElement	
isTextEdit		parentTextEdit	
lang	LANG=*string*	sourceIndex	
language	LANGUAGE= JAVASCRIPT | JSCRIPT | VBSCRIPT | VBS	style	STYLE=*string*
		tagName	
		title	TITLE=*string*
offsetHeight			

Methods
```
click contains  getAttribute insertAdjacentHTML
insertAdjacentText removeAttribute  scrollIntoView
setAttribute
```

Events
```
onclick ondblclick ondragstart onfilterchange onhelp
onkeydown onkeypress onkeyup onmousedown  onmousemove
onmouseout onmouseover onmouseup onselectstart
```

Collection	Description
filters	Collection of all the filter objects for an element.

```
<LISTING> <! following is rendered at a code listing on the screen>
   Sub MyRoutine(datToday)
     If datToday = "Saturday" Then
       strDestination = "The beach."
     Else
       strDestination = "The office again."
     End If
   End Sub
</LISTING>
```

348

Specifies a collection of hot spots for a client-side image map.

Properties	Attributes	Properties	Attributes
className	CLASS=*string*	offsetParent	
document		offsetTop	
event	\<event_name\>= *name of script*	offsetWidth	
		outerHTML	
id	ID=*string*	outerText	
innerText		parentElement	
isTextEdit		parentTextEdit	
lang	LANG=*string*	sourceIndex	
	NAME=*string*	style	STYLE=*string*
offsetHeight		tagName	
offsetLeft		title	TITLE=*string*

Methods
click contains getAttribute removeAttribute scrollIntoView
setAttribute

Events
onclick onbldclick ondragstart onfilterchange onhelp
onkeydown onkeypress onkeyup onmousedown onmousemove
onmouseout onmouseover onmouseup onselectstart

Collection	Description
areas	Collection of all the areas that make up the image map.

```
<MAP NAME="toolbar">
   <AREA SHAPE="RECT" COORDS="12,216,68,267" HREF="wrox.html">
   <AREA SHAPE="CIRCLE" COORDS="100,200,50" HREF="index.html">
</MAP>
```

MARQUEE

Creates a scrolling text marquee in the page.

Properties	Attributes	Properties	Attributes
accessKey		loop	LOOP=*number*
behavior	BEHAVIOR= ALTERNATE | SCROLL | SLIDE	offsetHeight	
		offsetLeft	
bgColor	BGCOLOR=*color*	offsetParent	
className	CLASS=*string*	offsetTop	
clientHeight		offsetWidth	
clientWidth		outerHTML	
dataFld	DATAFLD=*columnname*	outerText	
dataFormatAs	DATAFORMATAS=*string*	parentElement	
dataSrc	DATASRC=*id*	parentTextEdit	
direction	DIRECTION=DOWN | LEFT | RIGHT | UP	scrollAmount	SCROLLAMOUNT= *number*
document		scrollDelay	SCROLLDELAY=*number*
event	<event_name>= *name of script*	scrollHeight	
		scrollLeft	
height	HEIGHT=*string*	scrollTop	
hspace	HSPACE=*number*	scrollWidth	
id	ID=*string*	sourceIndex	
innerHTML		style	STYLE=*string*
innerText		tagName	
isTextEdit		title	TITLE=*string*
lang	LANG=*string*	trueSpeed	TRUESPEED
language	LANGUAGE= JAVASCRIPT | JSCRIPT | VBSCRIPT | VBS	vspace	VSPACE=*number*
		width	WIDTH=*number*

Methods
blur click contains focus getAttribute insertAdjacentHTML insertAdjacentText removeAttribute scrollIntoView setAttribute start stop

Events

onafterupdate onblur onbounce onclick ondblclick
ondragstart onfinish onfocus onhelp onkeydown onkeypress
onkeyup onmousedown onmousemove onmouseout onmouseover
onmouseup onresize onrowenter onrowexit onscroll
onselectstart onstart

Collection	Description
filters	Collection of all the filter objects for an element.

Renders the following block of text as individual items.

Properties	Attributes	Properties	Attributes
className	CLASS=*string*	offsetParent	
document		offsetTop	
event	<event_name>= *name of script*	offsetWidth	
		outerHTML	
id	ID=*string*	outerText	
innerHTML		parentElement	
innerText		parentTextEdit	
isTextEdit		sourceIndex	
lang	LANG=*string*	style	STYLE=*string*
language		tagName	
offsetHeight		title	TITLE=*string*
offsetLeft			

Methods

click contains getAttribute insertAdjacentHTML
InsertAdjacentText removeAttribute scrollIntoView
setAttribute

Events

onclick ondblclick ondragstart onfilterchange onhelp
onkeydown onkeypress onkeyup onmousedown onmousemove
onmouseout onmouseover onmouseup onselectstart

...MENU

Collection	Description
filters	Collection of all the filter objects for an element.

```
<MENU>
   <LI> This is an item in a menu
   <LI> This is another item in a menu
   <LI> And so is this one
</MENU>
```

META

Provides various types of unviewed information or instructions to the browser.

Properties	Attributes	Properties	Attributes
charset		name	
className		parentElement	
content	CONTENT=*string*	parentTextEdit	
document		sourceIndex	
httpEquiv	HTTP-EQUIV=*string*	tagName	
id		title	TITLE=*string*
isTextEdit		url	URL=*url*
lang			

Methods
contains getAttribute removeAttribute setAttribute

To store information in a document so that it can be read automatically by search engines or automated Web crawlers:

```
<META NAME="Updated" CONTENT "15-AUG-97">
<META NAME="Author" CONTENT="Wrox Press Limited">
<META NAME="Keywords" CONTENT="HTML Dynamic Web Internet">
<META NAME="Description" CONTENT="A page about Dynamic HTML">
```

A popular use for the **META** tag is to set HTTP values and redirect the browser to another page.

```
<META HTTP-EQUIV="REFRESH" CONTENT="10;URL=http://www.wrox.com">
<META HTTP-EQUIV="EXPIRES" CONTENT="Fri, 15 Aug 1997 12:00:00 GMT">
```

There are no Events for this tag.

352

Defines a Parameter in the <HEAD> of the page for use by text editing software.

Properties	Attributes	Properties	Attributes
className		parentElement	
document		parentTextEdit	
id		sourceIndex	
isTextEdit		tagName	
language		title	TITLE=*string*

Methods
contains getAttribute removeAttribute setAttribute

There are no Events for this tag.

Renders text without any text wrapping in the page.

Properties	Attributes	Properties	Attributes
	ID=*string*		TITLE=*string*
	STYLE=*string*		

There are no Methods or Events for this tag.

Defines the HTML to be displayed by browsers that do not support frames.

Properties	Attributes	Properties	Attributes
	ID=*string*		TITLE=*string*
	STYLE=*string*		

There are no Methods or Events for this tag.

NOSCRIPT

Defines the HTML to be displayed in browsers that do not support scripting.

Properties	Attributes	Properties	Attributes
id	ID=*string*	title	TITLE=*string*
style	STYLE=*string*		

There are no Methods or Events for this tag.

OBJECT

Inserts an object or other non-intrinsic HTML control into the page.

Properties	Attributes	Properties	Attributes
accessKey	ACCESSKEY=*string*	language	LANGUAGE= JAVASCRIPT | JSCRIPT | VBSCRIPT | VBS
align	ALIGN=ABSBOTTOM | ABSMIDDLE | BASELINE | BOTTOM | LEFT | MIDDLE | RIGHT | TEXTTOP | TOP		
		name	NAME=*string*
		offsetHeight	
		offsetLeft	
classid	CLASSID=*string*	offsetParent	
className	CLASS=*string*	offsetTop	
code	CODE=*string*	offsetWidth	
codeBase	CODEBASE=*string*	outerHTML	
codeType	CODETYPE=*string*	outerText	
data	DATA=*string*	parentElement	
dataFld	DATAFLD=*columnname*	parentTextEdit	
dataSrc	DATASRC=*id*	readyState	
disabled		sourceIndex	
document		style	STYLE=*string*
event	<event_name>= *name of script*	tabIndex	TABINDEX=*number*
height	HEIGHT=*string*	tagName	
id	ID=*string*	title	TITLE=*string*
isTextEdit		type	TYPE=*string*
lang	LANG=*string*	width	WIDTH=*number*

Methods
blur click contains focus getAttribute insertAdjacentHTML
insertAdjacentText removeAttribute scrollIntoView
setAttribute

Events
onafterupdate onbeforeupdate onblur onclick ondataavailable
ondatasetchanged ondatasetcomplete ondblclick ondragstart
onerror onerrorupdate onfilterchange onfocus onhelp
onkeydown onkeypress onkeyup onload onmousedown onmousemove
onmouseout onmouseover onmouseup onreadystatechange
onresize onrowenter onrowexit onselectstart

Collection	Description
filters	Collection of all the filter objects for an element.

```
<OBJECT ID="MyObject" CLASSID="clsid:AA45-6575-5C1E-7788-BB632C9E3453"
    WIDTH=200 HEIGHT=100 TYPE="application/x-oleobject"
    CODEBASE="http://mysite.com/activex/controls/controll.ocx">
    <PARAM NAME="StartValue" VALUE="12">
    <PARAM NAME="EndValue" VALUE="42">
    <PARAM NAME="ErrorMsg" VALUE="Panic">
</OBJECT>
```

OL

Renders lines of text with <LI> tags as an ordered list.

Properties	Attributes	Properties	Attributes
className	CLASS=*string*	offsetParent	
document		offsetTop	
event	<event_name>= *name of script*	offsetWidth	
		outerHTML	
id	ID=*string*	outerText	
innerHTML		parentElement	
innerText		parentTextEdit	
isTextEdit		sourceIndex	
lang	LANG=*string*	start	START=*number* | *string*
language	LANGUAGE= JAVASCRIPT | JSCRIPT | VBSCRIPT | VBS	style	STYLE=*string*
		tagName	
		title	TITLE=*string*
offsetHeight		type	TYPE=1 | a | A | i | I
offsetLeft			

Methods
click contains getAttribute insertAdjacentHTML
insertAdjacentText removeAttribute scrollIntoView
setAttribute

Events
onclick ondblclick ondragstart onfilterchange onhelp
onkeydown onkeypress onkeyup onmousedown onmousemove
onmouseout onmouseover onmouseup onselectstart

Collection	Description
filters	Collection of all the filter objects for an element.

See also **LI**, **UL**.

```
<OL>
   <LI> This is item one in an ordered list
   <LI> This is item two in an ordered list
</OL>
```

Denotes one choice in a **SELECT** element.

Properties	Attributes	Properties	Attributes
className	CLASS=*string*	offsetWidth	
document		parentElement	
event	`<event_name>`= *name of script*	parentTextEdit	
		selected	SELECTED
id	ID=*string*	sourceIndex	
isTextEdit		style	
language	LANGUAGE= JAVASCRIPT | JSCRIPT | VBSCRIPT | VBS	tagName	
		text	
		title	TITLE=*string*
offsetHeight		value	VALUE=*string*
offsetParent			

Methods
contains getAttribute removeAttribute scrollIntoView
setAttribute

```
<SELECT SIZE=1 ID="MyDropList">
   <OPTION VALUE="0.25"> 1/4 inch thick
   <OPTION VALUE="0.5"> 1/2 inch thick
   <OPTION VALUE="0.75" SELECTED> 3/4 inch thick
   <OPTION VALUE="1"> 1 inch thick
</SELECT>
```

```
<SELECT SIZE=12 ID=MySelectList" MULTIPLE>
   <OPTION VALUE="0723"> Active Server Pages
   <OPTION VALUE="0448"> VBScript Programming
   <OPTION VALUE="0464"> ActiveX Web Databases
   <OPTION VALUE="0707"> Professional DHTML
</SELECT>
```

There are no Events for this tag.

P

Denotes a paragraph.

Properties	Attributes	Properties	Attributes
	ALIGN=CENTER | LEFT | RIGHT	offsetHeight	
		offsetLeft	
className	CLASS=*string*	offsetParent	
document		offsetTop	
event	<event_name>= *name of script*	offsetWidth	
		outerHTML	
id	ID=*string*	outerText	
innerHTML		parentElement	
innerText		parentTextEdit	
isTextEdit		sourceIndex	
lang	LANG=*string*	style	STYLE=*string*
language	LANGUAGE= JAVASCRIPT | JSCRIPT | VBSCRIPT | VBS	tagName	
		title	TITLE=*string*

Methods
click contains getAttribute insertAdjacentHTML
insertAdjacentText removeAttribute scrollIntoView
setAttribute

Events
onclick ondblclick ondragstart onfilterchange onhelp
onkeydown onkeypress onkeyup onmousedown onmousemove
onmouseout onmouseover onmouseup onselectstart

Collection	Description
filters	Collection of all the filter objects for an element.

The P tag can be used on its own:

```
This sentence is separated from the next.<P> This is another paragraph.
```

or to enclose the text in a paragraph:

```
<P> This is one paragraph. </P> <P> This is another paragraph. </P>
```

Used in an **OBJECT** tag to set the object's properties.

Properties	Attributes	Properties	Attributes
	DATAFLD=*columnname*		NAME=*string*
	DATAFORMATAS=*string*		VALUE=*string*
	DATASRC=*id*		

See also **OBJECT, APPLET**.

There are no Methods or Events for this tag.

```
<OBJECT ID="MyObject" CLASSID="clsid:AA45-6575-5C1E-7788-BB632C9E3453"
   WIDTH=200 HEIGHT=100 TYPE="application/x-oleobject"
   CODEBASE="http://mysite.com/activex/controls/controll.ocx">
   <PARAM NAME="StartValue" VALUE="12">
   <PARAM NAME="EndValue" VALUE="42">
   <PARAM NAME="ErrorMsg" VALUE="Panic">
</OBJECT>
```

PLAINTEXT

Renders text in fixed-width type without processing tags.

Properties	Attributes	Properties	Attributes
className	CLASS=*string*	offsetLeft	
document		offsetParent	
event	<event_name>= *name of script*	offsetTop	
		offsetWidth	
id	ID=*string*	outerHTML	
innerHTML		outerText	
innerText		parentElement	
isTextEdit		parentTextEdit	
lang	LANG=*string*	sourceIndex	
language	LANGUAGE= JAVASCRIPT | JSCRIPT | VBSCRIPT | VBS	style	STYLE=*string*
		tagName	
offsetHeight		title	TITLE=*string*

Methods
click contains getAttribute insertAdjacentHTML
insertAdjacentText removeAttribute scrollIntoView
setAttribute

Events
onclick ondblclick ondragstart onfilterchange onhelp
onkeydown onkeypress onkeyup onmousedown onmousemove
onmouseout onmouseover onmouseup onselectstart

Collection	Description
filters	Collection of all the filter objects for an element.

```
<PLAINTEXT>
   All the text and HTML tags here will be rendered on the page without
   being processed by the browser. This means it will look like this on
   screen, and a <B> tag will show as a tag, and not change the text to
   bold. All the text will be in a fixed width font as well.
</PLAINTEXT>
```

360

Renders text in fixed-width type.

Properties	Attributes	Properties	Attributes
className	CLASS=*string*	offsetLeft	
document		offsetParent	
event	<event_name>= *name of script*	offsetTop	
		offsetWidth	
id	ID=*string*	outerHTML	
innerHTML		outerText	
innerText		parentElement	
isTextEdit		parentTextEdit	
lang	LANG=*string*	sourceIndex	
language	LANGUAGE= JAVASCRIPT | JSCRIPT | VBSCRIPT | VBS	style	STYLE=*string*
		tagName	
		title	TITLE=*string*
offsetHeight			

Methods
click contains getAttribute insertAdjacentHTML insertAdjacentText removeAttribute scrollIntoView setAttribute

Events
onclick ondblclick ondragstart onfilterchange onhelp onkeydown onkeypress onkeyup onmousedown onmousemove onmouseout onmouseover onmouseup onselectstart

Collection	Description
filters	Collection of all the filter objects for an element.

```
<PRE>
   Text here will be rendered in a fixed width font and the line breaks
   will be maintained, so this part will be on the second line.
</PRE>
```

S

Renders text in strikethrough type.

Properties	Attributes	Properties	Attributes
className	CLASS=*string*	offsetLeft	
document		offsetParent	
event	<event_name>= *name of script*	offsetTop	
		offsetWidth	
id	ID=*string*	outerHTML	
innerHTML		outerText	
innerText		parentElement	
isTextEdit		parentTextEdit	
lang	LANG=*string*	sourceIndex	
language	LANGUAGE= JAVASCRIPT | JSCRIPT | VBSCRIPT | VBS	style	STYLE=*string*
		tagName	
		title	TITLE=*string*
offsetHeight			

Methods
click contains getAttribute insertAdjacentHTML
insertAdjacentText removeAttribute scrollIntoView
setAttribute

Events
onclick ondblclick ondragstart onfilterchange onhelp
onkeydown onkeypress onkeyup onmousedown onmousemove
onmouseout onmouseover onmouseup onselectstart

Collection	Description
filters	Collection of all the filter objects for an element.

We can show a word in <S> strikethrough </S> format like this.

362

Renders text as a code sample listing.

Properties	Attributes	Properties	Attributes
className	CLASS=*string*	offsetLeft	
document		offsetParent	
event	<event_name>= *name of script*	offsetTop	
		offsetWidth	
id	ID=*string*	outerHTML	
innerHTML		outerText	
innerText		parentElement	
isTextEdit		parentTextEdit	
lang	LANG=*string*	sourceIndex	
language	LANGUAGE= JAVASCRIPT | JSCRIPT | VBSCRIPT | VBS	style	STYLE=*string*
		tagName	
		title	TITLE=*string*
offsetHeight			

Methods
```
click contains getAttribute insertAdjacentHTML
insertAdjacentText removeAttribute scrollIntoView
setAttribute
```

Events
```
onclick ondblclick ondragstart onfilterchange onhelp
onkeydown onkeypress onkeyup onmousedown onmousemove
onmouseout onmouseover onmouseup onselectstart
```

Collection	Description
filters	Collection of all the filter objects for an element.

```
<SAMP>
  ...
  x = sqr(y + b) * 2^e
  result = (x + y) / cos(t)
  ...
</SAMP>
```

SCRIPT

Specifies a script for the page that will be interpreted by a script engine.

Properties	Attributes	Properties	Attributes
className	CLASS=*string*	outerHTML	
document		outerText	
event	<event_name>= *name of script*	parentElement	
		parentTextEdit	
htmlFor	FOR=*string*	readyState	
id	ID=*string*	sourceIndex	
innerHTML		src	SRC=*url*
innerText		style	
isTextEdit		tagName	
	LANGUAGE= JAVASCRIPT | JSCRIPT | VBSCRIPT | VBS	text	
		title	TITLE=*string*

Methods
contains getAttribute insertAdjacentHTML insertAdjacentText
removeAttribute setAttribute

Events
onerror onload onreadystatechange

```
<SCRIPT LANGUAGE=JAVASCRIPT>
<!-- hide from older browsers
  // code goes here
-->
</SCRIPT>
```

Defines a list box or dropdown list.

Properties	Attributes	Properties	Attributes
accessKey	ACCESSKEY=*string*	multiple	MULTIPLE
	ALIGN=ABSBOTTOM | ABSMIDDLE | BASELINE | BOTTOM | LEFT | MIDDLE | RIGHT | TEXTTOP | TOP	name	NAME=*string*
		offsetHeight	
		offsetLeft	
		offsetParent	
		offsetTop	
className	CLASS=*string*	offsetWidth	
dataFld	DATAFLD=*colum-name*	outerHTML	
dataSrc	DATASRC=*id*	outerText	
disabled	DISABLED	parentElement	
document		parentTextEdit	
event	<event_name>= *name of script*	recordNumber	
form		selectedIndex	
id	ID=*string*	size	SIZE=*number*
IsTextEdit		sourceIndex	
lang	LANG=*string*	style	STYLE=*string*
language	LANGUAGE= JAVASCRIPT | JSCRIPT | VBSCRIPT | VBS	tabIndex	TABINDEX=*number*
		tagName	
		title	TITLE=*string*
		type	
length		value	

Methods
add blur click contains focus getAttribute
insertAdjacentHTML insertAdjacentText item remove
removeAttribute scrollIntoView setAttribute tags

Events
onafterupdate onbeforeupdate onblur onchange onclick
ondblclick ondragstart onerrorupdate onfilterchange onfocus
onhelp onkeydown onmouseout onmouseover onmouseup onresize
onrowenter onrowexit

...SELECT

Collection	Description
`filters`	Collection of all the filter objects for an element.
`options`	Collection of all the items in a `<SELECT>` element.

```
<SELECT SIZE=12 ID=MySelectList" MULTIPLE>
   <OPTION VALUE="0723"> Active Server Pages
   <OPTION VALUE="0448"> VBScript Programming
   <OPTION VALUE="0464"> ActiveX Web Databases
   <OPTION VALUE="0707"> Professional DHTML
</SELECT>
```

SMALL

Specifies that text should be displayed with a relatively smaller font than the current font.

Properties	Attributes	Properties	Attributes
`className`	`CLASS=`*string*	`offsetLeft`	
`document`		`offsetParent`	
`event`	`<event_name>=` *name of script*	`offsetTop`	
		`offsetWidth`	
`id`	`ID=`*string*	`outerHTML`	
`innerHTML`		`outerText`	
`innerText`		`parentElement`	
`isTextEdit`		`parentTextEdit`	
`lang`	`LANG=`*string*	`sourceIndex`	
`language`	`LANGUAGE=` `JAVASCRIPT` | `JSCRIPT` | `VBSCRIPT` | `VBS`	`style`	`STYLE=`*string*
		`tagName`	
`offsetHeight`		`title`	`TITLE=`*string*

Methods
```
click contains getAttribute insertAdjacentHTML
insertAdjacentText removeAttribute scrollIntoView
setAttribute
```

Events
onclick ondblclick ondragstart onfilterchange onhelp
onkeydown onkeypress onkeyup onmousedown onmousemove
onmouseout onmouseover onmouseup onselectstart

Collection	Description
filters	Collection of all the filter objects for an element.

We can show <SMALL>some of the text</SMALL> in a smaller font.

SPAN

Used with a style sheet to define non-standard attributes for text on the page.

Properties	Attributes	Properties	Attributes
className	CLASS=*string*	offsetLeft	
dataFld	DATAFLD=*columnname*	offsetParent	
dataFormatAs	DATAFORMATAS=HTML | TEXT	offsetTop	
		offsetWidth	
dataSrc	DATASRC=*id*	outerText	
document		parentElement	
event	<event_name>= *name of script*	parentTextEdit	
		scrollHeight	
id	ID=*string*	scrollLeft	
innerText		scrollTop	
isTextEdit		scrollWidth	
lang	LANG=*string*	sourceIndex	
language	LANGUAGE= JAVASCRIPT | JSCRIPT | VBSCRIPT | VBS	style	STYLE=*string*
		tagName	
		title	TITLE=*string*
offsetHeight			

367

...SPAN

Methods
blur click contains focus getAttribute insertAdjacentHTML
insertAdjacentText removeAttribute scrollIntoView
setAttribute

Events
onblur onclick ondblclick ondragstart onfilterchange
onfocus onhelp onkeydown onkeypress onkeyup onmousedown
onmousemove onmouseout onmouseover onmouseup onscroll
onselectstart

Collection	Description
filters	Collection of all the filter objects for an element.

```
<STYLE>
   SPAN {color:white; background-color:red}
</STYLE>

<P STYLE="color:green">
In a green paragraph, we can change <SPAN>some of the text to
white on red</SPAN> without changing anything else.
</P>
```

Renders text in strikethrough type.

Properties	Attributes	Properties	Attributes
className	CLASS=*string*	offsetLeft	
document		offsetParent	
event	<event_name>= *name of script*	offsetTop	
		offsetWidth	
id	ID=*string*	outerHTML	
innerHTML		outerText	
innerText		parentElement	
isTextEdit		parentTextEdit	
lang	LANG=*string*	sourceIndex	
language	LANGUAGE= JAVASCRIPT | JSCRIPT | VBSCRIPT | VBS	style	STYLE=*string*
		tagName	
		title	TITLE=*string*
offsetHeight			

Methods
click contains getAttribute insertAdjacentHTML
insertAdjacentText removeAttribute scrollIntoView
setAttribute

Events
onclick ondblclick ondragstart onfilterchange onhelp
onkeydown onkeypress onkeyup onmousedown onmousemove
onmouseout onmouseover onmouseup onselectstart

Collection	Description
filters	Collection of all the filter objects for an element.

We can show a word in <STRIKE>strikethrough</STRIKE> format like this.

STRONG

Renders text in boldface.

Properties	Attributes	Properties	Attributes
className	CLASS=*string*	offsetLeft	
document		offsetParent	
event	<event_name>= *name of script*	offsetTop	
		offsetWidth	
id	ID=*string*	outerHTML	
innerHTML		outerText	
innerText		parentElement	
isTextEdit		parentTextEdit	
lang	LANG=*string*	sourceIndex	
language	LANGUAGE= JAVASCRIPT | JSCRIPT | VBSCRIPT | VBS	style	STYLE=*string*
		tagName	
		title	TITLE=*string*
offsetHeight			

Methods
click contains getAttribute insertAdjacentHTML
insertAdjacentText removeAttribute scrollIntoView
setAttribute

Events
onclick ondblclick ondragstart onfilterchange onhelp
onkeydown onkeypress onkeyup onmousedown onmousemove
onmouseout onmouseover onmouseup onselectstart

Collection	Description
filters	Collection of all the filter objects for an element.

370

Specifies the style sheet for the page.

Properties	Attributes	Properties	Attributes
className		offsetWidth	
disabled	DISABLED	parentElement	
document		parentTextEdit	
id		readyState	
isTextEdit		sourceIndex	
offsetHeight		style	
offsetLeft		tagName	TITLE=*string*
offsetParent		type	TYPE=*string*
offsetTop			

Methods
click contains getAttribute insertAdjacentHTML
insertAdjacentText removeAttribute scrollIntoView
setAttribute

Events
onerror onload onreadystatechange

```
<STYLE>
  P {color:white;background-color:red}
</STYLE>
```

SUB

Renders text as a subscript using a smaller font than the current font.

Properties	Attributes	Properties	Attributes
className	CLASS=*string*	offsetLeft	
document		offsetParent	
event	<event_name>= *name of script*	offsetTop	
		offsetWidth	
id	ID=*string*	outerHTML	
innerHTML		outerText	
innerText		parentElement	
isTextEdit		parentTextEdit	
lang	LANG=*string*	sourceIndex	
language	LANGUAGE= JAVASCRIPT | JSCRIPT | VBSCRIPT | VBS	style	STYLE=*string*
		tagName	
		title	TITLE=*string*
offsetHeight			

Methods
click contains getAttribute insertAdjacentHTML insertAdjacentText removeAttribute scrollIntoView setAttribute

Events
onclick ondblclick ondragstart onfilterchange onhelp onkeydown onkeypress onkeyup onmousedown onmousemove onmouseout onmouseover onmouseup onselectstart

Collection	Description
filters	Collection of all the filter objects for an element.

To calculate the result multiply x₁ by x₂.

Renders text as a superscript using a smaller font than the current font.

Properties	Attributes	Properties	Attributes
className	CLASS=*string*	offsetLeft	
document		offsetParent	
event	<event_name>= *name of script*	offsetTop	
		offsetWidth	
id	ID=*string*	outerHTML	
innerHTML		outerText	
innerText		parentElement	
isTextEdit		parentTextEdit	
lang	LANG=*string*	sourceIndex	
	LANGUAGE= JAVASCRIPT | JSCRIPT | VBSCRIPT | VBS	style	STYLE=*string*
		tagName	
		title	TITLE=*string*
offsetHeight			

Methods
click contains getAttribute insertAdjacentHTML
insertAdjacentText removeAttribute scrollIntoView
setAttribute

Events
onclick ondblclick ondragstart onfilterchange onhelp
onkeydown onkeypress onkeyup onmousedown onmousemove
onmouseout onmouseover onmouseup onselectstart

Collection	Description
filters	Collection of all the filter objects for an element.

To calculate the result use x³ - y².

373

TABLE

Denotes a section of TR TD and TH tags organized into rows and columns.

Properties	Attributes	Properties	Attributes
align	ALIGN=CENTER | LEFT | RIGHT	id	ID=*string*
		innerText	
background	BACKGROUND=*string*	isTextEdit	
bgColor	BGCOLOR=*color*	lang	LANG=*string*
border	BORDER=*number*	language	LANGUAGE= JAVASCRIPT | JSCRIPT | VBSCRIPT | VBS
borderColor	BORDERCOLOR=*color*		
borderColorDark	BORDERCOLORDARK= *color*		
borderColorLight	BORDERCOLORLIGHT= *color*	offsetHeight	
		offsetLeft	
cellPadding	CELLPADDING=*number*	offsetParent	
cellSpacing	CELLSPACING=*number*	offsetTop	
className	CLASS=*string*	offsetWidth	
clientHeight		outerText	
clientWidth		parentElement	
cols	COLS=*number*	parentTextEdit	
dataFld		rules	RULES=ALL | COLS | GROUPS | NONE | ROWS
dataPageSize	DATAPAGESIZE= *number*		
dataSrc	DATASRC=*id*	scrollHeight	
document		scrollLeft	
event	<event_name>= *name of script*	scrollTop	
		scrollWidth	
frame	FRAME=ABOVE | BELOW | BORDER | BOX | INSIDES | LHS | RHS | VOID | VSIDES	sourceIndex	
		style	STYLE=*string*
		tagName	
		title	TITLE=*string*
height	HEIGHT=*string*	width	WIDTH=*number*

Methods

blur click contains focus getAttribute insertAdjacentHTML
insertAdjacentText nextPage prevPage refresh
removeAttribute scrollIntoView setAttribute

Events

```
onafterupdate onbeforeupdate onblur onclick ondblclick
ondragstart onfocus onhelp onkeydown onkeypress onkeyup
onmousedown onmousemove onmouseout onmouseover onmouseup
onresize onrowenter onrowexit onscroll onselectstart
```

Collection	Description
`filters`	Collection of all the filter objects for an element.
`rows`	Collection of all the rows in the table, including **THEAD**, **TBODY**, and **TFOOT**.

```
<TABLE BACKGROUND="wrox.gif" BORDER=1 WIDTH=100%>
    <THEAD>
        <TR>
            <TH COLSPAN=2> This is a heading cell</TH>
        </TR>
    </THEAD>
    <TBODY ALIGN-CENTER>
        <TR BGCOLOR=aliceblue>
            <TD This is a body detail cell</TD>
            <TD> And so is this one</TD>
        </TR>
    </TBODY>
    <TFOOT>
        <TR>
            <TD NOWRAP> This is a footer detail cell</TD>
            <TD> And so is this one</TD>
        </TR>
    </TFOOT>
<TABLE>
```

TBODY

Denotes a section of TR and TD tags forming the body of the table.

Properties	Attributes	Properties	Attributes
align	ALIGN=CENTER | LEFT | RIGHT	offsetHeight	
bgColor	BGCOLOR=*color*	offsetLeft	
className	CLASS=*string*	offsetParent	
document		offsetTop	
event	<event_name>= *name of script*	offsetWidth	
		parentElement	
id	ID=*string*	parentTextEdit	
isTextEdit		sourceIndex	
lang	LANG=*string*	style	STYLE=*string*
language	LANGUAGE= JAVASCRIPT | JSCRIPT | VBSCRIPT | VBS	tagName	
		title	TITLE=*string*
		vAlign	VALIGN=BASELINE | BOTTOM | CENTER | TOP

Methods
click contains getAttribute removeAttribute scrollIntoView
setAttribute

Events
onclick ondblclick ondragstart onfilterchange onhelp
onkeydown onkeypress onkeyup onmousedown onmousemove
onmouseout onmouseover onmouseup onselectstart

Collection	Description
filters	Collection of all the filter objects for an element.

376

Specifies a cell in a table.

Properties	Attributes	Properties	Attributes
align	ALIGN=CENTER | LEFT | RIGHT	language	LANGUAGE= JAVASCRIPT | JSCRIPT | VBSCRIPT | VBS
background	BACKGROUND=*string*		
bgColor	BGCOLOR=*color*	noWrap	NOWRAP
borderColor	BORDERCOLOR=*color*	offsetHeight	
borderColorDark	BORDERCOLORDARK= *color*	offsetLeft	
borderColorLight	BORDERCOLORLIGHT= *color*	offsetParent	
		offsetTop	
className	CLASS=*string*	offsetWidth	
clientHeight		parentElement	
clientWidth		parentTextEdit	
colSpan	COLSPAN=*string*	rowSpan	ROWSPAN=*number*
document		sourceIndex	
event	<event_name>= *name of script*	style	STYLE=*string*
		tagName	
height		title	TITLE=*string*
id	ID=*string*	vAlign	VALIGN=BASELINE | BOTTOM | CENTER | TOP
innerText			
isTextEdit			
lang	LANG=*string*	width	

Methods
blur click contains focus getAttribute insertAdjacentHTML
insertAdjacentText removeAttribute scrollIntoView
setAttribute

Events
onafterupdate onbeforeupdate onblur onclick ondblclick
ondragstart onfilterchange onfocus onhelp onkeydown
onkeypress onkeyup onmousedown onmousemove onmouseout
onmouseover onmouseup onresize onrowenter onrowexit
onselectstart

Collection	Description
filters	Collection of all the filter objects for an element.

TEXTAREA

Specifies a multi-line text input control.

Properties	Attributes	Properties	Attributes
accessKey	ACCESSKEY=*string*	offsetHeight	
	ALIGN=ABSBOTTOM | ABSMIDDLE | BASELINE | BOTTOM | LEFT | MIDDLE | RIGHT | TEXTTOP | TOP	offsetLeft	
		offsetParent	
		offsetTop	
		offsetWidth	
		outerText	
className	CLASS=*string*	parentElement	
clientHeight		parentTextEdit	
clientWidth		readOnly	READONLY
cols	COLS=*number*	rows	ROWS=*number*
dataFld	DATAFLD=*columnname*	scrollHeight	
dataSrc	DATASRC=*id*	scrollLeft	
disabled	DISABLED	scrollTop	
document		scrollWidth	
event	<event_name>= *name of script*	sourceIndex	
		status	
form		style	STYLE=*string*
id	ID=*string*	tabIndex	TABINDEX=*number*
innerText		tagName	
isTextEdit		title	TITLE=*string*
lang	LANG=*string*	type	
language	LANGUAGE= JAVASCRIPT | JSCRIPT | VBSCRIPT | VBS	value	
		wrap	WRAP=PHYSICAL | VIRTUAL | OFF
name	NAME=*string*		

Methods
blur click contains createTextRange focus getAttribute
insertAdjacentHTML insertAdjacentText removeAttribute
scrollIntoView select setAttribute

Events

onafterupdate onbeforeupdate onblur onchange onclick
ondblclick ndragstart onerrorupdate onfilterchange onfocus
onhelp onkeydown onkeypress onkeyup onmousedown onmousemove
onmouseout onmouseover onmouseup onresize onrowenter
onrowexit onscroll onselect onselectstart

Collection	Description
filters	Collection of all the filter objects for an element.

TFOOT

Denotes a set of rows to be used as the footer of a table.

Properties	Attributes	Properties	Attributes
align	ALIGN=CENTER | LEFT | RIGHT	offsetLeft	
		offsetParent	
bgColor	BGCOLOR=*color*	offsetTop	
className	CLASS=*string*	offsetWidth	
document		parentElement	
event	<event_name>= *name of script*	parentTextEdit	
id	ID=*string*	sourceIndex	
isTextEdit		style	STYLE=*string*
lang	LANG=*string*	tagName	
language	LANGUAGE= JAVASCRIPT | JSCRIPT | VBSCRIPT | VBS	title	TITLE=*string*
		vAlign	VALIGN=BASELINE | BOTTOM | CENTER | TOP
offsetHeight			

Methods

click contains getAttribute removeAttribute scrollIntoView
setAttribute

...TFOOT

Events

onclick ondblclick ondragstart onfilterchange onhelp
onkeydown onkeypress onkeyup onmousedown onmousemove
onmouseout onmouseover onmouseup onselectstart

Collection	Description
filters	Collection of all the filter objects for an element.

```
<TABLE BACKGROUND="wrox.gif" BORDER=1 WIDTH=100%>
   <THEAD>
      <TR>
         <TH COLSPAN=2> This is a heading cell</TH>
      </TR>
   </THEAD>
   <TBODY ALIGN-CENTER>
      <TR BGCOLOR=aliceblue>
         <TD This is a body detail cell</TD>
         <TD> And so is this one</TD>
      </TR>
   </TBODY>
   <TFOOT>
      <TR>
         <TD NOWRAP> This is a footer detail cell</TD>
         <TD> And so is this one</TD>
      </TR>
   </TFOOT>
<TABLE>
```

Denotes a header row in a table. Contents are centered within each cell and are bold.

Properties	Attributes	Properties	Attributes
align	ALIGN=CENTER | LEFT | RIGHT	noWrap	NOWRAP
background	BACKGROUND=*string*	offsetHeight	
bgColor	BGCOLOR=*color*	offsetLeft	
borderColor	BORDERCOLOR=*color*	offsetParent	
borderColorDark	BORDERCOLORDARK=*color*	offsetTop	
borderColorLight	BORDERCOLORLIGHT=*color*	offsetWidth	
		parentElement	
className	CLASS=*string*	parentTextEdit	
colSpan	COLSPAN=*string*	rowSpan	ROWSPAN=*number*
document		sourceIndex	
event	<event_name>= *name of script*	style	STYLE=*string*
id	ID=*string*	tagName	
isTextEdit		title	TITLE=*string*
lang	LANG=*string*	vAlign	VALIGN=BASELINE | BOTTOM | CENTER | TOP
language	LANGUAGE= JAVASCRIPT | JSCRIPT | VBSCRIPT | VBS		

Methods
click contains getAttribute removeAttribute scrollIntoView setAttribute

Events
onclick ondblclick ondragstart onhelp onkeydown onkeypress onkeyup onmousedown onmousemove onmouseout onmouseover onmouseup onselectstart

THEAD

Denotes a set of rows to be used as the header of a table.

Properties	Attributes	Properties	Attributes
align	ALIGN=CENTER | LEFT | RIGHT	offsetLeft	
		offsetParent	
bgColor	BGCOLOR=*color*	offsetTop	
className	CLASS=*string*	offsetWidth	
document		parentElement	
event	<event_name>= *name of script*	parentTextEdit	
		sourceIndex	
id	ID=*string*	style	STYLE=*string*
isTextEdit		tagName	
lang	LANG=*string*	title	TITLE=*string*
language	LANGUAGE= JAVASCRIPT | JSCRIPT | VBSCRIPT | VBS	vAlign	VALIGN=BASELINE | BOTTOM | CENTER | TOP
offsetHeight			

Methods
click contains getAttribute removeAttribute scrollIntoView setAttribute

Events
onclick ondblclick ondragstart onfilterchange onhelp onkeydown onkeypress onkeyup onmousedown onmousemove onmouseout onmouseover onmouseup onselectstart

Collection	Description
filters	Collection of all the filter objects for an element.

Denotes the title of the document, as used in the browser's window title bar.

Properties	Attributes	Properties	Attributes
className		parentTextEdit	
document		sourceIndex	
id	ID=*string*	tagName	
isTextEdit		text	
lang	LANG=*string*	title	TITLE=*string*
parentElement			

Methods
contains getAttribute removeAttribute setAttribute

```
<HTML>
   <HEAD>
      <TITLE> My new web page </TITLE>
   </HEAD>
   <BODY>
      Page contents
   </BODY>
</HTML>
```

There are no Events for this tag.

TR

Specifies a row in a table.

Properties	Attributes	Properties	Attributes
align	ALIGN=CENTER | LEFT | RIGHT	offsetHeight	
		offsetLeft	
bgColor	BGCOLOR=*color*	offsetParent	
borderColor	BORDERCOLOR=*color*	offsetTop	
borderColorDark	BORDERCOLORDARK= *color*	offsetWidth	
		parentElement	
borderColorLight	BORDERCOLORLIGHT= *color*	parentTextEdit	
className	CLASS=*string*	sourceIndex	
document		style	STYLE=*string*
event	<event_name>= *name of script*	tagName	
		title	TITLE=*string*
id	ID=*string*	vAlign	VALIGN=BASELINE | BOTTOM | CENTER | TOP
isTextEdit			
lang	LANG=*string*		
language	LANGUAGE= JAVASCRIPT | JSCRIPT | VBSCRIPT | VBS		

Methods
blur click contains focus getAttribute removeAttribute
scrollIntoView setAttribute

Events
onafterupdate onbeforeupdate onblur onclick ondblclick
ondragstart onfilterchange onfocusonhelp onkeydown
onkeypress onkeyup onmousedown onmousemove onmouseout
onmouseover onmouseup onresize onrowenter onrowexit
onselectstart

Collection	Description
cells	Collection of all the <TH> and <TD> cells in the row of a table.
filters	Collection of all the filter objects for an element.

384

Renders text in fixed-width type.

Properties	Attributes	Properties	Attributes
className	CLASS=*string*	offsetLeft	
document		offsetParent	
event	<event_name>= *name of script*	offsetTop	
		offsetWidth	
id	ID=*string*	outerHTML	
innerHTML		outerText	
innerText		parentElement	
isTextEdit		parentTextEdit	
lang	LANG=*string*	sourceIndex	
language	LANGUAGE= JAVASCRIPT | JSCRIPT | VBSCRIPT | VBS	style	STYLE=*string*
		tagName	
		title	TITLE=*string*
offsetHeight			

Methods
click contains getAttribute insertAdjacentHTML
insertAdjacentText removeAttribute scrollIntoView
setAttribute

Events
onclick ondblclick ondragstart onfilterchange onhelp
onkeydown onkeypress onkeyup onmousedown onmousemove
onmouseout onmouseover onmouseup onselectstart

Collection	Description
filters	Collection of all the filter objects for an element.

```
<TT>
This text will be shown in a fixed width font.
It comes from when documents were usually sent
from place to place on a teletype machine.
</TT>
```

U

Renders text underlined.

Properties	Attributes	Properties	Attributes
className	CLASS=*string*	offsetLeft	
document		offsetParent	
event	<event_name>= *name of script*	offsetTop	
		offsetWidth	
id	ID=*string*	outerHTML	
innerHTML		outerText	
innerText		parentElement	
isTextEdit		parentTextEdit	
lang	LANG=*string*	sourceIndex	
language	LANGUAGE= JAVASCRIPT | JSCRIPT | VBSCRIPT | VBS	style	STYLE=*string*
		tagName	
offsetHeight		title	TITLE=*string*

Methods
click contains getAttribute insertAdjacentHTML
insertAdjacentText removeAttribute scrollIntoView
setAttribute

Events
onclick ondblclick ondragstart onfilterchange onhelp
onkeydown onkeypress onkeyup onmousedown onmousemove
onmouseout onmouseover onmouseup onselectstart

Collection	Description
filters	Collection of all the filter objects for an element.

We can use this tag to <U> underline </U> some words.

386

Renders lines of text with **LI** tags as a bulleted list.

Properties	Attributes	Properties	Attributes
className	CLASS=*string*	offsetParent	
document		offsetTop	
event	<event_name>= *name of script*	offsetWidth	
		outerHTML	
id	ID=*string*	outerText	
innerHTML		parentElement	
innerText		parentTextEdit	
isTextEdit		sourceIndex	
lang	LANG=*string*	style	STYLE=*string*
language	LANGUAGE= JAVASCRIPT | JSCRIPT | VBSCRIPT | VBS	tagName	
		title	TITLE=*string*
		type	TYPE=1 | a | A | i | I
offsetHeight			
offsetLeft			

Methods
click contains getAttribute insertAdjacentHTML
insertAdjacentText removeAttribute scrollIntoView
setAttribute

Events
onclick ondblclick ondragstart onfilterchange onhelp
onkeydown onkeypress onkeyup onmousedown onmousemove
onmouseout onmouseover onmouseup onselectstart

Collection	Description
filters	Collection of all the filter objects for an element.

```
<UL>
   <LI> This is an item in an un-ordered list
   <LI> This is another item in an un-ordered list
</UL>
```

Se also **LI**, **OL**.

VAR

Renders text as a small fixed-width font.

Properties	Attributes	Properties	Attributes
className	CLASS=*string*	offsetLeft	
document		offsetParent	
event	<event_name>= *name of script*	offsetTop	
		offsetWidth	
id	ID=*string*	outerHTML	
innerHTML		outerText	
innerText		parentElement	
isTextEdit		parentTextEdit	
lang	LANG=*string*	sourceIndex	
language	LANGUAGE= JAVASCRIPT | JSCRIPT | VBSCRIPT | VBS	style	STYLE=*string*
		tagName	
		title	TITLE=*string*
offsetHeight			

Methods
click contains getAttribute insertAdjacentHTML
insertAdjacentText removeAttribute scrollIntoView
setAttribute

Events
onclick ondblclick ondragstart onfilterchange onhelp
onkeydown onkeypress onkeyup onmousedown onmousemove
onmouseout onmouseover onmouseup onselectstart

Collection	Description
filters	Collection of all the filter objects for an element.

Used to show the names of variables like <VAR>strTheValue</VAR> in the text

Inserts a soft line break in a block of NOBR text.

Properties	Attributes	Properties	Attributes
	CLASS=*string*		STYLE=*string*
	ID=*string*		TITLE=*string*
	LANGUAGE= JAVASCRIPT | JSCRIPT | VBSCRIPT | VBS		

```
<NOBR>
    This text will not break onto two lines in the browser window.
    This text will only break here <WBR>, and only if it won't fit on one line.
</NOBR>
```

There are no Methods or Events for this tag.

XMP

Renders text in fixed-width type used for example text.

Properties	Attributes	Properties	Attributes
className	CLASS=*string*	offsetLeft	
document		offsetParent	
event	<event_name>= *name of script*	offsetTop	
		offsetWidth	
id	ID=*string*	outerHTML	
innerHTML		outerText	
innerText		parentElement	
isTextEdit		parentTextEdit	
lang	LANG=*string*	sourceIndex	
language	LANGUAGE= JAVASCRIPT | JSCRIPT | VBSCRIPT | VBS	style	STYLE=*string*
		tagName	
offsetHeight		title	TITLE=*string*

Methods
click contains getAttribute insertAdjacentHTML
insertAdjacentText removeAttribute scrollIntoView
setAttribute

Events
onclick ondblclick ondragstart onfilterchange onhelp
onkeydown onkeypress onkeyup onmousedown onmousemove
onmouseout onmouseover onmouseup onselectstart

Collection	Description
filters	Collection of all the filter objects for an element.

```
<XMP>
  ...
  x = sqr(y + b) * 2^e
  result = (x + y) / cos(t)
  ...
</XMP>
```

390

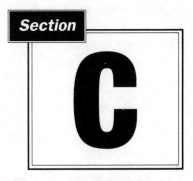

Style Sheet Properties

There are over 70 properties defined for the implementation of CSS in Dynamic HTML, and they are broken up into several major 'groups'. We've listed all of the properties below (by group), with some of the crucial information for each. We start with a summary of the units of measurement which can be used in the properties.

Units of Measurement

There are two basic categories of unit: relative and absolute (plus percentages). As a general rule, relative measures are preferred, as using absolute measures requires familiarity with the actual mechanism of display (e.g. what kind of printer, what sort of monitor, etc.).

Relative Units

Values: em, en, ex, px

em, **en** and **ex** are typographic terms, and refer to the sizes of other characters on display.
px refers to a measurement in screen pixels, which is generally only meaningful for display on computer monitors and depends on the user's display resolution setting.
In IE4, **em** and **ex** are the same as **pt**, and **en** is the same as **px**.

Absolute Units

Values: in, cm, mm, pt, pc

in gives the measurement in inches, **cm** gives it in centimetres, **mm** in millimetres, **pt** is in typeface points (72 to an inch), and **pc** is in picas (1 pica equals 12 points). These units are generally only useful when you know what the output medium is going to be, since browsers are allowed to approximate if they must.

Percentage

Values: Numeric

This is given as a number (with or without a decimal point), and is relative to a length unit (which is usually the font size of the current element). You should note that child elements will inherit the computed value, not the percentage value (so a child will not be 20% of the parent, it will be the same size as the parent).

Listing of Properties

There follows a listing of all the properties for use in Dynamic HTML, together with their equivalent scripting property in IE4, possible values, defaults, and other useful information. The properties are divided up into categories: **font** properties; **color** and **background** properties; **text** properties; **size** and **position** properties; **printing** properties; **filter** properties; and **other** properties.

Font Properties

font

Scripting Property:	font
Values:	<font-size>, [/<line-height>], <font-family>
Default:	Not defined
Applies to:	All elements
Inherited:	Yes
Percentage?:	Only on <font-size> and <line-height>

This allows you to set several font properties all at once, with the initial values being determined by the properties being used (e.g. the default for **font-size** is different to the default for **font-family**). This property should be used with multiple values separated by spaces, or a comma if specifying multiple font-families.

font-family

Scripting Property:	fontFamily
Values:	Name of a font family (e.g. New York) or a generic family (e.g. Serif)
Default:	Set by browser
Applies to:	All elements
Inherited:	Yes
Percentage?:	No

You can specify multiple values in order of preference (in case the browser doesn't have the font you want). To do so, simply specify them and separate multiple values with commas. You should end with a generic font-family (allowable values would then be **serif, sans-serif, cursive, fantasy**, or **monospace**). If the font name has spaces in it, you should enclose the name in quotation marks.

font-size

Scripting Property:	`fontSize`
Values:	`<absolute>`, `<relative>`, `<length>`, `<percentage>`
Default:	`medium`
Applies to:	All elements
Inherited:	Yes
Percentage?:	Yes, relative to parent font size

The values for this property can be expressed in several ways:

 Absolute size: legal values are **xx-small**, **x-small**, **small**, **medium**, **large**, **x-large**, **xx-large**

 Relative size: values are **larger**, **smaller**

 Length: values are in any unit of measurement, as described at the beginning of this section

 Percentage: values are a percentage of the parent font size

font-style

Scripting Property:	`fontStyle`
Values:	`normal`, `italic`, or `oblique`
Default:	`normal`
Applies to:	All elements
Inherited:	Yes
Percentage?:	No

This is used to apply styling to your font—if a pre-rendered font is available (e.g. New York Oblique) then that will be used if possible. If not, the styling will be applied electronically.

font-variant

Scripting Property:	`fontVariant`
Values:	`normal`, `small-caps`
Default:	`normal`
Applies to:	All elements
Inherited:	Yes
Percentage?:	No

Normal is the standard appearance, and is therefore set as the default. **Small-caps** uses capital letters that are the same size as normal lowercase letters.

font-weight

Scripting Property:	`fontWeight`
Values:	`normal`, `bold`, `bolder`, `lighter`—or numeric values from 100 to 900
Default:	`normal`
Applies to:	All elements
Inherited:	Yes
Percentage?:	No

Specifies the 'boldness' of text, which is usually expressed by stroke thickness. If numeric values are used, they must proceed in 100-unit increments (e.g. 250 isn't legal). `400` is the same as `normal`, and `700` is the same as `bold`.

Color and Background Properties

color

Scripting Property:	`color`
Values:	Color name or RGB value
Default:	Depends on browser
Applies to:	All elements
Inherited:	Yes
Percentage?:	No

Sets the text color of any element. The color can be specified by name (e.g. green) or by RGB-value. The RGB value can be expressed in several ways; in hex - "#FFFFFF", by percentage - "80%, 20%, 0%", or by value - "255,0,0".

background

Scripting Property:	`background`
Values:	`transparent`, `<color>`, `<URL>`, `<repeat>`, `<scroll>`, `<position>`
Default:	`transparent`
Applies to:	All elements
Inherited:	No
Percentage?:	Yes, will refer to the dimension of the element itself

Specifies the background of the document. `Transparent` is the same as no defined background. You can use a solid color, or you can specify the URL for an image to be used. The URL can be absolute or relative, but must be enclosed in parentheses and immediately preceded by `url:`.

```
BODY { background: url(http://foo.bar.com/image/small.gif) }
```

It is possible to use a color and an image, in which case the image will be overlaid on top of the color. The color can be a single color, or two colors that will be blended together. Images can have several properties set:

 <repeat> can be `repeat`, `repeat-x` (where **x** is a number), `repeat-y` (where **y** is a number) and `no-repeat`. If no repeat value is given, then `repeat` is assumed.

 <scroll> determines whether the background image will remain fixed, or scroll when the page does. Possible values are `fixed` or `scroll`.

<position> specifies the location of the image on the page. Values are by percentage (horizontal, vertical), by absolute distance (in a unit of measurement, horizontal then vertical), or by keyword (values are `top`, `middle`, `bottom`, `left`, `center`, `right`).

It is also possible to specify different parts of the background properties separately using these next five properties:

396

background-attachment

Scripting Property:	backgroundAttachment
Values:	fixed, scroll
Default:	scroll
Applies to:	All elements
Inherited:	No
Percentage?:	No

Determines whether the background will remain fixed, or scroll when the page does.

background-color

Scripting Property:	backgroundColor
Values:	transparent, <color>
Default:	transparent
Applies to:	All elements
Inherited:	No
Percentage?:	No

Sets a color for the background. This can be a single color, or two colors blended together. The colors can be specified by name (e.g. green) or by RGB-value (which can be stated in hex "#FFFFFF", by percentage "80%, 20%, 0%", or by value "255,0,0"). The syntax for using two colors is:

```
BODY { background-color: red / blue }
```

background-image

Scripting Property:	backgroundImage
Values:	<URL>, none
Default:	none
Applies to:	All elements
Inherited:	No
Percentage?:	No

You can specify the URL for an image to be used as the background. The URL can be absolute or relative, but must be enclosed in parentheses and immediately preceded by url:.

background-position

Scripting Properties:	backgroundPosition, backgroundPositionX, backgroundPositionY
Values:	<position> <length> top, center, bottom, left, right.
Default:	top, left
Applies to:	All elements
Inherited:	No
Percentage?:	No

Specifies the initial location of the background image on the page using two values, which are defined as a percentage (horizontal, vertical), an absolute distance (in a unit of measurement, horizontal then vertical), or using two of the available keywords.

background-repeat

Scripting Property:	`backgroundRepeat`
Values:	`repeat, repeat-x, repeat-y, no-repeat.`
Default:	`repeat`
Applies to:	All elements
Inherited:	No
Percentage?:	No

Determines whether the image is repeated to fill the page or element. If `repeat-x` or `repeat-y` are used, the image is repeated in only one direction. The default is to repeat the image in both directions.

Text Properties

letter-spacing

Scripting Property:	`letterSpacing`
Values:	`normal, <length>`
Default:	`normal`
Applies to:	All elements
Inherited:	Yes
Percentage?:	No

Sets the distance between letters. The length unit indicates an addition to the default space between characters. Values, if given, should be in units of measurement.

line-height

Scripting Property:	`lineHeight`
Values:	`<number>, <length>, <percentage> normal`
Default:	Depends on browser
Applies to:	All elements
Inherited:	Yes
Percentage?:	Yes, relative to the font-size of the current element

Sets the height of the current line. Numerical values are expressed as the font size of the current element multiplied by the value given (for example, 1.2 would be valid). If given by length, a unit of measurement must be used. Percentages are based on the font-size of the current font size, and should normally be more than 100%.

list-style

Scripting Property:	`listStyle`
Values:	`<keyword>, <position>, <url>`
Default:	Depends on browser
Applies to:	All elements
Inherited:	Yes
Percentage?:	No

Defines how list items are displayed. Can be used to set all the properties, or the individual styles can be set independently using the following styles.

list-style-image

Scripting Property:	`listStyleImage`
Values:	`none, <url>`
Default:	`none`
Applies to:	All elements
Inherited:	Yes
Percentage?:	No

Defines the URL of an image to be used as the 'bullet' or list marker for each item in a list.

list-style-position

Scripting Property:	`listStylePosition`
Values:	`inside, outside`
Default:	`outside`
Applies to:	All elements
Inherited:	Yes
Percentage?:	No

Indicates if the list marker should be placed indented or extended in relation to the list body.

list-style-type

Scripting Property:	`listStyleType`
Values:	`none, circle, disk, square, decimal, lower-alpha, upper-alpha, lower-roman, upper-roman`
Default:	`disk`
Applies to:	All elements
Inherited:	Yes
Percentage?:	No

Defines the type of 'bullet' or list marker used to precede each item in the list.

text-align

Scripting Property:	`textAlign`
Values:	`left, right, center, justify`
Default:	Depends on browser
Applies to:	All elements
Inherited:	Yes
Percentage?:	No

Describes how text is aligned within the element. Essentially replicates the `<DIV ALIGN=>` tag.

text-decoration

Scripting Properties:	`textDecoration, textDecorationLineThrough, textDecorationUnderline, textDecorationOverline`
Values:	`none, underline, overline, line-through`
Default:	`none`
Applies to:	All elements
Inherited:	No
Percentage?:	No

Specifies any special appearance of the text. Open to extension by vendors, with unidentified extensions rendered as an underline. This property is not inherited, but will usually span across any 'child' elements.

text-indent

Scripting Property:	`textIndent`
Values:	`<length>, <percentage>`
Default:	`Zero`
Applies to:	All elements
Inherited:	Yes
Percentage?:	Yes, refers to width of parent element

Sets the indentation values, in units of measurement, or as a percentage of the parent element's width.

text-transform

Scripting Property:	`textTransform`
Values:	`capitalize, uppercase, lowercase, none`
Default:	`none`
Applies to:	All elements
Inherited:	Yes
Percentage?:	No

 `capitalize` will set the first character of each word in the element as uppercase.

 `uppercase` will set every character in the element in uppercase.

 `lowercase` will place every character in lowercase.

`none` will neutralize any inherited settings.

vertical-align

Scripting Property:	`verticalAlign`
Values:	`baseline, sub, super, top, text-top, middle, bottom, text-bottom, <percentage>`
Default:	`baseline`
Applies to:	Inline elements
Inherited:	No
Percentage?:	Yes, will refer to the line-height itself

Controls the vertical positioning of any affected element.

 `baseline` sets the alignment with the base of the parent.

 `middle` aligns the vertical midpoint of the element with the baseline of the parent plus half of the vertical height of the parent.

`sub` makes the element a subscript.

`super` makes the element a superscript.

`text-top` aligns the element with the top of text in the parent element's font.

`text-bottom` aligns with the bottom of text in the parent element's font.

`top` aligns the top of the element with the top of the tallest element on the current line.

`bottom` aligns with the bottom of the lowest element on the current line.

Size and Border Properties

These values are used to set the characteristics of the layout 'box' that exists around elements. They can apply to characters, images, and so on.

border-top-color, border-right-color, border-bottom-color, border-left-color, border-color

Scripting Properties:	`borderTopColor, borderRightColor, borderBottomColor, borderLeftColor, borderColor`
Values:	`<color>`
Default:	`<none>`
Applies to:	Block and replaced elements
Inherited:	No
Percentage?:	No

Sets the color of the four borders. By supplying the URL of an image instead, the image itself is repeated to create the border.

border-top-style, border-right-style, border-bottom-style, border-left-style, border-style

Scripting Properties:	borderTopStyle, borderRightStyle, borderBottomStyle, borderLeftStyle, borderStyle
Values:	none, solid, double, groove, ridge, inset, outset
Default:	none
Applies to:	Block and replaced elements
Inherited:	No
Percentage?:	No

Sets the style of the four borders.

border-top, border-right, border-bottom, border-left, border

Scripting Properties:	borderTop, borderRight, borderBottom, borderLeft, border
Values:	<border-width>, <border-style>, <color>
Default:	medium, none, <none>
Applies to:	Block and replaced elements
Inherited:	No
Percentage?:	No

Sets the properties of the border element (box drawn around the affected element). Works roughly the same as the margin settings, except that it can be made visible.

 <border-width> can be thin, medium, thick, or as a unit of measurement.

<border-style> can be none, solid.

The color argument is used to fill the background of the element while it loads, and behind any transparent parts of the element. By supplying the URL of an image instead, the image itself is repeated to create the border. It is also possible to specify values for attributes of the border property separately using the border-width, border-style and border-color properties.

border-top-width, border-right-width, border-bottom-width, border-left-width, border-width

Scripting Properties:	borderTopWidth, borderRightWidth, borderBottomWidth, borderLeftWidth, borderWidth
Values:	thin, medium, thick <length>
Default:	medium
Applies to:	Block and replaced elements
Inherited:	No
Percentage?:	No

Sets the width of the border for the element. Each side can be set individually, or the border-width property used to set all of the sides. You can also supply up to four arguments for the border-width property to set individual sides, in the same way as with the margin property.

402

clear

Scripting Property:	`clear`
Values:	`none, both, left, right`
Default:	`none`
Applies to:	All elements
Inherited:	No
Percentage?:	No

Forces the following elements to be displayed below an element which is aligned. Normally, they would wrap around it.

clip

Scripting Property:	`clip`
Values:	`rect(<top><right><bottom><left>) , auto`
Default:	`auto`
Applies to:	All elements
Inherited:	No
Percentage?:	No

Controls which part of an element is visible. Anything that occurs outside the clip area is not visible.

display

Scripting Property:	`display`
Values:	`" ", none`
Default:	`" "`
Applies to:	All elements
Inherited:	No
Percentage?:	No

This property indicates whether an element is rendered. If set to **none** the element is not rendered, if set to `" "` it is rendered.

float

Scripting Property:	`styleFloat`
Values:	`none, left, right`
Default:	`none`
Applies to:	`DIV`, `SPAN` and replaced elements
Inherited:	No
Percentage?:	No

Causes following elements to be wrapped to the left or right of the element, rather than being placed below it.

height

Scripting Properties:	height, pixelHeight, posHeight
Values:	auto, <length>
Default:	auto
Applies to:	DIV, SPAN and replaced elements
Inherited:	No
Percentage?:	No

Sets the vertical size of an element, and will scale the element if necessary. The value is returned as a string including the measurement type (**px**, **%**, etc.). To retrieve the value as a number, query the **posHeight** property.

left

Scripting Properties:	left, pixelLeft, posLeft
Values:	auto, <length>, <percentage>
Default:	auto
Applies to:	All elements
Inherited:	No
Percentage?:	Yes, refers to parent's width

Sets or returns the left position of an element when displayed in 2D canvas mode, allowing accurate placement and animation of individual elements. The value is returned as a string including the measurement type (**px**, **%**, etc.). To retrieve the value as a number, query the **posLeft** property.

margin-top, margin-right, margin-bottom, margin-left, margin

Scripting Properties:	marginTop, marginRight, marginBottom, marginLeft, margin
Values:	auto, <length>, <percentage>
Default:	Zero
Applies to:	Block and replaced elements
Inherited:	No
Percentage?:	Yes, refers to parent element's width

Sets the size of margins around any given element. You can use **margin** as shorthand for setting all of the other values (as it applies to all four sides). If you use multiple values in **margin** but use less than four, opposing sides will try to be equal. These values all set the effective minimum distance between the current element and others.

overflow

Scripting Property:	overflow
Values:	none, clip, scroll
Default:	none
Applies to:	All elements
Inherited:	No
Percentage?:	No

This controls how a container element will display its content if this is not the same size as the container.

 none means that the container will use the default method. For example, as in an image element, the content may be resized to fit the container.

 clip means that the contents will not be resized, and only a part will be visible.

 scroll will cause the container to display scroll bars so that the entire contents can be viewed by scrolling.

padding-top, padding-right, padding-bottom, padding-left, padding

Scripting Properties:	paddingTop, paddingRight, paddingBottom, paddingLeft, padding
Values:	auto, <length>, <percentage>
Default:	Zero
Applies to:	Block and replaced elements
Inherited:	No
Percentage?:	Yes, refers to parent element's width

Sets the distance between the content and border of an element. You can use **padding** as shorthand for setting all of the other values (as it applies to all four sides). If you use multiple values in **padding** but use less than four, opposing sides will try to be equal. These values all set the effective minimum distance between the current element and others.

position

Scripting Property:	position
Values:	absolute, relative, static
Default:	relative
Applies to:	All elements
Inherited:	No
Percentage?:	No

Specifies if the element can be positioned directly on the 2D canvas.

 absolute means it can be fixed on the background of the page at a specified location, and move with it.

 static means it can be fixed on the background of the page at a specified location, but not move when the page is scrolled.

relative means that it will be positioned normally, depending on the preceding elements.

top

Scripting Properties:	`top, pixelTop, posTop`
Values:	`auto, <percentage>, <length>`
Default:	`auto`
Applies to:	All elements
Inherited:	No
Percentage?:	Yes, refers to parent's width

Sets or returns the vertical position of an element when displayed in 2-D canvas mode, allowing accurate placement and animation of individual elements. Value is returned as a string including the measurement type (**px**, **%**, etc.). To retrieve the value as a number, query the **posTop** property.

visibility

Scripting Property:	`visibility`
Values:	`visible, hidden, inherit`
Default:	`inherit`
Applies to:	All elements
Inherited:	No
Percentage?:	No

Allows the element to be displayed or hidden on the page. Elements which are hidden still take up the same amount of space, but are rendered transparently. Can be used to dynamically display only one of several overlapping elements

 visible means that the element will be visible.

 hidden means that the element will not be visible.

inherit means that the element will only be visible when its parent or container element is visible.

width

Scripting Properties:	`width, pixelWidth, posWidth`
Values:	`auto, <length>, <percentage>`
Default:	`auto`, except for any element with an intrinsic dimension
Applies to:	`DIV, SPAN` and replaced elements
Inherited:	No
Percentage?:	Yes, refers to parent's width

Sets the horizontal size of an element, and will scale the element if necessary. The value is returned as a string including the measurement type (**px**, **%**, etc.). To retrieve the value as a number, query the **posWidth** property.

z-index

Scripting Property:	zIndex
Values:	<number>
Default:	Depends on the HTML source
Applies to:	All elements
Inherited:	No
Percentage?:	No

Controls the ordering of overlapping elements, and defines which will be displayed 'on top'. Positive numbers are above the normal text on the page, and negative numbers are below. Allows a 2.5-D appearance by controlling the layering of the page's contents.

Printing Properties

page-break-after

Scripting Property:	pageBreakAfter
Values:	<auto>, <always>, <left>, <right>
Default:	<auto>
Applies to:	All elements
Inherited:	No
Percentage?:	No

Controls when to set a page break and on what page the content will resume, i.e. either the left or the right.

page-break-before

Scripting Property:	pageBreakBefore
Values:	<auto>, <always>, <left>, <right>
Default:	<auto>
Applies to:	All elements
Inherited:	No
Percentage?:	No

Controls when to set a page break and on what page the content will resume, i.e. either the left or the right.

Filter Properties

All filters are called with the keyword filter. There are two different types of filter, visual filters and transition filters. Transition filters are further divided into Blend Transition filters and Reveal Transition filters. All of these filters are called in the same way in cascading style sheets:

```
filter: filtername{fparameter1, fparameter2, etc}
```

There are 14 types of visual filter in all and two types of transition filter, all of them are documented.

Visual Filters

Scripting Property:	*object*.style.*filtername(fparameter1, etc)*
Values:	*filtername(fparameter1, fparameter2 etc)*
Default:	none
Applies to:	All elements
Inherited:	No
Percentage?:	No

Controls the manipulation of visible objects via any of a set of predefined filters.

A list of possible filter names and what they do follows:

filtername	description
alpha	sets a uniform transparency level
blur	creates a movement effect
chroma	makes one color transparent
dropshadow	makes a silhouette of an object
fliph	creates a horizontal mirror image
flipv	creates a vertical mirror image
glow	creates the effect that an object is glowing
grayscale	changes an object to monochromatic colors
invert	reverses all hue, saturation and brightness values
light	shines a light source onto an object
mask	creates a transparent mask from an object
shadow	creates a silhouette of an object offset from the object
wave	creates a sine wave distortion of an object along the x axis
xray	shows just the outline of an object

revealtrans

Scripting Property:	*object*.style.revealtrans(duration = <duration>, transition = <transition shape>)
Values:	revealtrans(duration = <duration>, transition = <transition shape>)
Default:	none
Applies to:	All elements
Inherited:	No
Percentage?:	No

Allows you reveal or cover up visual objects using one of 23 predefined patterns, specified by a code.

<duration> is the length of time that the transition will take to complete. This is specified in milliseconds.

<transition shape> is determined by the integer value assigned to it. The following shapes have the following values.

<Shape>	<Value>
Box In	0
Box Out	1
Circle In	2
Circle Out	3
Wipe Up	4
Wipe Down	5
Wipe Right	6
Wipe Left	7
Vertical Blinds	8
Horizontal Blinds	9
Checkerboard Across	10
Checkerboard Down	11
Random Dissolve	12
Split Vertical In	13
Split Vertical Out	14
Split Horizontal In	15
Split Horizontal Out	16
Strips Left Down	17
Strips Left Up	18
Strips Right Down	19
Strips Right Up	20
Random Bars Horizontal	21
Random Bars Vertical	22
Random	23

blendtrans

Scripting Property:	*object*.style.revealtrans(duration = <duration>)
Values:	blendTrans(duration = <duration>)
Default:	none
Applies to:	All elements
Inherited:	No
Percentage?:	No

Performs a fade in or fade out of selected visual objects.

409

`<duration>` is the length of time the transition should take to complete.

Other Properties

cursor

Scripting Property:	`cursor`
Values:	`auto, crosshair, default, hand, move, e-resize, ne-resize, nw-resize, n-resize, se-resize, sw-resize, s-resize, w-resize, text, wait, help`
Default:	`auto`
Applies to:	All elements
Inherited:	No
Percentage?:	No

Specifies the type of cursor the mouse pointer should be.

Unsupported CSS Properties

Internet Explorer 4 doesn't support the following CSS properties:

    `word-spacing`

`!important`

`first-letter pseudo`

`first-line pseudo`

`white-space`

410

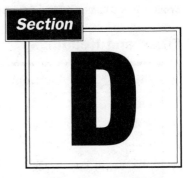
Common HTML Tags by Category

Here, we have listed some of the most commonly used tags by category. When you know what you want to do, but you're not sure which tag will achieve the desired effect, use the reference tables below to put you on the right track.

Document Structure

Tag	Meaning
`<!>`	Allows authors to add comments to code.
`<!DOCTYPE>`	Defines the document type. This is required by all HTML documents.
`<BASE>`	Specifies the document's base URL—its original location. It's not normally necessary to include this tag. It may only be used in HEAD section.
`<BODY>`	Contains the main part of the HTML document.
`<COMMENT>`	Allows authors to add comments to code. No longer recommended: use `<!>`.
`<DIV>`	Defines a block division of the BODY section of the document.
`<HEAD>`	Contains information about the document itself.
`<HTML>`	Signals the beginning and end of an HTML document.
`<LINK>`	Defines the current document's relationship with other resources. Used in HEAD section only.
`<META>`	Describes the content of a document.
`<NEXTID>`	Defines a parameter in the HEAD section of the document
`<SPAN>`	Defines an area for reference by a style sheet
`<STYLE>`	Specifies the style sheet for the page.

Titles and Headings

Tag	Meaning
<H1>	Heading level 1
<H2>	Heading level 2
<H3>	Heading level 3
<H4>	Heading level 4
<H5>	Heading level 5
<H6>	Heading level 6
<TITLE>	Identifies the contents of the document.

Paragraphs and Lines

Tag	Meaning
 	Inserts a line break.
<CENTER>	Centers subsequent text/images.
<HR>	Draws a horizontal rule.
<NOBR>	Prevents a line of text breaking.
<P>	Defines a paragraph.
<WBR>	Inserts a soft line break in a block of NOBR text.

Text Styles

Tag	Meaning
<ADDRESS>	Indicates an address. The address is typically displayed in italics.
<B>	Emboldens text.
<BASEFONT>	Sets font size to be used as default.
<BIG>	Changes the physical rendering of the font to one size larger.
<BLOCKQUOTE>	Formats a quote—typically by indentation
<CITE>	Renders text in italics.
<CODE>	Renders text in a font resembling computer code.
<DFN>	Indicates the first instance of a term or important word.
<EM>	Emphasized text—usually italic.
<FONT>	Changes font properties.
<I>	Defines italic text.
<KBD>	Indicates typed text. Useful for instruction manuals etc.

Tag	Meaning
`<LISTING>`	Renders text in a fixed-width font. No longer recommended - use `<PRE>`.
`<PLAINTEXT>`	Renders text in a fixed-width font without processing any other tags it may contain. May not be consistently supported across browsers - use `<PRE>`.
`<PRE>`	Pre-formatted text. Renders text exactly how it is typed, i.e. carriage returns, styles etc., *will* be recognized.
`<S> <STRIKE>`	Strike through. Renders the text as 'deleted' (crossed out).
`<SAMP>`	Specifies sample code and renders it in small font.
`<SMALL>`	Changes the physical rendering of a font to one size smaller.
`<STRONG>`	Strong emphasis—usually bold.
`<STYLE>`	Specifies the style sheet for the page.
`<SUB>`	Subscript.
`<SUP>`	Superscript.
`<TT>`	Renders text in fixed width, typewriter style font.
`<U>`	Underlines text. Not widely supported at present, and not recommended, as it can cause confusion with hyperlinks, which also normally appear underlined.
`<VAR>`	Indicates a variable.
`<XMP>`	Renders text in fixed width type, used for example text. No longer recommended, use `<PRE>` or `<SAMP>`.

Lists

Tag	Meaning
`<DD>`	Definition description. Used in definition lists with `DT` to define the term.
`<DIR>`	Denotes a directory list by indenting the text.
`<DL>`	Defines a definition list.
`<DT>`	Defines a definition term within a definition list.
`<LI>`	Defines a list item in any type of list other than a definition list.
`<MENU>`	Defines a menu list.
`<OL>`	Defines an ordered (numbered) list.
`<UL>`	Defines an unordered (bulleted) list.

Tables

Tag	Meaning
`<CAPTION>`	Puts a title above a table.
`<COL>`	Defines column width and properties for a table.
`<COLGROUP>`	Defines properties for a group of columns in a table.
`<TABLE>`	Defines a series of columns and rows to form a table.
`<TBODY>`	Defines the table body.
`<TD>`	Specifies a cell in a table.
`<TFOOT>`	Defines table footer.
`<TH>`	Specifies a header column. Text will be centered and bold.
`<THEAD>`	Used to designate rows as the table's header.
`<TR>`	Defines the start of a table row.

Links

Tag	Meaning
`<A>`	Used to insert an anchor, which can be either a local reference point or a hyperlink to another URL.
`<A HREF="url">`	Hyperlink to another document.
`<A NAME="name">`	Link to a local reference point.

Graphics, Objects, Multimedia and Scripts

Tag	Meaning
`<APPLET>`	Inserts an applet.
`<AREA>`	Specifies the shape of a "hot spot" in a client-side image map.
`<BGSOUND>`	Plays a background sound.
`<EMBED>`	Defines an embedded object in an HTML document.
`<IMG>`	Embeds an image or a video clip in a document.
`<MAP>`	Specifies a collection of hot spots for a client-side image map.
`<MARQUEE>`	Sets a scrolling marquee.
`<NOSCRIPT>`	Specifies HTML to be displayed in browsers which don't support scripting.
`<OBJECT>`	Inserts an object.
`<PARAM>`	Sets the property value for a given object.
`<SCRIPT>`	Inserts a script.

Forms

Tag	Meaning
<BUTTON>	Creates an HTML-style button.
<FIELDSET>	Draws a box around a group of controls.
<FORM>	Defines part of the document as a user fill-out form.
<INPUT>	Defines a user input box.
<LABEL>	Defines a label for a control.
<LEGEND>	Defines the text label to use in box created by a FIELDSET tag.
<OPTION>	Used within the SELECT tag to present the user with a number of options.
<SELECT>	Denotes a list box or drop-down list.
<TEXTAREA>	Defines a text area inside a FORM element.

Frames

Tag	Meaning
<FRAME>	Defines a single frame in a frameset.
<FRAMESET>	Defines the main container for a frame.
<IFRAME>	Defines a 'floating' frame within a document.
<NOFRAMES>	Allows for backward compatibility with non-frame compliant browsers.

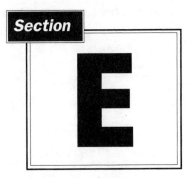

The Browser Object Model

The Dynamic HTML Object Model contains 12 **objects** and 15 **collections**. Most of these are organized into a strict hierarchy that allows HTML authors to access all the parts of the browser, and the pages that are loaded, from a scripting language like JavaScript or VBScript.

The Object Model In Outline

The diagram shows the object hierarchy in graphical form. It is followed by a list of the objects and collection, with a brief description. Then, each object is documented in detail, showing the properties, methods, and events it supports.

Note that not all the objects and collections are included in the diagram. Some are not part of the overall object model, but are used to access other items such as dialogs or HTML elements.

Section E - The Browser Object Model

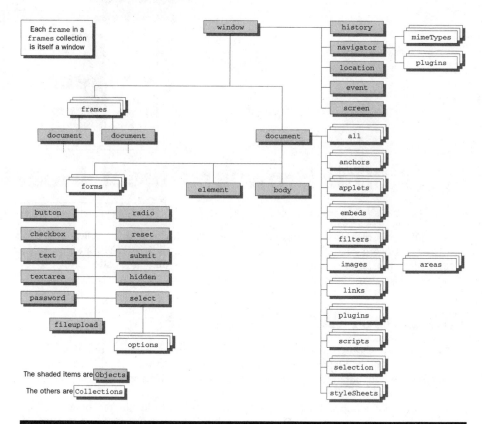

Object Name	Description
Document	An object that exposes the contents of the HTML document through a number of collections and properties.
Event	A global object that exposes properties that represent the parameters of all events as they occur.
History	Exposes information about the URLs that the client has previously visited.
Location	Exposes information about the currently displayed document's URL.
MimeType	An object that provides information about a MIME type.
Navigator	Exposes properties that provide information about the browser, or user agent.
Selection	Represents the currently active selection on the screen in the document.
Style	Represents an individual style element within a style sheet.
TextRange	Represents sections of the text stream making up the HTML document.

Object Name	Description
Screen	Exposes information about the client's monitor screen and system rendering abilities.
Window	Exposes properties, methods and events connected to the browser window or a frame.
StyleSheet	Exposes all the styles within a single style sheet in the styleSheets collection.

Collection Name	Description
all	Collection of all the tags and elements in the body of the document.
anchors	Collection of all the anchors in the document.
applets	Collection of all the objects in the document, including intrinsic controls, images, applets, embeds, and other objects.
areas	Collection of all the areas that make up the image map.
cells	Collection of all the <TH> and <TD> cells in the row of a table.
elements	Collection of all controls and elements in the form.
embeds	Collection of all the embed tags in the document.
forms	Collection of all the forms in the page.
frames	Collection of all the frames defined within a <FRAMESET> tag.
images	Collection of all the images in the page.
links	Collection of all the links and <AREA> blocks in the page.
options	Collection of all the items in a <SELECT> element.
plugins	An alias for collection of all the embeds in the page.
rows	Collection of all the rows in the table, including <THEAD>, <TBODY>, and <TFOOT>.
scripts	Collection of all the <SCRIPT> sections in the page.
filters	Collection of all the filter objects for an element.
imports	Collection of all the imported style sheets defined for a stylesheet object.
stylesheets	Collection of all the individual style property objects defined for a document.
mimeTypes	Collection of all the document and file types supported by the browser.

The Objects in Detail

This section documents all the properties, methods and events available for each object in the browser hierarchy.

The Document Object

Exposes the entire HTML content through its own collections and properties, and provides a range of events and methods to work with documents.

Property Name	Attribute Name	CSS Name	Description
activeElement			Identifies the element that has the focus.
alinkColor	ALINK		The color for active links in the page - i.e. while the mouse button is held down.
bgColor	BGCOLOR	background-color	Specifies the background color to be used for an element.
body			Read-only reference to the document's implicit body object, as defined by the <BODY> tag.
cookie			The string value of a cookie stored by the browser.
domain			Sets or returns the domain of the document for use in cookies and security.
fgColor	TEXT		Sets the color of the document foreground text.
lastModified			The date that the source file for the page was last modified, as a string, where available.
linkColor	LINK		The color for unvisited links in the page.
location			The full URL of the document.
parentWindow			Returns the parent window that contains the document.
readyState			Specifies the current state of an object being downloaded.

Property Name	Attribute Name	CSS Name	Description
referrer			The URL of the page that referenced (loaded) the current page.
selection			Read-only reference to the document's selection object.
title	TITLE		Provides advisory information about the element, such as when loading, or as a tooltip.
url	URL		Uniform Resource Locator (address) for the current document or in a <META> tag.
vlinkColor	VLINK		The color for visited links in the page.

Collections	Description
all	Collection of all the tags and elements in the body of the document.
anchors	Collection of all the anchors in the document.
applets	Collection of all the objects in the document, including intrinsic controls, images, applets, embeds, and other objects.
embeds	Collection of all the embed tags in the document.
forms	Collection of all the forms in the page.
frames	Collection of all the frames defined within a <FRAMESET> tag.
images	Collection of all the images in the page.
links	Collection of all the links and <AREA> blocks in the page.
plugins	An alias for collection of all the embeds in the page.
scripts	Collection of all the <SCRIPT> sections in the page.
styleSheets	Collection of all the individual style property objects defined for a document.

Method Name	Description
clear	Clears the contents of a selection or document object.

Table continued on following page

423

Method Name	Description
close	Closes a document forcing written data to be displayed, or closes the browser window.
createElement	Creates an instance of an image or option element object.
elementFromPoint	Returns the element at the specified x and y coordinates with respect to the window.
execCommand	Executes a command over the document selection or range.
open	Opens the document as a stream to collect output of write or writeln methods.
queryCommandEnabled	Denotes if the specified command is available for a document or TextRange.
queryCommandIndeterm	Denotes if the specified command is in the indeterminate state.
queryCommandState	Returns the current state of the command for a document or TextRange object.
queryCommandSupported	Denotes if the specified command is supported for a document or TextRange object.
queryCommandText	Returns the string associated with a command for a document or TextRange object.
queryCommandValue	Returns the value of the command specified for a document or TextRange object.
write	Writes text and HTML to a document in the specified window.
writeln	Writes text and HTML to a document in the specified window, followed by a carriage return.

Event Name	Description
onafterupdate	Occurs when transfer of data from the element to the data provider is complete.
onbeforeupdate	Occurs before transfer of changed data to the data provider when an element loses focus or the page is unloaded.
onclick	Occurs when the user clicks the mouse button on an element, or when the value of a control is changed.
ondblclick	Occurs when the user double-clicks on an element.
ondragstart	Occurs when the user first starts to drag an element or selection.

Event Name	Description
onerror	Occurs when an error loading a document or image arises.
onhelp	Occurs when the user presses the *F1* or *Help* key.
onkeydown	Occurs when the user presses a key.
onkeypress	Occurs when the user presses a key and a character is available.
onkeyup	Occurs when the user releases a key.
onload	Occurs when the element has completed loading.
onmousedown	Occurs when the user presses a mouse button.
onmousemove	Occurs when the user moves the mouse.
onmouseout	Occurs when the mouse pointer leaves the element.
onmouseover	Occurs when the mouse pointer first enters the element.
onmouseup	Occurs when the user releases a mouse button.
onreadystatechange	Occurs when the readyState for an object has changed.
onselectstart	Occurs when the user first starts to select contents of an element.

The Event Object

The global object provided to allow the scripting language to access an event's parameters. It provides the following properties:

Property Name	Description
altKey	Returns the state of the *Alt* key when an event occurs.
button	The mouse button, if any, that was pressed to fire the event.
cancelBubble	Set to prevent the current event from bubbling up the hierarchy.
clientX	Returns the *x* coordinate of the element, excluding borders, margins, padding, scrollbars, etc.
clientY	Returns the *y* coordinate of the element, excluding borders, margins, padding, scrollbars, etc.
ctrlKey	Returns the state of the *Ctrl* key when an event occurs.
fromElement	Returns the element being moved from for an onmouseover or onmouseout event.
keyCode	ASCII code of the key being pressed. Changing it sends a different character to the object.

Table continued on following page

Property Name	Description
offsetX	Returns the x coordinate of the mouse pointer when an event occurs, relative to the containing element.
offsetY	Returns the y coordinate position of the mouse pointer when an event occurs, relative to the containing element.
reason	Indicates whether data transfer to an element was successful, or why it failed.
returnValue	Allows a return value to be specified for the event or a dialog window.
screenX	Returns the x coordinate of the mouse pointer when an event occurs, in relation to the screen.
screenY	Returns the y coordinate of the mouse pointer when an event occurs, in relation to the screen.
shiftKey	Returns the state of the *Shift* key when an event occurs.
srcElement	Returns the element deepest in the object hierarchy that a specified event occurred over.
srcFilter	Returns the filter that caused the element to produce an **onfilterchange** event.
toElement	Returns the element being moved to for an **onmouseover** or **onmouseout** event.
type	Returns the name of the event as a string, without the 'on' prefix, such as 'click' instead of 'onclick'.
x	Returns the x coordinate of the mouse pointer relative to a positioned parent, or otherwise to the window.
y	Returns the y coordinate of the mouse pointer relative to a positioned parent, or otherwise to the window.

The History Object

Contains information about the URLs that the client has visited, as stored in the browser's History list, and allows the script to move through the list.

Properties	Description
length	Returns the number of elements in a collection.

Methods	Description
back	Loads the previous URL in the browser's History list.
forward	Loads the next URL in the browser's History list.
go	Loads a specified URL from the browser's History list.

The Location Object

Contains information on the current URL. It also provides methods that will reload a page.

PropertyName	AttributeName	Description
hash		The string following the # symbol in the URL.
host		The hostname:port part of the location or URL.
hostname		The hostname part of the location or URL.
href	HREF	The entire URL as a string.
pathname		The file or object path name following the third slash in a URL.
port		The port number in a URL.
protocol		The initial substring up to and including the first colon, indicating the URL's access method.
search		The contents of the query string or form data following the ? (question mark) in the complete URL.

MethodName	Description
assign	Loads another page. Equivalent to changing the `window.location.href` property.
reload	Reloads the current page.
replace	Loads a document, replacing the current document's session history entry with its URL.

The MimeType Object

Provides information about the page's MIME data type.

Properties	Attribute	Description
description		Returns a description of the MimeType.
enabledPlugin		Returns the plug-in that can handle the specified MimeType.
name	NAME	Specifies the name of the element, control, bookmark, or applet.
suffixes		A list of filename suffixes suitable for use with the specified MimeType.

427

The Navigator Object

This object represents the browser application itself, providing information about it's manufacturer, version, and capabilities.

Property Name	Description
appCodeName	The code name of the browser.
appName	The product name of the browser.
appVersion	The version of the browser.
cookieEnabled	Indicates if client-side cookies are enabled in the browser.
userAgent	The user-agent (browser name) header sent in the HTTP protocol from the client to the server.

Collection	Description
mimeTypes	Collection of all the document and file types supported by the browser.
plugins	An alias for collection of all the embeds in the page.

Method Name	Description
javaEnabled	Returns True or False, depending on whether a Java VM is installed and enabled.
taintEnabled	Returns False, included for compatibility with Netscape Navigator

The Screen Object

The **screen** object provides information to the scripting language about the client's screen resolution and rendering abilities.

Property Name	Description
bufferDepth	Specifies if and how an off-screen bitmap buffer should be used.
colorDepth	Returns the number of bits per pixel of the user's display device or screen buffer.
height	Returns the height of the user's display screen in pixels.
updateInterval	Sets or returns the interval between screen updates on the client.
width	Returns the width of the user's display screen in pixels.

The Selection Object

Returns the active selection on the screen, allowing access to all the selected elements including the plain text in the page.

Properties	Attribute	Description
type	TYPE	The type of the selection, i.e. a control, text, a table, or none.

Methods	Description
clear	Clears the contents of the selection.
createRange	Returns a copy of the currently selected range.
empty	Deselects the current selection and sets selection type to none.

The Style Object

This provides access to the individual style properties for an element. These could have been previously set by a style sheet, or by an inline style tag within the page.

Property Name	Attribute Name	CSS Name	Description
background	BACKGROUND		background Specifies a background picture that is tiled behind text and graphics.
background Attachment		background-attachment	Defines if a background image should be fixed on the page or scroll with the content.
background Color		background-color	Specifies the background color of the page or element.
background Image		background-image	Specifies a URL for the background image for the page or element.
background Position		background-position	The initial position of a background image on the page.

Table continued on following page

Property Name	Attribute Name	CSS Name	Description
background PositionX			The x coordinate of the background image in relation to the containing window.
background PositionY			The y coordinate of the background image in relation to the containing window.
Background Repeat		background-repeat	Defines if and how a background image is repeated on the page.
border	BORDER	border	Specifies the border to be drawn around the element.
borderBottom		border-bottom	Used to specify several attributes of the bottom border of an element.
borderBottom Color			The color of the bottom border for an element.
borderBottom Style			The style of the bottom border for an element.
borderBottom Width		border-bottom-width	The width of the bottom border for an element.
borderColor	BORDERCOLOR	border-color	The color of all or some of the borders for an element.
borderLeft		border-left	Used to specify several attributes of the left border of an element.
borderLeft Color			The color of the left border for an element.
borderLeft Style			The style of the left border for an element.
borderLeft Width		border-left-width	The width of the left border for an element.
borderRight		border-right	Used to specify several attributes of the right border of an element.
BorderRight Color			The color of the right border for an element.
BorderRight Style			The style of the right border for an element.

Property Name	Attribute Name	CSS Name	Description
BorderRight Width		border-right-width	The width of the right border for an element.
borderStyle		border-style	Used to specify the style of one or more borders of an element.
borderTop		border-top	Used to specify several attributes of the top border of an element.
borderTopColor			The color of the top border for an element.
borderTopStyle			The style of the top border for an element.
borderTop Width		border-top-width	The width of the top border for an element.
borderWidth		border-width	Used to specify the width of one or more borders of an element.
clear	CLEAR	clear	Causes the next element or text to be displayed below left-aligned or right-aligned images.
clip		clip	Specifies how an element's contents should be displayed if larger than the available client area.
color	COLOR	color	The text or foreground color of an element.
cssText			The text value of the element's entire STYLE attribute.
cursor		cursor	Specifies the type of cursor to display when the mouse pointer is over the element.
display		display	Specifies if the element will be visible (displayed) in the page.
filter		filter	Sets or returns an array of all the filters specified in the element's style property.

Table continued on following page

Property Name	Attribute Name	CSS Name	Description
font		font, @font-face	Defines various attributes of the font for an element, or imports a font.
fontFamily		font-family	Specifies the name of the typeface, or 'font family'.
fontSize		font-size	Specifies the font size.
fontStyle		font-style	Specifies the style of the font, i.e. normal or italic.
fontVariant		font-variant	Specifies the use of small capitals for the text.
fontWeight		font-weight	Specifies the weight (boldness) of the text.
height	HEIGHT	height	Specifies the height at which the element is to be drawn, and sets the **posHeight** property.
left		left	Specifies the position of the left of the element, and sets the **posLeft** property.
letter Spacing		letter-spacing	Indicates the additional space to be placed between characters in the text.
lineHeight		line-height	The distance between the baselines of two adjacent lines of text.
listStyle		list-style	Allows several style properties of a list element to be set in one operation.
listStyle Image		list-style-image	Defines the image used as a background for a list element.
listStyle Position		list-style-position	Defines the position of the bullets used in a list element.
listStyle Type		list-style-type	Defines the design of the bullets used in a list element.

Property Name	Attribute Name	CSS Name	Description
margin		margin	Allows all four margins to be specified with a single attribute.
margin Bottom		margin-bottom	Specifies the bottom margin for the page or text block.
marginLeft		margin-left	Specifies the left margin for the page or text block.
marginRight		margin-right	Specifies the right margin for the page or text block.
marginTop		margin-top	Specifies the top margin for the page or text block.
overflow		overflow	Defines how text that overflows the element is handled.
padding Bottom		padding-bottom	Sets the amount of space between the bottom border and content of an element.
paddingLeft		padding-left	Sets the amount of space between the left border and content of an element.
paddingRight		padding-right	Sets the amount of space between the right border and content of an element.
paddingTop		padding-top	Sets the amount of space between the top border and content of an element.
pageBreak After		page-break-after	Specifies if a page break should occur after the element.
pageBreak Before		page-break-before	Specifies if a page break should occur after the element.
pixelHeight			Sets or returns the height style property of the element in pixels, as a pure number, rather than a string.

Table continued on following page

Property Name	Attribute Name	CSS Name	Description
pixelLeft			Sets or returns the left style property of the element in pixels, as a pure number rather than a string.
pixelTop			Sets or returns the top style property of the element in pixels, as a pure number rather than a string.
pixelWidth			Sets or returns the width style property of the element in pixels, as a pure number rather than a string.
posHeight			Returns the value of the height style property in its last specified units, as a pure number rather than a string.
position		position	Returns the value of the position style property, defining whether the element can be positioned.
posLeft			Returns the value of the left style property in its last specified units, as a pure number rather than a string.
posTop			Returns the value of the top style property in its last specified units, as a pure number rather than a string.
posWidth			Returns the value of the width style property in its last specified units, as a pure number rather than a string.
styleFloat		float	Specifies if the element will float above the other elements in the page, or cause them to flow round it.

Property Name	Attribute Name	CSS Name	Description
textAlign		text-align	Indicates how text should be aligned within the element.
text Decoration		text-decoration	Specifies several font decorations (underline, overline, strikethrough) added to the text of an element.
text Decoration Blink			Specifies if the font should blink or flash. Has no effect in IE4.
text Decoration Line Through			Specifies if the text is displayed as strikethrough, i.e. with a horizontal line through it.
text Decoration None			Specifies if the text is displayed with no additional decoration.
text Decoration Overline			Denotes if the text is displayed as overline, i.e. with a horizontal line above it.
text Decoration Underline			Denotes if the text is displayed as underline, i.e. with a horizontal line below it.
textIndent		text-indent	Specifies the indent for the first line of text in an element, and may be negative.
text Transform		text-transform	Specifies how the text for the element should be capitalized.
top		top	Position of the top of the element, sets the posTop property. Also returns topmost window object.
vertical Align		vertical-align	Sets or returns the vertical alignment style property for an element.
visibility		visibility	Indicates if the element or contents are visible on the page.

Table continued on following page

Property Name	Attribute Name	CSS Name	Description
width	WIDTH	width	Specifies the width at which the element is to be drawn, and sets the **posWidth** property.
zIndex		z-index	Sets or returns the z-index for the element, indicating whether it appears above or below other elements.

MethodName	Description
getAttribute	Returns the value of an attribute defined in an HTML tag.
removeAttribute	Causes the specified attribute to be removed from the HTML element and the current page.
setAttribute	Adds and/or sets the value of an attribute in a HTML tag.

The StyleSheet Object

This object exposes all the styles within a single style sheet in the styleSheets collection

Property Name	Attribute Name	Description
disabled	DISABLED	Sets or returns whether an element is disabled.
href	HREF	The entire URL as a string.
id	ID	Identifier or name for an element in a page or style sheet, or as the target for hypertext links.
owningElement		Returns the style sheet that imported or referenced the current style sheet, usually through a **<LINK>** tag.
parentStyleSheet		Returns the style sheet that imported the current style sheet, or null for a non-imported style sheet.
readOnly	READONLY	Indicates that an element's contents are read only, or that a rule in a style sheet cannot be changed.

Property Name	Attribute Name	Description
type	TYPE	Specifies the type of list style, link, selection, control, button, MIME-type, rel, or the CSS language.

Collection	Description
imports	Collection of all the imported style sheets defined for a stylesheet object.

The TextRange Object

This object represents the text stream of the HTML document. It can be used to set and retrieve the text within the page.

Property Name	Description
htmlText	Returns the contents of a TextRange as text and HTML source.
text	The plain text contained within a block element, a TextRange or an <OPTION> tag.

Method Name	Description
collapse	Shrinks a TextRange to either the start or end of the current range.
compareEndPoints	Compares two text ranges and returns a value indicating the result.
duplicate	Returns a duplicate of a TextRange object.
execCommand	Executes a command over the document selection or range.
expand	Expands the range by a character, word, sentence or story so that partial units are completely contained.
findText	Sets the range start and end points to cover the text if found within the current document.
getBookmark	Sets String to a unique bookmark value to identify that position in the document.
inRange	Denotes if the specified range is within or equal to the current range.
isEqual	Denotes if the specified range is equal to the current range.

Table continued on following page

Method Name	Description
move	Changes the start and end points of a TextRange to cover different text.
moveEnd	Causes the range to grow or shrink from the end of the range.
moveStart	Causes the range to grow or shrink from the beginning of the range.
moveToBookmark	Moves range to encompass the range with a bookmark value previously defined in String.
moveToElementText	Moves range to encompass the text in the element specified.
moveToPoint	Moves and collapses range to the point specified in x and y relative to the document.
parentElement	Returns the parent element that completely encloses the current range.
pasteHTML	Pastes HTML and/or plain text into the current range.
queryCommand Enabled	Denotes if the specified command is available for a document or TextRange.
queryCommand Indeterm	Denotes if the specified command is in the indeterminate state.
queryCommandState	Returns the current state of the command for a document or TextRange object.
queryCommand Supported	Denotes if the specified command is supported for a document or TextRange object.
queryCommandText	Returns the string associated with a command for a document or TextRange object.
queryCommandValue	Returns the value of the command specified for a document or TextRange object.
scrollIntoView	Scrolls the element or TextRange into view in the browser, optionally at the top of the window.
select	Makes the active selection equal to the current object, or highlights the input area of a form element.
setEndPoint	Sets the end point of the range based on the end point of another range.

The Window Object

The window object refers to the current window. This can be a top-level window, or a window that is within a frame created by a <FRAMESET> in another document.

Property Name	AttributeName	CSS Name	Description
`client`			A reference that returns the navigator object for the browser.
`closed`			Indicates if a window is closed.
`default Status`			The default message displayed in the status bar at the bottom of the window.
`dialog Arguments`			Returns the arguments that were passed into a dialog window, as an array.
`dialogHeight`			Sets or returns the height of a dialog window.
`dialogLeft`			Sets or returns the x coordinate of a dialog window.
`dialogTop`			Sets or returns the y coordinate of a dialog window.
`dialogWidth`			Sets or returns the width of a dialog window.
`document`			Read-only reference to the window's document object.
`event`	`EVENT`		Read-only reference to the global event object.
`history`			Read-only reference to the window's history object.
`length`			Returns the number of elements in a collection.
`name`	`NAME`		Specifies the name of the window, frame, element, control, bookmark, or applet.
`navigator`			Read-only reference to the window's navigator object.

Table continued on following page

Property Name	AttributeName	CSS Name	Description
offScreen Buffering			Specifies whether to use off-screen buffering for the document.
opener			Returns a reference to the window that created the current window.
parent			Returns the parent window or frame in the window/frame hierarchy.
returnValue			Allows a return value to be specified for the event or a dialog window.
screen			Read-only reference to the global screen object.
self			Provides a reference to the current window.
status			Text displayed in the window's status bar, or an alias for the value of an option button.
top		top	Position of the top of the element, sets the posTop property. Also returns topmost window object.
window			Read-only reference to the current window object, same as _self.

MethodName	Description
alert	Displays an Alert dialog box with a message and an OK button.
blur	Causes a control to lose focus and fire its onblur event.
clearInterval	Cancels an interval timer that was set with the setInterval method.
clearTimeout	Cancels a timeout that was set with the setTimeout method.

MethodName	Description
close	Closes a document forcing written data to be displayed, or closes the browser window.
confirm	Displays a Confirm dialog box with a message and OK and Cancel buttons.
execScript	Executes a script. The default language is JScript.
focus	Causes a control to receive the focus and fires its onfocus event.
navigate	Loads another page (VBScript only). Equivalent to changing the window.location.href property.
open	Opens the document as a stream to collect output of write or writeln methods.
prompt	Displays a Prompt dialog box with a message and an input field.
scroll	Scrolls the window to the specified x and y offset relative to the entire document.
setInterval	Denotes a code routine to execute repeatedly every specified number of milliseconds.
setTimeout	Denotes a code routine to execute a specified number of milliseconds after loading the page.
showHelp	Opens a window to display a Help file.
showModalDialog	Displays a HTML dialog window, and returns the returnValue property of its document when closed.

EventName	Description
onbeforeunload	Occurs just before the page is unloaded, allowing the unload event to be cancelled.
onblur	Occurs when the control loses the input focus.
onerror	Occurs when an error loading a document or image arises.
onfocus	Occurs when a control receives the input focus.
onhelp	Occurs when the user presses the *F1* or *Help* key.
onload	Occurs when the element has completed loading.
onresize	Occurs when the element or object is resized by the user.
onscroll	Occurs when the user scrolls a page or element.
onunload	Occurs immediately before the page is unloaded.

Collections	Description
frames	Collection of all the frames defined within a `<FRAMESET>` tag.

HTML and Form Controls Cross Reference

Dynamic HTML provides the same integral control types as HTML 3.2. However, there are many more different properties, methods and events available now for all the controls.

The following tables show those that are most relevant to controls. For a full list and description of the properties, methods and events for each element check out Sections **A** and **B**.

Control Properties	checked	dataFld	dataFormatAs	dataSrc	defaultChecked	defaultValue	maxLength	readOnly	recordNumber	size	status	style	type	value
HTML button	✗	✓	✓	✓	✗	✗	✗	✓	✓	✗	✗	✗	✓	✓
HTML checkbox	✓	✓	✗	✓	✓	✗	✗	✓	✓	✗	✓	✓	✓	✓
HTML file	✗	✗	✗	✗	✗	✓	✗	✓	✓	✗	✗	✗	✓	✓
HTML hidden	✗	✓	✗	✓	✗	✗	✗	✓	✗	✗	✗	✗	✓	✓
HTML image	✗	✗	✗	✗	✗	✗	✗	✗	✓	✗	✗	✗	✓	✗
HTML password	✗	✓	✗	✓	✗	✓	✓	✓	✗	✗	✓	✗	✓	✓
HTML radio	✓	✓	✗	✓	✓	✗	✗	✓	✓	✗	✓	✗	✓	✓
HTML reset	✗	✗	✗	✗	✗	✗	✗	✗	✓	✗	✗	✗	✓	✓
HTML submit	✗	✗	✗	✗	✗	✗	✗	✗	✓	✗	✗	✗	✓	✓
HTML text	✗	✓	✗	✓	✗	✓	✓	✓	✓	✗	✓	✗	✓	✓
BUTTON tag	✗	✓	✓	✓	✗	✗	✗	✗	✗	✗	✗	✓	✓	✓
FIELDSET tag	✗	✗	✗	✗	✗	✗	✗	✗	✓	✗	✗	✗	✗	✗
LABEL tag	✗	✗	✗	✗	✗	✗	✗	✗	✗	✗	✗	✗	✗	✗
LEGEND tag	✗	✗	✗	✗	✗	✗	✗	✗	✓	✗	✗	✗	✗	✗
SELECT tag	✗	✓	✗	✓	✗	✗	✗	✗	✓	✓	✗	✗	✓	✓
TEXTAREA tag	✗	✓	✗	✓	✗	✗	✗	✓	✗	✗	✗	✓	✓	✓

Control Methods	add	blur	click	createTextRange	focus	item	remove	select
HTML button	✗	✓	✓	✗	✓	✗	✗	✓
HTML checkbox	✗	✓	✓	✗	✓	✗	✗	✓
HTML file	✗	✓	✓	✗	✓	✗	✗	✓
HTML hidden	✗	✗	✗	✗	✗	✗	✗	✗
HTML image	✗	✓	✓	✗	✓	✗	✗	✓
HTML password	✗	✓	✓	✗	✓	✗	✗	✓
HTML radio	✗	✓	✓	✗	✓	✗	✗	✓
HTML reset	✗	✓	✓	✗	✓	✗	✗	✓
HTML submit	✗	✓	✓	✗	✓	✗	✗	✓
HTML text	✗	✓	✓	✓	✓	✗	✗	✓
BUTTON tag	✗	✓	✓	✓	✓	✗	✗	✗
FIELDSET tag	✗	✓	✓	✗	✓	✗	✗	✗
LABEL tag	✗	✗	✓	✗	✗	✗	✗	✗
LEGEND tag	✗	✓	✓	✗	✓	✗	✗	✗
SELECT tag	✓	✓	✓	✗	✓	✓	✓	✗
TEXTAREA tag	✗	✓	✓	✓	✓	✗	✗	✓

Control Events	onafterupdate	onbeforeupdate	onblur	onchange	onclick	ondblclick	onfocus	onrowenter	onrowexit	onselect
HTML button	✗	✗	✓	✗	✓	✓	✓	✗	✗	✓
HTML checkbox	✓	✓	✓	✓	✓	✓	✓	✗	✗	✓
HTML file	✗	✗	✓	✓	✓	✓	✓	✗	✗	✓
HTML hidden	✗	✗	✗	✗	✗	✗	✗	✗	✗	✗
HTML image	✗	✗	✓	✓	✗	✓	✓	✗	✗	✓
HTML password	✗	✗	✓	✓	✓	✓	✓	✗	✗	✓
HTML radio	✓	✓	✓	✓	✓	✓	✓	✗	✗	✓
HTML reset	✗	✗	✓	✗	✓	✓	✓	✗	✗	✓
HTML submit	✗	✗	✓	✗	✓	✓	✓	✗	✗	✓
HTML text	✓	✓	✓	✓	✓	✓	✓	✗	✗	✓
BUTTON tag	✓	✓	✓	✗	✓	✓	✓	✓	✓	✗
FIELDSET tag	✓	✓	✓	✗	✓	✓	✓	✓	✓	✗
LABEL tag	✗	✗	✗	✗	✓	✓	✗	✗	✗	✗
LEGEND tag	✓	✓	✓	✗	✓	✓	✓	✓	✓	✗
SELECT tag	✓	✓	✓	✓	✓	✓	✓	✓	✓	✗
TEXTAREA tag	✓	✓	✓	✓	✓	✓	✓	✓	✓	✓

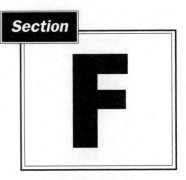
HTML Color Names and Values

Colors Sorted by Name

Color Name	Value	IE4 Color Constant
aliceblue	F0F8FF	htmlAliceBlue
antiquewhite	FAEBD7	htmlAntiqueWhite
aqua	00FFFF	htmlAqua
aquamarine	7FFFD4	htmlAquamarine
azure	F0FFFF	htmlAzure
beige	F5F5DC	htmlBeige
bisque	FFE4C4	htmlBisque
black	000000	htmlBlack
blanchedalmond	FFEBCD	htmlBlanchedAlmond
blue	0000FF	htmlBlue
blueviolet	8A2BE2	htmlBlueViolet
brown	A52A2A	htmlBrown
burlywood	DEB887	htmlBurlywood
cadetblue	5F9EA0	htmlCadetBlue
chartreuse	7FFF00	htmlChartreuse
chocolate	D2691E	htmlChocolate
coral	FF7F50	htmlCoral
cornflowerblue	6495ED	htmlCornflowerBlue
cornsilk	FFF8DC	htmlCornsilk
crimson	DC143C	htmlCrimson
cyan	00FFFF	htmlCyan
darkblue	00008B	htmlDarkBlue

Color Name	Value	IE4 Color Constant
darkcyan	008B8B	htmlDarkCyan
darkgoldenrod	B8860B	htmlDarkGoldenRod
darkgray	A9A9A9	htmlDarkGray
darkgreen	006400	htmlDarkGreen
darkkhaki	BDB76B	htmlDarkKhaki
darkmagenta	8B008B	htmlDarkMagenta
darkolivegreen	556B2F	htmlDarkOliveGreen
darkorange	FF8C00	htmlDarkOrange
darkorchid	9932CC	htmlDarkOrchid
darkred	8B0000	htmlDarkRed
darksalmon	E9967A	htmlDarkSalmon
darkseagreen	8FBC8F	htmlDarkSeaGreen
darkslateblue	483D8B	htmlDarkSlateBlue
darkslategray	2F4F4F	htmlDarkSlateGray
darkturquoise	00CED1	htmlDarkTurquoise
darkviolet	9400D3	htmlDarkViolet
deeppink	FF1493	htmlDeepPink
deepskyblue	00BFFF	htmlDeepSkyBlue
dimgray	696969	htmlDimGray
dodgerblue	1E90FF	htmlDodgerBlue
firebrick	B22222	htmlFirebrick
floralwhite	FFFAF0	htmlFloralWhite
forestgreen	228B22	htmlForestGreen
fuchsia	FF00FF	htmlFuchsia
gainsboro	DCDCDC	htmlGainsboro
ghostwhite	F8F8FF	htmlGhostWhite
gold	FFD700	htmlGold
goldenrod	DAA520	htmlGoldenRod
gray	808080	htmlGray
green	008000	htmlGreen
greenyellow	ADFF2F	htmlGreenYellow
honeydew	F0FFF0	htmlHoneydew
hotpink	FF69B4	htmlHotPink
indianred	CD5C5C	htmlIndianRed
indigo	4B0082	htmlIndigo
ivory	FFFFF0	htmlIvory
khaki	F0E68C	htmlKhaki

Color Name	Value	IE4 Color Constant
lavender	E6E6FA	htmlLavender
lavenderblush	FFF0F5	htmlLavenderBlush
lawngreen	7CFC00	htmlLawnGreen
lemonchiffon	FFFACD	htmlLemonChiffon
lightblue	ADD8E6	htmlLightBlue
lightcoral	F08080	htmlLightCoral
lightcyan	E0FFFF	htmlLightCyan
lightgray	D3D3D3	htmlLightGray
lightgreen	90EE90	htmlLightGreen
lightpink	FFB6C1	htmlLightPink
lightsalmon	FFA07A	htmlLightSalmon
lightseagreen	20B2AA	htmlLightSeaGreen
lightskyblue	87CEFA	htmlLightSkyBlue
lightslategray	778899	htmlLightSlateGray
lightsteelblue	B0C4DE	htmlLightSteelBlue
lightyellow	FFFFE0	htmlLightYellow
lime	00FF00	htmlLime
limegreen	32CD32	htmlLimeGreen
linen	FAF0E6	htmlLinen
magenta	FF00FF	htmlMagenta
maroon	800000	htmlMaroon
mediumaquamarine	66CDAA	htmlMediumAquamarine
mediumblue	0000CD	htmlMediumBlue
mediumorchid	BA55D3	htmlMediumOrchid
mediumpurple	9370DB	htmlMediumPurple
mediumseagreen	3CB371	htmlMediumSeaGreen
mediumslateblue	7B68EE	htmlMediumSlateBlue
mediumspringgreen	00FA9A	htmlMediumSpringGreen
mediumturquoise	48D1CC	htmlMediumTurquoise
mediumvioletred	C71585	htmlMediumVioletRed
midnightblue	191970	htmlMidnightBlue
mintcream	F5FFFA	htmlMintCream
mistyrose	FFE4E1	htmlMistyRose
moccasin	FFE4B5	htmlMoccasin
navajowhite	FFDEAD	htmlNavajoWhite
navy	000080	htmlNavy
oldlace	FDF5E6	htmlOldLace

449

Color Name	Value	IE4 Color Constant
olive	808000	htmlOlive
olivedrab	6B8E23	htmlOliveDrab
orange	FFA500	htmlOrange
orangered	FF4500	htmlOrangeRed
orchid	DA70D6	htmlOrchid
palegoldenrod	EEE8AA	htmlPaleGoldenRod
palegreen	98FB98	htmlPaleGreen
paleturquoise	AFEEEE	htmlPaleTurquoise
palevioletred	DB7093	htmlPaleVioletRed
papayawhip	FFEFD5	htmlPapayaWhip
peachpuff	FFDAB9	htmlPeachPuff
peru	CD853F	htmlPeru
pink	FFC0CB	htmlPink
plum	DDA0DD	htmlPlum
powderblue	B0E0E6	htmlPowderBlue
purple	800080	htmlPurple
red	FF0000	htmlRed
rosybrown	BC8F8F	htmlRosyBrown
royalblue	4169E1	htmlRoyalBlue
saddlebrown	8B4513	htmlSaddleBrown
salmon	FA8072	htmlSalmon
sandybrown	F4A460	htmlSandyBrown
seagreen	2E8B57	htmlSeaGreen
seashell	FFF5EE	htmlSeashell
sienna	A0522D	htmlSienna
silver	C0C0C0	htmlSilver
skyblue	87CEEB	htmlSkyBlue
slateblue	6A5ACD	htmlSlateBlue
slategray	708090	htmlSlateGray
snow	FFFAFA	htmlSnow
springgreen	00FF7F	htmlSpringGreen
steelblue	4682B4	htmlSteelBlue
tan	D2B48C	htmlTan
teal	008080	htmlTeal
thistle	D8BFD8	htmlThistle
tomato	FF6347	htmlTomato
turquoise	40E0D0	htmlTurquoise

Color Name	Value	IE4 Color Constant
violet	EE82EE	htmlViolet
wheat	F5DEB3	htmlWheat
white	FFFFFF	htmlWhite
whitesmoke	F5F5F5	htmlWhiteSmoke
yellow	FFFF00	htmlYellow
yellowgreen	9ACD32	htmlYellowGreen

Colors Sorted by Group

Color Name	Value	IE4 Color Constant
Blues		
azure	F0FFFF	htmlAzure
aliceblue	F0F8FF	htmlAliceBlue
lavender	E6E6FA	htmlLavender
lightcyan	E0FFFF	htmlLightCyan
powderblue	B0E0E6	htmlPowderBlue
lightsteelblue	B0C4DE	htmlLightSteelBlue
paleturquoise	AFEEEE	htmlPaleTurquoise
lightblue	ADD8E6	htmlLightBlue
blueviolet	8A2BE2	htmlBlueViolet
lightskyblue	87CEFA	htmlLightSkyBlue
skyblue	87CEEB	htmlSkyBlue
mediumslateblue	7B68EE	htmlMediumSlateBlue
slateblue	6A5ACD	htmlSlateBlue
cornflowerblue	6495ED	htmlCornflowerBlue
cadetblue	5F9EA0	htmlCadetBlue
indigo	4B0082	htmlIndigo
mediumturquoise	48D1CC	htmlMediumTurquoise
darkslateblue	483D8B	htmlDarkSlateBlue
steelblue	4682B4	htmlSteelBlue
royalblue	4169E1	htmlRoyalBlue
turquoise	40E0D0	htmlTurquoise
dodgerblue	1E90FF	htmlDodgerBlue
midnightblue	191970	htmlMidnightBlue
aqua	00FFFF	htmlAqua
cyan	00FFFF	htmlCyan

451

Color Name	Value	IE4 Color Constant
darkturquoise	00CED1	htmlDarkTurquoise
deepskyblue	00BFFF	htmlDeepSkyBlue
darkcyan	008B8B	htmlDarkCyan
blue	0000FF	htmlBlue
mediumblue	0000CD	htmlMediumBlue
darkblue	00008B	htmlDarkBlue
navy	000080	htmlNavy
Greens		
mintcream	F5FFFA	htmlMintCream
honeydew	F0FFF0	htmlHoneydew
greenyellow	ADFF2F	htmlGreenYellow
yellowgreen	9ACD32	htmlYellowGreen
palegreen	98FB98	htmlPaleGreen
lightgreen	90EE90	htmlLightGreen
darkseagreen	8FBC8F	htmlDarkSeaGreen
olive	808000	htmlOlive
aquamarine	7FFFD4	htmlAquamarine
chartreuse	7FFF00	htmlChartreuse
lawngreen	7CFC00	htmlLawnGreen
olivedrab	6B8E23	htmlOliveDrab
mediumaquamarine	66CDAA	htmlMediumAquamarine
darkolivegreen	556B2F	htmlDarkOliveGreen
mediumseagreen	3CB371	htmlMediumSeaGreen
limegreen	32CD32	htmlLimeGreen
seagreen	2E8B57	htmlSeaGreen
forestgreen	228B22	htmlForestGreen
lightseagreen	20B2AA	htmlLightSeaGreen
springgreen	00FF7F	htmlSpringGreen
lime	00FF00	htmlLime
mediumspringgreen	00FA9A	htmlMediumSpringGreen
teal	008080	htmlTeal
green	008000	htmlGreen
darkgreen	006400	htmlDarkGreen
Pinks and Reds		
lavenderblush	FFF0F5	htmlLavenderBlush
mistyrose	FFE4E1	htmlMistyRose

Color Name	Value	IE4 Color Constant
pink	FFC0CB	htmlPink
lightpink	FFB6C1	htmlLightPink
orange	FFA500	htmlOrange
lightsalmon	FFA07A	htmlLightSalmon
darkorange	FF8C00	htmlDarkOrange
coral	FF7F50	htmlCoral
hotpink	FF69B4	htmlHotPink
tomato	FF6347	htmlTomato
orangered	FF4500	htmlOrangeRed
deeppink	FF1493	htmlDeepPink
fuchsia	FF00FF	htmlFuchsia
magenta	FF00FF	htmlMagenta
red	FF0000	htmlRed
salmon	FA8072	htmlSalmon
lightcoral	F08080	htmlLightCoral
violet	EE82EE	htmlViolet
darksalmon	E9967A	htmlDarkSalmon
plum	DDA0DD	htmlPlum
crimson	DC143C	htmlCrimson
palevioletred	DB7093	htmlPaleVioletRed
orchid	DA70D6	htmlOrchid
thistle	D8BFD8	htmlThistle
indianred	CD5C5C	htmlIndianRed
mediumvioletred	C71585	htmlMediumVioletRed
mediumorchid	BA55D3	htmlMediumOrchid
firebrick	B22222	htmlFirebrick
darkorchid	9932CC	htmlDarkOrchid
darkviolet	9400D3	htmlDarkViolet
mediumpurple	9370DB	htmlMediumPurple
darkmagenta	8B008B	htmlDarkMagenta
darkred	8B0000	htmlDarkRed
purple	800080	htmlPurple
maroon	800000	htmlMaroon

Yellows

ivory	FFFFF0	htmlIvory
lightyellow	FFFFE0	htmlLightYellow

453

Color Name	Value	IE4 Color Constant
yellow	FFFF00	htmlYellow
floralwhite	FFFAF0	htmlFloralWhite
lemonchiffon	FFFACD	htmlLemonChiffon
cornsilk	FFF8DC	htmlCornsilk
gold	FFD700	htmlGold
khaki	F0E68C	htmlKhaki
darkkhaki	BDB76B	htmlDarkKhaki

Beiges and Browns

snow	FFFAFA	htmlSnow
seashell	FFF5EE	htmlSeashell
papayawhite	FFEFD5	htmlPapayaWhite
blanchedalmond	FFEBCD	htmlBlanchedAlmond
bisque	FFE4C4	htmlBisque
moccasin	FFE4B5	htmlMoccasin
navajowhite	FFDEAD	htmlNavajoWhite
peachpuff	FFDAB9	htmlPeachPuff
oldlace	FDF5E6	htmlOldLace
linen	FAF0E6	htmlLinen
antiquewhite	FAEBD7	htmlAntiqueWhite
beige	F5F5DC	htmlBeige
wheat	F5DEB3	htmlWheat
sandybrown	F4A460	htmlSandyBrown
palegoldenrod	EEE8AA	htmlPaleGoldenRod
burlywood	DEB887	htmlBurlywood
goldenrod	DAA520	htmlGoldenRod
tan	D2B48C	htmlTan
chocolate	D2691E	htmlChocolate
peru	CD853F	htmlPeru
rosybrown	BC8F8F	htmlRosyBrown
darkgoldenrod	B8860B	htmlDarkGoldenRod
brown	A52A2A	htmlBrown
sienna	A0522D	htmlSienna
saddlebrown	8B4513	htmlSaddleBrown

Whites and Grays

white	FFFFFF	htmlWhite
ghostwhite	F8F8FF	htmlGhostWhite

454

Color Name	Value	IE4 Color Constant
whitesmoke	F5F5F5	htmlWhiteSmoke
gainsboro	DCDCDC	htmlGainsboro
lightgray	D3D3D3	htmlLightGray
silver	C0C0C0	htmlSilver
darkgray	A9A9A9	htmlDarkGray
gray	808080	htmlGray
lightslategray	778899	htmlLightSlateGray
slategray	708090	htmlSlateGray
dimgray	696969	htmlDimGray
darkslategray	2F4F4F	htmlDarkSlateGray
black	000000	htmlBlack

Colors Sorted by Depth

Color Name	Value	IE4 Color Constant
white	FFFFFF	htmlWhite
ivory	FFFFF0	htmlIvory
lightyellow	FFFFE0	htmlLightYellow
yellow	FFFF00	htmlYellow
snow	FFFAFA	htmlSnow
floralwhite	FFFAF0	htmlFloralWhite
lemonchiffon	FFFACD	htmlLemonChiffon
cornsilk	FFF8DC	htmlCornsilk
seashell	FFF5EE	htmlSeashell
lavenderblush	FFF0F5	htmlLavenderBlush
papayawhip	FFEFD5	htmlPapayaWhip
blanchedalmond	FFEBCD	htmlBlanchedAlmond
mistyrose	FFE4E1	htmlMistyRose
bisque	FFE4C4	htmlBisque
moccasin	FFE4B5	htmlMoccasin
navajowhite	FFDEAD	htmlNavajoWhite
peachpuff	FFDAB9	htmlPeachPuff
gold	FFD700	htmlGold
pink	FFC0CB	htmlPink
lightpink	FFB6C1	htmlLightPink
orange	FFA500	htmlOrange

455

Color Name	Value	IE4 Color Constant
lightsalmon	FFA07A	htmlLightSalmon
darkorange	FF8C00	htmlDarkOrange
coral	FF7F50	htmlCoral
hotpink	FF69B4	htmlHotPink
tomato	FF6347	htmlTomato
orangered	FF4500	htmlOrangeRed
deeppink	FF1493	htmlDeepPink
fuchsia	FF00FF	htmlFuchsia
magenta	FF00FF	htmlMagenta
red	FF0000	htmlRed
oldlace	FDF5E6	htmlOldLace
linen	FAF0E6	htmlLinen
antiquewhite	FAEBD7	htmlAntiqueWhite
salmon	FA8072	htmlSalmon
ghostwhite	F8F8FF	htmlGhostWhite
mintcream	F5FFFA	htmlMintCream
whitesmoke	F5F5F5	htmlWhiteSmoke
beige	F5F5DC	htmlBeige
wheat	F5DEB3	htmlWheat
sandybrown	F4A460	htmlSandyBrown
azure	F0FFFF	htmlAzure
honeydew	F0FFF0	htmlHoneydew
aliceblue	F0F8FF	htmlAliceBlue
khaki	F0E68C	htmlKhaki
lightcoral	F08080	htmlLightCoral
palegoldenrod	EEE8AA	htmlPaleGoldenRod
violet	EE82EE	htmlViolet
darksalmon	E9967A	htmlDarkSalmon
lavender	E6E6FA	htmlLavender
lightcyan	E0FFFF	htmlLightCyan
burlywood	DEB887	htmlBurlywood
plum	DDA0DD	htmlPlum
gainsboro	DCDCDC	htmlGainsboro
crimson	DC143C	htmlCrimson
palevioletred	DB7093	htmlPaleVioletRed
goldenrod	DAA520	htmlGoldenRod
orchid	DA70D6	htmlOrchid

456

Color Name	Value	IE4 Color Constant
thistle	D8BFD8	htmlThistle
lightgray	D3D3D3	htmlLightGray
tan	D2B48C	htmlTan
chocolate	D2691E	htmlChocolate
peru	CD853F	htmlPeru
indianred	CD5C5C	htmlIndianRed
mediumvioletred	C71585	htmlMediumVioletRed
silver	C0C0C0	htmlSilver
darkkhaki	BDB76B	htmlDarkKhaki
rosybrown	BC8F8F	htmlRosyBrown
mediumorchid	BA55D3	htmlMediumOrchid
darkgoldenrod	B8860B	htmlDarkGoldenRod
firebrick	B22222	htmlFirebrick
powderblue	B0E0E6	htmlPowderBlue
lightsteelblue	B0C4DE	htmlLightSteelBlue
paleturquoise	AFEEEE	htmlPaleTurquoise
greenyellow	ADFF2F	htmlGreenYellow
lightblue	ADD8E6	htmlLightBlue
darkgray	A9A9A9	htmlDarkGray
brown	A52A2A	htmlBrown
sienna	A0522D	htmlSienna
yellowgreen	9ACD32	htmlYellowGreen
darkorchid	9932CC	htmlDarkOrchid
palegreen	98FB98	htmlPaleGreen
darkviolet	9400D3	htmlDarkViolet
mediumpurple	9370DB	htmlMediumPurple
lightgreen	90EE90	htmlLightGreen
darkseagreen	8FBC8F	htmlDarkSeaGreen
saddlebrown	8B4513	htmlSaddleBrown
darkmagenta	8B008B	htmlDarkMagenta
darkred	8B0000	htmlDarkRed
blueviolet	8A2BE2	htmlBlueViolet
lightskyblue	87CEFA	htmlLightSkyBlue
skyblue	87CEEB	htmlSkyBlue
gray	808080	htmlGray
olive	808000	htmlOlive
purple	800080	htmlPurple

457

Color Name	Value	IE4 Color Constant
maroon	800000	htmlMaroon
aquamarine	7FFFD4	htmlAquamarine
chartreuse	7FFF00	htmlChartreuse
lawngreen	7CFC00	htmlLawnGreen
mediumslateblue	7B68EE	htmlMediumSlateBlue
lightslategray	778899	htmlLightSlateGray
slategray	708090	htmlSlateGray
olivedrab	6B8E23	htmlOliveDrab
slateblue	6A5ACD	htmlSlateBlue
dimgray	696969	htmlDimGray
mediumaquamarine	66CDAA	htmlMediumAquamarine
cornflowerblue	6495ED	htmlCornflowerBlue
cadetblue	5F9EA0	htmlCadetBlue
darkolivegreen	556B2F	htmlDarkOliveGreen
indigo	4B0082	htmlIndigo
mediumturquoise	48D1CC	htmlMediumTurquoise
darkslateblue	483D8B	htmlDarkSlateBlue
steelblue	4682B4	htmlSteelBlue
royalblue	4169E1	htmlRoyalBlue
turquoise	40E0D0	htmlTurquoise
mediumseagreen	3CB371	htmlMediumSeaGreen
limegreen	32CD32	htmlLimeGreen
darkslategray	2F4F4F	htmlDarkSlateGray
seagreen	2E8B57	htmlSeaGreen
forestgreen	228B22	htmlForestGreen
lightseagreen	20B2AA	htmlLightSeaGreen
dodgerblue	1E90FF	htmlDodgerBlue
midnightblue	191970	htmlMidnightBlue
aqua	00FFFF	htmlAqua
cyan	00FFFF	htmlCyan
springgreen	00FF7F	htmlSpringGreen
lime	00FF00	htmlLime
mediumspringgreen	00FA9A	htmlMediumSpringGreen
darkturquoise	00CED1	htmlDarkTurquoise
deepskyblue	00BFFF	htmlDeepSkyBlue
darkcyan	008B8B	htmlDarkCyan
teal	008080	htmlTeal

Color Name	Value	IE4 Color Constant
green	008000	htmlGreen
darkgreen	006400	htmlDarkGreen
blue	0000FF	htmlBlue
mediumblue	0000CD	htmlMediumBlue
darkblue	00008B	htmlDarkBlue
navy	000080	htmlNavy
black	000000	htmlBlack

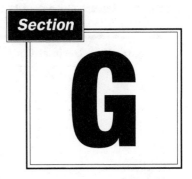
Special Characters in HTML

The following table gives you the codes you need to insert special characters into your HTML documents. Some characters have their own mnemonic names—for example, the registered trademark character can be written in HTML as &reg. Where there is no mnemonic name, you can insert the character simply by including its decimal code.

Character	Decimal Code	HTML	Description
"	&#34;	&quot;	Quotation mark
&	&#38;	&amp;	Ampersand
<	&#60;	&lt;	Less than
>	&#62;	&gt;	Greater than
			Non-breaking space
¡	&#161;	&iexcl;	Inverted exclamation
¢	&#162;	&cent;	Cent sign
£	&#163;	&pound;	Pound sterling
¤	&#164;	&curren;	General currency sign
¥	&#165;	&yen;	Yen sign
¦	&#166;	&brvbar;	Broken vertical bar
§	&#167;	&sect;	Section sign
¨	&#168;	&uml;	Diæresis/umlaut
©	&#169;	&copy;	Copyright
ª	&#170;	&ordf;	Feminine ordinal
«	&#171;	&laquo;	Left angle quote,
¬	&#172;	&not;	Not sign
-	&#173;	&shy;	Soft hyphen
®	&#174;	&reg;	Registered trademark
¯	&#175;	&macr;	Macron accent
°	&#176;	&deg;	Degree sign

Character	Decimal Code	HTML	Description
±	±	±	Plus or minus
²	²	²	Superscript two
³	³	³	Superscript three
´	´	´	Acute accent
µ	µ	µ	Micro sign
¶	¶	¶	Paragraph sign
·	·	·	Middle dot
¸	¸	¸	Cedilla
¹	¹	¹	Superscript one
º	º	º	Masculine ordinal
»	»	»	Right angle quote
¼	¼	¼	Fraction one quarter
½	½	½	Fraction one half
¾	¾	¾	Fraction three-quarters
¿	¿	¿	Inverted question mark
À	À	À	Capital A, grave accent
Á	Á	Á	Capital A, acute accent
Â	Â	Â	Capital A, circumflex
Ã	Ã	Ã	Capital A, tilde
Ä	Ä	Ä	Capital A, diæresis / umlaut
Å	Å	Å	Capital A, ring
Æ	Æ	Æ	Capital AE, ligature
Ç	Ç	Ç	Capital C, cedilla
È	È	È	Capital E, grave accent
É	É	É	Capital E, acute accent
Ê	Ê	Ê	Capital E, circumflex
Ë	Ë	Ë	Capital E, diæresis / umlaut
Ì	Ì	Ì	Capital I, grave accent
Í	Í	Í	Capital I, acute accent
Î	Î	Î	Capital I, circumflex
Ï	Ï	Ï	Capital I, diæresis /umlaut
Ð	Ð	Ð	Capital Eth, Icelandic
Ñ	Ñ	Ñ	Capital N, tilde
Ò	Ò	Ò	Capital O, grave accent
Ó	Ó	Ó	Capital O, acute accent
Ô	Ô	Ô	Capital O, circumflex
Õ	Õ	Õ	Capital O, tilde

Character	Decimal Code	HTML	Description
Ö	&#214;	&Ouml;	Capital O, diæresis / umlaut
×	&#215;	&times;	Multiplication sign
Ø	&#216;	&Oslash;	Capital O, slash
Ù	&#217;	&Ugrave;	Capital U, grave accent
Ú	&#218;	&Uacute;	Capital U, acute accent
Û	&#219;	&Ucirc;	Capital U, circumflex
Ü	&#220;	&Uuml;	Capital U, diæresis / umlaut
Ý	&#221;	&Yacute;	Capital Y, acute accent
Þ	&#222;	&THORN;	Capital Thorn, Icelandic
ß	&#223;	&szlig;	German sz
à	&#224;	&agrave;	Small a, grave accent
á	&#225;	&aacute;	Small a, acute accent
â	&#226;	&acirc;	Small a, circumflex
ã	&#227;	&atilde;	Small a, tilde
ä	&#228;	&auml;	Small a, diæresis / umlaut
å	&#229;	&aring;	Small a, ring
æ	&#230;	&aelig;	Small ae ligature
ç	&#231;	&ccedil;	Small c, cedilla
è	&#232;	&egrave;	Small e, grave accent
é	&#233;	&eacute;	Small e, acute accent
ê	&#234;	&ecirc;	Small e, circumflex
ë	&#235;	&euml;	Small e, diæresis / umlaut
ì	&#236;	&igrave;	Small i, grave accent
í	&#237;	&iacute;	Small i, acute accent
î	&#238;	&icirc;	Small i, circumflex
ï	&#239;	&iuml;	Small i, diæresis / umlaut
ð	&#240;	&eth;	Small eth, Icelandic
ñ	&#241;	&ntilde;	Small n, tilde
ò	&#242;	&ograve;	Small o, grave accent
ó	&#243;	&oacute;	Small o, acute accent
ô	&#244;	&ocirc;	Small o, circumflex
õ	&#245;	&otilde;	Small o, tilde
ö	&#246;	&ouml;	Small o, diæresis / umlaut
÷	&#247;	&divide	Division sign
ø	&#248;	&oslash;	Small o, slash
ù	&#249;	&ugrave;	Small u, grave accent
ú	&#250;	&uacute;	Small u, acute accent

Character	Decimal Code	HTML	Description
û	û	û	Small u, circumflex
ü	ü	ü	Small u, diæresis / umlaut
ý	ý	ý	Small y, acute accent
þ	þ	þ	Small thorn, Icelandic
ÿ	ÿ	ÿ	Small y, diæresis / umlaut

Remember, if you want to show HTML code in a browser, you have to use the special character codes for the angled brackets in order to avoid the browser interpreting them as start and end of tags.

464

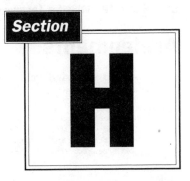

The VBScript Language

Array Handling

Dim—declares an array variable. This can be static with a defined number of elements or dynamic and can have up to 60 dimensions.

ReDim—used to change the size of an array variable which has been declared as dynamic.

Preserve—keyword used to preserve the contents of an array being resized. If you need to use this then you can only re-dimension the rightmost index of the array.

```
Dim strEmployees ()
ReDim strEmployees (9,1)

strEmployees (9,1) = "Phil"

ReDim strEmployees (9,2)            'loses the contents of element (9,1)
strEmployees (9,2) = "Paul"

ReDim Preserve strEmployees (9,3)   'preserves the contents of (9,2)
strEmployees (9,3) = "Smith"
```

LBound—returns the smallest subscript for the dimension of an array. Note that arrays always start from the subscript zero so this function will always return the value zero.

UBound—used to determine the size of an array.

```
Dim strCustomers (10, 5)
intSizeFirst = UBound (strCustomers, 1)     'returns SizeFirst = 10
intSizeSecond = UBound (strCustomers, 2)    'returns SizeSecond = 5
```

> The actual number of elements is always one greater than the value returned by **UBound** because the array starts from zero.

Assignments

Let—used to assign values to variables (optional).
Set—used to assign an object reference to a variable.

```
Let intNumberOfDays = 365

Set txtMyTextBox = txtcontrol
txtMyTextBox.Value = "Hello World"
```

Constants

Empty—an empty variable is one that has been created but not yet assigned a value.
Nothing—used to remove an object reference.

```
Set txtMyTextBox = txtATextBox      'assigns object reference
Set txtMyTextBox = Nothing          'removes object reference
```

Null—indicates that a variable is not valid. Note that this isn't the same as Empty.
True—indicates that an expression is true. Has numerical value –1.
False—indicates that an expression is false. Has numerical value 0.

Error constant:

Constant	Value
vbObjectError	&h80040000

System Color constants:

Constant	Value	Description
vbBlack	&h00	Black
vbRed	&hFF	Red
vbGreen	&hFF00	Green
vbYellow	&hFFFF	Yellow
vbBlue	&hFF0000	Blue
vbMagenta	&hFF00FF	Magenta
vbCyan	&hFFFF00	Cyan
vbWhite	&hFFFFFF	White

Comparison constants:

Constant	Value	Description
vbBinaryCompare	0	Perform a binary comparison.
vbTextCompare	1	Perform a textual comparison.
vbDatabaseCompare	2	Perform a comparison based upon information in the database where the comparison is to be performed.

Date and Time constants:

Constant	Value	Description
VbSunday	1	Sunday
vbMonday	2	Monday
vbTuesday	3	Tuesday
vbWednesday	4	Wednesday
vbThursday	5	Thursday
vbFriday	6	Friday
vbSaturday	7	Saturday
vbFirstJan1	1	Use the week in which January 1 occurs (default).
vbFirstFourDays	2	Use the first week that has at least four days in the new year.
vbFirstFullWeek	3	Use the first full week of the year.
vbUseSystem	0	Use the format in the regional settings for the computer.
vbUseSystemDayOfWeek	0	Use the day in the system settings for the first weekday.

Date Format constants:

Constant	Value	Description
vbGeneralDate	0	Display a date and/or time in the format set in the system settings. For real numbers display a date and time. For integer numbers display only a date. For numbers less than 1, display time only.

Table continued on following page

Constant	Value	Description
vbLongDate	1	Display a date using the long date format specified in the computers regional settings.
vbShortDate	2	Display a date using the short date format specified in the computers regional settings.
vbLongTime	3	Display a time using the long time format specified in the computers regional settings.
vbShortTime	4	Display a time using the short time format specified in the computers regional settings.

File Input/Output constants:

Constant	Value	Description
ForReading	1	Open a file for reading only.
ForWriting	2	Open a file for writing. If a file with the same name exists, its previous one is overwritten.
ForAppending	8	Open a file and write at the end of the file.

String constants:

Constant	Value	Description
vbCr	Chr(13)	Carriage return only
vbCrLf	Chr(13) & Chr(10)	Carriage return and linefeed (Newline)
vbLf	Chr(10)	Line feed only
vbNewLine	-	Newline character as appropriate to a specific platform
vbNullChar	Chr(0)	Character having the value 0
vbNullString	-	String having the value zero (not just an empty string)
vbTab	Chr(9)	Horizontal tab

Tristate constants:

Constant	Value	Description
TristateTrue	-1	True
TristateFalse	0	False
TristateUseDefault	-2	Use default setting

VarType constants:

Constant	Value	Description
vbEmpty	0	Un-initialized (default)
vbNull	1	Contains no valid data
vbInteger	2	Integer subtype
vbLong	3	Long subtype
vbSingle	4	Single subtype
vbDouble	5	Double subtype
vbCurrency	6	Currency subtype
vbDate	7	Date subtype
vbString	8	String subtype
vbObject	9	Object
vbError	10	Error subtype
vbBoolean	11	Boolean subtype
vbVariant	12	Variant (used only for arrays of variants)
vbDataObject	13	Data access object
vbDecimal	14	Decimal subtype
vbByte	17	Byte subtype
vbArray	8192	Array

Control Flow

For...Next—executes a block of code a specified number of times.

```
Dim intSalary (10)
For intCounter = 0 to 10
    intSalary (intCounter) = 20000
Next
```

For Each...Next Statement—repeats a block of code for each element in an array or collection.

471

```
For Each Item In Request.QueryString("MyControl")
   Response.Write Item & "<BR>"
Next
```

Do...Loop—executes a block of code while a condition is true or until a condition becomes true.

```
Do While strDayOfWeek <> "Saturday" And strDayOfWeek <> "Sunday"
   MsgBox ("Get Up! Time for work")
   ...
Loop


Do
   MsgBox ("Get Up! Time for work")
   ...
Loop Until strDayOfWeek = "Saturday" Or strDayOfWeek = "Sunday"
```

If...Then...Else—used to run various blocks of code depending on conditions.

```
If intAge < 20 Then
   MsgBox ("You're just a slip of a thing!")
ElseIf intAge < 40 Then
   MsgBox ("You're in your prime!")
Else
   MsgBox ("You're older and wiser")
End If
```

Select Case—used to replace **If...Then...Else** statements where there are many conditions.

```
Select Case intAge
Case 21,22,23,24,25,26
   MsgBox ("You're in your prime")
Case 40
   MsgBox ("You're fulfilling your dreams")
Case 65
   MsgBox ("Time for a new challenge")
End Select
```

Note that **Select Case** can only be used with precise conditions and not with a range of conditions.

While...Wend—executes a block of code while a condition is true.

```
While strDayOfWeek <> "Saturday" AND strDayOfWeek <> "Sunday"
   MsgBox ("Get Up! Time for work")
   ...
Wend
```

Functions

VBScript contains several functions that can be used to manipulate and examine variables. These have been subdivided into the general categories of:

  Conversion Functions

  Date/Time Functions

- Math Functions
- Object Management Functions
- Script Engine Identification Functions
- String Functions
- Variable Testing Functions

For a full description of each function, and the parameters it requires, see the VBScript Help file. This is installed by default in your **Docs/ASPDocs/VBS/ VBScript** subfolder of your IIS installation directory.

Conversion Functions

These functions are used to convert values in variables between different types:

Function	Description
Asc	Returns the numeric ANSI code number of the first character in a string.
AscB	As above, but provided for use with byte data contained in a string. Returns result from the first byte only.
AscW	As above, but provided for Unicode characters. Returns the **Wide** character code, avoiding the conversion from Unicode to ANSI.
Chr	Returns a string made up of the ANSI character matching the number supplied.
ChrB	As above, but provided for use with byte data contained in a string. Always returns a single byte.
ChrW	As above, but provided for Unicode characters. Its argument is a **Wide** character code, thereby avoiding the conversion from ANSI to Unicode.
CBool	Returns the argument value converted to a **Variant** of subtype **Boolean**.
CByte	Returns the argument value converted to a **Variant** of subtype **Byte**.
CDate	Returns the argument value converted to a **Variant** of subtype **Date**.
CDbl	Returns the argument value converted to a **Variant** of subtype **Double**.
CInt	Returns the argument value converted to a **Variant** of subtype **Integer**.
CLng	Returns the argument value converted to a **Variant** of subtype **Long**
CSng	Returns the argument value converted to a **Variant** of subtype **Single**

Table continued on following page

Function	Description
CStr	Returns the argument value converted to a **Variant** of subtype **String**.
Fix	Returns the integer (whole) part of a number.
Hex	Returns a string representing the hexadecimal value of a number.
Int	Returns the integer (whole) portion of a number.
Oct	Returns a string representing the octal value of a number.
Round	Returns a number rounded to a specified number of decimal places.
Sgn	Returns an integer indicating the sign of a number.

Date/Time Functions

These functions return date or time values from the computer's system clock, or manipulate existing values:

Function	Description
Date	Returns the current system date.
DateAdd	Returns a date to which a specified time interval has been added.
DateDiff	Returns the number of days, weeks, or years between two dates.
DatePart	Returns just the day, month or year of a given date.
DateSerial	Returns a **Variant** of subtype **Date** for a specified year, month, and day.
DateValue	Returns a **Variant** of subtype **Date**.
Day	Returns a number between **1** and **31** representing the day of the month.
Hour	Returns a number between **0** and **23** representing the hour of the day.
Minute	Returns a number between **0** and **59** representing the minute of the hour.
Month	Returns a number between **1** and **12** representing the month of the year.
MonthName	Returns the name of the specified month as a string.
Now	Returns the current date and time.
Second	Returns a number between **0** and **59** representing the second of the minute.
Time	Returns a **Variant** of subtype **Date** indicating the current system time.

Function	Description
TimeSerial	Returns a **Variant** of subtype **Date** for a specific hour, minute, and second.
TimeValue	Returns a **Variant** of subtype **Date** containing the time.
Weekday	Returns a number representing the day of the week.
WeekdayName	Returns the name of the specified day of the week as a string.
Year	Returns a number representing the year.

Math Functions

These functions perform mathematical operations on variables containing numerical values:

Function	Description
Atn	Returns the arctangent of a number.
Cos	Returns the cosine of an angle.
Exp	Returns **e** (the base of natural logarithms) raised to a power.
Log	Returns the natural logarithm of a number.
Randomize	Initializes the random-number generator.
Rnd	Returns a random number.
Sin	Returns the sine of an angle.
Sqr	Returns the square root of a number.
Tan	Returns the tangent of an angle.

Object Management Functions

These functions are used to manipulate objects, where applicable:

Function	Description
CreateObject	Creates and returns a reference to an ActiveX or OLE Automation object.
GetObject	Returns a reference to an ActiveX or OLE Automation object.
LoadPicture	Returns a picture object.

Script Engine Identification

These functions return the version of the scripting engine:

Function	Description
ScriptEngine	A string containing the major, minor, and build version numbers of the scripting engine.
ScriptEngineMajorVersion	The major version of the scripting engine, as a number.
ScriptEngineMinorVersion	The minor version of the scripting engine, as a number.
ScriptEngineBuildVersion	The build version of the scripting engine, as a number.

String Functions

These functions are used to manipulate string values in variables:

Function	Description
Filter	Returns an array from a string array, based on specified filter criteria.
FormatCurrency	Returns a string formatted as currency value.
FormatDateTime	Returns a string formatted as a date or time.
FormatNumber	Returns a string formatted as a number.
FormatPercent	Returns a string formatted as a percentage.
InStr	Returns the position of the first occurrence of one string within another.
InStrB	As above, but provided for use with byte data contained in a string. Returns the byte position instead of the character position.
InstrRev	As InStr, but starts from the end of the string.
Join	Returns a string created by joining the strings contained in an array.
LCase	Returns a string that has been converted to lowercase.
Left	Returns a specified number of characters from the left end of a string.
LeftB	As above, but provided for use with byte data contained in a string. Uses that number of bytes instead of that number of characters.
Len	Returns the length of a string or the number of bytes needed for a variable.
LenB	As above, but is provided for use with byte data contained in a string. Returns the number of bytes in the string instead of characters.
LTrim	Returns a copy of a string without leading spaces.

Function	Description
Mid	Returns a specified number of characters from a string.
MidB	As above, but provided for use with byte data contained in a string. Uses that numbers of bytes instead of that number of characters.
Replace	Returns a string in which a specified substring has been replaced with another substring a specified number of times.
Right	Returns a specified number of characters from the right end of a string.
RightB	As above, but provided for use with byte data contained in a string. Uses that number of bytes instead of that number of characters.
RTrim	Returns a copy of a string without trailing spaces.
Space	Returns a string consisting of the specified number of spaces.
Split	Returns a one-dimensional array of a specified number of substrings.
StrComp	Returns a value indicating the result of a string comparison.
String	Returns a string of the length specified made up of a repeating character.
StrReverse	Returns a string in which the character order of a string is reversed.
Trim	Returns a copy of a string without leading or trailing spaces.
UCase	Returns a string that has been converted to uppercase.

Variable Testing Functions

These functions are used to determine the type of information stored in a variable:

Function	Description
IsArray	Returns a **Boolean** value indicating whether a variable is an array.
IsDate	Returns a **Boolean** value indicating whether an expression can be converted to a date.
IsEmpty	Returns a **Boolean** value indicating whether a variable has been initialized.
IsNull	Returns a **Boolean** value indicating whether an expression contains no valid data

Table continued on following page

Function	Description
IsNumeric	Returns a **Boolean** value indicating whether an expression can be evaluated as a number.
IsObject	Returns a **Boolean** value indicating whether an expression references a valid ActiveX or OLE Automation object.
VarType	Returns a number indicating the subtype of a variable.

Variable Declarations

Dim—declares a variable.

Error Handling

On Error Resume Next—indicates that if an error occurs, control should continue at the next statement.
Err—this is the error object that provides information about run-time errors.

Error handling is very limited in VBScript and the **Err** object must be tested explicitly to determine if an error has occurred.

Input/Output

This consists of **Msgbox** for output and **InputBox** for input:

MsgBox

This displays a message, and can return a value indicating which button was clicked.

```
MsgBox "Hello There",20,"Hello Message","c:\windows\MyHelp.hlp",123
```

The parameters are:
"Hello There"—this contains the text of the message and is obligatory.
20—this determines which icon and buttons appear on the message box.

"Hello Message"—this contains the text that will appear as the title of the message box.

"c:\windows\MyHelp.hlp"—this adds a Help button to the message box and determines the help file that is opened if the button is clicked.

123—this is a reference to the particular help topic that will be displayed if the Help button is clicked.

The value of the icon and buttons parameter is determined using the following tables:

Constant	Value	Buttons
vbOKOnly	0	OK
vbOKCancel	1	OK Cancel
vbAbortRetryIngnore	2	Abort Retry Ignore
vbYesNoCancel	3	Yes No Cancel
vbYesNo	4	Yes No
vbRetryCancel	5	Retry Cancel
vbDefaultButton1	0	The first button from the left is the default.
vbDefaultButton2	256	The second button from the left is the default.
vbDefaultButton3	512	The third button from the left is the default.
vbDefaultButton4	768	The fourth button from the left is the default.

Constant	Value	Description	Icon
vbCritical	16	Critical Message	
vbQuestion	32	Questioning Message	
vbExclamation	48	Warning Message	
vbInformation	64	Informational Message	

Constant	Value	Description
vbApplicationModal	0	Just the application stops until user clicks a button.
vbSystemModal	4096	Whole system stops until user clicks a button.

To specify which buttons and icon are displayed you simply add the relevant values. So, in our example we add together **4 + 16** to display the Yes and No buttons, with Yes as the default, and to show the `Critical` icon.

You can determine which button the user clicked by assigning the return code of the `MsgBox` function to a variable:

```
intButtonClicked = MsgBox ("Hello There",35,"Hello Message")
```

Notice that brackets enclose the `MsgBox` parameters when used in this format. The following table determines the value assigned to the variable `intButtonClicked`:

Constant	Value	Button Clicked
vbOK	1	OK
vbCancel	2	Cancel
vbAbort	3	Abort
vbRetry	4	Retry
vbIgnore	5	Ignore
vbYes	6	Yes
vbNo	7	No

InputBox

This accepts text entry from the user and returns it as a string.

```
strTextEntered = InputBox ("Please enter your name","Login","John Smith",500, 500)
```

"`Please enter your name`"—this is the prompt displayed in the input box.
"`Login`"—this is the text displayed as the title of the input box.
"`John Smith`"—this is the default value displayed in the input box.
`500`—specifies the x position of the input box.
`500`—specifies the y position of the input box.

As with the `MsgBox` function, you can also specify a help file and topic to add a Help button to the input box.

480

Procedures

Call—optional method of calling a subroutine.
Function—used to declare a function.
Sub—used to declare a subroutine.

Other Keywords

Rem—old style method of adding comments to code.
Option Explicit—forces you to declare a variable before it can be used.

Visual Basic Run-time Error Codes

The following error codes also apply to VBA code and many will not be appropriate to an application built completely around VBScript. However, if you have built your own components then these error codes may well be brought up when such components are used.

Code	Description
3	Return without GoSub
5	Invalid procedure call
6	Overflow
7	Out of memory
9	Subscript out of range
10	This array is fixed or temporarily locked
11	Division by zero
13	Type mismatch
14	Out of string space
16	Expression too complex
17	Can't perform requested operation
18	User interrupt occurred
20	Resume without error
28	Out of stack space
35	Sub or Function not defined
47	Too many DLL application clients
48	Error in loading DLL

Code	Description
49	Bad DLL calling convention
51	Internal error
52	Bad file name or number
53	File not found
54	Bad file mode
55	File already open
57	Device I/O error
58	File already exists
59	Bad record length
61	Disk full
62	Input past end of file
63	Bad record number
67	Too many files
68	Device unavailable
70	Permission denied
71	Disk not ready
74	Can't rename with different drive
75	Path/File access error
76	Path not found

Table continued on following page

Code	Description
322	Can't create necessary temporary file
325	Invalid format in resource file
380	Invalid property value
423	Property or method not found
424	Object required
429	OLE Automation server can't create object
430	Class doesn't support OLE Automation
432	File name or class name not found during OLE Automation operation
438	Object doesn't support this property or method
440	OLE Automation error
442	Connection to type library or object library for remote process has been lost. Press OK for dialog to remove reference.
443	OLE Automation object does not have a default value
445	Object doesn't support this action
446	Object doesn't support named arguments
447	Object doesn't support current locale setting
448	Named argument not found
449	Argument not optional
450	Wrong number of arguments or invalid property assignment
451	Object not a collection
452	Invalid ordinal
453	Specified DLL function not found

Code	Description
454	Code resource not found
455	Code resource lock error
457	This key is already associated with an element of this collection
458	Variable uses an OLE Automation type not supported in Visual Basic
481	Invalid picture
500	Variable is undefined
501	Cannot assign to variable
1001	Out of memory
1002	Syntax error
1003	Expected ':'
1004	Expected ';'
1005	Expected '('
1006	Expected ')'
1007	Expected ']'
1008	Expected '{'
1009	Expected '}'
1010	Expected identifier
1011	Expected '='
1012	Expected 'If'
1013	Expected 'To'
1014	Expected 'End'
1015	Expected 'Function'
1016	Expected 'Sub'
1017	Expected 'Then'
1018	Expected 'Wend'
1019	Expected 'Loop'
1020	Expected 'Next'
1021	Expected 'Case'
1022	Expected 'Select'
1023	Expected expression
1024	Expected statement
1025	Expected end of statement
1026	Expected integer constant

Code	Description
1027	Expected 'While' or 'Until'
1028	Expected 'While', 'Until' or end of statement
1029	Too many locals or arguments
1030	Identifier too long
1031	Invalid number
1032	Invalid character
1033	Un-terminated string constant
1034	Un-terminated comment
1035	Nested comment
1036	'Me' cannot be used outside of a procedure
1037	Invalid use of 'Me' keyword
1038	'loop' without 'do'
1039	Invalid 'exit' statement
1040	Invalid 'for' loop control variable
1041	Variable redefinition
1042	Must be first statement on the line
1043	Cannot assign to non-ByVal argument

For more information about VBScript, visit Microsoft's VBScript site at:

`http://www.microsoft.com/vbscript/us/techinfo/`
`vbsdocs.htm`

A Tutorial in VBScript

This section is a brief tutorial on VBScript. We'll walk through the fundamentals, and along the way you will learn how to add VBScript to your existing web pages, the structure of the VBScript language, and how to use **event-driven** programming within your HTML documents.

What is VBScript?

VBScript, Microsoft's Visual Basic Scripting Edition, is a scaled down version of Visual Basic. While it doesn't offer the functionality of Visual Basic, it does provide a powerful, easy to learn tool that can be used to add interaction to your web pages. If you are already experienced in either Visual Basic or Visual Basic for Applications, you will find working with VBScript easy and should be immediately productive. Don't be concerned if you haven't worked in another version of Visual Basic. VBScript is easy to learn, even for the novice developer.

How to Use this Tutorial

This tutorial is a stand-alone introduction to VBScript. It is laid out in a series of five lessons. Each lesson introduces you to a new segment of the VBScript language. Along the way you will learn how to add calculations, formatting and validations to your web pages. At the end of each lesson is an exercise where you, the reader, get to try out your newly acquired knowledge by building web pages utilizing VBScript. The topics of the lessons are:

 An Introduction to VBScript—You will learn how to add VBScript into a web page and alternate methods for linking scripts with HTML

 Working with Variables—What would any language be without variables? Here you learn how to define and use variables in your script routines

Using Objects with VBScript—Java applets and ActiveX controls extend the HTML environment. In this lesson you will learn how to tie these objects together using VBScript

 Controlling Your VBScript Routines—Conditional statements (**If...Then...Else, Select...Case**) and looping (**For...Next** and **Do...Loop**) are the topic of this section

 Using VBScript with Forms—With VBScript you can validate forms before they are submitted. You see how in lesson 5

Step-by-step Exercises

As was mentioned above, each of the five lessons has a worked exercise, which demonstrates how to use the topics that were presented. Along the way you will find descriptions of each component of the example, so that by the end you will have a sound understanding of the lesson's topic.

A copy of the completed exercises can be found at
`http://rapid.wrox.co.uk/books/0685`. Each lesson will have two or
more completed examples that are referenced in the step-by-step instructions.

Lesson 1—Adding VBScript to Web Pages

Scripting languages, like JavaScript and VBScript, are designed as an extension
to HTML. The web browser receives scripts along with the rest of the web
document. It is the browser's responsibility to parse and process the scripts.
HTML was extended to include a tag that is used to incorporate scripts into
HTML—the `<SCRIPT>` tag.

The `<SCRIPT>` Tag

You add scripts into your web pages within a pair of `<SCRIPT>` tags. The
`<SCRIPT>` tag signifies the start of the script section, while `</SCRIPT>` marks
the end. An example of this is shown below:

```
<HTML>
<HEAD>
<TITLE>Working With VBScript</TITLE>
<SCRIPT LANGUAGE="VBScript">
  MsgBox "Welcome to my Web page!"
</SCRIPT>
```

The beginning `<SCRIPT>` tag includes a **LANGUAGE** argument that indicates the
scripting language that will be used. The **LANGUAGE** argument is required
because there is more than one scripting language. Without the **LANGUAGE**
argument, a web browser would not know if the text between the tags was
JavaScript, VBScript or another scripting language.

While technically you can place scripts throughout an HTML document using
pairs of `<SCRIPT>` tags, typically scripts are often found at either the top or
bottom of a Web document. This provides for easy reference and maintenance.

Handling Non-Supporting Browsers

Not all browsers support scripting languages. Some only support JavaScript.
Only Microsoft's Internet Explorer supports VBScript. You might be wondering
what happens to your scripts when non-supporting browsers encounter them.
Usually browsers will do what they do most frequently with text, they will
display your scripts as part of the web page. Obviously, this isn't the result you
had hoped for. One simple way to address this problem is to encase your
scripts in comment tags (`<!--` and `-->`). Below is our example script as it
appears with the addition of the comment tags:

```
<HTML>
<HEAD>
<TITLE>Working With VBScript</TITLE>
<SCRIPT LANGUAGE="VBScript">
<!--
  MsgBox "Welcome to my Web page!"
-->
</SCRIPT>
</HEAD>
</HTML>
```

Now, when a browser that does not support VBScript processes this page, it will view your script as a comment and simply ignore it.

Your First VBScript Exercise

The easiest way to learn any language is to work with it. So let's get right into exercise 1 and expose you to the process of using VBScript in your web pages. Just follow along with the step-by-step instructions to create your first script-enabled web page.

Exercise 1: Adding VBScript to a Web page

In this exercise, you will create an HTML document and add a simple script to respond to a click event generated by a command button. You will need to be familiar with creating and testing an HTML document. A completed copy of this part of the exercise can be found in the file **exer1_v1.htm**.

Creating the HTML Document

 Open up a text editor application and insert the following HTML code:

```
<HTML>
<HEAD>
<TITLE>Working With VBScript: Exercise 1</TITLE>
</HEAD>
<BODY>
    <H1>Your First VBScript Exercise</H1>
    <P> By utilizing VBScript you can give your web pages actions.
    Click on the button below to see what we mean. </P>
    <FORM NAME="frmExercise1">
        <INPUT TYPE="Button" NAME="cmdClickMe" VALUE="Click Me">
    </FORM>
</BODY>
</HTML>
```

Save the file and test it by loading it into Internet Explorer. The resulting page should be similar to the figure below.

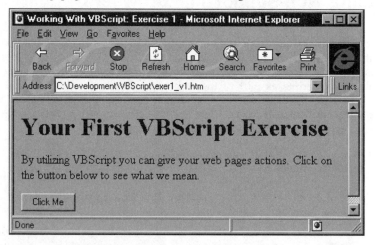

Try out the Click Me button. Does anything happen?

In the next part we will add a script to provide functionality for the Click Me command button. A completed copy of this part of the exercise can be found in the file `exer1_v2.htm`.

Adding VBScript

Re-open the HTML document that you created in part 1, if necessary. Modify the document adding the lines shown with shading below:

```
<HTML>
<HEAD>
<TITLE>Working With VBScript: Exercise 1</TITLE>
</HEAD>
<BODY>
    <H1>Your First VBScript Exercise</H1>
    <P> By utilizing VBScript you can give your Web pages actions.
    Click on the button below to see what we mean. </P>
    <FORM NAME="frmExercise1">
        <INPUT TYPE="Button" NAME="cmdClickMe" VALUE="Click Me">
        <SCRIPT FOR="cmdClickMe" EVENT="onClick" LANGUAGE="VBScript">
          MsgBox "A simple example of VBScript in action."
        </SCRIPT>
    </FORM>
</BODY>
</HTML>
```

Save the file and test it by loading it into Internet Explorer. Try out the Click Me button. The result is shown below:

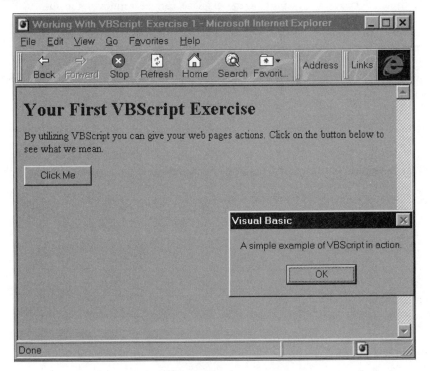

How It Works

Let's take a look at the three lines of code that you added. We want you to have a firm understanding of what the VBScript code is doing and how it is implemented within the HTML document. The first line defines a script. The **FOR** argument specifies that this script is for the button named **cmdClickMe**, the name we have given our command button with the HTML **<INPUT>** tag. The **EVENT** argument says that this script should be run when the button is clicked. The **LANGUAGE** argument states that this is a VBScript module.

```
<SCRIPT FOR="cmdClickMe" EVENT="onClick" LANGUAGE="VBScript">
```

The second line is the only line of VBScript in this HTML document. The **MsgBox** function simply displays a message dialog. You will see more of the **MsgBox** function later in this tutorial. The third line marks the end of our script.

In the previous part, we simply inserted the VBScript module right after the HTML tag that defined the command button. While this method is functional, it is not the preferred approach. HTML by itself can be confusing to read with all of its tags and text. Adding VBScript into the middle all of this just makes it even more complicated. A more organized alternative is to place all of your script together within the HTML document. The following steps introduce you to this approach.

A completed copy of this part of the exercise can be found in the file **exer1_v3.htm**.

Preferred Method to Include VBScript

 Re-open the HTML document that you created in part 2, if necessary, and remove the lines that you added there:

```
<SCRIPT FOR="cmdClickMe" EVENT="onClick" LANGUAGE="VBScript">
  MsgBox "A simple example of VBScript in action."
</SCRIPT>
```

 Modify the document adding the scripting lines as shown in the light shading below:

```
<HTML>
<HEAD>
<TITLE>Working With VBScript: Exercise 1</TITLE>
<SCRIPT LANGUAGE="VBScript">
<!-- Instruct non-IE browsers to skip over VBScript modules.
  Sub cmdClickMe_OnClick
    MsgBox "A simple example of VBScript in action."
  End Sub
-->
</SCRIPT>
</HEAD>
<BODY>
  <H1>Your First VBScript Exercise</H1>
  <P> By utilizing VBScript you can give your Web pages actions.
  Click on the button below to see what we mean. </P>
```

```
<FORM NAME="frmExercise1">
  <INPUT TYPE="Button" NAME="cmdClickMe" VALUE="Click Me">
</FORM>
</BODY>
</HTML>
```

Save the file and test the file by loading it into Internet Explorer. When you try out the Click Me button, the result is the same as the previous example.

How It Works

This second method starts with the same `<SCRIPT>` tag as the previous example. At the center of this script are three lines that provide the functionality for our page. The first line defines a sub-procedure called **cmdClickMe_OnClick**. This will be executed any time that the control **cmdClickMe** is clicked. This type of procedure is referred to as an *event* procedure. The event is the user clicking the button. The procedure that we associate with this event is executed every time the button is clicked.

```
Sub cmdClickMe_OnClick
```

On the second line we find the **MsgBox** function again, while the third line marks an end to our subroutine.

Don't get too hung up on understanding all of the details of this right now, you will see plenty more examples along the way.

Summary

That's it—you just created your first VBScript-enabled web page. Along the way you have learned:

 How to add VBScript into your web pages

 Ways to tie HTML and VBScript together to provide functionality to your pages

Why you should encase your VBScript modules within HTML comments

Next up we will look at what VBScript has to offer in the way of variables.

Lesson 2—Working with Variables

A variable is a named location in computer memory that you can use for storage of data during the execution of your scripts. You can use variables to:

 Store input from the user gathered via your web page

Save data returned from functions

Hold results from calculations

An Introduction to Variables

Let's look at a simple VBScript example to clarify the use of variables. This procedure is included in the file **exam_2a.htm**.

```
Sub cmdVariables_OnClick
   Dim Name
   Name = InputBox("Enter your name: ")
   MsgBox "The name you entered was " & Name
End Sub
```

The first line of this example defines a sub procedure associated with the click event of a command button named **cmdVariables**.

On the second line we declare a variable named **Name**. We are going to use this variable to store the name of the user when it is entered. The third line uses the **InputBox** function to first prompt for, and then return, the user's name. You will see more of the **InputBox** function later in this tutorial. The name it returns is stored in the **Name** variable.

The fourth line uses the **MsgBox** function to display the user's name. Finally, the sub procedure completes on line five.

Exactly how, and where, variables are stored is not important. What you use them for, and how you use them is important. That is what we will be looking at next.

Declaring Variables

There are two methods for declaring variables in VBScript, explicitly and implicitly. You usually declare variables explicitly with the **Dim** statement:

```
Dim Name
```

This statement declares the variable **Name**. You can also declare multiple variables on one line as shown below, although it is preferable to declare each variable separately:

```
Dim Name, Address, City, State
```

Variables can be declared implicitly by simply using the variable name within your script. This practice is not recommended. It leads to code that is prone to errors and more difficult to debug.

You can force VBScript to require all variables to be explicitly declared by including the statement **Option Explicit** at the start of every script. Any variable that is not explicitly declared will then generate an error.

Variable Naming Rules

When naming variables the following rules apply:

 They must begin with an alphabetic character

- They cannot contain embedded periods
- They must be unique within the same scope. There is more on scopes later in this lesson
- They must be no longer than 255 characters

Variants and Subtypes

VBScript has a single data type called a **variant**. Variants have the ability to store different types of data. The types of data that a variant can store are referred to as **subtypes**. The table below describes the subtypes supported by VBScript.

Subtype	Description of Uses for Each Subtype
Byte	Integer numbers between 0 to 255
Boolean	True and False
Currency	Monetary values
Date	Date and time
Double	Extremely large numbers with decimal points
Empty	The value that a variant holds before being used
Error	An error number
Integer	Large integers between –32,768 and 32,767
Long	Extremely large integers (–2,147,483,648 and 2,147,483,647)
Object	Objects
Null	No valid data
Single	Large numbers with decimal points
String	Character strings

Assigning Values

You assign a value to a variable by using the following format:

```
Variable_name  =  value
```

The following examples demonstrate assigning values to variables:

```
Name = "Larry Roof"
HoursWorked = 50
Overtime = True
```

Scope of Variables

The scope of a variable dictates where it can be *used* in your script. A variable's scope is determined by where it is *declared*. If it is declared within a procedure, it is referred to as a **procedure-level** variable and can only be used within that procedure. If it is declared outside of any procedure, it is a **script-level** variable and can be used throughout the script.

The example below demonstrates both script-level and procedure-level variables.

```
<SCRIPT>
   Dim counter
   Sub cmdButton_onClick
      Dim temp
   End Sub
</SCRIPT>
```

The variable `counter` is a script-level variable and can be utilized throughout the script. The variable `temp` exists only within the `cmdButton_onClick` sub-procedure.

Constants

VBScript does not provide support for constants, such as you find in other programming languages. You can work around this by assigning values to variables that you have defined as shown in the example below. Here, **TAX_RATE** is our constant.

```
<SCRIPT>
   Dim TAX_RATE
   TAX_RATE = .06
   Function CalculateTaxes
      CalculateTaxes = CostOfGoods * TAX_RATE
   End Function
</SCRIPT>
```

Arrays

The VBScript language provides support for arrays. You declare an array using the `Dim` statement, just as you did with variables:

```
Dim States(50)
```

The statement above creates an array with 51 elements. Why 51? Because VBScript arrays are **zero-based**, meaning that the first array element is indexed 0 and the last is the number specified when declaring the array.

You assign values to the elements of an array just as you would a variable, but with an additional reference (the index) to the element in which it will be stored:

```
States(5) = "California"
States(6) = "New York"
```

Arrays can have multiple dimensions—VBScript supports up to 60. Declaring a two dimensional array for storing 51 states and their capitals could be done as follows:

```
Dim StateInfo(50,1)
```

To store values into this array you would then reference both dimensions.

```
StateInfo(18,0) = "Michigan"
StateInfo(18,1) = "Lansing"
```

VBScript also provides support for arrays whose size may need to change as the script is executing. These arrays are referred to as **dynamic arrays**. A dynamic array is declared without specifying the number of elements it will contain:

```
Dim Customers()
```

The **ReDim** statement is then used to change the size of the array from within the script:

```
ReDim Customers(100)
```

There is no limit to the number of times an array can be re-dimensioned during the execution of a script. To preserve the contents of an array when you are re-dimensioning, use the **Preserve** keyword:

```
ReDim Preserve Customers(100)
```

Your Second VBScript Exercise

In this exercise we will create a page that performs a simple calculation involving sub-totals, sales tax and final totals. Follow the step-by-step instructions that will introduce you to using variables with VBScript. In this exercise you will create an HTML document which contains a script that will retrieve data from a web page, perform calculations and output a result. A completed copy of this part of the exercise can be found in the file **exer2_v1.htm**.

Creating the HTML Document

Open up a text editor and insert the following HTML code:

```
<HTML>
<HEAD>
<TITLE>Working With VBScript: Exercise 2</TITLE>
</HEAD>
<BODY>
<H1>Your Second VBScript Exercise</H1>
<P> Variables can be used to store and manipulate values. To
see a demonstration of this enter a quantity and unit price
in the fields below and click the "Calculate Cost" button.</P>
<FORM NAME="frmExercise2">
  <TABLE>
    <TR>
      <TD><B>Quantity:</B></TD>
      <TD><INPUT TYPE="Text" NAME="txtQuantity" SIZE=5></TD>
    </TR>
    <TR>
      <TD><B>Unit price:</B></TD>
      <TD><INPUT TYPE="Text" NAME="txtUnitPrice" SIZE=5></TD>
    </TR>
  </TABLE>
  <BR>
```

493

```
<INPUT TYPE="Button" NAME="cmdCalculate" VALUE="Calculate Cost">
</FORM>
</BODY>
</HTML>
```

 Save the file, and load it into Internet Explorer. The result is shown
below.

In this part we will be adding a script to provide functionality for when the
Calculate Cost command button is clicked. A completed copy of this part of the
exercise can be found in the file **exer2_v2.htm**.

Adding VBScript

Re-open the HTML document that you created in part 1, if necessary.
Modify the document adding the scripting lines as shown by the
shading:

Please note that the apostrophes ' are there to comment out code—there is more
on this on the next page—and the _ at the end of the line **Subtotal =
document.frmExercise2.txtQuantity.value_** is a coding convention
which is telling you to type the following line on the same line as this one and
to discard the _.

```
<HTML>
<HEAD>
<TITLE>Working With VBScript: Exercise 2</TITLE>
<SCRIPT LANGUAGE="VBScript">
<!-- Add this to instruct non-IE browsers to skip over VBScript modules.
Option Explicit

Sub cmdCalculate_OnClick
   Dim AmountofTax
   Dim CRLF
   Dim Message
   Dim Subtotal
   Dim TABSPACE
   Dim TAX_RATE
   Dim TotalCost

' Define our constant values.
   TAX_RATE = 0.06
```

```
    CRLF = Chr(13) & Chr(10)
    TABSPACE = Chr(9)

' Perform order calculations.
    Subtotal = document.frmExercise2.txtQuantity.value _
             * document.frmExercise2.txtUnitPrice.value
    AmountofTax = Subtotal * TAX_RATE
    TotalCost = Subtotal + AmountofTax

' Display the results.
    Message = "The total for your order is:"
    Message = Message & CRLF & CRLF
    Message = Message & "Subtotal:" & TABSPACE & "$" & Subtotal & CRLF
    Message = Message & "Tax:" & TABSPACE & "$" & AmountofTax & CRLF
    Message = Message & "Total:" & TABSPACE & "$" & TotalCost
    MsgBox Message,,"Your Total"
End Sub
-->
</SCRIPT>
</HEAD>
<BODY>
    ...
```

Save the file and test it by loading it into Internet Explorer. Enter 100 into the Quantity field and 10 into the Unit Price field. Try out the Calculate Cost button. The result is shown below:

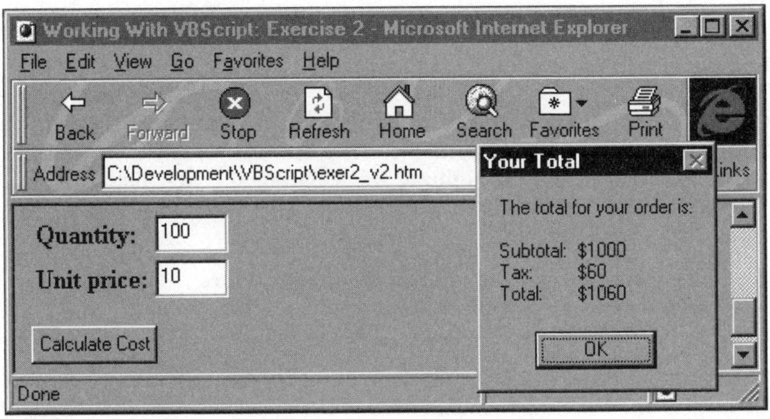

How It Works

What should be obvious right from the start is that this script is far more involved than the one used with Exercise 1. Don't be intimidated by its size. As with the previous lesson, we will work through this script line-by-line.

After the starting `<SCRIPT>` tag and HTML comment we find:

```
Option Explicit
```

Do you remember what this statement does? It forces you to declare all of your variables.

Next we create a sub procedure for the click event of the `cmdCalculate` button.

495

```
Sub cmdCalculate_OnClick
```

Following that we declare seven variables, three of which we are going to use as constants. They can be identified by the fact that they are all in uppercase. In VBScript, case doesn't matter (though it does in JavaScript). We are using it to make the script easier to read. Are the variables procedure-level or script-level variables? They are procedure-level since they are declared within a procedure.

In VBScript, anything after an apostrophe is a comment. As such, they are ignored when the script is processed. Comments can appear on a line by themselves or at the end of a line of script. Comments at the end of a line are referred to as inline comments.

```
' Define our constant values.
```

The constants are assigned values in the following lines. **Chr()** is a VBScript function that returns the character associated with a specified ASCII code. ASCII codes 13, 10 and 9 are carriage return, line feed and tab, respectively.

```
CRLF = Chr(13) & Chr(10)
TABSPACE = Chr(9)
```

The next line demonstrates how values are taken from a form on a web page, and used within a script. The two fields on our form were named **txtQuantity** and **txtUnitPrice** in their HTML **<INPUT>** tags. The form was named **frmExercise2**. Here we are referencing our web document, then the form, then the input field and finally the **value** of that field. The value associated with each field contains what the user entered into that field on the web page. The ***** says to multiply the value of the first field, **txtQuantity**, by the second field, **txtUnitPrice**.

> The commonly used VBScript operands are **+ for addition, – for subtraction, * for multiplication and / for division.**

The result of this calculation is then stored in the variable **Subtotal**. Next we perform some additional calculations. Finally, we display the result of our calculations using the **MsgBox** function. The ampersand character, **&**, is used to concatenate two strings.

As with the previous lesson, don't get too worried about understanding all of the details of this example right now. As you continue to work with VBScript you will begin to pick up the language.

Summary

That completes Exercise 2. You just created a web page that interacts with the user to gather data, perform calculations and present results—the fundamental components of most applications. Along the way you have learned:

 The types of variables that VBScript supports

How to declare and use variables within a script

A technique to work around the absence of constants in VBScript

What a comment line is in a script

In the next lesson we will look at objects. You will learn what they are and how they are used with VBScript.

Lesson 3—Objects and VBScript

Objects, both in the form of Java applets and ActiveX controls, enhance the functionality that is provided with HTML. By using VBScript you can extend the capabilities of these controls, integrating and manipulating them from within your scripts. In this lesson we will look at how you can utilize the power of objects with VBScript.

Scripting with objects involves two steps:

 Adding the object to your web page using HTML

Writing script procedures to respond to events that the object provides

Adding Objects to Your Web Pages

Since this is a VBScript tutorial, rather than an HTML tutorial, we will offer only a limited discussion of how to add an object to a web page. Objects, whether they're Java applets or ActiveX controls are added to a page with the **<OBJECT>** tag. The properties, or characteristics, of the object are configured using the **<PARAM>** tag. Typically you will see an object implemented using a single **<OBJECT>** tag along with several **<PARAM>** tags. The following HTML code demonstrates how an ActiveX control might appear when added to a page:

```
<OBJECT ID="lblTotalPay" WIDTH=45 HEIGHT=24
CLASSID="CLSID:978C9E23-D4B0-11CE-BF2D-00AA003F40D0">
<PARAM NAME="ForeColor" VALUE="0">
<PARAM NAME="BackColor" VALUE="16777215">
<PARAM NAME="Caption" VALUE="">
<PARAM NAME="Size" VALUE="1582;635">
<PARAM NAME="SpecialEffect" VALUE="2">
<PARAM NAME="FontHeight" VALUE="200">
<PARAM NAME="FontCharSet" VALUE="0">
<PARAM NAME="FontPitchAndFamily" VALUE="2">
<PARAM NAME="FontWeight" VALUE="0">
```

Linking VBScript with Objects

Once you have added a control to your web page, it can be configured, manipulated and responded to through its properties, methods and events. **Properties** are the characteristics of an object. They include items like a caption, the foreground color and the font size. **Methods** cause an object to perform a task. **Events** are actions that are recognized by an object. For instance, a command button recognizes an **onclick** event.

497

> The Script Wizard found in the Microsoft ActiveX Control Pad can be used to identify events provided by a control, and to generate script to respond to these events.

For the most part, you will be focusing on properties and events. An example of setting properties for a label control is shown in the following example.

```
<SCRIPT LANGUAGE="VBScript">
Sub cmdCalculatePay_onClick
    Dim HoursWorked
    Dim PayRate
    Dim TotalPay

    HoursWorked = InputBox("Enter hours worked: ")
    PayRate = InputBox("Enter pay rate: ")
    TotalPay = HoursWorked * PayRate

    lblTotalPay.caption = TotalPay
End Sub
</SCRIPT>
```

The **caption** property of the label control, **lblTotalPay**, is set equal to the results of our calculation with the script line:

```
document.frmPayrate.lblTotalPay.caption = TotalPay
```

Object properties are referenced within your scripts using the same format shown in Exercise 2.

Your Third VBScript Exercise

In Exercise 3 we modify the web page created in Exercise 2. These modifications will be made so that we can display the results of our calculations not with the **MsgBox** function, but rather to ActiveX objects that are part of the page. Just follow the step-by-step instructions below to begin learning how to use VBScript with ActiveX.

Exercise 3: Working with Objects

In this exercise, you will create an HTML document that contains a script that will retrieve data from a web page, perform calculations and output a result back to the web page.

Testing the HTML Document

 Load the file **exer3_v1.htm** into a text editor. This is the HTML component of this exercise already typed in for you. Look over the HTML document. It contains three ActiveX label controls named **lblSubtotal**, **lblTaxes** and **lblTotalCost**. Save the file under a different name. We are going to be modifying this source and wouldn't want to work with the original.

 Test the file by loading it into Internet Explorer. The result is shown below. I'd have you try out the **Calculate Cost** button, but you have probably already figured out from the previous two exercises that it doesn't do anything.

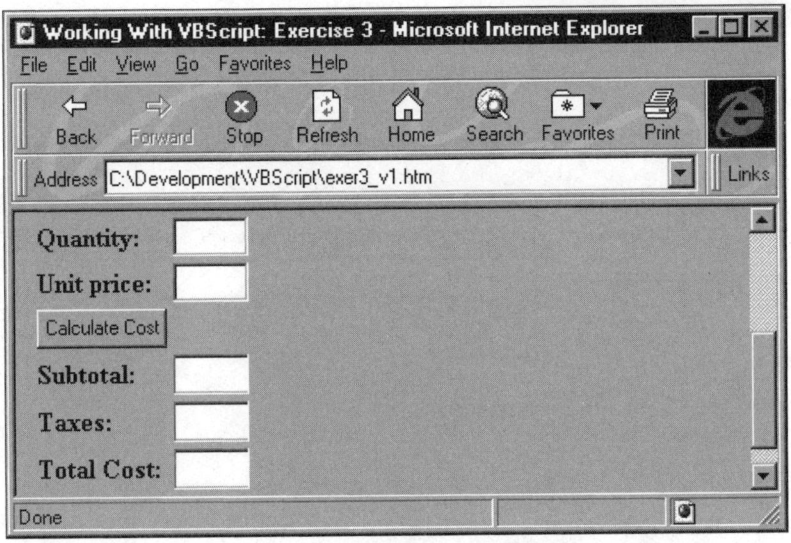

As we did in Exercise 2, we will now add a script to provide functionality for the Calculate Cost command button's click event. A completed copy of this part of the exercise can be found in the file **exer3_v2.htm**.

Adding VBScript

We're going to modify the document, by adding the scripting lines as shown by the shading below:

```
<HTML>
<HEAD>
<TITLE>Working With VBScript: Exercise 3</TITLE>
<SCRIPT LANGUAGE="VBScript">
<!-- Add this to instruct non-IE browsers to skip over VBScript modules.
Option Explicit

Sub cmdCalculate_OnClick
  Dim AmountofTax
  Dim Subtotal
  Dim TAX_RATE
  Dim TotalCost

' Define our constant values.
  TAX_RATE = 0.06

' Perform order calculations.
  Subtotal = document.frmExercise3.txtQuantity.value _
           * document.frmExercise3.txtUnitPrice.value
  AmountofTax = Subtotal * TAX_RATE
  TotalCost = Subtotal + AmountofTax

' Display the results.
  document.frmExercise3.lblSubtotal.caption = Subtotal
  document.frmExercise3.lblTaxes.caption = AmountofTax
  document.frmExercise3.lblTotalCost.caption = TotalCost
End Sub
-->
</SCRIPT>
</HEAD>
...
```

Save the file and test it by loading it into Internet Explorer. Enter 100 into the Quantity field and 10 into the Unit Price field. Try out the Calculate Cost button. The result is shown below:

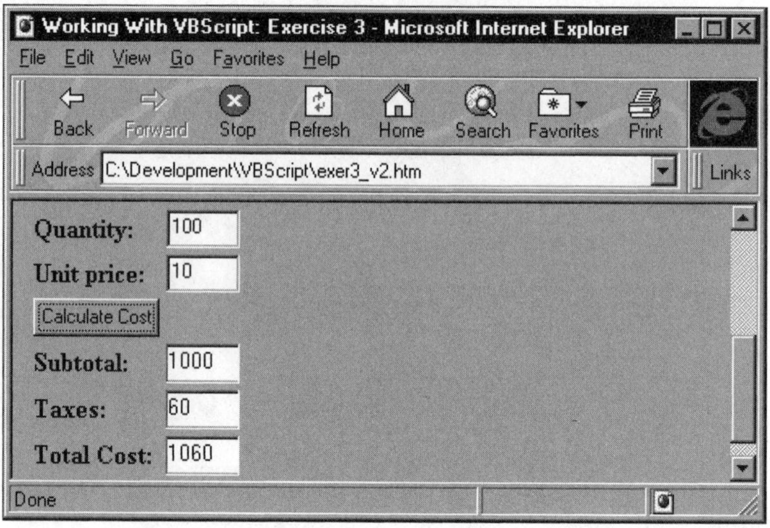

How It Works

Exercise 3 was just a modification of Exercise 2. As such, we will focus on how they differ, rather than going over the script line by line again.

There were minimal changes involving variable declarations and the defining of constant values. We simply didn't need them in this version, so they were removed.

```
Dim AmountofTax
Dim Subtotal
Dim TAX_RATE
Dim TotalCost

' Define our constant values.
TAX_RATE = 0.06
```

We won't discuss the method used to calculate the subtotal, taxes and total amount, as it is identical between the two versions.

The way results are displayed is different in Example 3. The script has been modified to remove the **MsgBox** function and in its place we set the **caption** property of three label controls.

```
' Display the results.
document.frmExercise3.lblSubtotal.caption = Subtotal
document.frmExercise3.lblTaxes.caption = AmountofTax
document.frmExercise3.lblTotalCost.caption = TotalCost
```

The format used when referencing properties is:

document	Our web document
frmExercise3	The form on which the ActiveX controls were placed
lblTaxes	The name of the control
caption	The property to set

Hopefully, by this point you are starting to get comfortable reading and working with VBScript. The best way to strengthen your knowledge of VBScript is to take some of the examples that we have been working with in the first three lessons and modify them to suit your own needs.

Summary

Well that's it for Exercise 3. I know, objects are a pretty hefty topic for a small lesson. What we wanted to do was to give you an exposure to objects and how they can be utilized in VBScript Along the way, you have learned:

 What objects are and how they could be used with VBScript

About properties, methods and events

Next is a lesson in how you can control your script files using conditional and looping statements.

Lesson 4—Controlling Your VBScript Routines

VBScript allows you to control how your scripts process data through the use of **conditional** and **looping** statements. By using conditional statements you can develop scripts that evaluate data and use criteria to determine what tasks to perform. Looping statements allow you to repetitively execute lines of a script. Each offers benefits to the script developer in the process of creating more complex and functional web pages.

Conditional Statements

VBScript provides two forms of conditional statements:

- `If..Then..Else`
- `Select..Case`

If..Then..Else

The `If..Then..Else` statement is used, first to evaluate a condition to see if it is true or false and second, depending upon the condition, to execute a statement or set of statements. Rather than discussing an `If` statement in theory, we will examine some examples to see how they work.

501

The simplest version of an `If` statement is one that contains only a condition and a single statement:

```
If AmountPurchased > 10000 Then DiscountAmount = AmountPurchased * .10
```

In this example statement the condition is:

```
If AmountPurchased > 10000
```

which simply checks to see if the contents of the variable **AmountPurchased** is greater than ten thousand. If it is, the condition is true. In this simple version of the `If` statement when the condition is true the following statement is executed:

```
DiscountAmount = AmountPurchased * .10
```

Next we will look at a more complicated version of the `If` statement. In this version we will perform a series of statements when the condition is true:

```
If AmountPurchased > 10000 Then
   DiscountAmount = AmountPurchased * .10
   Subtotal = AmountPurchased - DiscountAmount
End If
```

In this form of the `If` statement, one or more statements can be executed when the condition is true, by placing them between the `If` statement on top and the **End If** statement on the bottom.

The next form of the `If` statement uses the **If..Then..Else** format. This version of the `If` statement differs from the two previous versions in that it will perform one set of statements if the condition is true and another set when the condition is false:

```
If AmountPurchased > 10000 Then
   DiscountAmount = AmountPurchased * .10
   Subtotal = AmountPurchased - DiscountAmount
Else
   HandlingFee = AmountPurchased *.03
   Subtotal = AmountPurchased + HandlingFee
End If
```

In this example when the condition is true, that is the customer's order is over $10,000, they receive a 10% discount. When the order is under $10,000, they are charged a 3% handling fee.

The final version of the `If` statement that we will look at is the **If..Then..Else If**. In this form the `If` statement checks each of the conditions until it either finds one that is true or an **Else** statement:

```
If AmountPurchased > 10000 Then
   DiscountAmount = AmountPurchased * .10
   Subtotal = AmountPurchased - DiscountAmount
Else If AmountPurchased > 5000 Then
   DiscountAmount = AmountPurchased * .05
```

```
      Subtotal = AmountPurchased - DiscountAmount
   Else
      HandlingFee = AmountPurchased *.03
      Subtotal = AmountPurchased + HandlingFee
   End If
```

In this example the customer receives a 10%discount for orders over $10000, a 5% discount for orders over $5000 and a handling fee of 3% for orders under $5000.

As you see, VBScript offers you plenty of options when it comes to `If` statements.

Select Case

The `Select Case` statement provides an alternative to the `If..Then..Else` statement, providing additional control and readability when evaluating complex conditions. It is well suited for situations where there are a number of possible conditions for the value being checked. Like the `If` statement the `Select Case` structure checks a condition, and based upon that condition being true, executes a series of statements.

The syntax of the `Select Case` statement is:

```
Select Case condition
   Case value
   Case value
   ...
   Case Else
End Select
```

For example, the following `Select` statement assigns different shipping fees based upon the State where the order is being sent:

```
Select Case Document.frmOrder.txtState.Value
   Case "California"
      ShippingFee= .04
   Case "Florida"
      ShippingFee = .03
   Case Else
      ShippingFee = .02
End Select
```

The `Select Case` statement checks each of the `Case` statements until it finds one that will result in the condition being true. If none are found to be true, it executes the statements within the `Case Else`.

> Even though it is not required, always include a Case Else when working with Select Case statements to process conditions that you may not have considered possible. For these conditions you can display something as simple as a message dialog to inform you that a branch was executed that you hadn't planned for.

Looping Statements

VBScript provides four forms of looping statements:

- For..Next
- For Each..Next
- Do..Loop
- While..Wend

These four statements can be divided into two groups. The **For** statements are best used when you want to perform a loop a specific number of times. The **Do..While** and **While..Wend** statements are best used to perform a loop an undetermined number of times.

For..Next

The **For..Next** structure is used when you want to perform a loop a specific number of times. It uses a counter variable, which is incremented or decremented with each repetition of the loop. The following example demonstrates a simple **For** loop:

```
For counter = 1 To 12
   result = 5 * counter
   MsgBox counter & " times 5 is " & result
Next counter
```

The variable **counter** is the numeric value being incremented or decremented. The number 1, defines the start of the loop, 12 the end of the loop. When this loop executes it will display twelve dialog box messages, each containing the product of multiplying five times the counter as it runs from 1 to 12.

In this example, the variable **counter** is incremented by 1 with each loop. Optionally, we could control how we wanted the counter to be modified through the addition of the **Step** argument:

```
For counter = 1 To 12 Step 2
   result = 5 * counter
   MsgBox counter & " times 5 is " & result
Next counter
```

This slight modification to the loop results in only the products of the odd numbers between 1 and 12 being displayed. If you want to create a countdown loop, where the number is decremented with each loop simply use a negative value with the **Step** argument as shown in the following example:

```
For counter = 12 To 1 Step -1
   result = 5 * counter
   MsgBox counter & " times 5 is " & result
Next counter
```

Note that in a decrementing loop the starting number is greater than the ending number.

504

For Each..Next

The `For Each..Next` is similar to the `For..Next` loop but instead of repeating a loop for a certain number of times, it repeats the loop for each member of a specified collection. The discussion of collections and their use is outside of the scope of this tutorial. The `For Each..Next` structure is detailed elsewhere in the book.

Do..Loop

The `Do..Loop` structure repeats a block of statements until a specified condition is met. Normally, when using a `Do..Loop`, the condition being checked is the result of some operation being performed within the structure of the loop. Two versions of this structure are provided the `Do..While` and the `Do..Until`.

Do..While

A `Do` loop that contains the `While` keyword will be performed as long as the condition being tested is true. You have the option of checking the condition at the start of the loop, as in the form:

```
Do While   condition
    statement
    statement
    ...
Loop
```

Or at the end of the loop as shown in the following example:

```
Do
    statement
    statement
    ...
Loop While   condition
```

The difference between these two formats is that the first example may never perform the statements included within its structure while the second example will always perform its statements at least once.

Do..Until

A `Do` loop that contains the `Until` keyword will continue to loop as long as the condition being tested is false. As with the `Do..While` structure, you have the option of checking the condition at the start of the loop as in the form:

```
Do   Until   condition
    statement
    statement
    ...
Loop
```

Or at the end of the loop as shown in the following example:

```
Do
    statement
    statement
    ...
Loop Until  condition
```

One use for a **Do..Loop** is shown in the example below:

```
password = InputBox("Enter your password:")
Do Until password = "letmein"
  Msgbox "Invalid password - please try again."
  password = InputBox("Enter you password:")
Loop
```

In this example we ask the user to enter a password before performing the conditional part of the **Do..Loop** the first time. The result is that, if they enter the correct password the first time, the statements within the loop's structure will never be performed. If the user were to enter an invalid password then the statements within the **Do..Loop** structure would be performed, a message would be displayed and the user would be prompted to re-enter their password.

While..Wend

The **While..Wend** structure loops as long as the condition being checked is true. If the condition is true, the **While..Wend** statement operates similar to the **Do..Loop** structure but without its flexibility.

The structure for the **While..Wend** statement is:

```
While  condition
    statement
    statement
    ...
Wend
```

Your Fourth VBScript Exercise

In this exercise we continue to extend the functionality of our web page. New features provided by this exercise are:

 A combo box from which the user can select products

A utomatic pricing of products as they are selected

Discounting purchase prices based upon the size of the order

As with the first three exercises simply follow the step-by-step instructions below to begin to learn how to use conditional and looping statements with your scripts.

Exercise 4: Working with Objects

In this exercise you will create an HTML document which contains a script that will retrieve data from a web page, perform calculations and output a result

506

back to the web page. Additionally it will look up prices for products and provide discounts based upon the order size.

Testing the HTML Document

Open up a text editor application and load the file **exer4_v1.htm**. This is the HTML component of this exercise already typed in for you.

Look over the HTML document. Note the addition of an ActiveX combo box control, **cmbProducts**, and additional label controls. Scroll to the bottom of the document where you will find a script that fills the combo box with the available products as shown in the following code fragment.

```
<SCRIPT LANGUAGE="VBScript">
<!--
    document.frmExercise4.cmbProducts.addItem "NEC MultiSync E1100"
    document.frmExercise4.cmbProducts.addItem "NEC MultiSync P1150"
    document.frmExercise4.cmbProducts.addItem "NEC MultiSync E750"
-->
</SCRIPT>
```

Test the file by loading it into Internet Explorer. The resulting page is shown below. You can forget about testing the Calculate Cost button, we've been down that road before.

```
┌─────────────────────────────────────────────────────────────┐
│ ⬚ Working With VBScript: Exercise 4 - Microsoft Internet Explorer │ _ □ X │
│  File  Edit  View  Go  Favorites  Help                          │
│   ⇐      ⇒      ⊗      ↻     ⌂     ⊕    📁▼   🖨    (e)         │
│  Back  Forward  Stop  Refresh Home  Search Favorites Print       │
│ ┌─────────────────────────────────────────────────────────┐    │
│ │Address C:\Development\VBScript\exer4_v1.htm           ▼ │ Links│
│ ├─────────────────────────────────────────────────────────┤ ▲  │
│ │ Monitor:            [                   ▼]               │    │
│ │ Quantity:           [                    ]               │    │
│ │ [Calculate Cost]                                         │    │
│ │ Unit Cost:          [          ]                         │    │
│ │ Subtotal before discount: [          ]                   │    │
│ │ Discount:           [          ]                         │    │
│ │ Subtotal after discount:  [          ]                   │    │
│ │ Taxes:              [          ]                         │    │
│ │ Total Cost:         [          ]                       ▼ │    │
│ ├─────────────────────────────────────────────────────────┤    │
│ │Done                                          ⬚           │    │
│ └─────────────────────────────────────────────────────────┘    │
```

We will now add a script to provide functionality for the Calculate Cost command button, as well as when a product is selected from the combo box control. A completed copy of this part of the exercise can be found in the file **exer4_v2.htm**.

507

Adding VBScript

Modify the document by adding the shaded lines of script:

```
<HTML>
<HEAD>
<TITLE>Working With VBScript: Exercise 4</TITLE>
<SCRIPT LANGUAGE="VBScript">
<!-- Add this to instruct non-IE browsers to skip over VBScript modules.
Option Explicit

Sub cmdCalculate_OnClick
  Dim AmountofDiscount
  Dim AmountofTax
  Dim DISCOUNT_LIMIT
  Dim DISCOUNT_RATE
  Dim SubtotalBefore
  Dim SubtotalAfter
  Dim TAX_RATE
  Dim TotalCost

' Define our constant values.
  DISCOUNT_LIMIT = 1000
  DISCOUNT_RATE = .10
  TAX_RATE = 0.06

' Calculate the subtotal for the order.
  SubtotalBefore = document.frmExercise4.txtQuantity.value _
                 * document.frmExercise4.lblUnitCost.caption

' Check to see if the order is large enough to offer discounts.
  If (SubtotalBefore > DISCOUNT_LIMIT) Then
    AmountofDiscount = SubtotalBefore * DISCOUNT_RATE
  Else
    AmountofDiscount = 0
  End If
  SubtotalAfter = SubtotalBefore - AmountofDiscount

' Calculate taxes and total cost.
  AmountofTax = SubtotalAfter * TAX_RATE
  TotalCost = SubtotalAfter + AmountofTax

' Display the results.
  document.frmExercise4.lblSubtotalBefore.caption = SubtotalBefore
  document.frmExercise4.lblDiscount.caption = AmountofDiscount
  document.frmExercise4.lblSubtotalAfter.caption = SubtotalAfter
  document.frmExercise4.lblTaxes.caption = AmountofTax
  document.frmExercise4.lblTotalCost.caption = TotalCost
End Sub

Sub cmbProducts_Change()
  Select Case document.frmExercise4.cmbProducts.value
    Case "NEC MultiSync E1100"
      document.frmExercise4.lblUnitCost.caption = 1590
    Case "NEC MultiSync P1150"
      document.frmExercise4.lblUnitCost.caption = 880
    Case "NEC MultiSync E750"
      document.frmExercise4.lblUnitCost.caption = 1940
    Case Else
      document.frmExercise4.lblUnitCost.caption = 0
  End Select
End Sub
-->
</SCRIPT>
</HEAD>
...
```

508

Save the file, and test it in Internet Explorer. Select a product from the combo box. Notice how the Unit Cost field is automatically updated as shown below.

```
┌─────────────────────────────────────────────────────────────┐
│ Working With VBScript: Exercise 4 - Microsoft Internet Explorer │ _ □ X │
├─────────────────────────────────────────────────────────────┤
│ File  Edit  View  Go  Favorites  Help                         │
│   ←      ⇒      ⊗      🗘     🏠     🔍      🗖▼     🖨         │
│  Back  Forward  Stop  Refresh  Home  Search  Favorites  Print  │
│ Address C:\Development\VBScript\exer4_v2.htm          ▼ │ Links│
├─────────────────────────────────────────────────────────────┤
│  Monitor:              [NEC MultiSync E1100 ▼]                │
│  Quantity:             [              ]                        │
│  [Calculate Cost]                                             │
│  Unit Cost:            [         1590]                         │
│  Subtotal before discount: [          ]                       │
│  Discount:             [              ]                        │
│  Subtotal after discount: [           ]                       │
│  Taxes:                [              ]                        │
│  Total Cost:           [              ]                        │
├─────────────────────────────────────────────────────────────┤
│ Done                                                          │
└─────────────────────────────────────────────────────────────┘
```

 Enter 10 into the Quantity field. Try out the Calculate Cost button. The result is shown below.

```
┌─────────────────────────────────────────────────────────────┐
│ Working With VBScript: Exercise 4 - Microsoft Internet Explorer │ _ □ X │
├─────────────────────────────────────────────────────────────┤
│ File  Edit  View  Go  Favorites  Help                         │
│   ←      ⇒      ⊗      🗘     🏠     🔍      🗖▼     🖨         │
│  Back  Forward  Stop  Refresh  Home  Search  Favorites  Print  │
│ Address C:\Development\VBScript\exer4_v2.htm          ▼ │ Links│
├─────────────────────────────────────────────────────────────┤
│  Monitor:              [NEC MultiSync E1100 ▼]                │
│  Quantity:             [           10]                        │
│  [Calculate Cost]                                             │
│  Unit Cost:            [         1590]                         │
│  Subtotal before discount: [    15900]                        │
│  Discount:             [         1590]                         │
│  Subtotal after discount: [    14310]                         │
│  Taxes:                [        858.6]                         │
│  Total Cost:           [      15168.6]                         │
├─────────────────────────────────────────────────────────────┤
│ Done                                                          │
└─────────────────────────────────────────────────────────────┘
```

How It Works

Exercise 4 has two new features, the automatic price lookup and the discount feature. We will look at how each is implemented separately.

Product Lookup

The lookup feature is implemented via the **cmbProducts_Change** event procedure. As you might have remembered, the ActiveX combo box control that we added to your HTML document was given the name **cmbProducts**. This control supports a **change** event, which is triggered every time the user selects an item from the list. We simply make use of the **Select Case** statement to check the value of the control. Now, in our example, these values are hard coded. In a real life application we would normally pull these from a data source.

```
Sub cmbProducts_change()
   Select Case document.frmExercise4.cmbProducts.value
      Case "NEC MultiSync E1100"
         document.frmExercise4.lblUnitCost.caption = 1590
      Case "NEC MultiSync P1150"
         document.frmExercise4.lblUnitCost.caption = 880
      Case "NEC MultiSync E750"
         document.frmExercise4.lblUnitCost.caption = 1940
      Case Else
         document.frmExercise4.lblUnitCost.caption = 0
   End Select
End Sub
```

> **Even though the combo box control can only contain one of the three monitors, we still employ a** Case Else **branch. This is simply a good programming habit to develop.**

Discounting Orders

The script used to implement discounts begins by defining some constants, setting the discount limit at $1000 and a discount rate of 10%. Our discounting process begins by calculating the subtotal of the order before discounts and taxes are applied.

Discounting is then applied through the use of an **If..Then..Else** statement. We compare our subtotal amount against the constant **DISCOUNT_LIMIT**. If our amount is greater than the limit, the discount amount is calculated and stored in the variable **AmountofDiscount**. If it is less than, or equal to, the limit, the discount amount is set to 0.

```
' Check to see if the order is large enough to offer discounts.
  If (SubtotalBefore > DISCOUNT_LIMIT) Then
    AmountofDiscount = SubtotalBefore * DISCOUNT_RATE
  Else
    AmountofDiscount = 0
  End If
```

The value of the variable **AmountofDiscount** is subsequently subtracted from the subtotal. Next we calculate the taxes and total cost of the order. We complete the script by displaying the order information on the web page.

Extending this application

In this example I set the discount limit at $1,000. What would we have to change in our script to set the limit at a more reasonable amount of say, $100,000?

Summary

Can you believe how far our original application has progressed? Now we have a page that receives user input, performs price lookups, calculates discount amounts and displays the complete order information on the web page, all without having to go back to the web server.

In this chapter you were introduced to:

 Conditional statements, which allow you to selectively execute blocks of statements

 Looping statements that provide you with a way to repetitively execute blocks of statements

Now that we can input, manipulate and display data, it is time to learn how to validate the data, before sending it on to a web server.

Lesson 5—Using VBScript with Forms

As the popularity of web page forms increase, so does the need to be able to validate data before the client browser submits it to the web server. As a scripting language, VBScript is well suited for this task. Once the form has been validated, the same script can be used to forward the data on to the server. In this lesson we will look at both the process of validating and submitting forms.

Validating Your Forms

The process of validating forms involves checking the form to see if:

 All of the required data is proved

The data provided is valid

Meticulous data validation scripts can be tedious to code but are well worth their return in verifying the quality of the data.

The validation example that we will be examining does not contain anything new in the way of VBScript. We are simply using the elements that we have learned in the previous lessons in a new way. Before reading any further you may find if beneficial to ponder how you would validate an HTML form using the VBScript techniques that you have learned.

Okay, are you through pondering? Let's look at an example to give you an idea of what is possible when it comes to validating forms.

511

Checking Form Input

This example is pretty simple. It has a single field in which the user can enter their age and a single command button that is used to submit their age to the server. A copy of this example can be found in exam_5a.htm.

```
<HTML>
<HEAD>
<TITLE>Working With VBScript: Example 5a</TITLE>

<SCRIPT LANGUAGE="VBScript">
<!-- Instruct non-IE browsers to skip over VBScript modules.
Option Explicit

Sub cmdSubmit_OnClick
' Check to see if the user entered anything.
  If (Len(document.frmExample5a.txtAge.value) = 0) Then
    MsgBox "You must enter your age before submitting."
    Exit Sub
  End If

' Check to see if the user entered a number.
  If (Not(IsNumeric(document.frmExample5a.txtAge.value))) Then
    MsgBox "You must enter a number for your age."
    Exit Sub
  End If

' Check to see if the age entered is valid.
  If (document.frmExample5a.txtAge.value < 0) Or _
     (document.frmExample5a.txtAge.value > 100) Then
    MsgBox "The age you entered is invalid."
    Exit Sub
  End If

' Data looks okay so submit it.
  MsgBox "Thanks for providing your age."
  document.frmExample5a.submit
End Sub
-->
</SCRIPT>

</HEAD>
<BODY>
<H1>A VBScript Example on Variables</H1>
<P> This example demonstrates validation techniques in VBScript. </P>
<FORM NAME="frmExample5a">
  <TABLE>
    <TR>
      <TD>Enter your age:</TD>
      <TD><INPUT TYPE="Text" NAME="txtAge" SIZE="2"></TD>
    <TR>
      <TD><INPUT TYPE="Button" NAME="cmdSubmit" VALUE="Submit"></TD>
      <TD></TD>
    </TR>
  </TABLE>
</FORM>
</BODY>
</HTML>
```

How It Works

The heart of this validation script is found in the click event procedure for the cmdSubmit command button. We start by checking if the user entered anything at all into the field using VBScript's **Len** function. This function returns the length of a string. If the length is 0, the data is invalid. We inform the user and exit the submit procedure via the **Exit Sub** statement:

```
' Check to see if the user entered anything.
If (Len(document.frmExample5a.txtAge.value) = 0) Then
  MsgBox "You must enter your age before submitting."
  Exit Sub
End If
```

Next we check to see if what the user entered is a numeric value. The VBScript function **IsNumeric** returns a true value when it is a number. If not, we tell the user and exit:

```
' Check to see if the user entered a number.
If (Not(IsNumeric(document.frmExample5a.txtAge.value))) Then
  MsgBox "You must enter a number for your age."
  Exit Sub
End If
```

Our final check involves verifying that the age they entered seems reasonable for our environment. I have determined that no age less than 0 or greater than 100 is acceptable. Using an **If..Then** statement we can check the value of the input field against this criteria:

```
' Check to see if the age entered is valid.
If (document.frmExample5a.txtAge.value < 0) Or _
   (document.frmExample5a.txtAge.value > 100) Then
  MsgBox "The age you entered is invalid."
  Exit Sub
End If
```

That's it. While this example is by no means the most detailed validation script you will encounter it provides you with a basis of what is possible with VBScript.

Submitting Your Forms

Compared to validation, the process of submitting a form is simple. In our example we've used a normal HTML button with the Submit caption that is tied to an event procedure that both validates and at the same time submits the form. In Chapter 5, we've demonstrated how to use function **MyButton_onSubmit**, as an alternative.

The code that we would have to add to our previous example to submit the form is shown below:

```
' Data looks okay so submit it.
MsgBox "Thanks for providing your age."
document.frmExample5a.submit
```

The **MsgBox** statement lets the user know that their data has been processed. The form is then submitted by invoking the Submit method of the form object. As we saw in lesson 3 on objects, methods cause an object to perform a task. Here we are using the **submit** method of our form to cause the form to submit its data, just as if we had used a **submit** control.

Your Fifth VBScript Exercise

With this exercise we will add scripts to validate and submit the form that we have been constructing in the previous four lessons.

Exercise 5: How to Validate and Submit a Form

In this exercise you will create an HTML document which contains a script that will retrieve data from a web page, perform calculations, and output results back to the web page. Additionally it will lookup prices for products and provide discounts based upon the order size. Finally, it will validate data and submit the web page form to a server.

Testing the HTML Document

Open up the file **exer5_v1.htm** in a text editor. This is the HTML component of this exercise. Look over the HTML document. Note the addition of a command button **cmdSubmit**, which will be used to submit our form to a web server, after validation. Load the file up into Internet Explorer and it should look like the illustration below:

Next we will add the script that will handle the validation and submit our form. A completed copy of this part of the exercise can be found in the file **exer5_v2.htm**.

```
Sub cmdCalculate_OnClick
    Dim AmountofDiscount
```

514

```
      Dim AmountofTax
      Dim DISCOUNT_LIMIT
      Dim DISCOUNT_RATE
      Dim SubtotalBefore
      Dim SubtotalAfter
      Dim TAX_RATE
      Dim TotalCost

    ' Perform validation checks before process anything. While this is not
    ' everything that we could check, it provides an example of how you can
    ' validate data.
      If (Len(document.frmExercise5.txtQuantity.value) = 0) Then
        MsgBox "You must enter a quantity."
        Exit Sub
      End If

      If (Not IsNumeric(document.frmExercise5.txtQuantity.value)) Then
        MsgBox "Quantity must be a numeric value."
        Exit Sub
      End If

      If (Len(document.frmExercise5.cmbProducts.value) = 0) Then
        MsgBox "You must select a product."
        Exit Sub
      End If

    ' Define our constant values.
      DISCOUNT_LIMIT = 1000
      DISCOUNT_RATE = .10
      TAX_RATE = 0.06

    ' Calculate the subtotal for the order.
      SubtotalBefore = document.frmExercise5.txtQuantity.Value _
    * document.frmExercise5.lblUnitCost.Caption

    ' Check to see if the order is large enough to offer discounts.
      If (SubtotalBefore > DISCOUNT_LIMIT) Then
        AmountofDiscount = SubtotalBefore * DISCOUNT_RATE
      Else
        AmountofDiscount = 0
      End If
      SubtotalAfter = SubtotalBefore - AmountofDiscount

    ' Calculate taxes and total cost.
      AmountofTax = SubtotalAfter * TAX_RATE
      TotalCost = SubtotalAfter + AmountofTax

    ' Display the results.
      Document.frmExercise5.lblSubtotalBefore.Caption = SubtotalBefore
      Document.frmExercise5.lblDiscount.Caption = AmountofDiscount
      Document.frmExercise5.lblSubtotalAfter.Caption = SubtotalAfter
      Document.frmExercise5.lblTaxes.Caption = AmountofTax
      Document.frmExercise5.lblTotalCost.Caption = TotalCost
    End Sub

    ' Submit this order for processing.
    Sub cmdSubmit_onClick
    MsgBox "Your order has been submitted."
     document.frmExercise5.submit
    End Sub

    Sub cmbProducts_Change()
      Select Case Document.frmExercise5.cmbProducts.Value
        Case "NEC MultiSync E1100"
          Document.frmExercise5.lblUnitCost.Caption = 1590
        Case "NEC MultiSync P1150"
          Document.frmExercise5.lblUnitCost.Caption = 880
```

515

```
        Case "NEC MultiSync E750"
           Document.frmExercise5.lblUnitCost.Caption = 1940
        Case Else
           Document.frmExercise5.lblUnitCost.Caption = 0
    End Select
End Sub
```

Save the file and test it by loading it into Internet Explorer. Without entering anything into the Quantity field click the Calculate Costs button. The following dialog will be displayed:

Enter the letter A into the Quantity field and click the Calculate Costs button. You will see the following dialog:

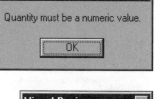

Enter a value of 10 into the Quantity field and once again click the Calculate Costs button. This time you will see the following dialog:

Finally, select the NEC MultiSync E1100 monitor from the combo box. Clicking the Calculate Costs button followed by the Submit Order button will leave you with the following:

How It Works

The script that was added to Exercise 5 has two components, one which validates the form and one that submits the form. We will look at each component separately.

Form Validation

The validation of our form is handled by the event procedure associated with the button named `cmdCalculate`. You should note that this is only an example of what is possible in the way of validation and is by no means a comprehensive validation script.

We start by checking the length of the Quantity field to determine if the user has entered anything. VBScript's `Len` function is well suited for this purpose. If we find that the length is zero, the user is informed and we exit the event procedure.

Next we check to make sure that the Quantity field contains a numeric value. For this we use VBScript's `IsNumeric` function. An order would never be valid without selecting a product first so we check the value of the Monitor combo box, again using the `Len` function.

If we pass all of these validations the cost of the order is calculated and displayed.

Submitting the Form

The submitting of the form is handled within the event procedure for the button named `cmdSubmit`. When the user clicks this button first a message box is displayed to confirm with the user that the order has been processed and then the form is submitted.

> Normally we would include the script for both validating a form and submitting it in the same event procedure. I chose to separate them in this example so that it would be easier to understand.

Summary

That wraps up our application and our tutorial on VBScript. In this short space we've covered some of the basic ways you can use VBScript in a web page. We started with a simple example that displayed a message box and built it into a program that accepted, processed, displayed, validated and submitted data. What's left for you? Coupled with the reference and the examples in the book, you can try modifying and tweaking some of the examples. Take some of the techniques that were presented and integrate them into your own web pages. Script writing, like any development skill, requires practice and perseverance.

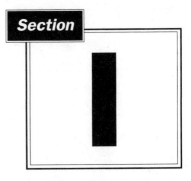
JavaScript Reference

General Information

JavaScript is included in an HTML document with the **\<SCRIPT>** tag. Here's an example:

```
<HTML>
<HEAD>

<!-- wrap script in comments
<script language = "JavaScript">
 script code goes here
</SCRIPT>
-->

</HEAD>
<BODY>
 HTML goes here
</BODY>
</HTML>
```

The following points should be kept in mind:

 By placing JavaScript code in the **\<HEAD>** section of the document you ensure that all the code has been loaded before an attempt is made to execute it.

 The script code should be wrapped in an HTML comment tag to stop older (non-JavaScript) browsers from displaying it.

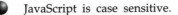 JavaScript is case sensitive.

Values

JavaScript recognizes the following data types:

 strings—"Hello World"

numbers—both integers (86) and decimal values (86.235)

boolean—true or false

A null (*no value*) value is assigned with the keyword **null**.

JavaScript also makes use of 'special characters' in a similar way to the C++ programming language:

Character	Function
\n	newline
\t	tab
\f	form feed
\b	backspace
\r	carriage return

You may 'escape' other characters by preceding them with a backslash (\), to prevent the browser from trying to interpret them. This is most commonly used for quotes and backslashes, or to include a character by using its octal (base 8) value:

```
document.write("This shows a \"quote\" in a string.");
document.write("This is a backslash: \\");
document.write("This is a space character: \040.");
```

Variables

JavaScript is a **loosely typed** language. This means that variables do not have an explicitly defined variable type. Instead, every variable can hold values of various types. Conversions between types are done automatically when needed, as this example demonstrates:

```
x = 55;     // x is assigned to be the integer 55
y = "55"; // y is assigned to be the string "55"
y = '55';   // an alternative using single quotes

z = 1 + y;
<!-- even though y is a string, it will be automatically
 converted to the appropriate integer value so that 1 may
 be added to it. -->

document.write(x);
<!-- the number 55 will be written to the screen. Even
 though x is an integer and not a string, Javascript will
 make the  necessary conversion for you. -->

n = 3.14159;  // assigning a real (fractional) number
n = 0546;     // numbers starting 0 assumed to be octal
n = 0xFFEC;   // numbers starting 0x assumed to be hex
n = 2.145E-5; // using exponential notation
```

Variable names must start with either a letter or an underscore. Beyond the first letter, variables may contain any combination of letters, underscores, and digits. JavaScript is case sensitive, so **this_variable** is not the same as **This_Variable**.

520

Variables do not need to be declared before they are used. However, you may use the **var** keyword to explicitly define a variable. This is especially useful when there is the possibility of conflicting variable names. When in doubt, use **var**.

```
var x = "55";
```

Assignment Operators

The following operators are used to make assignments in JavaScript:

Operator	Example	Result
=	x = y	x equals y
+=	x += y	x equals x plus y
-=	x -= y	x equals x minus y
*=	x *= y	x equals x multiplied by y
/=	x /= y	x equals x divided by y
%=	x %= y	x equals x modulus y

Each operator assigns the value on the right to the variable on the left.

```
x = 100;
y = 10;
x += y;  // x now is equal to 110
```

Equality Operators

Operator	Meaning
==	is equal to
!=	is not equal to
>	is greater than
>=	is greater than or equal to
<	is less than
<=	is less than or equal to

Other Operators

Operator	Meaning
+	Addition
-	Subtraction
*	Multiplication

Operator			Meaning
/			Division
%			Modulus
++			Increment
--			Decrement
-			Unary Negation
&	or	AND	Bitwise AND
|	or	OR	Bitwise OR
^	or	XOR	Bitwise XOR
<<			Bitwise left shift
>>			Bitwise right shift
>>>			Zero-fill right shift
&&			Logical AND
||			Logical OR
!			Not

String Operators

Operator	Meaning
+	Concatenates strings, so `"abc"` + `"def"` is `"abcdef"`
>	Compare strings in a case-sensitive way. A string is 'greater' than
>=	another based on the Latin ASCII code values of the characters,
<	starting from the left of the string. So `"DEF"` is greater than `"ABC"`
<=	and `"DEE"`, but less than `"abc"`.

Comments

Operator	Meaning
`// a comment`	A single line comment
`/* this text is a` `multi-line comment */`	A multi-line comment

Input/Output

In JavaScript, there are three different methods of providing information to the user, and getting a response back.

Alert

This displays a message with an OK button.

```
alert("Hello World!");
```

Confirm

Displays a message with both an OK and a Cancel button. True is returned if the OK button is pressed, and false is returned if the Cancel button is pressed.

```
confirm("Are you sure you want to quit?");
```

Prompt

Displays a message and a text box for user input. The first string argument forms the text that is to be displayed above the text box. The second argument is a string, integer, or property of an existing object, which represents the default value to display inside the box. If the second argument is not specified, "<undefined>" is displayed inside the text box.

The string typed into the box is returned if the OK button is pressed. False is returned if the Cancel button is pressed

```
prompt("What is your name?", "");
```

523

Control Flow

There are two ways of controlling the flow of a program in JavaScript. The first involves **conditional** statements, which follow either one branch of the program or another. The second way is to use a **repeated iteration** of a set of statements.

Conditional Statements

JavaScript has one conditional statement:

`if..then..else`–used to run various blocks of code—depending on conditions. These statements have the following general form in JavaScript:

if (*condition*)
   {
 code to be executed if condition is true
   }
else
   {
 code to be executed if condition is false
   };

In addition:

 The `else` portion is optional.

 `if` statements may be nested.

 Multiple statements must be enclosed by braces.

Here is an example:

```
person_type = prompt("What are you ?", "");
if (person_type == "cat")
  alert("Here, have some cat food.")
else
{
  if (person_type == "dog")
    alert("Here, have some dog food.")
  else
  {
    if (person_type == "human")
      alert("Here have some, er, human food!");
  };
};
```

Notice that the curly brackets are only actually required where there is more than one statement within the block. Like many other constructs, they can be omitted where single statements are used. The final semi-colon is mandatory:

if (*condition*)
   code to be executed if condition is true
else
   code to be executed if condition is false;

524

Loop Statements

for—executes a block of code a specified number of times.

```
for (i = 0; i = 10; i++)
{
  document.write(i);
}
```

while—executes a block of code while a condition is true.

```
while (condition)
{
  statements to execute ...
}
```

break— will cause an exit from a loop regardless of the condition statement.

```
x = 0;
while (x != 10)
{
  n = prompt("Enter a number or 'q' to quit", "");
  if (n == "q")
  {
    alert("See ya");
    break;
  }
}
```

continue— will cause the loop to jump immediately back to the condition statement.

```
x = 0;
while (x != 1)
{
  if (!(confirm("Should I add 1 to n ?")))
  {
    continue;
    // the following x++ is never executed
    x++;
  }
  x++;
}
alert("Bye");
```

Built-in Functions

JavaScript provides a number of built-in functions that can be accessed within code.

525

Function	Description
`escape`(*char*)	Returns a string of the form %*XX* where *XX* is the ASCII encoded value of *char*.
`eval`(*expression*)	Returns the result of evaluating the numeric expression *expression*
`isNaN`(*value*)	Returns a Boolean value of **true** if *value* is not a legal number.
`parseFloat`(*string*)	Converts *string* to a floating-point number.
`ParseInt`(*string*, *base*)	Converts *string* to an integer number with the base of *base*.
`typeOf`(*object*)	Returns the data type of *object* as a string, such as `"boolean"`, `"function"`, etc.

Built-in Objects

JavaScript provides a set of built-in data-type objects, which have their own set of properties, and methods—and which can be accessed with JavaScript code.

Array Object

The **Array** object specifies a method of creating arrays and working with them. To create a new array, use:

```
cats = new Array();      // create an empty array
cats = new Array(10);    // create an array of 10 items

// or create and fill an array with values in one go:
cats = new Array("Boo Boo", "Purrcila", "Sam", "Lucky");
```

Properties	Description
`length`	A read/write Integer value specifying the number of elements in the array.

Methods	Description
`join`([*string*])	Returns a string containing each element of the array, optionally separated with *string*.
`reverse`()	Reverses the order of the array.
`sort`([*function*])	Sorts the array, optionally based upon the results of a function specified by *function*.

Early versions of JavaScript had no explicit array structure. However, JavaScript's object mechanisms allow for easy creation of arrays:

526

```
function MakeArray(n)
{
  this.length = n;
  for (var i = 1; i <= n; i++)
    this[i] = 0;
  return this
}
```

With this function included in your script, you can create arrays with:

```
cats = new MakeArray(20);
```

You can then populate the array like this:

```
cats[1] = "Boo Boo";
cats[2] = "Purrcila";
cats[3] = "Sam";
cats[4] = "Lucky";
```

Boolean Object

The **Boolean** object is used to store simple yes/no, true/false values. To create a new Boolean object, use the syntax:

```
MyAnswer = new Boolean([value])
```

If *value* is **0**, **null**, omitted, or an empty string the new Boolean object will have the value **false**. All other values, *including the string* **"false"**, create an object with the value **true**.

Methods	Description
toString()	Returns the value of the Boolean as the string **"true"** or **"false"**.
valueOf()	Returns the primitive numeric value of the object for conversion in calculations.

Date Object

The **Date** object provides a method for working with dates and times inside of JavaScript. New instances of the **Date** object are invoked with:

```
newDateObject = new Date([dateInfo])
```

dateInfo is an optional specification for the date to set in the new object. If it is not specified, the current date and time are used. *dateInfo* can use any of the following formats:

milliseconds (*since midnight GMT on January 1st 1970*)
year, month, day (e.g. 1997, 0, 27 is 27th Jan 1997)
year, month, day, hours, minutes, seconds
month day, year hours:minutes:seconds
(e.g. September 23, 1997 08:25:30)

527

Methods	Description
getDate()	Returns the day of the month as an Integer between 1 and 31.
getDay()	Returns the day of the week as an Integer between 0 (Sunday) and 6 (Saturday).
getHours()	Returns the hours as an Integer between 0 and 23.
getMinutes()	Returns the minutes as an Integer between 0 and 59.
getMonth()	Returns the month as an Integer between 0 (January) and 11 (December).
getSeconds()	Returns the seconds as an Integer between 0 and 59.
getTime()	Returns the number of milliseconds between January 1, 1970 at 00:00:00 GMT and the current **Date** object as an Integer.
getTimeZoneOffset()	Returns the number of minutes difference between local time and GMT as an Integer.
getYear()	Returns the year (generally minus 1900 - i.e. only two digits) as an Integer.
parse(*dateString*)	Returns the number of milliseconds in a date string, since Jan. 1, 1970 00:00:00 GMT.
setDate(*dayValue*)	Sets the day of the month where *dayValue* is an Integer between 1 and 31.
setHours(*hoursValue*)	Sets the hours where *hoursValue* is an Integer between 0 and 59.
setMinutes(*minutesValue*)	Sets the minutes where *minutesValue* is an Integer between 0 and 59.
setMonth(*monthValue*)	Sets the month where *monthValue* is an Integer between 0 and 11.
setSeconds(*secondsValue*)	Sets the seconds where *secondsValue* is an Integer between 0 and 59.
setTime(*timeValue*)	Sets the value of a **Date** object where *timeValue* is and integer representing the number of milliseconds in a date string, since Jan. 1, 1970 00:00:00 GMT.
setYear(*yearValue*)	Sets the year where *yearValue* is an Integer (generally) greater than 1900.
toGMTString()	Converts a date from local time to GMT, and returns it as a string.
toLocaleString()	Converts a date from GMT to local time, and returns it as a string.
UTC(*year, month, day* [,*hrs*] [,*min*] [,*sec*])	Returns the number of milliseconds in a date object, since Jan. 1, 1970 00:00:00 Universal Coordinated Time (GMT).

Function Object

The **Function** object provides a mechanism for compiling JavaScript code as a function. A new function is invoked with the syntax:

```
functionName = new Function(arg1, arg2, ..., functionCode)
```

where **arg1, arg2,** etc. are the arguments for the function object being created, and **functionCode** is a string containing the body of the function. This can be a series of JavaScript statements separated by semi-colons.

Properties	Description
arguments[]	A reference to the **Arguments** array that holds the arguments that were provided when the function was called.
caller	Specifies the function that called the **Function** object.
prototype	Provides a way for adding properties to a **Function** object.

Arguments Object

The **Arguments** object is list (array) of arguments in a **Function** object.

Properties	Description
length	An Integer specifying the number of arguments provided to the function when it was called.

Math Object

Provides a set of properties and methods for working with mathematical constants and functions. Simply reference the **Math** object, then the method or property required:

```
MyArea = Math.PI * MyRadius * MyRadius;
MyResult = Math.floor(MyNumber);
```

Properties	Description
E	Euler's Constant e (the base of natural logarithms).
LN10	The value of the natural logarithm of 10.
LN2	The value of the natural logarithm of 2.
LOG10E	The value of the natural logarithm of E.
LOG2E	The value of the base 2 logarithm of E.
PI	The value of the constant π (pi).
SQRT1_2	The value of the square root of a half.
SQRT	The value of the square root of two.

Methods	Description
abs (*number*)	Returns the absolute value of *number*.
acos (*number*)	Returns the arc cosine of *number*.
asin (*number*)	Returns the arc sine of *number*.
atan (*number*)	Returns the arc tangent of *number*.
atan2 (*x, y*)	Returns the angle of the polar coordinate of a point *x*, *y* from the *x*-axis.
ceil (*number*)	Returns the next largest Integer greater than *number,* i.e. rounds up.
cos (*number*)	Returns the cosine of *number*.
exp (*number*)	Returns the value of *number* as the exponent of *e*, as in e^{number}.
floor (*number*)	Returns the next smallest Integer less that *number,* i.e. rounds down.
log (*number*)	Returns the natural logarithm of *number*.
max (*num1, num2*)	Returns the greater of the two values *num1* and *num2*.
min (*num1, num2*)	Returns the smaller of the two values *num1* and *num2*.
pow (*num1, num2*)	Returns the value of *num1* to the power of *num2*.
random ()	Returns a random number between 0 and 1.
round (*number*)	Returns the closest Integer to *number* i.e. rounds up *or* down to the nearest whole number.
sin (*number*)	Returns the sin of *number*.
sqrt (*number*)	Returns the square root of *number*.
tan (*number*)	Returns the tangent of *number*.

Number Object

The Number Object provides a set of properties that are useful when working with numbers:

```
MyArea = Math.PI * MyRadius * MyRadius;
MyResult = Math.floor(MyNumber);
```

Properties	Description
MAX_VALUE	The maximum numeric value represented in JavaScript (~1.79E+308).
MIN_VALUE	The minimum numeric value represented in JavaScript (~2.22E-308).
NaN	A value meaning 'Not A Number'.
NEGATIVE_INFINITY	A special value for negative infinity ("-Infinity").
POSITIVE_INFINITY	A special value for infinity ("Infinity").

530

Methods	Description
toString([*radix_base*])	Returns the value of the number as a string to a radix (base) of 10, unless specified otherwise in *radix_base*.
valueOf()	Returns the primitive numeric value of the object.

String Object

The **string** object provides a set of methods for text manipulation. To create a new string object, the syntax is:

```
MyString = new String([value])
```

where **value** is the optional text to place in the string when it is created. If this is a number, it is converted into a string first.

Properties	Description
length	An Integer representing the number of characters in the string.

Methods	Description
anchor("*nameAttribute*")	Returns the original string surrounded by <A> and </A> anchor tags, with the **NAME** attribute set to "*nameAttribute*".
big()	Returns the original string enclosed in <BIG> and </BIG> tags.
blink()	Returns the original string enclosed in <BLINK> and </BLINK> tags.
bold()	Returns the original string enclosed in <B> and </B> tags.
charAt(*index*)	Returns the single character at position *index* within the **String** object.
fixed()	Returns the original string enclosed in <TT> and </TT> tags.
fontcolor("*color*")	Returns the original string surrounded by <FONT> and </FONT> tags, with the **COLOR** attribute set to "*color*".
fontsize("*size*")	Returns the original string surrounded by <FONT> and </FONT> anchor tags, with the **SIZE** attribute set to "*size*".
indexOf(*searchValue* [,*fromIndex*])	Returns first occurrence of the string *searchValue* starting at index *fromIndex*.
italics()	Returns the original string enclosed in <I> and </I> tags.

531

Methods	Description
`lastIndexOf` (*searchValue* [,*fromIndex*])	Returns the index of the last occurrence of the string *searchValue*, searching backwards from index *fromIndex*.
`link` ("*hrefAttribute*")	Returns the original string surrounded by `<A>` and `</A>` link tags, with the `HREF` attribute set to "*hrefAttribute*".
`small()`	Returns the original string enclosed in `<SMALL>` and `</SMALL>` tags.
`split` (*separator*)	Returns an array of strings created by separating the `String` object at every occurrence of *separator*.
`strike()`	Returns the original string enclosed in `<STRIKE>` and `</STRIKE>` tags.
`sub()`	Returns the original string enclosed in `<SUB>` and `</SUB>` tags.
`substring` (*indexA*, *indexB*)	Returns the sub-string of the original `String` object from the character at *indexA* up to and including the one **before** the character at *indexB*.
`sup()`	Returns the original string enclosed in `<SUP>` and `</SUP>` tags.
`toLowerCase()`	Returns the original string with all the characters converted to lowercase.
`toUpperCase()`	Returns the original string with all the characters converted to uppercase.

Reserved Words

The following are reserved words that can't be used for function, method, variable, or object names. Note that while some words in this list are not currently used as JavaScript keywords, they have been reserved for future use.

abstract	else	int	super
boolean	extends	interface	switch
break	false	long	synchronized
byte	final	native	this
case	finally	new	throw
catch	float	null	throws
char	for	package	transient
class	function	private	true
const	goto	protected	try
continue	if	public	typeof
default	implements	reset	var
delete	import	return	void
do	in	short	while
double	instanceof	static	with

Support and Errata

One of the most irritating things about any programming book can be when you find that a bit of code you've just spent an hour typing simply doesn't work. You check it a hundred times to see if you've set it up correctly and then you notice the spelling mistake in the variable name on the book page. Grrrr! Of course, you can blame the authors for not taking enough care and testing the code, the editors for not doing their job properly, or the proofreaders for not being eagle-eyed enough, but this doesn't get around the fact that mistakes do happen.

We try hard to ensure no mistakes sneak out into the real world, but we can't promise you that this book is 100% error free. What we can do is offer the next best thing by providing you with immediate support and feedback from experts who have worked on the book and try to ensure that future editions eliminate these gremlins. The following sections will take you step by step through how to post errata to our web site to get that help:

 Finding a list of existing errata on the web site

 Adding your own errata to the existing list

 What happens to your errata once you've posted it (why doesn't it appear immediately?)

and how to mail a question for technical support:

 What your e-mail should include

 What happens to your e-mail once it has been received by us

Finding an Errata on the Web Site

Before you send in a query, you might be able to save time by finding the answer to your problem on our web site, **http:\\www.wrox.com**. Each book we publish has its own page and its own errata sheet. You can get to any book's page by using the drop down list box on our web site's welcome screen.

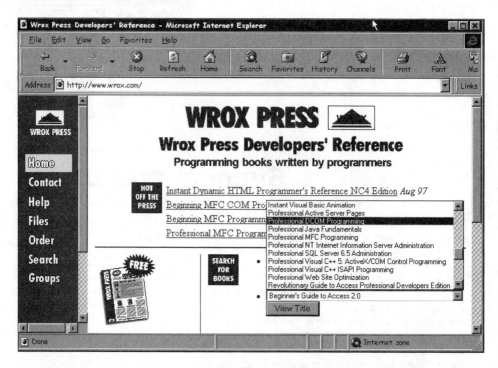

From this you can locate any book's home page on our site. Select your book and click View Title to get the individual title page:

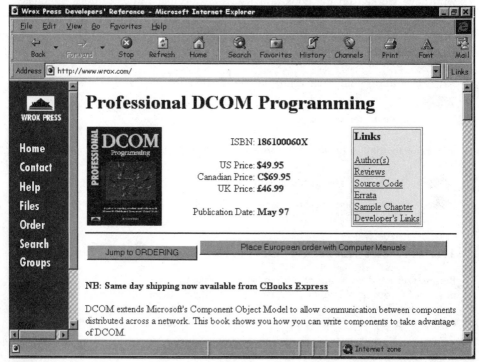

Each book has a set of links. If you click on the Errata link, you'll immediately be transported to the errata sheet for that book:

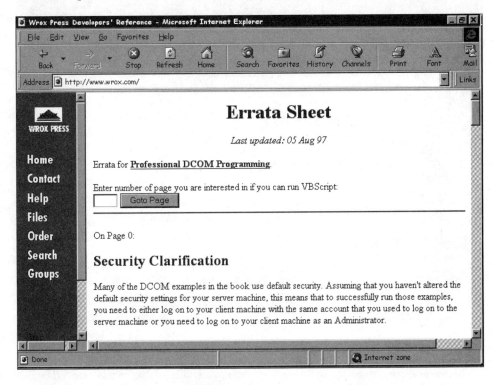

If you're using Internet Explorer 3.0 or later, you can jump to errors more quickly using the text box provided. The errata lists are updated on daily basis, ensuring that you always have the most up-to-date information on bugs and errors.

Adding an Errata to the Sheet Yourself

It's always possible that you may not find your error listed, in which case you can enter details of the fault yourself. It might be anything from a spelling mistake to a faulty piece of code in a book. Sometimes you'll find useful hints that aren't really errors on the listing. By entering errata you may save another reader some hours of frustration and, of course, you will be helping us to produce even higher quality information. We're very grateful for this sort of guidance and feedback. Here's how to do it:

Find the errata page for the book, then scroll down to the bottom of the page, where you will see a space for you to enter your name (and e-mail address for preference), the page the errata occurs on and details of the errata itself. The errata should be formatted using HTML tags - the reminder for this can be deleted as you type in your error.

Once you've typed in your message, click on the **Submit** button and the message is forwarded to our editors. They'll then test your submission and check that the error exists, and that any suggestions you make are valid. Then your submission, together with a solution, is posted on the site for public consumption. Obviously this stage of the process can take a day or two, but we will endeavor to get a fix up sooner than that.

E-mail Support

If you wish to directly query a problem in the book with an expert who knows the book in detail then e-mail **support@wrox.com**, with the title of the book and the last four numbers of the ISBN in the Subject field of the e-mail. A typical e-mail should include the following things:

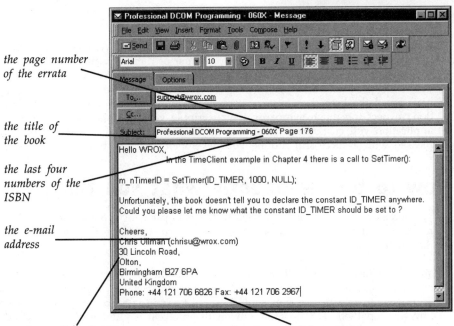

the page number of the errata

the title of the book

the last four numbers of the ISBN

the e-mail address

the snail mail address

the phone and fax numbers

We won't send you junk mail. We need details to help save your time and ours. If we need to replace a disk or CD we'll be able to get it to you straight away. When you send an e-mail it will go through the following chain of support;

Customer Support

Your message is delivered to one of our customer support staff who are the first people to read it. They have files on the most frequently asked questions and will answer anything immediately. They answer general questions about the books and web site.

Editorial

Deeper queries are forwarded on the same day to the technical editor responsible for that book. They have experience with the programming language or particular product and are able to answer detailed technical questions on the subject. Once an issue has been resolved, the editor can post the errata to the web site.

The Author(s)

Finally, in the unlikely event that the editor can't answer your problem, he/she will forward the request to the author. We try to protect the author from any distractions from writing. However, we are quite happy to forward specific requests to them. All Wrox authors help with the support on their books. They'll mail the customer and editor with their response, and again, all readers should benefit.

539

What we can't answer

Obviously with an ever growing range of books and an ever-changing technology base, there is an increasing volume of data requiring support. While we endeavor to answer all questions about a book, we can't answer bugs in your own programs that you've adapted from our code. So, while you might have loved the help desk system examples in our Active Server Pages book, don't expect too much sympathy if you cripple your company with a live application you customized from chapter 12. But do tell us if you're especially pleased with a successful routine you developed with our help.

How to tell us exactly what you think!

We understand that errors can destroy the enjoyment of a book and can cause many wasted and frustrated hours, so we seek to minimize the distress that they can cause.

You might just wish to tell us how much you liked or loathed the book in question. Or you might have ideas about how this whole process could be improved. In which case you should e-mail **feedback@wrox.com**. You'll always find a sympathetic ear, no matter what the problem is. Above all you should remember that we do care about what you have to say and we will do our utmost to act upon it.

INSTANT

Dynamic HTML

Index

E

H

J

P

X

Y

Z

Professional Dynamic HTML IE4 Programming

Authors: Various   ISBN: 1861000707
Price: $49.95   C$69.95   £46.99

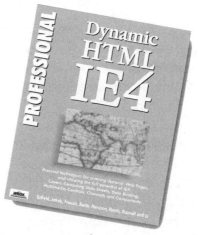

There's no doubt that many people will be using the new version of Microsoft's Internet Explorer browser. As well as supporting Dynamic HTML, the latest and most exciting version of HTML, it also offers lots of other new features. This book looks at what you can do with IE4, and - more importantly for the developer and HTML author - how you can program for it. We cover Dynamic HTML in depth, and explore ways of using the whole Active Desktop environment. This includes Active Desktop Components, dynamic linking to server-side databases, subscriptions and channel technology. Providing you are reasonably familiar with HTML up to version 3.2, and have tinkered with scripting languages before, you'll find everything you need to know here.

Professional Active Server Pages

Authors: Various   ISBN: 1861000723
Price: $44.95   C$62.95   £41.99

Active Server Pages is simply the easiest way to build dynamic sites. This book assumes you are familiar with simple HTML Web pages, and have at least some knowledge of Visual Basic or VBA. It starts with a full review of the background and workings of this new technology to get you up to speed, then

quickly moves on to discuss the ways it can be used in the real world. We take ASP further than other books, showing you just what is possible. There's a discussion of client/server design topics, a full reference section, and plenty of real-world examples. This is one book you just can't afford to be without.